IDEALISM

IDEALISM
The History of a Philosophy

Jeremy Dunham, Iain Hamilton Grant and Sean Watson

ACUMEN

© 2011 Jeremy Dunham, Iain Hamilton Grant and Sean Watson

This book is copyright under the Berne Convention.
No reproduction without permission.
All rights reserved.

First published in 2011 by Acumen

Acumen Publishing Limited
4 Saddler Street
Durham
DH1 3NP
www.acumenpublishing.co.uk

ISBN: 978-1-84465-240-2 (hardcover)
ISBN: 978-1-84465-241-9 (paperback)

British Library Cataloguing-in-Publication Data
A catalogue record for this book is available
from the British Library.

Printed and bound in the UK by MPG Books Group.

CONTENTS

Acknowledgements	vii
Note on the text	viii
Abbreviations	ix
Introduction	1

I Ancient idealism
1. Parmenides and the birth of ancient idealism	10
2. Plato and Neoplatonism	19

II Idealism and early modern philosophy
3. Phenomenalism and idealism I: Descartes and Malebranche	34
4. Phenomenalism and idealism II: Leibniz and Berkeley	59

III German idealism
5. Immanuel Kant: cognition, freedom and teleology	89
6. Fichte and the system of freedom	116
7. Idealist philosophy of nature: F. W. J Schelling	129
8. Hegel and Hegelianism: mind, nature and logic	144

IV British idealism
9. British absolute idealism: from Green to Bradley	159
10. Personal idealism: from Ward to McTaggart	175
11. Naturalist idealism: Bernard Bosanquet	190
12. Criticisms and persistent misconceptions of idealism	201

13. Actual occasions and eternal objects: the process metaphysics of Alfred North Whitehead — 210

V Contemporary idealisms

14. Self-organization: the idea in late-twentieth-century science — 223
15. Contemporary philosophical idealism — 256

Notes — 299
Bibliography — 312
Index — 327

ACKNOWLEDGEMENTS

I owe an enormous debt of gratitude to a great number of staff working at the University of the West of England who have, both during my undergraduate and graduate study, helped and inspired me beyond measure; in particular Iain Hamilton Grant, Dave Green, Peter Jowers, John Sellars and Sean Watson. I must dedicate an extra special thanks to Hamid Danesh and Georgina Oliver at Human Rights Aid, and Alison Assiter and Havi Carel, without whose help and support I would have been unable to complete the work on this book. Finally I want to express my great gratitude to my family and Stephanie Allan for their unconditional love and support.
Jeremy Dunham

I would like to thank my colleagues Alison Assiter, Havi Carel, Jeremy Dunham, Darian Meacham, John Sellars and Sean Watson of the University of the West of England for their inspiring presence. Tristan Palmer is due all our gratitude for his patience and encouragement throughout this project. Finally, I would like to offer belated gratitude to Karin Littau for putting up with my absence for so long during the preparation of this book and to Graham Harman for blogging intensively about it.
Iain Hamilton Grant

I would like to thank my colleagues Jeremy Dunham, Iain Hamilton Grant and Peter Jowers for the many inspirational hours that we have spent together discussing the contents of this book. Two other colleagues, Alison Assiter and Lita Crociani-Windland, have offered thoughts and comments on this work, for which I am grateful. Finally I would like to thank Lorraine Kirby, whose support and patience have made my contribution to this project possible.
Sean Watson

We would like to dedicate this book to our former colleague Peter Jowers (Rieupeyroux) whose influence on this book was felt yet missed throughout.

NOTE ON THE TEXT

Many and various rules for the capitalization of important terms are adopted in translating and writing works of philosophy. We have adopted the practice of capitalizing where a work or author being cited would or does capitalize (as in Hegel or Bradley, for example). There are two major exceptions to this rule: the term "Absolute" is so prone to being read adjectivally that we have capitalized all its substantive uses throughout; similarly, references to the "Idea" in the overtly Platonic sense are capitalized in order to avoid assimilating it too easily to everyday usages and understandings. Why this is so will become clear in the text.

ABBREVIATIONS

A   Leibniz, *Sämtliche Schriften und Briefe* (1923–). Cited by series, volume and page number.

Ak.   *Immanuel Kants gesammelte Schriften* (1902). Cited by volume number (in roman numerals).

AG   Leibniz, *Philosophical Essays* (1989a).

AT   Descartes, *Oeuvres de Descartes* (1974–89). Cited by volume and page number.

CA   Leibniz, *The Leibniz–Arnauld Correspondence* (1967). Page references refer to the *Die Philosophischen Schriften* (1875–90), vol. 2, which are cited alongside the translation in Mason's edition.

CDB   Leibniz, *The Leibniz–Des Bosses Correspondence* (2007). The original Latin is printed on the page facing the translation.

CP   Leibniz, *Confessio Philosophi: Papers Concerning the Problem of Evil* (2005).

CPR   Kant, *Critique of Pure Reason* (1929). Cited by A/B editions.

CSM   Descartes, *The Philosophical Writings of Descartes* (1984–91). Cited by volume and page number.

DMR   Malebranche, *Dialogues on Metaphysics and on Religion* (1997b).

DSR   Leibniz, *De Summa Rerum: Metaphysical Papers, 1675–1676* (1992b).

E   Leibniz, *Opera Philosophicae quae exstant Latina, Gallica, Germanica omnia* (1839–40).

ET   Proclus, *The Elements of Theology* (1963).

G   Leibniz, *Die Philosophischen Schriften* (1875–90). Cited by volume and page number.

GA   Fichte, *Gesamstausgabe der Bayerischen Akademie der Wissenschaften* (1976–). Cited by series, volume and page number.

GBW   Berkeley, *The Works of George Berkeley Bishop of Cloyne* (1948–57).

GM   Leibniz, *Mathematische Schriften* (1848–63). Cited by volume and page number.

ABBREVIATIONS

L	Leibniz, *Gottfried Wilhelm Leibniz: Philosophical Papers and Letters* (1989).
M	Rescher, *G. W. Leibniz's Monadology* (1992). Cited by section number.
NE	Leibniz, *New Essays on Human Understanding* (1992a). Page numbers refer to the *Sämtliche Schriften und Briefe*, series VI, volume vi (A VI.vi), which are the only page numbers used in this edition.
OCM	Malebranche, *Oeuvres completes de Malebranche* (1958–67). Cited by volume and page number.
PHK	Berkeley, *A Treatise Concerning the Principles of Human Knowledge*. In *GBW*, cited by section number.
PR	Whitehead, *Process and Reality* (1929).
SAT	Malebranche, *The Search After Truth* (1997a).
SW	Schelling, *Schellings Werke* (1856–61).
T	Leibniz, *The Theodicy* (1985). Cited by section number.
TNG	Malebranche, *Treatise on Nature and Grace* (1992).
W	Fichte, *Fichtes Werke herausgegeben von Immanuel Hermann Fichte* (1971). Cited by volume and page number.
WFNS	Woolhouse & Francks, *Leibniz's "New System" and Associated Contemporary Texts* (1997).
WLS	Wiener, *Leibniz Selections* (1951).

INTRODUCTION

The idealist tradition in philosophy stretches from the earliest beginnings of the subject, and extends to the present. There has never been a moment in the history of philosophy when there has not existed an idealist current: for every Locke and Hume there is a Berkeley, just as for every Russell and Moore there is a Whitehead and for every contemporary philosophical naturalist there is a John Leslie and a T. L. S. Sprigge. While this very ubiquity makes a survey of the entire range of idealist philosophy a difficult and obscure undertaking, the present philosophical situation affords good reasons to do so.

First, idealism is once again at the core of mainstream philosophical problems. The same issues that make a survey of idealism as such difficult, however, make any extant idealism partial with respect to that tradition. In consequence, portraits of idealism emerge that, while depicting only local features, tend inexorably to be confused with the entire landscape. Most contemporary idealism, for example, is preoccupied with constructing a metaphysics on the basis of a normativity posed as an alternative to naturalism. While this has, of course, been one theme in the history of idealism, it does not exhaust it.

Second, therefore, there is a need for an account of idealism that sets out its central problems such that contemporary, historical and unacknowledged idealisms can be coordinated within its general landscape. Despite the enormous and growing scholarly interest in idealism, such interest tends by definition to focus on specific philosophers, schools or periods, rather than addressing idealism as such. Thus, German idealism, surely one of the most inventive periods in the entire history of philosophy, continues to attract enormous scholarly and philosophical energy, while the emerging historical consciousness of the analytic philosophical tradition has brought about a return to the problems that defined that tradition against its idealist precursors. Nevertheless, few works cover both, let alone other tributaries of idealist philosophy.

Third, while we hope to restore relatively unnoticed dimensions of historical idealisms to contemporary attention, we seek not only to contextualize contemporary idealism, but also to engage the philosophical resources idealism offers across a range of problems that extend beyond the history of philosophy. On the one hand, we wish to engage a debate concerning what idealism is. On the other, we wish to extend the range of environments in which contributions and developments of idealist problematics may be found. Chief among these environments is that of the natural sciences. While idealism has a long history of engagement with cosmology and the philosophy of nature, contemporary focus tends to be on providing alternatives to the predominant naturalistic tendency in philosophy. Yet this is not the only way in which idealism engages with the problem of nature. Idealism has often, for example, engaged in productive exchanges with the natural sciences. Our hope in so doing is to promote contemporary philosophical engagements with idealism and the problem of nature.

We take seriously our responsibilities to the figures and concepts we treat, and have endeavoured as far as we can not to distort them. Yet the presence of the set of problems through which we shall consider idealism will of course be registered in our accounts, perhaps to the consternation of the reader in that philosophers will emerge from our discussions in a relatively unfamiliar context. We hope the virtues of direct engagement outweigh the vices of what distortion remains inevitable. Moreover, we cannot, even within the framework we have set ourselves for this project, pretend to completeness. We have had to omit large swathes of idealism's varieties and history,[1] sometimes, frankly, owing to a lack of the relevant knowledge, sometimes owing to space and sometimes to prior decision. Two such decisions should be mentioned at the outset. The first concerns the relative subjugation of the ethical and political to the metaphysical dimensions of idealism. This reflects (a) the relatively widespread extant discussions of the former as contrasting with the relative paucity of those of the latter dimensions; (b) our concern to foreground these last, especially given the current predominance of normative idealism; and (c) our contention that philosophy in general, but idealist philosophy in particular, faces a considerable challenge from the problems of nature that normativism rather avoids than meets.

The second such decision concerns our address to the natural sciences in what follows. In particular as regards the science of biology, it is hard to avoid the problem Kant bequeathed philosophers in the *Critique of Judgement*. Kant's famous despair over the prospect of discovering a "Newton of the blade of grass" (Ak. V.400),[2] that is, over the adequacy of mechanistic materialism to explanation in the life sciences, centres on the number and kinds of causes operative in nature. With the development of the sciences of complexity, the same problem recurs regarding what kind of cause "organization" is or involves. At one level, then, the natural sciences call out for philosophical interpretation. At another, however, forms of philosophy are implicit in science's accounts of the phenomena it investigates. Sometimes this becomes explicit, as is Bernard d'Espagnat's (2006) redeployment of Kant's noumenon for particle physics; Julian Barbour's (2003) celebration of the cosmological pertinence of Leibniz; Stuart Kauffman's direct address to Kant's third *Critique* (see ch. 14); or in Roland Omnès' (1999) plea that philosophers cease to worry about scientific method or epistemology and provide the sort of conceptual orientation for intelligibility as such to which Plotinus is better suited than Popper. Our rationale for exploring the idealism we find in contemporary biology (chs 14–15) concerns the concepts involved in the explanation of natural phenomena. What Bernard Bosanquet (1911) called "the morphology of knowledge" is most fully developed, philosophers are apt to contend, in logic; yet if logic is conceived, as, for example, Hegel did, as "the science of things grasped in thoughts" (Hegel 1991: 156), then, wherever concepts are deployed, that morphology is evidenced in the grappling of thought with things. It seems to us, therefore, an arbitrary limitation of the concept that it be exclusively discovered in philosophy.

A further reason, however, to pursue idealism *through* naturalism is precisely to unsettle the contemporary normativist consensus as regards what idealism *is*. Since Socrates explained his disappointment with natural history in explaining the nature of things, idealism has negotiated its concerns with the philosophy of nature, more overtly on some occasions than others. Nature is a central element of Platonism's architecture, as is its reinvention by the rationalists; Kant and the German idealists were centrally concerned with nature, with only Fichte rejecting any form of naturalism as philosophically important. Among the British idealists, James Ward agitated for the reintroduction of finality and creativity into physics, while Bosanquet sought to unite Hegel and Darwin. Alfred North Whitehead followed Schelling's "real idealism" in the direction of a speculative philosophy of nature, while John Leslie returns to Platonism to explain cosmogony.

That the naturalistic dimension of idealism's history is not well known is to some degree due to some central confusions over what idealism in fact holds. This is relatively unsurprising given the ferocious oversimplifications formulated in G. E. Moore's (1903) so-called "refutation" of it, and the relative silence surrounding idealism following the success of analytic philosophy in deposing its forebears. Accordingly, two aspects in particular of these criticisms ought to be addressed before we discuss what we take to be idealism's core principles. These are (a) that idealism is *anti-realist* in that it argues that reality, for idealism, is something essentially "mind-dependent"; and (b) that idealism is *anti-naturalistic*, in so far as it disputes that matter is the basis of all existence.

IDEALISM AS ANTI-REALISM

Idealism is frequently characterized, especially following Berkeley, as "anti-realist", meaning that it disputes the mind-independent reality of the world. According to some accounts of Berkeleyan idealism, that existence consists solely of perceptions, means that there can by definition be no mind-independent existence. Yet Berkeley was clearly disputing the constitution of things with the corpuscular philosophers. That he offers a theory of the world as constituted by other than tiny, spatiotemporally extended material spheres suggests that his philosophy is precisely an attempt to characterize reality. To call Berkeley an anti-realist is therefore to beg the question concerning the character of reality.

The Berkeleyan corollary, however, that idealism is the position that reality is mind-dependent, has proved extraordinarily resilient to correction. Six out of eight contemporary dictionaries and encyclopaedias of philosophy we consulted presented idealism as the theory that reality is mind-dependent. The thesis is part and parcel of the general anti-realist charge, but makes the additional assertion that whatever reality is, it cannot exist independently of a mind that observes or thinks it. Where idealists are concerned, however, to promote the fundamentality of mindedness, they do not have in mind some reality other than the one common to us all. Idealism, in other words, tends to be motivated not by scepticism, but rather by systematic completeness. Consider, for example, the panpsychist idealism of the sort that T. L. S. Sprigge (ch. 15) maintains and draws from F. H. Bradley (ch. 9). The revelation that the universe is panpsychist may well entail that reality turns out to be something other than we had previously conceived it to be, but it does not entail that reality is eliminated, or that its fundamental character has changed. As with the anti-realism charge, the deep claim about universal mindedness is not destructive, but rather constitutive of reality.

This means that the idealist, rather than being anti-realist, is in fact additionally a realist concerning elements more usually dismissed from reality. Chief among these is the Idea, as Plato understood it. Plato (ch. 2) is often erroneously interpreted as holding that what is not the Idea has no existence whatsoever, or that *only* the Idea exists. Yet as Socrates puts it in the *Phaedo* (100d), the Idea of Beauty or "beauty itself" is the *cause*, the *reason why*, of the existence of beautiful things. An idealism that is a realism concerning Ideas is not therefore committed *only* to the existence of Ideas, but rather to the claim that any adequate ontology must include *all* existence, including the existence of the Ideas and the becomings they cause. Idealism, that is, is not anti-realist, but realist precisely about the existence of Ideas.

IDEALISM AND ANTI-SCIENCE

One of the motives behind Berkeley's idealism (ch. 4) was to dispute with what he called the "minute philosophers", who earned their name by virtue of maintaining that the real nature of things consisted entirely of atomic entities. In other words, Berkeley was disputing the adequacy of mechanistic materialism not only as an explanatory model, but as an ontology. Now the claim is often made that this amounts to being anti-science, and yet it is clearly not so. Rather, Berkeley opposes a particular scientific account in explaining things. In some senses, then, the claim that idealism is anti-science is of a piece with the claim that it is anti-realist: philosophers committed to the mind-dependent existence of entities cannot maintain, it is held, the existence of a physical reality. We know of no idealist for whom this is true. Kant's transcendental idealism (ch. 5), for instance, is premised on Newtonianism having the nature of the physical universe fundamentally right, a point Kant had maintained since his first major book, *Universal Natural History and Theory of the Heavens* (1755). As already noted, Kant's problematization of the adequacy of mechanistic materialism for explaining the phenomena of life is not so much anti-science as intra-science, a fact corroborated by the scientists who began theorizing in acknowledged accordance with his strictures concerning natural history. Again, Kant worries about the lack of human remains in the emergent fossil record precisely because this makes the "kingdom of ends" he sees it as our moral duty to create dependent on the contingencies of physical nature: should an earthquake strike, all finite rational intellect might conceivably vanish in the upheaval. Additionally, Kant's immediate contribution was not simply to provide philosophers hell-bent on denying reality with a means of consistently doing so, but also to give philosophical impetus to natural scientists such as Christoph Girtanner and Johann Friedrich Blumenbach in what we would now call biology, to Johann Christian Reil in what would now be known as the neurosciences, and to Johann Heinrich Lambert in physics. Lastly, when Kant disputes the right of chemistry to be accounted a science (rather than a technique), he does so not in an anti-scientific spirit, but in support of the mathematical grounds of what he holds to be true science.

Of Kant's immediate successors, while Fichte did pursue the elimination of all that is unfree from nature (ch. 6), Schelling spent his entire career developing and situating the philosophy of nature as a fundamental department of philosophy (ch. 7), while at the same time maintaining the existence of the Absolute. Thus Schelling committed himself to precisely the kind of inclusive ontology we noted to be a hallmark of idealism's realism, while the organicist theory of nature we associate with the Romantic period owes much to Hegel (ch. 8).

Again, the portrait of the British idealists we receive from the triumphalist literature of the "analytic revolution" is of philosophers with no concern for nature and its sciences. Yet this is consistently untrue: the avowedly speculative philosopher Bosanquet (ch. 11), for instance, contested so-called "realist" philosophers such as C. D. Broad and Samuel Alexander regarding their "emergentist" thesis of mind, which had an enormous influence in psychology and biology (C. Lloyd Morgan, William McDougall and James Ward, the last often considered the "Godfather of Emergentism", owing to his theory of creative synthesis). Then, as now, emergentism was the thesis that mind is a late acquisition, a relatively rare product that is as natural as rivers but with properties not to be discovered elsewhere in nature. Bosanquet, who was committed to a synthesis of Hegel and Darwin, despite the former's supposedly infamous denial of the reality of evolution,[3] in explaining the origins of logic, proposed against the realists that "nature moulds mind" through evolutionary process. Similarly, the impact of Einsteinian relativity on the idealists was enormous, prompting not only Bertrand Russell, but also H. Wildon Carr, J. S. Haldane and Whitehead (ch. 13), to write significant works on it. This impact is significant not only in that it illustrates idealism's attention to the sciences, but also in so far as it reveals that idealism, far from being antiscience, disputes the adequacy of mechanistic materialism to real nature. This amounts to arguing that idealism is the sole philosophical means by which to arrive at an adequate theory of matter in so far as this must involve an explanation of the existence of all phenomena, including the Ideas about which idealists are realists. These theses will form an important strand in our account of idealism throughout this book.

WHAT IDEALISM IS

If we put together our view that idealism is realist about ideas with the argument that the philosophy of nature forms a crucial component of it, we arrive at a conception not of the two-worlds idealism beloved of interpretations of Plato, but of a one-world inflationary idealism. The world of change, birth and decay is not a world causally isolated from that of the Ideas since, as the *Phaedo*, for instance, makes clear, the Idea has as its nature to be causal in respect of becomings.

This is the Platonism maintained by idealists, a Platonism of "immanent law" or causal efficacy. Not only, that is, do idealists such as Bosanquet dispute the two-worlds interpretation (1912: 260–61), but, as a result of idealism's realism concerning Ideas, they will be committed in turn to a single world that has Ideas as features of its actual existence or nature, as Gernot Böhme has recently argued (2000: 18). Similarly, the Hegelian Absolute is not other than the world, but it *is* the world to the fullest extent of its powers; Whitehead's "eternal objects" are not situated outside or beyond actual entities, but are their articulators, their possibilizers; Schelling's Absolute "is the universe"; and even Bradley, that most apparently conspicuous "two-worlds" idealist, is committed to a single world that our partial and limited epistemological and practical perspectives are condemned to misconstrue.

To be a realist concerning Ideas entails having a theory of what they are. One of the reasons the two-worlds interpretation of Plato has such purchase is that textbooks of metaphysics present the Platonic Idea as a version of the medieval theory of universals. Nominalist critics of universals held that they have no real existence other than in our mind (Boethius) or God's (Augustine), since what really exist are particulars only. When we manufacture universals, we merely "equate what is unequal", as Nietzsche maintained. Such universals, therefore, correspond to the "abstract universals" criticized by Berkeley. There is no "red in itself", such critics hold, but only red things. How could anyone argue that universals are *more* real than the world of particulars, and that they occupy a separate and eternal realm?

If we hold the Idea to be equivalent to the abstract universal, we will arrive at a poor view of Platonism. This is why it is so important to examine not only the themes of the various disputes tracked across Plato's dialogues, but also what the Neoplatonists (ch. 2) made of these: the One that is the source of all things, with matter as the lowest ebb of its productivity; the One whose power is augmented by production, while its productions lack sufficient power to return to it. These Platonists share a commitment to the causal dimension of the Idea, integrating it into the world as its immanent reason for being what it is, as Whitehead clearly saw. Clearly, abstract universals do not possess a causal dimension of the sort Platonism hypothesizes the Idea does. While the Platonic Idea certainly acts as a "form" or "paradigm", it is *actual* in itself whereas, as Sprigge (1983: 11) writes, the abstract universal remains merely a set of *possible* forms. We must not therefore confuse the Idea with the abstract universals of medieval and modern philosophy.

The other modern candidate for equivalence with the Idea is the concrete universal. Introduced by Hegel, it was enthusiastically embraced as core to many of the British idealists, especially Bradley, and remained central even to Sprigge's ontology. Hegel contrasts the "abstract universality" of mere collections or sets, and "concrete universality", which develops into real particularity. What makes the concrete universal concrete is precisely its development, which tends always to the production of particulars or singulars. Without this development, it remains abstract. According to the ordinary understanding, Hegel writes, the concept is an example of a universal in so far as it is without particularities; such a concept, however, remains undetermined and therefore abstract, since the increase in determination is an increase in

7

particularity. In so far as the Concept determines itself to particularity, then and only then does its generality relate to its particularization so as to form the concrete universal (Hegel 1991: 239–41). In keeping with Hegel's general organicism, then, the concrete universal is for him the "metabolic" relation between system and product.

Hegel's understanding of the concrete universal survives in Bosanquet's account of the "plastic unity of an inclusive system" (1924: 62) and in Josiah Royce's: "The universal is no abstraction at all, but a perfectly concrete whole, since the facts are, one and all, not mere examples of it, but are embraced in it, are brought forth by it as its moments, and exist only in relation to one another and to it" (1892: 224). Crucially, then, the concrete universal is inseparable from its moments. It is accordingly immanent to its particulars because they derive from it. Bradley adds an additional dimension to this "organic mereology" in his *Principles of Logic*. On the one hand, Bradley considers the concrete universal to be the whole of reality. On the other, he takes it to constitute a denial of the concreteness of particulars *qua* particulars. In other words, there are no particulars that do not derive their existence from the universal, while universality exists independently of particulars. Since, however, particulars have "internal diversity of content" (Bradley 1922: 187), none is indivisible or atomic, making it a concrete universal in turn. Where Hegel's organicism makes particularity into a moment of the universal's self-development, thus introducing the causal dimension of the Idea, Bradley adds to it the idea of *organization* as internal complexity all the way down. Gilles Deleuze overtly equates the Idea with the concrete universal, opposing it, as does Hegel, to the "concepts of the understanding", which retain a non-reciprocal relation with their exemplars (1994: 173).

The concrete universal, or the whole determined by the particulars it generates and that differentiate it in turn, is the Idea exactly as Platonism conceived it: as the *cause* of the approximations of becomings to particular forms, and as the "setting into order of this universe" (*Ti.* 53a)[4] from disorder (*ataxia*), as organization. When idealism is therefore presented as realism concerning the Idea, this means: *first*, that the Idea is causal in terms of organization; second, that this is an organization that is not formal or abstract in the separable sense, but rather concretely relates part to whole as the whole; and third, therefore that such an idealism is a *one-world* idealism that must, accordingly, take nature seriously.

This is the variety of idealism the present book is concerned to identify and defend as it is at once less ubiquitous in the secondary literature and more indebted to the tradition's origins than others of its variants. We shall, however, provide this defence within the full range of idealist positions, rather than seeking to reduce them all to our favoured formula. This context is at once historical and contemporary since, as we shall see, contemporary idealisms tend overwhelmingly to leave nature behind. Finally, it is contemporary in the sense that this is a philosophical exercise, a thinking grasp of things more generally, an attempt to make explicit what lies implicit in a philosophy we thought we had already displaced.

1. PARMENIDES AND THE BIRTH OF ANCIENT IDEALISM

INTRODUCTION: ON THE VERY IDEA OF ANCIENT IDEALISM

At the end of the nineteenth century, Benjamin Jowett, Plato's translator and the teacher of many of British idealism's earlier leading lights, had no qualms about asserting, in the introduction to his translation of the *Republic*, that Plato "is the father of idealism in philosophy, in politics, in literature" (1902: 105). In contemporary philosophy, however, the claim that there is such a thing as "ancient idealism" is controversial. This is because for many philosophers, G. E. Moore's claim that "modern idealism, if it asserts any general conclusion about the universe at all, asserts that it is *spiritual*" (1903: 433), for all its vagueness, remains an accurate account of idealism.[1] Thus we find Moore's very loose "definition" repeated in Miles Burnyeat's influential paper "Idealism and Greek Philosophy", which uses it to argue that idealism:

> whether we mean by that Berkeley's own doctrine that *esse est percipi* or a more vaguely conceived thesis to the effect that everything is in some substantial sense mental or spiritual, is one of the very few major philosophical positions which did not receive its first formulation in antiquity. (1982: 3–4)

Rather than, with Moore, seeking to "refute" idealism as such, Burnyeat's contention, as Bernard Williams suggests, is that:

> idealism and the historical consciousness are the only two really substantial respects in which later philosophy is removed from Greek philosophy, as opposed to its pursuing what are recognizably the same types of preoccupation as Greek philosophy pursued. (2008: 6)

If idealism is the view that the universe is spirit or mind, as Burnyeat and Williams, following Moore, maintain it to be, then while it would not seem absurd to find *precursors* of idealism in what Plato reports as Anaxagoras' view that "it is intelligence [*nous*] that arranges and causes all things" (*Phd.* 97b–c), or in Parmenides' much-discussed proposition that "thinking and being are the same" (DK28 B3),[2] we could not claim these philosophers *to be* idealists, because "we do not find" the claim that "nothing ultimately exists except minds and their experiences ... in the ancient world" (B. Williams 2008: 5).

Yet even if we concede that, as a matter of fact, no such "monism of mind" occurred in the ancient world, it would be a mistake to conflate genus with species. That is, it is at best, as we shall see throughout this book, foolhardy to claim that idealism as such is simply a spiritualist or mentalist monism. At one level, it is the *monistic* claim regarding mind that is most bothersome to these critics; "I take it", writes Burnyeat, "that if the label 'idealism' is of any historical use at all, it indicates a form of monism" (1982: 8). The reason for the unease such a monistic mentalism provokes is that, at first sight, it deprives reality of material existence.[3] On this view, there is a straightforwardly exclusive disjunction between idealism and materialism: either one or the other; not both. Such a disjunction would mean that the robust, naturalistic and pre-philosophical[4] realism Burnyeat affirms of the Greeks would, under idealism, be "whittled away" (Inge 1923: vol. 2, 42). This realism is based on the insistence that "it is our nature and our experience of the world that explain the concepts we have, not the other way round. The world is as it is independently of us, and shapes our thought accordingly" (Burnyeat 1982: 22).

Yet the conclusion that idealism is inherently anti-realist or "immaterialist" is open to question. First, let us consider realism. Burnyeat bases his Greek realism on the obviousness of the existence of the external world, its bald there-ness; yet he prejudges the *nature* of this reality as material *and therefore not ideal*. It is one thing to impute inconsistent positions to the folk philosophy that Burnyeat wishes to protect from post-Cartesian sophisticates; it is quite another, however, to impute to this realism a preformulated exclusive disjunction between materialist and idealist explanations, not least since realism is not the exclusive philosophical orientation of materialists; according to at least one early-twentieth-century British idealist philosopher, for example, "thought-adaptation in relation to the environment has always been the peculiar pride and province of objective idealism" (Bosanquet 1911: vol. ii, 275).

A version of the same problem arises in regard to the presupposition that materialism is simply the antithesis of idealism. A consistent materialism must be a monism concerning the nature of existents. Accordingly, there could be nothing that existed that was not also material. No consistent materialism could therefore argue that anything existent was other than material, including the causes and the contents of mental phenomena.[5] There could therefore be nothing that was purely mental that would not at the same time be equally purely material. Thus, as Galen Strawson has recently noted, while we might accept that:

> materialism … is the view that every real concrete phenomenon is physical in every respect …, a little more needs to be said[;] for experiential phenomena … are the only real, concrete phenomena that we can know with certainty to exist, and as it stands this definition of materialism doesn't even rule out idealism … from qualifying as a form of materialism! (2008: 23)

Rather than opposing one another, the monistic dimension makes the distinction suspect. It would, in other words, be futile to protest, as Burnyeat does, against the proposition that "the universe is mental" if all possible universes were of this nature, as a monist must hold. There could be nothing "unnatural" in such a universe, nor anything unreal about its constituents, nor, by virtue of the monism, any additional "material" element on which it all rested. In other words, the idealist is a *realist* to the extent that she formulates propositions concerning the nature of the universe. For a *subjective* idealism to differ from this, it would have to allow either that (a) there is some portion of the *objective* universe that experience or mind cannot reach; or that (b) conscious, subjective experience – the only sort of experience there is – can know only itself. Since Burnyeat finds the philosophical conditions necessary to idealism given in the apparent subjectivism of Descartes' epistemology, there is good reason to assume that it is (b) that he takes to provide the model of what he has in mind as idealism.[6]

As Richard Sorabji has urged against Burnyeat, however, not all idealism is a response to epistemological scepticism. According to Sorabji (1983: 288), therefore, there are in fact idealisms in the ancient world, for instance in the acccount of the genesis of matter from the immaterial in the fourth-century philosopher Gregory of Nyssa. Further, and in direct contradiction to Burnyeat's case that idealism cannot exist prior to Descartes, Dermot Moran has argued that John Scottus Eriugena's ninth-century philosophy is exactly *subjective*, "in the sense that all spatiotemporal reality is understood as immaterial, mind dependent, and lacking in independent existence", and *idealist*, "in the Hegelian sense, whereby all finite reality is understood to require infinite reality for its full intelligibility and completion" (1989: 81). The problem these idealists, ancient and medieval, confront is how to form a philosophical system of *all* things, not some. This is not because they are engaged in *denying* the existence of this or that element of things, or in "whittling away one of the terms" (Inge 1923: vol. 2, 42), but, on the contrary, are seeking to combine them. Again, to quote Bosanquet, "in a theory which has to face the universe as a whole, nothing which is can be treated as if it were not. The attempt to do so at once convicts the theory which attempts it of arbitrary superficiality" (1927: 22).

If Gregory therefore seeks to combine the immaterial and the material, as Eriugena does mind-dependence and the totality, we can conclude, against Burnyeat's scruples that admitting the existence of ancient idealism would damage the Greeks' native realism, that one of the problems facing idealists from Gregory through Hegel to Bosanquet is precisely the problem of an inclusivist monism, not the eliminative immaterialism Burnyeat fears. As we shall see in what follows, this inclusivism is the hallmark of the great idealist systems of Leibniz, Hegel and Whitehead. Since these philosophers do in fact draw on ancient sources, we need be less interested in whether there was an ancient idealist philosophy than in what idealist philosophers have made of what they take to be their ancient precursors, and the inventors of some of their most important concepts.

Bosanquet's formulation of idealism as inclusivist monism draws on the vocabulary of the initiator of monism and, indeed, of systematic metaphysics, Parmenides of Elea. While some will therefore protest that "Parmenides is not, as some have said, the 'father of idealism'; on the contrary, all materialism depends on his view of reality" (Burnet 1930: 182), we have already seen that idealism does not rule out materialism, and will see in what follows that the problems first formulated by Parmenides play a decisive role in the development, in successive ages, of idealist philosophy, as Charles H. Kahn acknowledges: "Parmenides' monism … had an important development in ancient and medieval philosophy and significant parallels in modern monism since Spinoza and Hegel. The identification of Mind and Being; that is, of cognition with its object" (2009: 163).

PARMENIDES AND THE IDENTITY OF BEING AND THINKING

The 150 extant lines constituting the writings of Parmenides of Elea take the form of a two-part poem, the first part called the *Way of Truth* and the second, the *Way of Appearance*.[7] Following a prologue or "proem", in which the narrator is carried by a chariot of the sun through the gates of night and day to the abode of a goddess who promises him that he will "learn all things" (DK28 B1; "Both the unmoved heart of rounded truth, and what seems to mortals, in which there is no true belief …, [s]till, you shall learn them too, and come to see how beliefs must exist in an acceptable form, all-pervasive as they together are"),[8] the goddess next informs the narrator of the two "ways of seeking". The first is the "path of Trust, for Truth attends it" and the second, "the way that it is not and that it must not be" (DK28 B2). Both methods are vital, since the latter provides the rule in accordance with which to assess what cannot be. The problem of "what is not", here announced for the first time, marks the beginning of Parmenides' complex ontology and its relation to epistemology, in so far as it opposes truth not to falsity or to belief, but to "what *is* not". We cannot know what is not, the goddess then advises, because "there is no end to it". Yet there is another sense to the unknowability of what is not, a sense that, were its translation not so hotly disputed, we could say is made clear in fragment B3, which in F. M. Cornford's translation runs: "For it is the same thing that can be thought and that can be" (DK28 B3). Cornford's objection to the identification of thinking and being postulated by fragment B3 is, therefore, that it leads to the *panpsychism* that Plato finds through Parmenides – "all things think" (*Prm.* 132c) – and that Hegel (1969: 84) identifies with the Eleatics in general.[9] It is against the risk of pansychism, rather than that of idealism, that Cornford justifies his translation:

> I cannot believe that Parmenides meant: "To think is the same thing as to be." He nowhere suggests that his One Being thinks, and no Greek of his date or for long afterwards would have seen anything but nonsense in the statement that "*A exists*" means the same thing as "*A thinks*". (1939: 34n1)

Cornford's translation is not the only one; the simplest translation of the fragment runs "for thinking and being are the same" (Phillips 1955: 553), from which we can conclude, argues E. D. Phillips, disputing Cornford and John Burnet, that "Parmenides can be called an idealist, who believes that what can be thought must be real" (1955: 556). This is closer to the sense that most overtly idealist commentators on Parmenides have settled on, as for example in Hegel, who explicates it thus: "thinking is therefore identical with its Being, for there is nothing other than Being" (1970a: vol. 18, 289–90). Hegel makes Parmenides' indeterminate being into the starting point for systematic thinking in general.[10] We find support for this account of the fragment in Plotinus:

> The contemplation must be the same as the contemplated, and Intellect the same as the intelligible; for, if not the same, there will not be truth; for the one who is trying to possess beings [*ta onta*] will possess an impression different from the realities, and this is not truth. (*Enn.* V.3.5)

Plotinus' concern with the "realities" or beings (*ta onta*) as grounding the identity of contemplation and what is contemplated and therefore producing truth exactly echoes Parmenides. The passage therefore draws attention to the objective dimension of the identity of what is and what is thought. This is why Hegel takes "indeterminate Being" as the cornerstone of a system of an *objective* idealism – not because it can then be determined by and for thinking, but because, following Parmenides' starting point, *thinking starts necessarily from being*, from "what is".

However, there is also a *subjective* idealism associated with the reading "being and thinking are the same". Writing in 1935, Heidegger outlines the reasoning that leads to this "customary" view of the fragment. If, "thinking and being are the same", then:

> because thinking remains a subjective activity, and thinking and Being are supposed to be the same according to Parmenides, everything becomes subjective. There are no beings in themselves. But such a doctrine, so the story goes, can be found in Kant and German Idealism. Parmenides already basically anticipated their doctrines. (2000: 145)

The reason for this parody is not that Heidegger considers Parmenides' poem *not* to be a vital stimulus to the German idealists, but rather that thinking would become *all* that there is. If "thinking and being are the same" is read as "being is nothing other than what is thought by thinking", it follows that nothing *but* thinking "is". This is how Bernard Williams construes fragment B3, which has allowed, he claims, "some interpreters [to] have claimed that Parmenides believed being and thought to be one, that nothing existed except thought" (2008: 21). Berkeley's argument that, since everything perceived is an idea, there must be an "infinite mind" to perceive them is taken as the exemplar for Burnyeat and Williams; but even Berkeley does not conclude that "nothing exists except thought", claiming instead that such an "infinite mind should be necessarily inferred from the bare existence of the sensible world" (GBW II.213). Similarly, the subjective idealisms we find, for example, in Sprigge (2006) and in Fichte, who waxes very Parmenidean when he argues that "self-consciousness is the identity of thinking and being" (1992: 382 n.),[11] add importantly "objective" qualifications to subjectivity. For such subjective idealisms, the model is best expressed by Bradley:

> We have experience in which there is no distinction between my awareness and that of which I am aware. There is an immediate feeling, a knowing and being in one, with which knowledge begins; and though this is in a manner transcended, it nevertheless remains throughout as the present foundation of my known world. (Bradley 1914: 159–60)

Bradley is explicit that, although my experience has a "finite centre", it would be a "fundamental and disastrous mistake" to call it subjective (*ibid.*: 189). He is concerned, in other words, with that point in experience where precisely being and thinking become one, in other words, when knowing occurs, when experience is as much objective as subjective. Such a position would construe fragment B3 not primarily as a thesis concerning being, but as one concerning knowing. This epistemological or phenomenological approach is echoed and acknowledged by Kahn as expressly Parmenidean (2009: 157). Kahn accordingly proposes that "[t]he 'is' which Parmenides proclaims is not primarily existential but veridical: it asserts not only the reality but the determinate being-so of the knowable object, as the ontological 'content' or correlate of true statement" (*ibid.*: 155). It makes no sense for Kahn to argue that the result is subjective in the restrictive sense, precisely because all knowledge, if it is knowledge at all, must have "what is" as its content. He thus argues that in fragment B3, it is the *noein*, the thinking, that is "reduced" to being and never the contrary: "the mind does not impose its forms but receives them from the object it knows" (*ibid.*: 166). Although Kahn does not self-describe as an idealist of any sort, the claim as to the fundamental inalienability of being from knowing he proposes would be equally at home in Plato, Hegel or, as he acknowledges (*ibid.*: 157), Bradley.

The three positions – panpsychist, objective and subjective idealism – derived from Parmenides' fragment B3, show that the philosophical *problem* of idealism consists in (a) how the identity of being and thinking exhausts what is, and (b) which determines the other. Regardless, then, of whether we may claim Parmenides as an idealist, his formulations remain key to determining what idealism became. Importantly, we have seen that none of the idealists, Berkeley included, *simply* pass off thought as *all there is to being*.

It follows from the identity of being and thinking, or of what is and what is thought, that nothing additional can exist. It is here we first encounter the monistic implications of Parmenides' thought. The monism is formulated in accordance with the two ways announced by the goddess in the proem. According to the *Way of Truth*, "it is, and cannot not be"; while according to the *Way of Appearance*, "it is not, and it must not be" (DK28 B2).[12] From the first formulation that "It is", the longest of the extant fragments, B8, deduces the following properties of being: it cannot have been created, nor can it be destroyed, since to be created, it must have arisen. To have arisen, it must not have been there, so if it arose, this must have been from nothing. But what is not cannot be; therefore, it cannot have arisen. Nor can it have been created by something else, since there could be nothing other than what is except what is not, which cannot be, and so on. Nor can it contain any void, since this would be other than being, and therefore nothing; nor can it have parts, since by what could parts of being be separated, if not nothingness?

Nor can it have come into being at any time, nor become anything in the future, since either It is, or It is not: "if it is, then it is now, all at once" (Burnet 1930: 181).

Discussing not-being, therefore, immediately presents problems: if what is not cannot be thought or spoken of, then either mentioning it, as the goddess does, constitutes a simple self-contradiction, or thinking of x is not sufficient to warrant a claim that x exists, apparently contradicting fragment B3. For this reason, the goddess instructs the investigator to "use reason" and "the test I have announced" in order to "restrain your thinking from this way of seeking" (DK28 B7). The force of the test is therefore purely logical, and constitutes an early formulation of the principle of non-contradiction. *Not* to follow the results of the test will therefore involve the enquirer in an endless series of failed determinations of not-being, when all that can be said about it is that "it is not". In other words, Parmenides is not arguing that contradictions in thinking "what is" are not possible, but, on the contrary, that *because* they are, a test is necessary in order that enquiry into "what is" does not suffer the infinite detours of "what is not". Logically and ontologically, therefore, not-being constitutes a limit to "what is" and what can be thought.

Yet if "what is not" can be thought *even as a limit*, or if thinking about not-being does take place, then not-being is in fact thinkable; it would then not be true that thinking thinks only what is (fragment B3) unless "what is" includes "what is not". Yet this is expressly what Parmenides denies. As Kahn puts it,

> A real distinction between knowledge and its object, or between language and the world, is excluded by his rigid dichotomy [of what is and what is not]. Such a distinction is all the more alien to his philosophy insofar as the logical laws (excluded middle, non-contradiction, identity) which he has discovered in thought and in language are understood by him as construing the very structure of the real. (2009: 165)

Thus Parmenides' axioms outline a problem for any systematic, monistic philosophy. If all is one, as the *Way of Truth* claims, then all that is must be accounted for in its terms. Parmenides does this by *negation*: the one is *un*created, *in*destructible, *does not* come into being, *has no* parts, and so on. The problem is, if being and thinking are the same, and yet what-is-not cannot be thought, how is negation thinkable? If the goddess's test is solely logical, then there must be a divide between the logical (what can be thought) and the ontological (what is), marring the consistency of the system. If, as Kahn has it, the logical laws of thought constitute the very structure of reality, then "what is not" must *be*. One solution to this is to argue that the difference lies in the *content* of thought: the thought of what is, that is, has an object, whereas the thought of what is not has none whatsoever. Would it then remain true, however, that "thinking and being are the same", or would a better translation run "for it is the same thing that can be thought and can be" (Cornford 1939: 31; Burnet 1930: 173), since this would allow that "what is not" cannot be thought, without sacrificing consistency?

The problem of negation continues to play a major role in the development of idealism, most especially in Hegel's dialectic (see ch. 8). Plato's attempted accommodation of not-being, against Parmenidean strictures, is crucial in the subsequent development of idealism, and we turn to it in Chapter 2. Yet Parmenides' renown is equally due to his advocacy of this direct contact between thought and reality. There are accordingly many realist accounts of the same identity in subsequent idealists. Bosanquet, for example, argues that "It is all but impossible to distinguish nature from mind; to separate them is impossible" (1912: 367); Whitehead, that "No entity can be conceived in complete abstraction from the system of the universe" (PR 3). As a simultaneous testament to the range of Parmenides' identity thesis, and warning against an oversimplified account of idealism as inherently anti-naturalistic, both retain their idealism within a naturalistic framework.

2. PLATO AND NEOPLATONISM

PLATONIC IDEAS

While Parmenides presented his philosophy in poetic metre, Plato's prefered medium is the display of dialectic in dramatic form. This presents certain problems when we set out to identify what does and does not count as Plato's own philosophy: positions are given as characters, or characters as positions, and their implications are worked out in live discussion, with all its digressions, illustrations and false starts. A degree of caution must therefore be exercised when we attribute a theory to Plato, in the sense "Plato held that …". That said, the problems addressed in his dialogues form the corpus of Platonic philosophy, both in his work and, as we shall see, in Neoplatonism. When, therefore, in what follows we attribute a position or a thesis, we are attributing it to "Platonism", although we shall take care to note what justification there might be for attributing these positions to Plato. The resulting problems will therefore form the basis of this outline of key elements of Platonism for the idealist tradition.

The first such problem concerns Parmenides' conclusions regarding what is not, or not-being. Plato engages it in the *Sophist*, which argues that not-being takes two forms: first, there is *to me on*, absolute not-being or "what is not". The Eleatic Stranger, who takes Socrates' usual role as the primary interlocutor in the dialogue, presents Theaetetus with Parmenides' argument that "he who undertakes to say 'not-being' [*me on*] says nothing at all" (*Soph.* 237e), but adds an important qualification: things can be said of "what is not", despite the fact that it is "no thing". Indeed, in speaking of "things which are not" or "that which is not", we cannot avoid attributing the qualities of plurality or unity to not-being (238b–39b), as Parmenides' goddess does: the way of not-being is endless.

So far, the Stranger is only exploring the consequences of Parmenidean restrictions on what can be said about what is not, contravening the goddess's advice to "hold back thy thought from this way of inquiry" (DK28 B6), but not contradicting Parmenides' theses. It remains the case, in other words, that not-being cannot be correctly described, that "what is not, cannot be thought". Does it follow from this, however, that whatever is not absolute not-being, absolutely is? To demonstrate that it does not, the Stranger asks Theaetetus to state what an image is. Theatetus answers that an image is a likeness, copied from reality, but is "of the same sort" (*Soph*. 240a) as reality. That is, an image is, *qua* image, a real thing in that it is not itself something nonexistent; but it is also the "opposite of real", something that, as the Stranger clarifies the point, "though not really existing [*ouk on*], really does exist" (240b). This is the second account of not-being. Second, therefore, whereas *me on* is "absolute not-being" (*to me on auto kath' auto*; 238c), *ouk on* is "other than being and therefore not-being [*ouk on*]" (256e). As Hegel would helpfully put it, *me on* is indeterminate, and *ouk on* determinate negation (1969: 82; 1991: 147). The former negates, that is, *indiscriminately*, as when Being as such is negated. The latter negates in a determinate manner, as when we say "he's not *really* tall" to distinguish one relatively tall person from another. The Stranger's conclusion is that "When we say not-being [*me on*], we speak, I think, not of something that is the opposite of being, but only of something different" (*Soph*. 257b).

The distinction of indeterminate from determinate negation, or of *me on* from *ouk on*, allows the Stranger to criticize Parmenides' ontological monism. The question is: is Being one or many? Determinate negation (*x is not y*) makes it possible to conceive Being as many. Through a series of arguments concerning the names of Being (Is Being *also* unity? Is the name of Being something or nothing?), echoing Plato's argument in the *Parmenides* (141e) that a purely monistic philosophy could not even say of the One that it exists (if it were and had a name, it would be minimally two), the Stranger next asks whether being is a whole of parts. If it is, then it *is not* unity, since it is *both* whole *and* parts; if not, then either wholeness is real, or being is, but not both, since "being a whole" is not one but many.

Drawing back from the progress of the Stranger's arguments for the moment, the *Sophist* here makes use of the distinction between indeterminate and determinate negation against Parmenides' account of Being. Hence, towards the conclusion of the famous "Battle of Gods and Giants", between materialists and idealists, the latter grouping contains and differentiates between both Parmenidean monists and the "lovers of Ideas" who argue that Being is a plurality (*Soph*. 249c–d). Platonism's advocacy of a plurality of Ideas as "what really are" is therefore drawn out from Parmenides' rigid dichotomy between Being and its indeterminate negation (the absolute antithesis of being) precisely by means of determinate negation or distinction (*x* is not a *y*). As Spinoza noted, this is because all determination of a thing depends not on its "being, but on the contrary, its non-being" (Spinoza 2002: 892), each determinate thing being determinate by virtue of being distinct from every other thing. Similarly in Platonic ontology, each Idea[1] is exactly and only what it is, "itself for itself": the Idea of Beauty, or Beauty itself, is what there *is* of Beauty; but Plato can assert the real being of Beauty precisely because it differs from other Ideas, such as the Good and the True, in a manner that Parmenides could not. "True being", as the Stranger puts it, "consists in certain intelligible and bodiless Ideas" (*Soph.* 246b). Equally, by distinguishing the Ideas from everything else, Platonic ontology accommodates becoming in a manner ruled out by Parmenidean monism. The Stranger therefore defines "being and the universe" as consisting both of rest *and* motion (249d), without compromising the *being* of rest or motion themselves.

What, then, is the Idea? Every philosophy student learns that Plato understands by the Idea a real being existing independently of its being thought or instantiated in "physical reality". Yet the problem of *what the Idea is* develops throughout his dialogues. The dialogues most expressly devoted to exploring what has become known as "Plato's theory of Ideas" are the *Phaedo* (65c–78e, 97b–105c), where it is introduced, the *Parmenides* (128e–137c), where it is critically examined, and the *Sophist*, which revises the theory. To answer the question "What is the Idea?", we shall look at what remains constant throughout these developments.

Socrates offers the first theory of Ideas as unchanging and absolute true being in the *Phaedo*:

> Absolute equality, absolute beauty, any absolute existence, true being – do they ever admit of any change whatsoever? Or does each absolute essence, since it is uniform and exists by itself [*auto kath' auto*], remain the same and never in any way admit of any change? "It must", said Cebes, "necessarily remain the same, Socrates". (*Phd.* 78d)

Plato defines an Idea as *auto kath' auto*. Sometimes translated as "absolute *X*" or "*X* itself", its literal translation is "itself by itself". Each thing that sensibly and physically becomes – the four-dimensional furniture of the everyday world – does so in accordance with the "unique Idea" in which those sensible things that approximate it "participate" (101c) in order to "become" in the particular way they do (i.e. by participating in the Idea "Man", an animal does not become "horse"). Asked how it is that "two" becomes, Socrates responds that nobody knows of any other way:

> by which anything can come into existence than by participating in the proper being [*ousias*] of each thing in which it participates, and therefore [we can] accept no other cause of the existence of

two than participation in duality, and whatever is to be one must
participate in unity. (*Ibid.*)

The thesis is clear: "participation" is what causes the coming-into-existence of particulars, whether these are abstract entities such as numbers, or concrete beautiful things (100c). If participation in the Ideas is to explain how particulars become the particulars they become, or how they come into existence, then the Idea itself must be something that does not come into existence, since, if it were not so, the theory would be viciously regressive. This would mean that Idea and becoming are *different in kind*, leading to the problem, examined at length in the *Parmenides* (130a–35c), as to how becomings participate in the Idea at all.

In the dialogue bearing his name, Parmenides' first criticism of Socrates' theory is to construe the existing-by-itself (*auto kath' auto*) nature of the Idea *globally*, so that Socrates' theory has "separated apart on the one side Ideas themselves and on the other the things that participate in them", an attribution Socrates accepts (*Prm.* 130b). The separation of the Ideas from concrete particulars now accomplished, Parmenides is free to pose the problem of how two things that are different in kind can have anything in common, or how physical things can have any relation whatsoever to Ideas different in kind from them. Parmenides' famous arguments pose Socrates the following dilemma, known as the third man argument:[2] either concrete particulars and the Idea in which they participate are all instances of the same property and therefore not separate; or they are entirely different, and therefore unrelated. In the former case, if the theory of Ideas is true, then a second-level Idea is necessary in order to impart the quality in question to the first Idea and its participants, so that the initial problem forms an infinite regress. Thus Socrates must revert to the view that they are different, proposing that, rather than being a thing like other things, "each of these Ideas is a thought, which cannot properly exist anywhere but in a mind" (132b).

It is striking that Socrates accepts the global construal of the separateness argument. Separateness, however, need not be a property of the Ideas *en masse*. Separateness also follows simply from the Ideas being exactly what they are, no more and no less, so that their separation is not *from* becomings, but rather *different from other Ideas*. This is why the problem of the combination of the Ideas and the problem of determinate negation assume the importance they do in the *Sophist*. It is by this means that Plato initially distinguishes his theory of "what really is" from Parmenides' theory: rather than the One Being, being is *many*, comprising all the Ideas, on the one hand and, as we have seen, all becoming on the other. Yet this means that "being" must be shared by *all* that is: all ideas and, to the extent that they participate in an Idea, all becomings. In other words, there is in Platonism a *hierarchy* of

Ideas, with the Good at its apex. For this reason, the *Sophist* raises the issue of what is at stake in describing the Ideas by means of terms such as "being", "by itself", "apart" and "from the others" (*Soph.* 252c). If Ideas possess these qualities then, according to the theory that things receive what character they have from the Ideas they participate in, it must be that the *Phaedo*'s Idea of Beauty, for example, "participates in" or is "combinable with" the Idea of Being, but not with that of Motion or Rest. It turns out that the Ideas are not free-standing and isolated, each "itself by itself", but are internally complex or, as the Stranger puts it, "in every one of the Ideas there is much that it *is* and an indefinite number of things that it *is not*" (256e).

In other words, being is many ("there is much that is") *because* what *X* is, is different from all ("an indefinite number") the things "that it is not". One Idea is not another, for instance, but neither is it other than an Idea nor a concrete particular. In other words, the *Sophist* does not concede that the separateness of the Ideas constitutes "another world", as popular Platonism has it, but is rather of a piece with the world of becomings, or nature. The Idea in Platonism is a problem solved by intelligence but also by nature: intelligence investigates the precise complexion of the Idea at issue, just as nature resolves the problem of endless becoming by approximation to the Ideas.

This "one-world" account of Platonism is now contrary to the popular view, but it was not always so. Bosanquet, for instance, consistently argues against "Plato's so-called dualism", noting that "this splitting-up of Plato's universe into two persistent extremes is part of the easy-going centrifugal attitude against which our whole thesis will prove to be a protest" (1912: 8).[3] In *A Companion to Plato's Republic for English Readers* he notes that the Idea is always conceived by Plato as "inherently connect[ed] with his idea of causation" (1925: 241), as in its initial presentation in the *Phaedo*, where the theory is consequent upon an enquiry into "the cause of generation and decay" (*Phd.* 95e–6a). The causal Idea becomes explicit later in that dialogue: "If anything is beautiful besides beauty itself [*auto to kalon*] it is beautiful for no other reason than because it partakes of beauty itself" (100c). Thus, while Cornford (1935: 78–9) notes that the *Phaedo* simply ducks the issue of participation, the dialogue does in fact address the issue precisely in causal terms. Clearly, however, we are not dealing with the kind of "efficient" causation such as is evident in the transmission of impetus from one object to another. The causation at issue is *final*, that is, "teleological", as Cornford (1932: 63–4) notes. The Idea does not push nature into existence; rather, nature becomes in the way it does, generates and decays, by virtue of the Idea that draws it, as Plato's cosmology has it, from its "contra-rational [*alogou*] and aleatoric power" (*Phlb.* 28d) to the "setting into order this Universe" (*Ti.* 53a–b).

Plato thus renegotiates the monism of Parmenidean Being by virtue of a more complex account of negation as difference than Parmenides' strict dichotomy could allow. The core qualification of the Idea as "itself by itself" need not be understood as a two-worlds theory, but on the contrary, as many philosophers have urged, as a one-world account stretching from the causes of physical becoming to those of intelligibility. It is Plotinus who carries both the systematic and the causal dimensions of Platonism further, and it is to his extraordinary philosophy that we now turn.

PLOTINUS AND NEOPLATONISM

Plotinus, an Egyptian, founded a school in Rome in 245 CE whose members have, since the late eighteenth century, been known as Neoplatonists. Their period of activity, the last great flowering of ancient philosophy, ended with the Emperor Justinian closing Plato's Athenian Academy in 529 and banishing the philosophers.

Having a formidable history behind them, the Neoplatonists were concerned to synthesize the knowledges their precedent philosophies furnished them with. In this, they follow the practices of Plato, whose metaphysics fused Heraclitean becoming with Parmenidean Being; and of Aristotle, who begins most of his major treatises with accounts of his predecessors' theories. In Simplicius' commentaries on Aristotle's works, the Neoplatonist scholar provides us with a great deal of ancient philosophical materials that would otherwise not have come down to us, including much of Parmenides' poem. Similarly, Neoplatonist philosophers such as Proclus, Iamblichus, Damascius and Olympiodorus wrote commentaries on Plato's works.

Commentary, however, is not simply exegetical or scholarly in the restrictive sense. Reading any of these works betrays a clear agenda: to synthesize the works of the major historical philosophers into a single system. Here is Plotinus setting out the parameters of this research programme: "Now we must consider that some of the blessed philosophers of ancient times have found out the truth; but it is proper to investigate which of them have attained it most completely, and how we too could reach an understanding about these things" (*Enn.* III.7.1).[4] Clearly, although Plotinus wrote no commentaries himself, the practice of commentary contributed towards this goal in producing not simply a compendium of philosophers' views, as Aristotle's histories tend to do, but attempts to ascertain the "completeness" of the truth each presents. Since we know in advance that none has "truth itself", these attempts are themselves subject to "completion" by the commentator-philosopher.

The Neoplatonic practice of "co-mentation" or *thinking with* previous philosophers – a practice that survives into modernity most obviously in Hegel's *Lectures on the History of Philosophy* – was particularly focused on realizing the "harmony" of Plato's and Aristotle's doctrines. Such harmony depended also on rendering each philosopher self-consistent, so that a significant element of what might critically be called revisionism is necessarily involved in the Neoplatonic project.[5] Their basic means for achieving this was to search for "first principles" to provide foundations. Discovering the self-consistency of each philosopher entails that each had a discoverable system; unifying these systems then becomes the task of the Neoplatonic philosopher.

The notion that philosophy, regardless of how little systematic form it may appear to possess, always articulates a system, entails the highly Platonic thesis that the elements of philosophy are essentially unchanging and fixed. As opposed, then, to Hegel's developmental history of philosophy, the Neoplatonists eliminated historical accident from systematic, intelligible form, a form that Hegel himself said was achieved best not in Plotinus' better known *Enneads*, but in Proclus, who, in his *Elements of Theology*, "distinguished himself from Plotinus, not least because with him, Neoplatonic philosophy by this time attained a general systematic order and a developed form" (Hegel 1970a: vol. 19, 469).

What remains implicit in the *Enneads* is systematically set out in the *Elements*; while this remains a powerful prejudice,[6] Hegel's interest is clearly aroused by Proclus because of the presupposition that reason grants immanent access to the real or, in Plotinus' terms, that "Being and Intellect are therefore one nature" (*Enn.* V.9.8). The crucial question is: *what* nature? How many natures are there in the Plotinian universe? William Ralph Inge, for instance, argues that for Plotinus, "Reality … is not a purely objective realm, existing apart from the mind", but makes being *dependent* on "being thought" in precisely the manner that worries Burnyeat; for Inge, even "Matter standing alone is only thinkable if it is invested with a spurious substantiality" (1923: vol. 1, 137–8). This same construal of Plotinus' "one nature" is equally evident in the work of contemporary scholars such as Maria Luisa Gatti, who characterizes Plotinus' philosophy as a "'contemplationist metaphysics', in which contemplation, as creative, constitutes the reason for the being of everything" (Gatti 1996: 33). Both make Plotinus' metaphysics into a precursor of the subjective idealisms found in Berkeley or in Fichte (see chs 4 and 6, respectively), for whom the only reality there is depends on mind for its being.[7]

There are two remaining alternatives. Inge directly disputes one of these, which he calls the "panlogicist" account most often associated with Hegel. Noting the triadic structure of Plotinus' "hypostases" (literally, a hypostasis is a constantly underlying element) – the One, Intellect and Soul – Inge adds the following qualification: "In Plotinus the triad is important, but it does not dominate the whole of his thought, as it does that of Proclus and Hegel" (1923: vol. 1, 122). It is not the formalism alone, however, but rather its combination with the Parmenidean identity of thought and being that Inge is rejecting. For in such a case, formalism is not a mere formalism, added as a human artefact for conceptual convenience, but rather the nerve uniting thinking and being, and, in consequence, an *objective* structure. Hence the idealists' fascination with logic, as simultaneously the enquiry into being's self-determination in and as thought; and into thinking's becoming structurally self-conscious. Thus, in Hegel's words, "the task of philosophy determines itself by making the unity of thinking and being, its foundational idea, objective, and conceiving this" (1970a: vol. 20, 314). If the *objectivity* of the unity of thinking and being is idealism's prize, it must still be asked whether it is won if this objectivity is only *made*, or whether its "being conceived" is a sufficient condition for its being in the first place. In other words, there remains the problem of the real instantiation of logic, of the *logos*; or, otherwise put, of the reality of the Ideas.

The third variation on the Parmenidean identity we find in Neoplatonic philosophy concerns this structure not only as conceived by a subject, however universal it might be; but rather as being's *own* structures. This provides us with a third, "naturalistic" strand of idealism, whose legatees are Leibniz, Schelling and Bosanquet (see chs 4, 7 and 11, respectively), so that Neoplatonism's systematic ambitions encompass idealism's three major subsequent variants: subjective, objective and naturalistic, respectively. Accordingly, while disputes may be mounted regarding which particular type of idealism is represented by which particular philosopher, Neoplatonism sets out the parameters for all subsequent developments in idealist philosophy.

In what follows, we shall consider Plotinus and Proclus to be offering a naturalistic account, but without determining yet what Plotinus' "one nature" might be. We shall also consider it as starting, therefore, from Platonic questions and problems, not least the problem of the differentiation of the Ideas explored in the *Sophist*. It is in this regard, moreover, that the term "Neoplatonist" is appropriate, in so far as it is integral to all the accounts Plato's dialogues offer concerning the theory of Ideas that they are always and invariably, that is, eternally, what they are. In its Neoplatonic variant, Platonism achieves a consistency that Plato's interrogations could not supply. Neoplatonism combines the Platonic Idea with core Aristotelian problems concerning the nature of the changeable, of *physis*, nature or "generation", to form a complete, that is, a systematic and inclusive ontology of thinking and being "of one nature".

FIRST PRINCIPLES: THE GOOD BEYOND BEING

In a text of fundamental importance for the Neoplatonic philosophers, the *Republic*'s famous simile of the sun provides an excellent map on which we may locate the starting points from which their problems emerge.

The common starting point for Plotinus and Proclus concerns what Gatti calls "the principal problem of Greek metaphysics", namely, "why and how do a many derive from One?" (1996: 28; cf. Dillon in Proclus 1987: xvi; Remes 2008: 41). This already represents a transformation of the problems posed in the *Parmenides* (131a–c) concerning the "one over many", since at issue is not the *separability* of the Ideas from particulars, but the *derivation* or *production* of the many from or by the one. Plotinus offers two accounts of the "procession" (*proodos*) of the many from the one:

> But there is a need for the One from which the many derives to exist before the many: for in every number series the one comes first. But in the case of number-series people do say this; for the successive numbers are [the result of] composition; but in the series of realities, what necessity is there now for there to be some one here too from which the many derive? (*Enn.* V.3.12)

Plotinus considers first formal, and then real, series. In the former, there is always something before the many, from which the latter emerges by "composition" (*syntheseis*) or addition (1 + 1 + 1 + ...). The procession of realities from the One, however, is not by composition, but by the necessity that if there is to be one, something must cause it. "All that exists", Proclus clarifies, "proceeds from a single first cause" (ET 11); yet of what kind? The efficient, formal, material and final causes Aristotle identifies in the *Physics* (194b16–5a2) or the "kind of causality" Socrates presents in the *Phaedo* (100d)? The question of the kinds of cause (ET 7–13, 56–65, 75–86, 97–112), of "principles" (Damascius 2010) or "firsts" (Plotinus), assumes central importance in the Neoplatonic philosophy. At this point, then, the contrast between the composition of the numbers consequent on the one, and the order exemplified by the real series, focuses the problem of the nature and kinds of causality. Just as the *Phaedo*'s enquiries into the "causes of everything" led Socrates from natural history to "other kinds of cause" (*Phd.* 96a–8a), the *Republic*'s simile of the sun leads from natural causes to the causes of being. The sun "not only makes things visible", but:

> causes the processes of generation, growth and nourishment, without itself being such a process. The Good therefore may be said to be the source not only of the intelligibility of the objects of knowledge, but also of their being and reality; yet it is not itself that reality, but is beyond it, and superior to it in dignity and power.
> (*Resp.* 509c)

The Idea of the Good therefore provides the Neoplatonists with their paradigmatic concept of the first cause or "principle" (*Enn.* VI.7.15). They do not consider it true because Plato says it is, but rather ask, "how can the best of realities possibly not be the Good?" (VI.7.23), before filling out this cause with all the powers necessary to the best of realities. Thus, "if there is something from which all things come, there is nothing stronger than it, but things are less than it" (*ibid.*). The *before* and *after*, and the *greater* and *lesser* power, become key to understanding Neoplatonism. Thus, since the Good is the source of the "objects of knowledge", that is, the Ideas, and since the Ideas are "true beings", the Good cannot be a part of the being it produces (one among many) but must be "beyond being". On the other hand, it exceeds being both in dignity (or value)[8] and in power; the excess of the Good over being is therefore quantifiable in terms of greater or lesser *power*: "Every productive cause is superior to that which it produces" (ET 7).

For Plotinus, power is immanently differentiating. That is, differences in power constitute the hierarchy of realities or "hypostases" – Good or One, Intellect and higher and lower Soul – that compose being, as in the following passage:

> For that Good is the principle .... Intellect therefore had the power from him to generate and to be filled full of its own offspring, since the Good gave what he did not himself have. But from the Good himself who is one there were many for this Intellect; for it was unable to hold the power which it received and broke it up and made the one power many, that it might be able so to bear it part by part. (*Enn*. VI.7.15)

What the Good gave that it did not have is Intellect and its offspring. If the Good is the principle, and if Intellect has power – "for intelligence is a kind of movement" (VI.7.35) – then the cause of the *objects* of knowledge (the offspring of Intellect, or the Ideas) and of their *being* and *reality*, is a power that by definition exceeds being. In a direct inversion of Aristotle's thesis that "from the potential [*dunamis*] the actual [*energeia*] is always produced by an actual thing, e.g. man by man; musician by musician" (*Metaph.* 1049b24–5), that is, that actuality precedes potentiality, Plotinus argues that it is only *from* a productive power that being arises. The "productive power of all things" (*Enn*. III.8.10) is the source of the actual and thus transcends it. It is simply because being depends on such power that it can contain less power than its source: "What then is more deficient than the One? That which is not one; it is therefore many" (V.3.15). Since it cannot grasp the power of the Good immediately, Intellect contemplates the objects it produces *singly* yet each as related to the One that exceeds it, "making the one power many"; each resultant Idea is differentiated from the others precisely by its share of the power of the Good. As Proclus explains, "for partition dissipates and dissolves the potency of the individual, but indivisibility, compressing and concentrating it, keeps it self-contained without exhaustion or diminution" (ET 86).

Moreover, being differentiated each from the other according to the share of power manifest in their being, the One differentiates in accordance with power. Were the One merely one among many, "it would not be the absolute One" (*Enn.* V.3.13). Therefore, "since the nature of the One is generative of all things it is not any one of them" (VI.9.3). Hence the Plotinian formula that the One or Good is "solitary and alone" (VI.7.25) depends on the differentiating power it exerts and that cannot be equalled. All of being descends in a hierarchy of differentials of power in relation to the maximum power of the One. It is through the measurement, or evaluation, of this difference that the structure of being is caused. Thus the causal relations that generate being are also evaluations of beings, each evaluation existing as a level of being, proceeding from the One that generates all form to the formless not-one of matter itself, which is relative incapacity, or the lowest value of power.

The One, as the power of generation, is "efficient" in Aristotle's sense (*Ph.* 194b30), as Plotinus states: "The First is the power which causes motion and rest, so that it is beyond them" (*Enn.* III.9.7). Like "the beautiful itself", however, it is also a final cause, since "all things desire the Good" (VI.7.20), while the Good itself remains "impassive" or unmoved. The reference to desire invokes the doctrine of final causes from which Aristotle fashioned the rudiments of his life sciences (see Lennox 2001).

We would, however, be equally mistaken in considering Neoplatonic systems to be governed by teleological relations as we would Plato to be unconcerned with causes. Rather, they are governed by a "principle of differentiation into unequals" or, as Pauliina Remes calls it, a "principle of non-reciprocal dependence" (2008: 43): what comes after depends on what precedes it; but what precedes does not depend on what succeeds it.

The principle of differentiation into unequals applies not only between realities, but to realities themselves, and even to the Good. Thus, "the One is always perfect and therefore produces everlastingly; and its product is less than itself" (*Enn.* V.1.6). Realities are unequal in several respects: (a) in respect of power and value; (b) in respect of priority and posteriority; (c) in respect of generator and generated. All these inequalities are entailed in the Plotinian concept of cause, a concept that Proclus formalized thus: "Every effect remains in its cause, proceeds from it, and reverts upon it" (ET 35). Thus, to the efficient cause of being must be added the final cause of the Good. Since all things desire the Good, which is nevertheless unique and alone, the power that produces is also responsible for the power that pursues "reversion" (*epistrophe*) towards the Good. Reversion is the turning back of contemplation on to its cause or principle, but as contemplation rather than production or "procession" (*proohodos*) from the One. Since "Intellect is not that Good" (*Enn*. V.1.7), it cannot recover the entirety of the Good that causes the being and reality of its objects; the circuit of production, in other words, cannot be perfectly closed in thought alone.

Thus, immanently differentiated and differentiating, Plotinus' philosophical system determines what must follow if there is a cause of being that is *prior* to it. Given only this priority or antecedence, there follows the entire "cosmos", or ordered, beautiful whole.

What remains to be seen, finally, is which of the variants of idealism Plotinus' extraordinary speculative philosophy supports. To assess this, we shall revert to the problem discussed at the beginning of Chapter 1: the Parmenidean identity of thinking and being.

Plotinus cites this identity several times throughout the *Enneads*, but V.1.4 offers a lengthier discussion of the problem. Beginning from the proposition that, since the One is the productive source of the many-that-are, and since what is are the Ideas, "Intellect is all things". At one level, this certainly suggests a plausible alliance between Plotinus and subjective idealism. Hence Inge's (1923: vol. 1, 138) identification of Plotinus' real-idealism with Bradley's (see ch. 9). Yet the envelopment of the Ideas within the broader problem of causation upsets this equation, in so far as it invokes what is genuinely new in Plotinus: prior and posterior as the categories of ontogenesis, or the genesis of being. If Intellect is "all things", as *Enneads* V.1.4 claims, what are these things that the Intellect is? Plotinus unfolds the problem: "Each of them is Intellect and Being, and the whole is universal Intellect and Being, Intellect making Being exist in thinking it, and Being giving Intellect thinking and existence by being thought" (*ibid.*). Each reality being differentiated according to its share of power, Intellect makes Being exist *in thinking it*; yet thinking depends on Being in order that there is something to be thought at all. In attempting to distinguish the prior from the posterior, Plotinus draws the conclusion that "the cause of thinking is something else, which is also cause of being; they both therefore have a cause other than themselves" (*ibid.*). Being and thinking are the same, but the commonality of their cause differentiates them: what is first in being and thinking is their cause, "the productive power of all things" (III.8.10).

From Plotinus, then, we inherit a metaphysics in which power is not, as the Eleatic Stranger from Plato's *Sophist* proposes, identified with being (*Soph.* 247e), but, rather, precedes it. That the "becoming of being" (*Phlb.* 26d8) has a logic of anteriority and posteriority – that "by nature, production always leads, and the generated product follows" (27a4) – is the outcome of five hundred years of attempts to forge a system of the identity of thinking and being. Whether the becoming of being or ontogenesis is static or dynamic; whether power or eternal substance lies at the ground of all things; whether a God might initiate all becoming while remaining as its ground; whether mind might be excised from nature altogether; all these are philosophical possibilities speculatively developed from these initiating interrogations of the single problem bequeathed to philosophy by Parmenides.

Neoplatonism supplies Plato's interrogations of power, becoming and being with systematic form, leaving the source of being, its ground of becoming, asymmetrical with respect to its products. In the process, a philosophy of nature is given where nature, since it participates in the Idea, becomes inseparable from it. Hence, following Proclus' *Elements of Theology* or "first philosophy", there is an *Elements of Physics*. The fundamental problem systematic philosophical idealism must hereafter address is whether the system is a closed one, that is, whether one or all *epistrophai* can recover the entire *proodos*: whether the source is immanently identical with its thinking. Where Plotinus, Berkeley, Schelling and Bradley would respond in the negative, Spinoza and Hegel propose that the identity of thought and being comprise the beginning and the end of systematic philosophy. It is this question of asymmetry, as we shall see, rather than the reducibility of being to thinking, that differentiates idealist philosophies even to the present: for every investigation of cosmogenesis from the Good (Leslie 2007) there is another (Rescher 2000) claiming the irreducible excess of being over thinking; neither, however, renounces nature.

CONCLUSION: THE ACTUALITY OF ANCIENT IDEALISM

In Plato and Plotinus, as in Hegel, dialectic is the means whereby the world makes itself intelligible. For Hegel, Logic is "the science of things grasped in thoughts", and Dialectic the means whereby these "thought-determinations" are thinkable. "The Logical", he writes, "is to be sought in a system of thought-determinations in which the antithesis between subjective and objective … disappears" (1991: 56). Accordingly, concerned neither with thoughts to the exclusion of things, nor with things to the exclusion of thoughts, Logic makes the antitheses of thinking and being, of subject and object, possible in the first place. Dialectic, as "the very nature of thinking" (*ibid.*: 35), then thinks both sides of these antitheses along with their contradictions; but in so far as these antitheses are not merely formal offences against a rule of reasoning, such as affirming both p and not-p of a single subject X, Dialectic discovers the full actuality of these antitheses as "the reason immanent in the world" (*ibid.*: 56).

Yet the preconditions for Hegel's thinking are far from original to him, having been established among the ancients. Starting, as does Hegel, from the Dialectic as the method by which "being, reality, and eternal immutability" (*Phlb.* 58a4) are organized, well-proportioned and true, Plato describes it as making true causes intelligible to the extent that "the power of the Good … takes refuge in the nature of the Beautiful" (64e4–5), that is, that power is found within the proportionate arrangement of the Ideas. Yet it is not a power to push something into existence that the Idea possesses, but rather a power to draw existents towards it. Dialectic therefore immediately distinguishes intelligible from natural causes, in that it is the power of the former to differentiate and combine the Ideas involved in the articulation of being, while that of the latter is to produce, one after the other, the "things of this universe" (59a3) without reference to the cause of the All.

This distinction in turn provokes Plotinus' claim that Dialectic "is the science which can speak about everything in a reasoned and orderly way" (*Enn.* I.3.4.1–3), since it articulates the "essential nature of each thing" and "traverses the intelligible whole" (I.3.4.13–17). From this whole, nothing is excluded; in addition to the whole, it "deals with things and has real beings as a kind of material for its activity" (I.3.5.5–12), so that even natural science borrows intimately from it. Plotinus therefore distinguishes dialectic from logic in that the one is expressed in the grain of being, while the other is a separate tool, an organon, used only by philosophers. Hence, as one of the identity thesis's most recent adherents, John McDowell, writes: "there is no ontological gap between the sort of thing one can mean, or generally the sort of thing one can think, and the sort of thing that can be the case. When one thinks truly, what one thinks is what is the case" (1996: 27). Proponents of dialectic advocate the identity of thought and being not only owing to their realism, but also because they claim it as philosophy's task to discover the reason in nature, not merely how to organize our thoughts in isolation from what they are of, as though reason sprang into being with finite rational beings, as a novel element in the world. This is why nature is not a side issue, but rather an immediate problem for all three. In Plato, nature is productive power; in Plotinus, it is next in order of derivation from the "real beings" that are the activity of the dialectic, as it were, in "material" form (*Enn.* I.3.5.12); in Hegel, dialectic explicates the "innermost nature" of the world (1991: 56); and in McDowell, "the world exerts a rational influence on our thinking" (1996: 34).

If being, the world or nature are to exert such an influence on thinking as McDowell suggests, and if this influence is itself rational, this invokes a further worry concerning idealist – or idealist-like – metaphysics that also has its grounds in ancient philosophy, and which has an epistemic and a metaphysical dimension. The epistemic dimension of the problem is given, for instance, in Schelling's *Philosophical Investigations into the Essence of Human Freedom*, where he writes of the "ancient doctrine that like is recognized by like" (2006: 10), and references it to Empedocles, Pythagoras, Plato and Sextus Empiricus. The metaphysical dimension of the problem is sourced by Sorabji to the fourth-century philosopher Gregory of Nyssa, and poses the question of whether "a cause needs to be somehow like its effect". Gregory writes:

> If God is matterless, where does matter come from? How can quantity come from non-quantity, the visible from the invisible, some thing with limited bulk and size from what lacks magnitude and limits? And so also for the other characteristics seen in matter: how or whence were they produced by one who had nothing of the kind in his own nature? (Quoted in Sorabji 1983: 290)

Gregory's solution is that quantity, visibility, size and limitation are ideas that, "when they combine, turn into matter", that is, into a body. The only alternative is the absurdity that "a corporeal substance existing outside the minds of spirits should be produced out of nothing by the mere will of a spirit" (*ibid.*: 291), which does not so much resolve as restate the problem Gregory identifies. Now while Sorabji seeks in Gregory the lineaments of a precursor for Berkeley with which to refute Burnyeat's thesis that there could be no ancient idealism, we can here note again that the epistemic and the metaphysical are in fact two dimensions of the one problem. That is, it is only by isolating thinking from being that the problem arises. If, that is, we begin from some version of Parmenides' identity thesis, then the knowing at issue already has a causal component, in so far as the likeness of the known and knowing would be the effect of the latter's being produced. Extracting the causal dimension from knowing, in other words, is precisely what isolates thinking from being, or mind from nature.

The identity, however, does not only enable the reconnection of mind to nature as effect to cause. As the example of the medieval philosopher Eriugena shows, accepting a causal connection between knower and known as the ground of their likeness is no barrier to asserting the priority of mind over nature: "the intellection of all things", he writes, "is the being of all things" (1976: II.559). In this respect, Moran comments, "Eriugena is articulating an idealist thesis of the dependence of being on mind" (1989: 143). Accordingly, the unity of knower and known entails that "we are not other than our power of knowing" (*ibid.*: 144). Regardless, however, of the causal direction – whether from nature to mind or mind to nature – neither Gregory's nor Eriugena's discussions of knowing and being depart from the identity thesis propounded by Parmenides. Both, moreover, follow Plato and Plotinus in asserting the actuality of the causal connection, of the power articulating the relations between Ideas and being.

It is this threefold relation – logic, nature, mind – that forms the conceptual space occupied by idealism and, indeed, by all philosophy. Whether such a relation can ground a systematic philosophy is the gamble idealism prosecutes against the whole of reality.

3. PHENOMENALISM AND IDEALISM I: DESCARTES AND MALEBRANCHE

Descartes' move towards an egocentric philosophy of the *cogito* is one of the most important, radical and often discussed moments in the history of philosophy. Whitehead wrote in 1929 that:

> [Descartes] laid down the principle, that those substances which are the subjects enjoying conscious experiences, provide the primary data for philosophy, namely, themselves as in the enjoyment of such experience. This is the famous subjectivist bias which entered into modern philosophy through Descartes. In this doctrine Descartes undoubtedly made the greatest philosophical discovery since the age of Plato and Aristotle. (PR 159)

In a seminal paper, Burnyeat fleshed out this claim and, through a careful analysis of texts that Berkeley used as proof of predecessors from Greek philosophy, argued that prior to Descartes there were no examples of philosophical idealism whatsoever. In addition, Burnyeat put forward the even stronger thesis that it was not even *possible* to conceive of idealism prior to Descartes, as idealism requires the subjective epistemological shift that Descartes acquired through hyperbolic scepticism: a shift that used tools not available to even the ancient Greek sceptics.

In a recent article, Darren Hibbs (2009: 646) claims to find four definitions of idealism in Burnyeat's work. He lists them:

> D1: The doctrine that everything is in some substantial sense mental or spiritual.
> D2: The doctrine that the world is essentially structured by the categories of our thought.
> D3: The doctrine that *esse* is *percipi*.
> D4: The doctrine that mind and the contents of mind are all that exists.

Hibbs suggests in the conclusion of his paper that D1 is the only definition of the available four that has the "latitude required to capture the diversity of the idealist tradition" (2009: 651). However, Burnyeat's claim that idealism "was not possible" before Descartes depends on the D3 and D4 definitions of idealism, which are unnecessarily restrictive, and, as the present work shows, cannot capture the diverse range of philosophies commonly referred to as idealist.[1] While Burnyeat has argued that Plotinus could not have been an out-and-out idealist, Hibbs[2] argues that Plotinus certainly *conceived* of an idealism of the D1 type even if he ultimately failed to defend it. This, Hibbs argues, means that Burnyeat's strong thesis – "it was not possible to conceive of D1 idealism prior to Descartes" (Hibbs 2009: 650) – should be rejected in favour of the weaker thesis: "Although it was possible to conceive of D1 idealism prior to Descartes, there was no philosophical *motivation* to adopt such a position" (*ibid.*, emphasis added).

Throughout this chapter, we shall develop two key arguments while concurrently outlining the development of the idealist tradition in early modern philosophy through expositions of Descartes, Malebranche, Leibniz and Berkeley. First, we shall argue that Hibbs's conclusion points towards an important factor regarding the history of idealism that he himself does not flesh out: that what is important in Descartes' philosophy is not only the subjectivist move that made the phenomenalist position conceivable but also the fact that he introduced the *motivation* for defending such a view by advancing a fully developed mechanistic theory of the extended world that attempted to explain every aspect of physical nature. However, Descartes' theory of extension (*res extensa*) can in no way account for consciousness or life, while at the same time his fully developed theory of thinking substance (*res cogitans*) *can* account for extension without the postulation of a separate substance. Thus, the idealist systems of Berkeley and Leibniz are developed in response to the theory of *res extensa* and its failure to explain adequately the existence of life and matter.

The second key argument is that all four of the definitions of idealism that can be found in Burnyeat's article fail to act as historically useful definitions of idealism because they all fail to identify the importance of the "idea" for *idea*lism. When Descartes made the important philosophical step towards phenomenal idealism, he did so by taking Platonic idealism and changing its central domain of operation. Rather than using the "Ideas" in order to explain the cosmological production of physical reality, he used them in order to explain the phenomenological production of our experienced reality. "Ideas" for Descartes are Platonic in the sense that they are the innate archetypes common to all rational beings. There can be no doubt that Descartes made an important and novel move, but in order to make this move he used an idealist structure that he borrowed from Plato. Descartes then developed a new and interesting *form* of idealism rather than being the first to make idealism possible. This is what Descartes saw and Burnyeat missed.

THE *MEDITATIONS* AND THE MOVE TO SUBJECTIVE PHENOMENALISM

In the first two of his *Meditations on First Philosophy*, Descartes develops a number of powerful arguments aimed towards bringing into doubt our sensory experience and thus paving the way towards his epistemology of "clear and distinct" ideas. Descartes does this by taking the reader through several stages of doubt, which increase in severity, starting from "common-sense" doubt: the doubt we should acquire merely from noticing that sometimes the objects we see are in reality different from the way they appear to be. To use Gassendi's example, a tower that appears circular from a distance may turn out, on closer inspection, to be square. Descartes concludes from these observations that "it is prudent never to trust completely those who have deceived us even once" (AT VII.18; CSM II.12).

The second stage of doubt is the argument from dreams. This stage is of the utmost importance in the context of phenomenalist idealism because it is at this point that Descartes proceeds from *local* to *global* scepticism. He questions whether or not the senses could deceive him regarding the beliefs of which he is the most certain, such as the fact that he really has a body and that he really is sitting by the fire. To his own question, he responds that he has been sure that he was sitting by the fire on a number of occasions only to discover that he was actually dreaming. After analysing these similar experiences, he claims that "there are never any sure signs by means of which being awake can be distinguished from being asleep" (AT VII.19; CSM II.13). Margaret Wilson (1978) points out that there are a number of possible ways that we can read this argument:

DA1: I cannot be absolutely certain whether or not I am at this moment dreaming.[3]
DA2: I cannot know whether or not I am ever truly awake. It could be the case that I am always dreaming.[4]
DA3: "I cannot say why I should unquestioningly regard waking experience of physical objects as real or veridical, when there are no marks to distinguish it from the 'illusions of dreams'" (1978: 23).[5]

The interpretation of the argument from dreams that Wilson defends (DA3) points to a very important fact regarding the possibility of our sense experience. When I am awake, sitting next to a fire or playing with wax, I presume that there is something real "out there" beyond my own *cogito* that is causing these sensory experiences: the wax in my hand really exists as an object beyond my thoughts, I really do have a body and it really is the fire that is the causal source of the warmth. The problem is that often I have had very similar experiences while dreaming. I believe that I am walking along and that I can see objects; however, when I wake up I presume that there were no real objects causing these sensations and that my body had been lying in bed for the duration. While all these experiences appeared to be true, they were in fact caused without the aid of any external objects. If Descartes is right to claim in this first meditation that there are no distinct signs to distinguish whether we are awake or asleep, then what is important regarding this temporary conclusion is that if visions can be produced in dream states without any external objects, then we have absolutely no reason to believe that there *must* be external objects "out there" causing the experiences we enjoy when we are awake. "The dreaming argument brings out the fact that we do not accept this assumption universally (we don't accept it in the case of dreams). It raises the question whether we are then entitled to accept the assumption ('with certainty') in any case at all" (Wilson 1978: 27). Despite the importance of the dreaming argument, Descartes argues that there are some truths that it cannot put into doubt and that the truths of geometry and arithmetic are just as true whether one is sleeping or awake. What could possibly put the latter kind of truth into doubt? Of course, the answer is Descartes' *evil demon* argument, perhaps the most famous argument in the history of philosophy. It could be the case that an evil demon has tricked us into thinking that $2 + 2 = 4$ when in fact $2 + 2 = 5$. However, it is important to note that this level of hyperbolic doubt is available to Descartes only because he makes God prior to reason in his ontology. God is the creator of logic, the truths of mathematics and all forms of reason; therefore, if God were an evil demon rather than an all-perfect non-deceiver then he could trick us regarding these foundational truths. Leibniz and Spinoza avoid the evil demon problem by denying the possibility that God could be *prior* to reason. For Spinoza this would imply interventionism, which he denies, and for Leibniz it would imply the unacceptable conclusion that God does not act according to reason. For both, in contrast to Descartes, truth is the guarantor of itself. However, Burnyeat argues that it was owing to Descartes' radical level of doubt that he was able to make the historically significant "subjectivist" move. Descartes believed that he was the first philosopher truly capable of refuting the sceptics because he used the sceptics' very methods, pushed them even further than they had intended to go and, as a result, managed to achieve certainty. The ancient sceptics doubted that we could find any valid criterion that could be used infallibly to ascertain whether our sensations are either true or false representations of reality. However, Descartes starts by making us suppose that all our sensations are false and then asks us if there is anything that we could be sure of in this context.

> The Pyrrhonists argued that you cannot determine what is true and what is false without first settling on a criterion of truth. And they made sure that no proposed criterion would hold good under examination. But Descartes can go the other way round. He has got a truth without applying a criterion, and he can use this unassailable truth to fix the criterion of truth. (Burnyeat 1982: 39)

Descartes finds, in the second meditation, the one truth regarding which not even an evil demon could trick him, and this is, of course, *ego sum, ego existo*: I am, I exist. As long as I am thinking it cannot be the case that I am nothing. It is only if nothing could enjoy predicates such as "thinking" that it could be wrong to infer my existence from my thinking. Since to predicate "thinking" of nothing would affirm that nothingness is something, and since this is contradictory, we can conclude that this is not possible, therefore it must be the case that as long as I am thinking, I exist. Importantly, we can also conclude from this that thoughts are real things even if the objects that they are supposed to represent do not in truth exist. Descartes cements this point further by returning to the dream argument:

> [I]t is also the same "I" who has sensory perceptions, or is aware of bodily things as it were [*tanquam*] through the senses. For example, I am now seeing light, hearing a noise, feeling heat. However, all these things are false, for I am asleep. Yet I certainly *seem* to see, to hear, and to be warmed. This cannot be false; what is called "having a sensory perception" is strictly just this, and in this restricted sense of the term it is simply thinking.
> (AT VII.29; CSM II.19, trans. mod.)

Regardless of whether or not we can finally be certain of anything else, we can be certain of *tanquam* sensations: sensations that seem *as if* they are the product of external stimuli, but can be caused without external stimuli and therefore do not require external stimuli in order to exist. Descartes then rebuilt his ontology from this one certain truth and by doing so he made one of the most revolutionary moves in the history of philosophy and introduced a subjectivist bias that philosophy has not managed to shake off 350 years later.

In the course of the *Meditations* Descartes gradually grounds certain knowledge of the true on clear and distinct ideas, those ideas represented most ideally in geometrical knowledge, through several arguments for the existence of God as infinitely perfect and in possession of a "non-deceiving" nature. However, the subjective turn made by Descartes means that we shall always know the mind better than we know the body.[6] Exactly why is made clear in a response to the empiricist Gassendi. Gassendi argued that

Descartes had done nothing to prove that the mind is better known than the body. For our knowledge of the body is developed through numerous rich scientific analyses that give us facts that go far beyond the vulgar, while, in the course of the *Meditations*, all Descartes has told us about the human mind is that it is "a thing that doubts, affirms etc." (AT VII.276; CSM II.192), which tells us nothing above what we already knew. If Descartes is to prove that we know the mind better than we know the body, we must perform a kind of scientific analysis of the mind. Descartes responded by arguing that Gassendi had failed to realize just how different the mind and the body are and that he continues to think of the mind in bodily terms. The mind is simply not susceptible to scientific analysis in the same way that the body is. However, this does not mean that we cannot know the mind. To know a substance, Descartes argues, is to know its attributes. Every time we discover an object's attribute in the material world, such as "that wax is hard", we discover a corresponding attribute about the mind: "that it has the *power to know* that wax is hard". Thus, Descartes' subjective turn makes it, if we accept his principles, logically impossible to know matter better than mind, because we always know matter through our mind.

DESCARTES' MECHANIST NATURAL PHILOSOPHY

While Descartes' "subjectivist revolution" is undoubtedly of the greatest importance for the history of philosophy, it is important not to forget how revolutionary his philosophy of the natural world would have seemed to his contemporary readership. In fact, it is reported that Malebranche, the most famous of all the occasionalist philosophers, was so excited when he read Descartes' *Treatise on Man* that he had violent palpitations of the heart and had to leave the work at frequent intervals for the sake of his own health (see Schmaltz 2002). This was the impact of such a powerful anti-scholastic work.

Descartes' blanket application of mathematics to the study of the physical world is clear in the *Meditations*. One of his key epistemological conclusions is that in fact we know the world outside us better through our understanding (our mental reasoning) than we do from our senses. We conceive of the world through the senses in terms of its secondary qualities (i.e. non-extended qualities such as colour, temperature, weight, etc.), but these are qualities that do not exist in the things themselves. Rather, the external world out there can be truly and completely defined in terms of its geometrical mathematical qualities: "The nature of body consists not in weight, hardness, colour, or the like, but simply in extension" (AT VII.42; CSM I.224). Extension is simply length, breadth and depth. It is the physical realization of the mathematics of geometry.

In *The World* and in the *Principles of Philosophy* Descartes develops from this key premise a mechanist cosmology. The fundamental principles of his cosmology are:

1. There is no distinction between space, place, or corporeal substance; thus, there is no such thing as the void.
2. There is no fixed place in the universe. There is nothing anywhere that is not changing.
3. There are no atoms. Every body is indefinitely divisible.

In addition to these key features, Descartes outlined the laws of motion that he considered as fundamental for the universe. The cornerstone of his physical theory is the law of the conservation of motion. He argued that "God is the primary cause of motion; and he always preserves the same quantity of motion in the universe" (AT VIIIA.61; CSM I.240). Motion, he argued, has both a general cause and a particular cause. The general cause is God himself and the preservation of the quantity of motion within the system of the universe is a reflection of the perfection of God who always acts in constant and immutable ways. The "particular" causes are what Descartes refers to as the "laws of nature", to which God always conforms (see AT VIIIA.62–5; CSM I.240–42). These are the ingredients of a mechanist cosmology from which he believed the entire workings and diversity of the universe could be constructed. Let us consider an idealized version of Descartes' universe simplified down to twenty "parts" of matter (Fig. 1).[7]

1	2	3	4	5
6	7	8	9	10
11	12	13	14	15
16	17	18	19	20

Figure 1. A simplified Cartesian universe.

Let us say that, in this simplified universe, these twenty parts of matter compose space. As Descartes denies the existence of the void, he believes that all motion in general must be circular. This is because there is no "place" outside the plenum for any "part" of matter to move to: all matter can only move to a place previously occupied by another part of matter. In addition, according to the second of Descartes' three laws of motion, while the motion of matter is in general vortical, it is a vortical motion made up of rectilinear movements. The individual movement of each body can only be rectilinear, because only rectilinear motion can occur at an instant of time. So if block 1 moved to block 6 this would not leave an empty space where block 1 was, but, rather, block 6 would have to move too, in order to accommodate block 1's movement. Block 6 would then move to block 11, and every connecting piece of matter would move round, leaving block 2 in the place of block 1. Every piece of matter is connected to every other bit of matter and extension continues indefinitely in every direction. As there is no fixed place in the universe, motion is relative; therefore when block 1 moved to block 6, it would be just as true to say, rather than block 1 moving to block 6, that block 12 had moved to block 7. There would be no way to tell whether it is actually the inner six blocks moving or the outer fourteen: both stories are true. Each block only moves relative to every other block. In fact the true story would be that every block is in motion, rather than merely the outer or inner blocks alone. Descartes used his theory to avoid giving an answer to the question whether the Ptolemaic or Copernican theory is true or false; rather, for Descartes, all things move relative to each other and therefore both are in their own way correct. From one perspective the Earth is moving around the Sun and from the other the Sun around the Earth. There is no fixed centre of the universe because no position is fixed in the universe. When we look at things they appear to have a fixed place, because they retain a fixed place relative to other positions, but on a wider scale the conglomerate is moving around. It is our "thought" that determines the fixed place of matter.

All parts of matter are merely length, breadth and depth and contain no secondary qualities in themselves. As matter is everywhere "homogeneous", there must be some way in which the difference we observe is individualized out of this homogenous mass. Descartes argues that all variety is dependent on the motion of matter. It is important at this point that we make clear exactly what he meant by the term "motion". Descartes makes an important distinction between the common vulgar conception of motion and the more precise sense in which he intends to use it: "Motion, in the ordinary sense of the term, is simply *the action by which a body travels from one place to another*" (AT VIIIA.53; CSM I.233). He then goes on to say:

> If, on the other hand, we consider what should be understood by *motion*, not in common usage but in accordance with the truth of the matter ... we may say that *motion is the transfer of one piece of matter, or one body, from the vicinity of the other bodies which are in immediate contact with it, and which are regarded as being at rest, to the vicinity of other bodies*. By "one body" or "one piece of matter" I mean whatever is transferred at a given time, even though this may in fact consist of many parts which have different motions relative to each other. And I say "the transfer" as

> opposed to the force or action which brings about the transfer, to show that motion is always in the moving body as opposed to the body which brings about the movement. The two are not normally distinguished with sufficient care; and I want to make it clear that the motion of something that moves is, like the lack of motion in a thing which is at rest, a mere mode of that thing and not itself a subsistent thing, just as shape is a mere mode of the thing which has shape. (AT VIIIA.53–4; CSM I.233)

Despite the important role that motion and shape play for the role of individuation, motion is not itself a force or power which exists in nature itself. As Gary Hatfield writes: "Motion is fundamental to Descartes' system of nature, but it is not itself causally fundamental. God is the cause of motion" (1979: 140). Different parts of matter move at various speeds; those parts of matter that combine to form units do so by combining through their various relationships of speed. Bodies are not different substances but rather different parts of *res extensa* individuated by their motions. The story of how these various complexes, such as the human body, are formed is a causal story of parts causing parts to act on other parts in various ways. The movements of all bodies are determined by all the movements of previous bodies and those bodies in turn are determined by all the movements of all other previous bodies and so on to infinity. Bodies unite through relationships of constraint and by having fixed and related speeds of motions that they communicate to each other. Bodies external to these united bodies have different degrees of speed and motion and are not in any way constrained.

For Descartes, the bodies formed from *res extensa*, being merely mathematical forms, have no causal power of their own. They cannot put themselves into motion and they cannot cause motion in other things without divine concurrence. However, Descartes did not see this as a weak point of his system but rather the logical result of the mathematization of the physical world. In fact, he uses this fact about the physical world as another argument for the existence of God. He provides his proof as follows:

> [T]he nature of time is such that its parts are not mutually dependent, and never coexist. Thus, from the fact that we now exist, it does not follow that we shall exist a moment from now, unless there is some cause – the same cause which originally produced us – which continually reproduces us ... that is to say, which keeps us in existence ... For we easily understand that there is no power in us enabling us to keep ourselves in existence. We also understand that he who has so great a power that he can keep us in existence ... is God. (AT VII.13; CSM I.200)

DESCARTES AND MIND–BODY INTERACTION

As we have seen, Descartes argued that there exist two distinct substances, *res extensa* and *res cogitans*. These substances are radically different and share none of the same attributes. *Res extensa* is passive, mathematically analysable, shape. It is infinitely divisible and it has a spatiotemporal reality. *Res cogitans*, on the other hand, is active, it thinks, affirms and wills. It is indivisible and has no spatially extended reality. Descartes' immediate readers, such as Gassendi and Princess Elizabeth of Bohemia, as well as commentators for hundreds of years, have been perplexed regarding how two such radically different substances could possibly interact. Gassendi could not see how it could be possible that one could cause an effect in the other if there is no way that either one could be in contact with the other, given that they share no similar attribute through which they could interact. It is clear, however, that Descartes did not consider this a serious objection. He wrote to Gassendi:

> [T]he whole problem contained in such questions arises simply from a supposition that is false and cannot in any way be proved, namely that, if the soul and the body are two substances whose nature is different, this prevents them from being able to act on each other. (AT VII.213; CSM II.275)[8]

Daisie Radner (1985) argues that the key problem with mind–body interaction is that it is incoherent with Descartes' key principles. For example, in the third meditation, Descartes puts forward the causal adequacy principle as a metaphysical truth that needs no defence. The causal adequacy principle states that an effect must derive its reality from its cause and a cause cannot communicate reality to its effect unless it possesses this reality to give; *nothing can come from nothing*. On the one hand, we have extended body, which has as its attributes breadth, length and depth, and, on the other hand, we have thinking substance, which perceives and wills. How can extended matter cause "sensation"? The reality of the effect must be included in the cause yet there is no sensation in extension. Therefore, Radner argues, body–mind causation is incoherent given Descartes' metaphysical principles. However, it is arguable that Descartes does not violate his own causal principle because he does not claim that bodies communicate sensations to minds in this way. It is not the body that causes sensations in the mind; rather, the mind causes its own sensations in accordance with the reports that it reads from the "signs" or "cerebral patterns" given to it by the brain. Descartes provides his clearest exposition of this theory in the *Comments on a Certain Broadsheet*:

> [I]f we bear well in mind the scope of our senses and what it is

exactly that reaches our faculty of thinking by way of them, we must admit that in no case are the ideas of things presented to us by the senses just as we form them in our thinking. So much so that there is nothing in our ideas which is not innate to the mind or the faculty of thinking, with the sole exception of those circumstances which relate to experience, such as the fact that we judge that this or that idea which we now have immediately before our mind refers to a certain thing situated outside us. We make such a judgement not because these things transmit the ideas to our mind through the sense organs, but because they transmit something which, at exactly that moment, gives the mind occasion to form these ideas by means of the faculty innate to it. Nothing reaches our mind from external objects through the sense organs except certain corporeal motions ... But neither the motions themselves nor the figures arising from them are conceived by us exactly as they occur in the sense organs ... Hence it follows that the very ideas of the motions themselves and of the figures are innate in us. The ideas of pain, colours, sounds and the like must be all the more innate if, on the occasion of certain corporeal motions, our mind is to be capable of representing them to itself, for there is no similarity between these ideas and the corporeal motions.
(AT VIIIB.358–9; CSM I.304)

The nerves and the brain contain a "fine air or wind", which Descartes called the "animal spirits". These animal spirits are the active powers that transmit the reports of the senses to the brain and actions from the brain to other parts of the body and they are powered by the fire of the heart. However, we must not confuse "animal spirits" with anything soul-like. They are rather very small bodies that move very quickly, they are like jets of flame, ultimately still corporeal and explainable mechanically. These bodies are constantly moving around the human body, entering into the brain's cavities and leaving through its pores. From the pores they are conducted into the nerves and the muscles. Animal spirits send reports from the sensory organs to the brain, which form certain cerebral patterns and motions. On the *occasion* of these motions, the mind reads the states, or "signs" as Descartes refers to them at times, and then the mind actively causes itself to form images from its own innate resources. The mind gathers none of its images from outside itself and the role of the body is simply to explain why the mind has its image at one point in time rather than another. It is a trigger that instructs the mind to bring a certain arrangement of innate ideas into consciousness. This is still a causal relationship but it is one that is "inefficacious" on behalf of the body.[9] The physical cause is a secondary or remote cause while the efficacious primary cause is the mind itself. It is the mind's active power that brings forth the image.

IDEAS AND IDEALISM

At first sight it might appear that Descartes' philosophy is as far from Platonic idealism as it possibly could be. He did not consider necessary truths to be eternally true in a Platonic sense. God brought necessary truths into existence through his own will and if he were to choose to do so he could change them at any point in time. However, Descartes made an important shift in the history of the concept of the "Idea" by making it refer to the contents of the human mind rather than eternal archetypes or Ideas in the mind of God. It is at exactly this point, as Nicholas Jolley (1990) notes, that Descartes' Platonic inheritance becomes clear. Descartes does not use the concept "idea" for want of a better term, but because he wants to retain the archetypal implication of the concept. The Platonic Ideas are the forms that exist as part of our own minds, which, if triggered by the right external motions, are brought into consciousness. Jolley points out the importance of the book of Genesis for Descartes' philosophy. For Descartes, man is made in the image of God; therefore, the ideas previously restricted to the mind of God are now brought forth into the minds of all rational human beings: "The mind of man, like the mind of God, does not need to go outside itself. This is perhaps the basic reason why Descartes thought that 'idea' was the most appropriate term for the forms of human perception" (*ibid.*: 30). For Descartes, the ideas fulfil the same role in the creation of qualities in human consciousness as they play more generally for the creation of qualities in all of reality for the Platonic idealists.[10]

While Descartes' move to a mental Platonic idealism may be more consistent within Descartes' own system than the account suggested by Radner, Wilson is right to argue that this model brings problems of its own. In terms of mind–body interaction, it merely shifts the problem rather than providing a solution. She writes:

> The model suggests that the mind perceives external bodies by virtue of perceiving, or otherwise recognizing, something *else*: traces or motions in the brain. But it neither explains how it is possible for the mind to do *this*, nor tells us why the question of how the mind does this is not as legitimate as the original question about how perception of external things takes place. (1999b: 54)

The most important issue for this current discussion is how close this brings Descartes to monist phenomenal idealism (in which independent physical extension is denied in favour of mind dependence), and how weak his epistemological defence against being an immaterialist is. Yet the same thing brings him close to Platonism, too, since he claims in effect that the fundamentally real is the eternal mathematical structure of any and all possibilia, which mind has the power to grasp by virtue of its own innate structures. It is no surprise that dreams are virtually indistinguishable from waking experience, because the source of *tanquam* sensations is the same source as real sensations: innate ideas. The only difference is that real sensations have a greater sense of duration attached to them because there is a consistent substratum to which they refer, rather than the mere contingency of dreams. Descartes defends the reality of matter by appeal to a non-deceiving God. These sensations must come from extended matter, otherwise God would be a deceiver, which would contradict his nature. However, this epistemological defence seems a particularly weak part of Descartes' philosophy. In addition, why must this substratum be a substance that differs in its principal attribute from *res cogitans*? The predicament Descartes leaves philosophy with is that the picture of *res extensa* he presents so clearly cannot produce life, matter and activity without constant intervention from God; while, on the other hand, *res cogitans* can produce its entire sensual world without any aid from external objects whatsoever. In addition, how external objects could cause sensations in the first place is still a difficult problem for Cartesian philosophers.

Jolley claims that Descartes subscribes to what he calls a "dustbin or grab-bag conception of the mind" (1990: 57). By this he means that Descartes has provided a complete picture of what the world of extension is like and everything that it is capable of doing given his conception of natural philosophy. Everything that cannot be explained by extension alone is put in the "grab-bag" and is to be explained by mind. However, what Jolley does not point out is that this philosophical "dustbin" ends up becoming more powerful than the theory of *res extensa*. It is clear, then, that Descartes has left the door wide open for a phenomenalist idealism, into which Cartesian philosophy, pushed to its limits, might easily have turned.

MALEBRANCHE AND THE NEW PHILOSOPHY OF IDEAS

The idealism of Nicolas Malebranche further develops Descartes' philosophy, bringing the "Idea" to centre stage. While Malebranche's philosophy endorses the subjectivist move, presenting idealism as a philosophy that explains the production of mental phenomena, at the same time, he rejects Descartes' psychology of innate ideas. Malebranche explicitly revives Platonic Ideas and synthesizes Descartes' philosophy with the metaphysics of Augustine.

He argues that Platonic Ideas are the true ground of both our phenomenal experiences and the physical world, but those Ideas are not innate to the structure of our own minds but rather have an ontological existence solely in God: "Human beings", Malebranche wrote, "are not their own lights unto themselves" (OCM XII–XIII.64; DMR 32).

Malebranche's philosophy is Cartesian in that he accepts a dualistbetween account of mind and matter and considers thought to be the essence of mind just as extension is the essence of matter. However, Malebranche's conception of the faculties of the mind is quite different from Descartes' in a number of important ways.[11] For Malebranche, the mind has two faculties: the *understanding* and the *will*. The understanding is the passive faculty of receiving ideas, while the mind's "motion", so to speak, is the will and its *inclinations*. Malebranche accepted Descartes' thesis that motion is imparted to matter by God, and continually coordinated by him, but, unlike Descartes, he understood a similar process to be at play in the mind. The configuration of pattern and figure in the extended world is a purely passive process, which is dependent on the efficacy of God for its motion. Likewise, the reception of ideas in the mind is a purely passive process, which is dependent on the inclinations of the will and God's efficacy. Just as extended matter in motion will continue in a straight line unless interrupted, so the inclinations of the mind will continue towards good unless disrupted by external causes. For Malebranche, then, the Cartesian philosophy is not anti-scholastic enough. While Descartes rejects terms such as "nature" and "faculty" in his explanation of the material world, Malebranche complained that Descartes and his followers seem to have no problem resurrecting these concepts for their explanation of the "powers" of the mind:

> They criticise those who say that fire burns by its *nature* or that it changes certain bodies into glass by a natural *faculty*, and yet some of them do not hesitate to say that the human mind produces in itself the ideas of all things by its nature, because it has the *faculty* of thinking. But, with all due respect, these terms are no more meaningful in their mouth than in the mouth of the Peripatetics.
> (Elucidation X, OCM III.144; SAT 622)

Both mind and matter are capable of movement but to say that matter has its own "power" to produce its own movement, or that mind has a "faculty" to produce ideas is to beg the question: what *exactly* is this power? What is this faculty? However hard he tries, Malebranche claims, the idea of force, power, efficacy in nature, seems inconceivable and thus, foreshadowing Hume, he is convinced that those who claim to find such forces in nature advance what they do not properly understand.

Malebranche argues that the understanding perceives Ideas in three distinct ways. First, through the *pure understanding* it perceives universals, common notions and the Ideas of perfection. These species of perceptions are referred to as "pure intellections" because they do not require images of corporeal things. We can have a complete conception of a triangle by knowing all its properties without forming a corporeal picture of it in our mind. We need not form a pictorial representation of these "Ideas". This form of knowledge, for Malebranche, is the most reliable and valuable kind of knowledge. The second form of perception, the *imagination,* forms pictorial representations when the objects perceived are not really present to the senses. While I can know the Idea of a triangle without picturing one through the pure understanding, I can picture it through the imagination, or, if a real triangle were in front of me, I would use the third kind of perception, the *senses*, to form a pictorial representation of what is really "out there". As for Descartes, our sensory perceptions are not to be trusted as reliable sources for truth regarding external stimuli. What is reported to our mind via the senses is primarily for the maintenance and preservation of our bodies (OCM I.126–9; SAT 51–2).

Malebranche accepted Descartes' important distinction between the primary and secondary qualities in our perception and considered it to be one of the most important post-Augustinian philosophical discoveries. Secondary qualities (i.e. non-extended qualities such as colour, temperature, weight, etc.) are, for Malebranche, entirely the product of our own mind. They help us create corporeal representations of the Ideas via the imagination or the senses and they exist for the purpose of helping us live healthy lives and enable us to avoid danger in the material world. The secondary qualities serve a very particular purpose and should not be trusted as adequate tools for the acquisition of truth. We are able to know the primary qualities of the material world most reliably through our understanding because it is through our understanding alone that we know the "Ideas" without the aid of secondary qualities. The Ideas are Malebranche's epistemological anchor and he believes that because of them his system is far more secure from scepticism than the system left by Descartes. So what exactly is an Idea?

IDEAS, PRE- AND POST-CARTESIAN, AND THE VISION IN GOD

In a famous passage from *The Search After Truth* Malebranche attempts to answer the question "What is an Idea?" He writes:

> I think everyone agrees that we do not perceive objects external to us by themselves. We see the sun, the stars, and an infinity of

objects external to us; and it is not likely that the soul should leave the body to stroll about the heavens, as it were, in order to behold all these objects. Thus, it does not see them by themselves, and our mind's immediate object when it sees the sun, for example, is not the sun, but something that is intimately joined to our soul, and this is what I call an *idea*. Thus, by the word *idea*, I mean here nothing other than the immediate object, or the object closest to the mind, when it perceives something, i.e., that which affects and modifies the mind with the perfection it has of an object.

(OCM I.413–14; SAT 217)

That there is an important distinction between the sun "out there" and the representation of the sun that we form in our own mind is clearly shown by our imaginings of beings that are "not really there". Malebranche provides us with an example of a golden mountain: when we think about a golden mountain, this mountain does not exist in the exterior world of extension, but something *does* exist. There is always an "Idea" that we perceive, and this Idea is real regardless of any reality attaching or not to its object. For when we think of a golden mountain it is impossible that we are thinking of nothing, for nothing possesses no properties. If our image of a golden mountain possessed no properties then we could not distinguish it from our imagining of a silver dragon, because strictly speaking to think of either of those things would be to think of nothing at all. This thesis is not exclusive to Malebranche but what is original is where he locates these ideas. The ideas that we perceive cannot exist in our own minds, for reasons that will be explained below, but, rather, must exist in God, echoing the medieval Platonist view of the location of the Ideas.[12] All our experiences are made possible via the efficacious Ideas of God.

Malebranche puts forward an enumeration of all the possible sources from which ideas could originate and argues that there is only one possible source that agrees with reason: God. The possible sources are as follows: (a) bodies; (b) our soul produces and annihilates the ideas itself; (c) all ideas are *innate* to the soul; (d) the soul contains all the perfections it perceives; (e) we see the ideas in God. He then argues that:

(a) It cannot be the bodies themselves that *impress* these ideas on the external senses because it is not in the nature of body to transmit such images. The "peripatetic" theory, that bodies transmit resembling species to our external senses, contains too many inconsistencies to be taken seriously. The species transmitted would themselves need to be little bodies, but the whole of space is filled with such bodies: "they must run against and batter each other from all directions … hence they cannot make objects visible"' (OCM I.419; SAT 220). Malebranche also argues that problems of perspective are inexplicable via this explanation. When we see an object close up it appears larger than when far away. Are the species sent by the bodies thus smaller when further away then when they are closer? How does this process work? Similarly, when we perceive a perfect cube, the species of bodies sent by its sides are unequal. How can this be explained via this model? There are, Malebranche argues, too many inexplicable difficulties in the peripatetic model. Here, Malebranche makes clear his Platonic antipathy to Aristotelianism.

(b) Ideas cannot be our own creations that we create and annihilate ourselves. For this would imply a veritable creation *ex nihilo*. In fact, Malebranche argues that to create ideas ourselves merely from the material impressions would be further against reason than complete creation *ex nihilo*. This is because material impressions contain nothing that could be used as an ingredient for a "spiritual" Idea. They are the products of completely different substances. If we were to attempt to create an angel from a stone, we would first of all have to annihilate the stone, because it in no way contains any of the necessary ingredients for angel production. Yet, to create an idea from a material impression is analogous to creating an angel from a stone in that it is equally impossible. Even if we possessed such a divine power there would still be a further problem: in order to produce the idea of a circle, you would need an idea of the circle from which to copy it. You could not create a circle if you did not have an Idea of it first, but if you already have an Idea of a circle then you need not produce one yourself and therefore you cannot be the cause of your own Ideas.

(c) That all Ideas are innate and exist in our mind "awaiting" a trigger is against Malebranche's conception of God. He argues that God always produces things by the "simplest means". God always acts according to reason and never produces more when less could do the job just as efficiently. There are an infinite number of Ideas. For every triangle we consider there are an infinite number of possible variations: "the altitude can be infinitely increased or decreased while the base remains the same" (OCM I.429; SAT 226). To produce the infinite set of Ideas in every soul would be against God's method. It would be contrary to reason to create the Ideas so many times when they could be created just the once, in God, for all to share.

(d) Before concluding that we see all things in God, Malebranche considers the view that our soul contains all the perfections that it perceives. Much of what we do perceive is due to the soul. All secondary qualities, sensations and affects (pleasure, pain, cold, heat, colours, sounds, odours, tastes, love, hatred, etc.) are modifications of the soul. However, the theory that ideas are perfections of the mind suffers from two key problems. First, it fails to appreciate how different "Ideas" are to the "modifications of the mind". Ideas are eternal, immutable, necessary, infinite, universal and so on, whereas the modifications of the mind are particular, contingent, variable. They are a different ontological kind and therefore the former cannot be a type of the latter. The second key problem is theological: it is natural vanity that persuades us that we contain all the perfections necessary and thus we elevate our perception of ourselves to the divine and consider ourselves a light unto ourselves even though only God is a light unto himself.

After these negative arguments against all other possible sources, Malebranche puts forward a positive argument for his "vision in God" thesis, the first part of which goes as follows:

1. All things that act on the mind must be, by their very nature, efficacious.
2. Ideas act upon the mind.
3. Therefore [by 1 & 2] Ideas must be efficacious.
4. In order for X to affect Y, Y must be in a real sense subordinate to X; otherwise it would simply resist its affection.
5. Ideas affect the mind. [repeating point 2]
6. Ideas must be ontologically superior to mind. [by 4 & 5]

Malebranche presents his "hierarchy of being" most clearly in his tenth Elucidation. Not only are there eternal, necessary and immutable truths, he argues, but there must also be a "necessary and immutable order among them" (OCM III.138; SAT 618); this can be demonstrated in geometric fashion. God, as an infinitely perfect being, must necessarily obey universal reason. It is also clear that God must have more perfections (positive reality) than any other being (by the very definition of God). His love must *necessarily* be directed primarily at his own being, for, as the most superior existent being, he deserves the most love. He will then, by the order of reason, love those beings that are closest in perfection to himself. As minds, Malebranche argues, are closer in perfection to bodies, minds must be ontologically superior to bodies.

7. Minds are ontologically superior to bodies.
8. Bodies cannot act upon minds and thus cannot be the source of Ideas. [by 6 & 7]
9. The only being superior to mind is God.
10. God must be the source of our Ideas. [by 6, 7 & 9]

We are now in a better position to understand exactly what Ideas are and exactly what role they play in perception. There is an important distinction between the "Ideas" and mere modifications because the soul's modes are "changeable, particular, contingent, obscure and shadowy", while the Ideas are "immutable, general to all intelligences, eternal and necessary, clear and luminous and efficacious". While Descartes argued that in a sense God was "above" reason and responsible for its creation and could well have chosen another form of reason or logic, Malebranche sternly rejected this "voluntarist" view. According to Malebranche, there is a necessary and immutable order of Ideas that are "co-eternal" or "consubstantial" with God and determine the universal truths. If it were not for this necessary and immutable order, then God could, according to his will, make it so that twice four equals nine, that what is now beautiful is ugly and what is now good is bad. Ideas, then, are eternal, immutable, infinite and necessary. The Idea of infinite intelligible extension exists co-eternally with God and illuminates our perceptions. Ideas are the fundamental ingredients of our experience, without which we would perceive nothing at all. In the *Dialogues on Metaphysics and Religion* his mouthpiece Theodore asks Aristes to suppose that:

> God annihilated all the beings He created, except you and me, your body and mine ... Let us suppose further that God impresses all the same traces on our brains, or rather He presents all the same ideas to our minds which we have in our minds now. On this supposition, Aristes, in which world would we spend the day? Would it not be in an intelligible world? Now, take note, it is in this world that we exist and live, although the bodies we animate live and walk in another. It is that world which we contemplate, admire, and sense. But the world which we look at or consider in turning our head in all directions, is simply matter, which is invisible by itself and has none of all those beauties that we sense and admire when we look at it ... on the supposition that the world is annihilated and that God nonetheless produces the same traces in our brains, or rather that He presents to our mind the same ideas that are produced in the presence of objects, we would still see the same beauties. Hence, the beauties we see are not material beauties but intelligible beauties rendered sensible as a consequence of laws of the union of soul and body; since the assumed annihilation of matter does not carry with it the annihilation of those beauties we see when we look at the objects surrounding us. (OCM XII–XIII.38; DMR 10–11)

Visibility is not a property of bodies; we see all bodies through the Ideas. While such a view may lead us to scepticism regarding the existence of the material world, Malebranche believed that his theory of Ideas provides epistemic security. This is because the Ideas that we perceive are the very same Ideas that God used as the blueprints from which he created the physical world. The Ideas account just as much for the production of physical reality as they do for the production of phenomenological reality. Therefore, when we perceive a triangle, the very Idea of that triangle, which was the blueprint for its creation, is brought forth into our consciousness.

As Steven Nadler (1992) notes in his important *Malebranche and Ideas*, if the Ideas are the eternal archetypes for both physical and phenomenological reality, then this means that they cannot be understood as being in any way pictorial or visual-like. They are the complete logical concepts from which a material being can be constructed and thus include all its possible extended formations. If an Idea were pictorial, it would be merely a representation from a certain perspective and would not be capable of all the detail necessary to act as a blueprint for a physical realization. The distinction between "perceiving" an Idea through the pure understanding, on the one hand, or through sensation or imagination, on the other, is essential here. To perceive an Idea through the pure understanding is to meditate over its complete concept. It is to understand the logical concept rather than to form any pictorial image. To perceive the Idea through sensations or the imagination is to perceive the Idea through the modifications of the mind. It is to, in a sense, "realize" the Idea through secondary qualities. As Jolley (1990) notes, in a way Malebranche anticipates the modern "adverbial" theory of perception. This is because when I "look at" the black square that is my computer case in front of me, I am realizing the "Idea" of the square "blackly". When I watch a sunset, I am realizing the sun "redly", "orangely", "mauvely" and through whatever other wonderful secondary qualities my mind uses to animate this beautiful scene. However, we must remember that for Malebranche it is the Ideas that are causally efficacious: they are the "power" behind perceptual experience; it is the Ideas that in a sense "light up" the secondary qualities and make them available to the mind. It is the ideas that "govern" (*regle*) the mind and conduct the imagination.

For Malebranche, then, there are always two parts to every sensation that we have: we experience both a "pure" Idea and a "modification" of the mind and they are connected according to the laws of the union of soul and body that God has considered most fit, in accordance with the laws of simplicity. God plays a double causal role in all our experiences. God is at once the cause of our perceptions of the Ideas as they exist "in" him and also the cause of our mental modifications. Even though the modifications of the mind are the property of our soul and are not in God, so to speak, it is still God to whom we owe the privilege of the power of the will, without which we could not advance from one perception to the next.

In his Elucidation X, Malebranche explains that the "Ideas" are not a collection of separate beings related to the world in such a way that there is a specific Idea for each material existent. There is not an Idea of the sun, an Idea of the horse, an Idea of the chair I am sitting on and so on; rather, there is an Idea of infinite intelligible extension that can be varied in an infinite number of ways depending on how we perceive it. When I look at the sun, it is not really the physical sun that I see but rather the Idea of infinite intelligible extension from a particular perspective. The Idea of an infinite intelligible extension helps Malebranche out of some possible theological objections. If everything in God must be eternal and immutable, then how can it be the case that we see all things through the Ideas, as the Idea of the sun appears larger or smaller depending on its distance from the horizon? How can the Idea of sun, which must be immutable, change size? The answer is that the infinite intelligible extension never changes; what is part of God forever stays the same. Our particular perceptions are composed of this general extension and realized via our sensations, and we perceive this same extension from various different perspectives. We perceive an Idea from various parts of this intelligible extension via colour and thus we perceive it as in motion; however, despite the perception of motion there is no motion in the infinite Idea itself. The fact that this extension is an infinite whole is further evidence that it cannot be a property of our finite minds: as Theodore professes to Aristes:

> Simply consider that this idea of an infinite intelligible extension must indeed have a great deal of reality since you cannot comprehend it, and whatever effort of mind you make, you cannot exhaust it. Consider that it is impossible for it to be a mere modification of your mind, since the infinite cannot actually be the modification of something finite. Say to yourself: my mind cannot comprehend this vast idea. It cannot measure it. Thus it infinitely surpasses my mind … [M]odifications of beings cannot extend beyond the beings of which they are modifications, because the modifications are simply those same beings existing in a particular way.
> (OCM XII–XII.43; DMR 14–15)

OCCASIONALISM

Malebranche is probably best known for his doctrine of occasionalism, which is, unfortunately, still widely known through what are, arguably, two key misinterpretations put forward by Leibniz in his *New System* (WFNS §§12–13). According to Leibniz, (a) occasionalism is an attempted solution to the mind–body problem, which (b) introduces God as a *deus ex machina* who props up the Cartesian system through perpetual miracles (G IV.483; WFNS 17). The reason why the first part of Leibniz's accusation is incorrect is because the interaction between minds and bodies is not the central problem for occasionalism; rather, the problem for Malebranche is the problem of causation between *all* created beings. He argues that no created being possesses causal power; thus, of course, bodies cannot affect minds, but, in addition, bodies cannot affect other bodies. Extension consists solely in relations of distance and there is nothing in it that could act as a source of power from which it could cause motion in other parts of extension. While Aristotle believed the inner motion of natural bodies to be so evident that it was not in need of defence, Malebranche considers this trust in the testimony of the senses pitiful. While we may observe one ball A move owing to the effect of an encounter with another ball B, reason proves that B cannot possibly be the cause of the movement in A because there is no power in extension for ball B to communicate to ball A.

Malebranche refers to the belief in natural powers as the "*most dangerous error of the philosophy of the ancients*" (OCM II.309; SAT 446). Natural causal powers are theologically dangerous for Malebranche because they attribute powers to nature, and therefore admiration, when the powers are God's alone. It is to attribute divinity to nature and to put forward a pagan, rather than a Christian, philosophy. To claim that the powers in nature can produce their work without intelligence, he argues, is nonsense. How can we believe that the beauty of nature, which displays a wisdom far surpassing the intelligence of philosophers, has been produced without intellect? But, if these powers are in nature then they are the true causes of our pleasure and pain and should therefore be loved and feared as such. However, in reality, such love and fear should only be directed at God, because God is the true (and exclusive) cause of all motion. Malebranche's key argument is that there can only be one true cause and that cause is the one true God. All natural causes are only *occasional* causes. Malebranche's definition of a "true cause" as equivalent to "necessary connection" is absolutely essential to his argument: "A true cause as I understand it is one such that the mind perceives a necessary connection between it and its effect" (OCM II.316; SAT 450). He then argues for occasionalism as follows:

1. There are bodies and there are minds.
2. Bodies contain nothing that could contribute to movement.
3. If bodies do not cause their own movement, then minds must be the cause of this movement. [by 1 & 2]

4. For finite minds we find that there is no necessary connection between the will of the mind and the movement in bodies.

In order to understand point 4, consider the way in which your common sense tells you that you move your arm. You "will" your arm to move and it moves. Most of the time this works fine, but, on occasion, your arm may not move; maybe you are just waking up and your arm is dead and thus you cannot make it move. As it is possible that on willing the movement of your arm it does not move, there can be no necessary connection between the willing and the movement. For Malebranche, if the movement is not a necessary consequence of the will, then the willing is not the true cause. He expands on this point further by explaining that when we will our arm to move we have no real knowledge of how or why the arm is moving. We do not understand our animal spirits, nerves or muscles; rather, God alone has true knowledge of all the operations of the body and God alone is the true cause of the movement.

5. Minds do not move bodies so therefore point 3 is false. [by 4]
6. As God is an infinitely perfect being, everything he wills must necessarily occur (because there is nothing greater than his will that could restrict it). There is, therefore, a necessary connection between the will of God and its outcome.
7. As necessary connections only exist between God and the movements he wills, then God can be the only true cause, by the very definition of true cause. All other causes are therefore only *occasional*.

At this point it seems that Leibniz was wrong to claim that occasionalism is merely a solution to the mind–body problem, but what about the second part of his accusation? Does occasionalism equate to a metaphysics of perpetual miracles? The answer to this question is no, and the explanation will help us understand exactly what an *occasional* cause is. Rather than replace traditional causation with miracles, Malebranche replaces it with "laws". God's wisdom is displayed through the production of an enormous amount of beauty through very simple laws. Reason is co-eternal with God and God is able to conceive of an infinite number of possible worlds that he could construct from this logic. God's laws are constructed on the basis of these possible worlds, but he considers not only the work that such laws will produce but also the laws themselves, which Malebranche calls God's "ways". The relation between his work and his ways is essential: to improve the work would be to worsen the ways, and vice versa. God chose the best possible combination, but not the best possible world. In his *Treatise on Nature and Grace*, Malebranche writes that these laws are constant and immutable, and that God established the laws of the communication of motion and provided necessity in a natural world that would otherwise be merely contingent: "laws so simple and at the same time so fruitful that they serve to produce everything beautiful that we see in the world" (OCM V.32; TNG 118). As true cause of the motion of the universe and the inclinations of the will, God always follows these natural laws. On the *occasion* that one ball hits another, the motion that is transferred from one to the other is the motion of God; it is God's very power. Ball *A* is the occasional cause of the movement of ball *B* because of the laws imparted to nature by God's will. However, it is always God who provides the causal power. When I look at the pile of books in front of me, it provides the occasion for God to cause the idea of these books realized by the senses of my soul. The ideas occur not because my mind is united to my body but rather because my mind is united to God.

FROM MALEBRANCHE TO LEIBNIZ

Malebranche plays an important role in the development of modern philosophy and his role is beginning to be recognized in Anglo-American philosophical commentary thanks to the work of Jolley (1990), Nadler (1992), Pyle (2003) and others. Malebranche's work is not only an interesting and original development of the Cartesian philosophy but also an extraordinary synthesis of pre- and post-Cartesian idealism. Malebranche's system, perhaps more than that of any other philosopher, overtly highlights the importance of understanding the dual meaning of the philosophical concept "Idea", and while he claimed that Descartes did not go far enough in his move from scholasticism, he simultaneously argued that he had gone too far in his move away from Platonism.

While Malebranche plays such an interesting role in the history of idealism, he also plays a fascinating role in the development of empiricism. His critique of sense experience and his emphasis on the distinction between the complete "contingency" of the material world against the necessity of the geometric world of eternal Ideas, his critique of causality and denial of powers make him, arguably, one of the most important, and underappreciated, influences on the philosophy of Hume.

Malebranche's metaphysics, even more than Descartes', is a clear reflection of the problem of extension in early modern philosophy. The move from scholasticism to mechanism brought with it a conception of the material world that is perfectly analysable mathematically but capable of very little else. This is, of course, not a problem for Malebranche; if anything it is one of the key merits of the Cartesian system. It highlights the inertness of matter and thus the importance of the role of God for all existence, and returns all the powers wrongly attributed to nature back to God. Malebranche was not alone in this "supernaturalism" and in fact it was a general trend in early mechanical conceptions of nature to attribute this power to God. As Keith Hutchison (1983) notes, while it is often presumed that the mechanical materialism of the Scientific Revolution was an important step towards Enlightenment naturalism, it was also a significant interruption. Both Descartes and Malebranche, in fact, used the mechanistic natural philosophy as a way to advance a radical supernaturalism. The move from immanent causation to "laws of nature" was at the same time an opportunity to increase the power of God's causal efficacy from merely mediate to immediate. This move was not exclusive to philosophers and theologians but rather was the dominant tendency of seventeenth-century mechanistic science. Both Boyle and Newton saw that the inactivity of matter supported the powers of God. Hutchison cites a passage from Boyle that could just as easily have come from Malebranche's *Dialogues*:

> [I]t is intelligible to me, that God should at the beginning impress the determinate motions upon the parts of matter, and guide them, as he thought requisite, for the primordial constitution of things; and that even since he should ... maintain those powers, which he gave the parts of matter, to transmit their motion ... to one another. But I cannot conceive, how a body devoid of understanding and sense ... can moderate and determinate its own motions, especially so as to make them comfortable to laws, that it has not knowledge or apprehension of. (1983: 298)

When Samuel Clarke acted as Newton's spokesman in the *Leibniz–Clarke Correspondence*, he argued that the fact that Newton's mechanism allowed God to have continuous contact with the world made his theory preferable over Leibniz's. Leibniz took fundamental issue with this Cartesian conception of extension. Leibniz's idealism is an important break from and critique of this general move towards supernaturalism. For Leibniz, such a conception introduces numerous insoluble problems of a physical, metaphysical and theological nature.

4. PHENOMENALISM AND IDEALISM II: LEIBNIZ AND BERKELEY

LEIBNIZ'S IDEALISMS

Leibniz, like Malebranche, constructed a philosophical system that is both a Platonic and a phenomenalist idealism. For both Leibniz and Malebranche, God is the ground of Ideas, forms or, as Leibniz often calls them, possibles,[1] and, at the same time, he is the only immediate object of perception. Leibniz claimed that his system could be seen as a development of Malebranche's and that it is to him that he owed his basic metaphysical principles (GM II.294; WFNS 56). However, Leibniz's system differs greatly from Malebranche's owing to his novel conception of substance. There is only one kind of substance in Leibniz's ontology, a reconceptualization of the Aristotelian substantial form, a true unity that he refers to as a "simple substance" or, in his mature metaphysics, as a monad. While Descartes defended the existence of God, extension and thought as three different kinds of substance, Leibniz defends the existence of an infinite number of substances, monads, all of the same kind, differing only according to the distribution of what Leibniz refers to as primitive passive power. In correspondence with the Cartesian Buchard De Volder, Leibniz attempted to highlight the similarity between his concept of substance and the Aristotelian conception by distinguishing between: "(1) the primitive entelechy, i.e. the soul; (2) primary matter, i.e. primitive passive power; (3) the complete monad formed by these two" (G II.252; L 530). A monad is a composition of forces, active and passive, and all monads share this composition except for God, who is the primitive uncreated monad, and who alone is without limitations and thus *actus purus*.

59

Forces and monads

As we discussed in Chapter 3, Leibniz objects to Malebranchian occasionalism because he believes that the continual creation of God hypothesis is equivalent to perpetual miracles. In addition, he believes that a maximally perfect God would create beings that are capable, owing to their own power, of continuing to exist and to obey the commands of God. For Leibniz we cannot admit, by pain of contradiction, that God is both maximally perfect and that at the same time his creations perish at the moment of inception. In his *On Nature Itself* (1698), Leibniz presents an important objection to occasionalism, which can be formalized as follows:

1. God is maximally perfect.
2. A God whose creations immediately perish would not be as perfect as a God whose creations live on.
3. The occasionalist doctrine sees God's commands as producing immediate effects that then immediately perish.
4. The occasionalist doctrine is necessarily false. [by 1, 2 & 3]
5. If created things are to have a lasting effect then they must contain some form of causal power (force) by which they can keep themselves in existence and continue to obey God's laws.
6. We cannot have a conception of God worthy of his glory without at the same time acknowledging that the created world possesses causal powers by which it keeps itself in existence: "something from which the series of phenomena follow in accordance with the prescript of the first command" (G IV.507; AG 159). [by 1, 2 & 5]

The role this allows Leibniz's God is one in which he can be used to explain the creation of the universe, or why the laws of nature are the way they are; however, if God is to be used as an explanation of anything other than that, then the explanation must ultimately refer back to the moment of the creation of the universe. God created the world but the world he created is so perfect that he no longer needs to intervene in its operations. The key non-theological conclusion of this theological argument is that nature cannot be causally powerless. There must be something in nature that causes it to act and keeps it in existence and this cannot be God alone because God does not intervene in nature.

Leibniz also objected to the Cartesian theory of extended substance because he argued that such a conception of the material world is unable to account for the diversity of physical phenomena. Descartes argued that from motion and extension he could construct the world. Leibniz, however, cannot see how either motion or extension can be considered as "primitive" principles from which such a construction could be made. Both principles, he argues, are derivative, rather than primitive:

> That extension constitutes the common nature of corporeal substance I find asserted by many, with much confidence, but never proved ... Indeed, the notion of extension is not a primitive one but is resolvable. For an extended being implies the idea of a continuous whole in which there is a plurality of things existing simultaneously. To speak of this more fully, there is required in extension, the notion of which is relative, a something which is extended or continued as whiteness is in milk, and that very thing in a body which constitutes its essence; the repetition of this, whatever it may be, is extension. (G IV.364; L 390)

Descartes used motion as his principle of individuation. Matter, which would otherwise be homogeneous, obtains character through its various motions. Leibniz finds this conception of individuation problematic. One key problem is that, for Descartes, there is actually no real way of telling what "section" of matter is actually moving. Motion is defined by the change of position in relation to other sections in its close vicinity (see AT VIIIA 53; CSM I.233).

Whether or not we assert that a section of matter is moving or at rest is an arbitrary choice and, as Leibniz quipped, even our own eye could be the centre of the universe. Leibniz concluded from this point that:

> [I]f there is nothing more in motion than this reciprocal change, it follows that there is no reason in nature to ascribe motion to one thing rather than to others. The consequence of this will be that there is no real motion. Thus, in order to say that something is moving, we will require not only that it change its position with respect to other things but also that there be within itself a cause of change, a force, an action. (G IV.369; L 393)

The key point to this argument is that the "force" that individuates matter must be something internal to it. The principle of individuation cannot be placed on to a homogeneous mass from above. Difference must be primary, not derivative, and Descartes' theory of extension simply cannot account for this primary difference. Leibniz concluded that there must be some kind of essential property structure from which things are composed. From the empirical observation that there are aggregates and structures in our world, we can conclude that these composites are composed of more basic parts. The complexity of this aggregation is almost incomprehensible, but at the most fundamental level there must be basic properties or qualities from which the aggregations are made; otherwise the relations would be merely related to other relations and so on to infinity, which would lead to a vicious regress with nothing for the relations to be related to. Both Leibniz and Descartes agreed that material atoms could not be the ultimate constituents of the universe because everything material can be divided into smaller material parts, but, for Leibniz, if matter is composed of something smaller than "any given quantity" then extension must ultimately be produced by something non-extended. The natural world must have non-spatiotemporal constituents as its prerequisites. This should have been the conclusion to Descartes' metaphysics. These non-extended constituents (monads) are the true unities in nature and the ultimate forces from which extended nature derives its power.

This leads us to another of Leibniz's metaphysical arguments against Descartes' natural philosophy. On the basis of the foregoing, Leibniz argued that if matter were merely extension then there could be no true unities in nature and only aggregates. All true unities must have some metaphysical substantial union. A sandcastle does not have a true substantial union, but is merely an aggregate, whereas I, on the other hand, am not merely an aggregate, but a substantial union whereby all of my organs work together and create a single being – a unity. For Leibniz, no real unity can be discovered in extended matter alone, only aggregation; however, in the metaphysical realm, substantial union can be found and it is at this level that my unity can be explained. The true unities from which the world is composed are Leibniz's monads: non-spatiotemporal substances that are the true purveyors of qualities and phenomena.

Aristotelian entelechies and Leibnizian forces

In Leibniz's work we find many attempts to highlight the similarity between his theory of monads and the scholastic–Aristotelian theory of entelechies and primary matter; however, in Leibniz's metaphysics the roles that activity and passivity play are very different. For the scholastics, the active entelechy plays the key role as the individuator of the homogeneous primary matter, which in itself cannot exist except as a bare potency. In Aquinas' *De Principiis Naturae*, during a discussion of potentiality, he distinguishes between matter and form by defining matter as that *from which* generation proceeds while form is that *to which* generation proceeds. Matter is the formless that is actualized via form. Bronze is a matter out of which an artist may make a statue by supplying it with form. Bronze is not, however, *primary matter* because in whatever state the bronze is in, when an artist is supplied with this metal alloy, it will always already have some form. For Aquinas, primary matter is the completely formless, homogeneous and passive matter that has only potential being and is actualized only when active form individualizes it through the imparting of qualities (2007: 160). The entelechy provides the otherwise merely potent primary matter with its form. In so far as active force is the supplier of qualities, Leibniz's active force does not differ from entelechy, but, for Leibniz, the role of individuator is not assigned to the active force but rather to the passive. Without primary passive force all monads would be pure activity. They would possess every single possible positive attribute and express them all to an infinite degree; they would be pure act, like God (E 466; WLS 506). Primitive passive force, then, cannot be a mere potency, like prime matter. Rather, it is necessary and essential to a monad because it restricts the activity of a monad and therefore distinguishes it from God. Leibniz writes that "a primary activity or substantial thing is given which varies according to the disposition of passive matter" (G II.171; WLS 161). Each monad is individuated to the extent that primary passive force restricts its activity. Therefore, each individual monad has its own primitive passive force, which is essential to it and from which it cannot be separated (CA 120). The primitive active and primitive passive forces are both primitive in so far as, except in the case of God, one can never exist without the other.

The other key respect in which Leibniz's monads differ from substantial forms is that the active force of a monad does not wait to be triggered by an external substance. Aristotelian and scholastic possibilities are, Leibniz argues, dead, bare and without exigency. However, Leibniz believes that the true lesson of the Cartesian problem of interaction is that there can be no inter-substantial causal relations; therefore, these scholastic inactive potentials must be mere fictions, as a substance cannot be triggered from an outside substance. All action must arise from a substance's own source; consequently all monads are entirely self-sufficient. In a draft of the *New System* Leibniz wrote:

> By "force" or "potency" I do not mean a power or a mere faculty, which is only a bare possibility for action, and which, being itself dead, as it were, never produces an action without being excited from outside; instead I mean *something midway between power and action*, something which involves an effort, an act, an entelechy-for force passes into action by itself so long as nothing prevents it. That is why I consider it to be what constitutes substance, since it is the principle of action, which is its characteristic feature. (WFNS 22, emphasis added)

When Leibniz refers to force, then, he is referring to "power" but, as he writes in the *New Essays on Human Understanding* (NE 169; cf. 112), understood in a fuller sense as not only mere possibility but also the *endeavour* (*conatus*) to bring itself in action.

The combination of primitive active and passive force completes a monad and consequently forms what Leibniz refers to as its "law of the series". This law is the inscription of everything that will ever happen to it. The temporal succession of phenomena, of which the monad is the base, is the realization of this law. Every future state of a monad could be gathered from its current state if interrogated by an infinite intellect. Once God has created the monads, they unfold according to their law without any interaction with other monads; a simple substance "is naturally impeded only from within by itself" (CDB 369). Leibniz's world is made up of an infinity of self-sufficient monads all marching to their own tune as if a world apart, although in perfect harmony with every other monad. This is why Leibniz claims that the past is pregnant with the future. From the moment of its creation, every future state has been programmed into each monad and it cannot break from its own internal destiny. In addition, it expresses every other monad's current state within its being and this is how it is harmonized with its monadic community. This expression is pre-programmed by God rather than being in any way *caused* by other monads. So monads are windowless; nothing can come into or out of any monad. This means that Leibniz avoids the problems of causation that haunted Descartes; he needs no explanation of how one substance affects another. Each monad is the cause of its own internal states. There is intra-monadic causation (a monad causes its own actions) but no inter-monadic causation. No monad exerts a causal influence over any other monad. But still, in a sense they do. Every monad acts *as if* they were causally influenced by every other monad. A monad's perceptions truly are the perceptions of every other monad's actual state, and it truly is through the aggregation of these states that the appearance of the external world occurs. However, if every other monad were destroyed except for one, the remaining monad would still act in exactly the same way and have perceptions of an external world in exactly the same way, even though the extended world outside this monad would not be produced. Leibniz claims that the monads are synchronized with each other like an infinite number of clocks that have all been constructed to chime at exactly the same time.

Perceptions and phenomenalism

Leibniz often suggests that there is a direct link between active and passive force and distinct and confused perception. It is key to Leibniz's phenomenalist idealism that one understands perceptions as modifications of primitive powers; hence Leibniz writes: "Substances have metaphysical matter or passive power insofar as they express something confusedly; active, insofar as they express it distinctly" (G VII.322; L 365). In a letter to De Volder, Leibniz tells him:

> I think it is obvious that primitive forces can be nothing but the internal strivings [*tendentia*] of simple substances, strivings by means of which they pass from perception to perception in accordance with a certain law of their nature, and at the same time harmonize with one another, representing the same phenomena of the universe in different ways, something that must necessarily arise from a common cause. (G II.275; AG 181)

The relation of primitive passive power to primitive active power makes up the monad's law of the series. It is the non-temporal foundation from which the temporal series of perceptions emerge. Our perceptions are "modes" of this non-temporal ground. Leibniz calls these modifications "derivative forces", which, like the primitive forces, are both active and passive (distinct and confused). These perceptions are also representations or expressions of our universe, which is made up of an infinity of monads. Every part of matter in this universe, be it a rock, a bug or an atom, is an aggregate of aggregates of monads. Daniel Garber's (1985: 29) description of this as "big bugs which contain smaller bugs, which contain smaller bugs still, and all the way down" is quite apt, as long as we understand by "bug" an organized collection of monads, of which one monad dominates while the rest are subordinate. While God has a fixed concept of the universe as a whole, in the created world of monads there is no single world to correspond to this concept, but rather an infinity of monads that all represent this concept of the universe but from their own individual perspective. Each monad represents one part of God's concept better than any other monad, and it is as a collection of monads each representing one part of the universe better than any other that they make up the entire concept. Our perceptions are "expressions" of this world of monads. Of expressions, Leibniz writes:

> One thing *expresses* another (in my terminology) when there exists a constant and fixed relationship between what can be said of one and of the other. This is the way that a perspectival projection expresses its ground-plan. Expression is common to all forms, and it is a genus of which natural perception, animal sensation and intellectual knowledge are species. (CA 112)

Our perceptions of the world do not copy the world as a photocopier copies an image but represent the world in so far as there is a fixed relation between the monads and our perceptions. In the *Theodicy* Leibniz writes:

> The projections in perspective of the conic sections of the circle show that one and the same circle may be represented by an ellipse, a parabola and a hyperbola, and even by another circle, a straight line and a point. Nothing appears so different nor so dissimilar as these figures; and yet there is an exact relation between each point and every other point. (T §357)

When we perceive external objects we do not see monads as they really are because monads do not really look like anything; they have no spatiotemporal properties. They are composed exclusively of internal perceptions and the appetite to pass from one perception to another. This does not mean, however, that what we see is false or an illusion. Our perceptions are in reality actual "expressions" of this external world even if there is no true resemblance.

Platonic Ideas and the best possible world

Since Benson Mates's (1986) influential work on Leibniz it has become popular in the secondary literature, with some justification, to refer to Leibniz as a "nominalist". Indeed, Leibniz professes that the only things that exist within his ontology are individual substances and the active qualities they are composed of. There is no "third realm" of abstract entities that these substances partake in. In the *New Essays*, he claims that the "thorniest brambles" of the scholastics: "disappear in a flash if one is willing to banish abstract entities, to resolve that in speaking one will ordinarily use only concrete terms and will allow no terms into learned demonstrations except ones which stand for substantial subjects" (NE 217–18). However, regardless of Leibniz's apparent professions of nominalism there is in his system an overt Platonic idealism. Leibniz makes a distinction between God's *understanding* and God's *will* and in God's understanding exists an infinity of Platonic Ideas, which Leibniz refers to as "simple forms", as well as the eternal necessary logical truths and the laws of beauty, goodness and justice. These forms are co-eternal with God and thus do not depend on his will. They are the basic qualities from which all things are composed and they are infinite in number. Because the forms are co-eternal with, rather than created by, God, God is not to blame for the existence of evil:

> Evil springs, rather, from the *Forms* themselves in their detached state, that is, from the ideas that God has not produced by an act of his will, anymore than he thus produced numbers and figures, and all possible essences which one must regard as eternal and

> necessary; for they are in the ideal region of the possibles, that is, in the divine understanding. (T §335)

By God's will he chooses to create the best of all possible worlds, but he does so according to the possible forms that he did not choose to create. According to Leibniz, the best world is the one with the greatest variety in combination with the greatest possible order (M §58). In God himself all possibles are compossible: they can all exist together, because they all exist in unlimited maximum perfection. God cannot create a being equivalent in perfection for to do so would be to create a being indiscernible from himself. All created substances must therefore include some level of imperfection, and from imperfection comes incompossibility; this means that some possible substances cannot co-exist in the same possible worlds as one another. In order to choose the best world God must weigh up all the worlds and find the combination of compossible substances that best accords with his rules of maximal variety and order. The result of this deliberation is the blueprint for our universe in which we exist (T §225).

At this point, Leibniz's Platonism appears to be quite similar to that of Malebranche's: from the deliberation on his own Ideas God creates the best possible world. What makes Leibniz's Platonism so very different from Malebranche's is that for Malebranche souls cannot contain the forms, as forms are infinite and the soul merely finite, the forms exist exclusively within the mind of God and he alone is our light. For Leibniz, too, God is our light, he alone is the source of our ideas, but, at the moment of the creation of the monads, he creates us with the infinity of forms as part of our individual essence. The difference is that while in God all forms exist in maximal perfection, in individual monads they exist in various degrees of imperfection. To return to our earlier discussion of force, the forms exist within us as perfect in so far as we have active force and imperfect in so far as we have passive force. To tie this together with Leibniz's phenomenalism we perceive the essences clearly to the extent that they exist perfectly within us and confusedly to the degree that they are imperfect. Every created monad shares with God the infinity of perceptions of all possibles, but differs from God in that it expresses these possibles confusedly.

For Leibniz to be is to be active; this means that all forms are in some sense active at all times and, as they are reproduced in every single monad, they are always active in every single monad. As we "perceive" each of these forms to the extent that they are active, we have some perception of every single form at any moment of time; "every mind is omniscient in a confused way" (A VI.3.524; DSR 85). Leibniz, of course, does not believe that we have conscious perceptions of all these forms, but every conscious perception, which Leibniz refers to as "apperception", is accompanied by an infinity of minute perceptions of which we are not aware. As he writes in an early work, "the perception of a sensible quality is not one perception, but an aggregate of infinitely many perceptions" (A VI.3.515; DSR 71). The infinitely many perceptions are the "differentiae of thoughts" (A VI.3.521; DSR 81) from which our conscious thoughts arise. Weaker perceptions can combine together to form greater perceptions, which on their own would not be enough to break into our consciousness. The sound of the sea is made up of multiple waves, each of which would not, on its own, be loud enough to enter into our consciousness (see McRae 1976: 36). We do not hear the individual waves, but the overall sound, an integral of all the differentials. Leibniz calls these perceptions "confused" perceptions, as we perceive a confused whole rather than the individual parts. Most of our perceptions remain completely unconscious. Standing by the sea in Brighton, we still confusedly perceive what is going on in China, although with such a low degree of perception that it is nowhere near consciousness. There is an infinite continuum of complexity from distinctness to confusedness, which spans from our present situation as most distinct, all the way down to all of our past and future happenings, even further down towards all of the past and future happenings of every created monad, reaching as far as all possibility whatever. Those perceptions that enter our conscious thought and that we thus "apperceive" are those with the greatest strength: the most distinct perceptions. For example, if we were listening intently to birdsong and then a loud rock group started playing equidistant from us, the sound of the birdsong (presuming that the bird would continue to sing rather than fly to find a more peaceful habitat) would disappear from our thought while the sound of the rock band would take over.

The minute perceptions are the impulses that drive our very being. All of our thoughts and volitions depend on them.

> Every impression has an effect, but the effects are not always noticeable. When I turn one way rather than another, it is often because of a series of tiny impressions of which I am not aware but which make one movement slightly harder than the other. All our undeliberated actions result from a conjunction of minute perceptions; and even our customs and passions, which have so much influence when we do deliberate, come from the same source; for these tendencies come into being gradually, and so without the minute perceptions we would not have acquired these noticeable dispositions. (NE 115–16)

Minute perceptions determine our behaviour and whenever we act, for example if we choose to turn left rather than right, it is because our minute perceptions have made that decision more appealing than the alternative. Leibniz claims we can take for a model the German word for the balance of the clock, *Unruhe*, which also means disquiet. There is always a "disquiet": minute sufferings that, even though below consciousness, propel us towards the desire for good like "so many little springs trying to unwind and so driving our machine along" (NE 166).

In what sense is Leibniz a "phenomenalist"?

The extent to which Leibniz can be classified as an "idealist" philosopher has been the subject of a considerable amount of debate in the contemporary secondary literature. In this literature, "idealism" is generally used to refer to a doctrine of "austere monadism" that admits only "spiritual substances" into ontology, and which considers "matter" to have only a "phenomenal" reality, that is, it exists only in the minds of perceivers and has no real existence outside these minds. This literature contrasts such "idealist" scepticism with a "realist" position with respect to matter. The "realist" interpreters of Leibniz have taken up a variety of stances. Some believe that Leibniz was not an idealist for his entire philosophical career and that corporeal substances play an important part in his metaphysics in his "middle period" (see Garber 2009). Others believe that Leibniz was exclusively a "realist" with respect to matter throughout his mature philosophy and some have even argued that both a "realist" and an "idealist" theory can be read in Leibniz's works, even those from the same period (see Hartz 2006).

Despite the rise in popularity of such realist interpretations in recent years, the austere monad interpretation is still without doubt the most popular and has received the most defenders.[2] Those who interpret Leibniz in this manner claim that the real aggregation that makes "bodies" as we perceive them is performed by our perception. The harmony of our perceptions combined with the harmony of the infinite monads causes the perception of bodies. This means that we perceive the distinction between primitive and derivative forces in a phenomenalist sense. The non-spatiotemporal forces (monads) are the true existents: they are the "true atoms of nature" (G VI.607; L 643). Secondary matter is not truly an existent but a phenomenon. It is a perception that is coordinated with everyone else's perception because we all see things in similar ways. There is a true background of non-spatiotemporal monads that "ground" these visions but the secondary matter is the product of the workings of our perceptions. There are numerous passages in Leibniz's corpus to support the "austere monadist" interpretation, and it is not for nothing that it enjoys such success. Two particularly important passages are:

> [I]t is not necessary to say that matter is nothing, but it is sufficient to say that it is a phenomenon, like the rainbow. (AG 307)

> I don't really eliminate body, but reduce it to what it is. For I show that corporeal mass, which is thought to have something over and above simple substances, is not a substance, but a phenomenon resulting from simple substances, which alone have unity and absolute reality. I relegate derivative forces to the phenomena. (G II.275; AG 181)

These two passages, as well as many others, seem to support unambiguously the austere monadist interpretation. However, the rise in popularity of the realist view has brought with it some compelling arguments. Much rests on how we are to understand "phenomena". As Wilson (1999a) points out, the "immaterialist" interpretations of Leibniz assume that what Leibniz means by phenomena is pretty much what Berkeley means by phenomena. Wilson questions this assumption and claims that it is probably the case that what Berkeley and Leibniz mean by "phenomena" and "perception" is, in fact, different. Pauline Phemister follows this question and develops a line of argument to support the corporeal substance interpretation. She highlights a letter to De Volder where Leibniz claims that phenomena can "always be divided into lesser phenomena which could be observed by other, more subtle, animals and we can never arrive at smallest phenomena" (G II.268; AG 179; see Phemister 2005: 168). Indeed, this principle of divisibility is essential to Leibniz's physics and biology, *but* Phemister notes that the phenomena that are being discussed here categorically cannot be inner perceptions because perceptions are indivisible; they have no parts to divide. The distinction between monads and phenomena, then, is not a distinction between the "really real" and our inner perceptions but rather a distinction between monads, which have no spatiotemporal reality, and therefore cannot be perceived in themselves, and that which is the "result" of the monadic network, namely secondary matter, which is *real phenomena*. Real unities, like ourselves, are "corporeal substances" possessing true substantial unities and a corporeal body composed of an infinity of other substances. Bread, on the other hand, is not a true unity; its body is merely an aggregate of other corporeal substances and in this sense its substantial unity is provided only by our perceptions.

Phemister's argument is important because if "phenomena" can be read in Leibniz's texts as not referring to mere perceptions but to a real physical world then many of the quotes that seem to defend an austere monadist interpretation can be read in a corporeal realist sense. However, Phemister's argument is not entirely convincing. First, it relies on the premise that for Leibniz a "perception" cannot be divided; however, this seems to be easily contradicted by textual evidence and, for example, Leibniz writes that "the perception of a sensible quality is not one perception, but an aggregate of infinitely many perceptions" (A VI.3.515; DSR 71). In addition, the fact that phenomena are infinitely divisible, as the quote points out, and therefore constructed of no basic phenomenal parts, is one of the key defences for an austere monadist interpretation.

For the austere monadist interpreter Donald Rutherford, when Leibniz refers to an "organic body" he is not referring to a real material entity in some sense "produced" or "created" by these monads; rather, it is a kind of shorthand for "a plurality of monads, which happen to give the appearance of being an extended object when apprehended by other finite monads" (1995b: 218). Against other Leibniz scholars, such as Garber, who have claimed that Leibniz's discussion of "corporeal substance", particularly in the 1680s and 1690s, suggests an earlier matter-realist theory, Rutherford claims that even in the *Discourse on Metaphysics* and other contemporaneous writings, corporeal substance does not signify anything above and beyond "substantial forms". What is real in a body for Leibniz, he claims, is the active and passive force of substantial forms.

Rutherford puts forward an extremely important argument in order to defend this view. According to the realist interpretation, bodies have two key ingredients: (a) a substantial form (or monad); and (b) other corporeal substances, which, in turn, are formed of other corporeal substances and so on *ad infinitum*. Ingredient (a) is a building block from which things can be constructed; substantial forms combine with other substantial forms and aggregates are formed, such as the aggregate that we call our human body. Ingredient (b), on the other hand, provides us with nothing analogous to a building block. In fact, all corporeal substances are merely formed of more corporeal substances, and there are no final "basic" corporeal components. Rutherford concludes from this that this is because the only real things are ingredient (a), the substantial forms; ingredient (b) is merely phenomenal. To be a body, then, is to be a plurality of monads that express themselves in harmony. When we look at the objects in front of us, there is an organization of monads that mutually express themselves in relation to each other which form the ground of these objects. What this means is that our perception of the external world is not merely equivalent to a "well-ordered dream", but rather what we see is a representation of the order of harmonious and supersensible monads. Rutherford writes:

> Within the best of all possible worlds, each monad does not simply express itself as an embodied creature, in addition, it is guaranteed that there exist monads answering to the content of its perception

> of itself as embodied – monads expressing themselves as the functional components of that body. Under this condition, we can speak of the latter monads as "resulting" in an aggregate that is identifiable with the organic body of the dominant monad.
>
> (1995b: 256)

Finally, Rutherford claims that Leibniz uses the term "corporeal substance" continuously, not in order to suggest anything truly "corporeal" in his metaphysical world, but rather to highlight the important part played by the dominant monads in harmonizing with the other subordinate monads that make up its body, and by representing the body as its body even when the subordinate monads that make it up change.

LEIBNIZ, MALEBRANCHE, BERKELEY AND VISION IN GOD

For Leibniz and Malebranche as well as for Berkeley, to whom we will soon turn, there is no possibility of receiving our sensations from external objects. For all three extension has none of the required powers for causing an effect on the mind. Ultimately, all three conclude that the only being capable of providing us with the Ideas responsible for the production of our phenomenal experiences is God. For Malebranche, this doctrine means that the eternal and infinite "Ideas" cannot exist in the minds of finite beings. To perceive any Idea is to participate in God's eternal essence and God is our only light. For Leibniz, God replicates this very infinite and eternal essence in every single substance; every monad is omniscient, albeit confusedly. Our phenomenal experience is grounded by this replication and we perceive as mirrors of God. Our perceptions are "expressions" of the created world of monads, which all auto-create their phenomenal world, according to God's plan. God is the only immediate object of perception because God imparted every phenomenal quality into each monad at the moment of its inception. Leibniz moves from a vision *in* God thesis to vision *by* God. God is still each monad's only "light".

As we shall see, for Berkeley, too, it is God alone who is responsible for our "ideas of sense", although he rejects important elements of both the Malebranchian and Leibnizian theories of divine illumination. He criticizes Malebranche for the supposition of a "useless" causally inactive external world of which we have no evidence and no reason to believe and argues that neither he nor anyone else could make sense of Malebranche's theory that we see the external world by way of God's own eternal essence alone. Against Leibniz, our ideas are not "expressions" of an external world: ideas resemble only other ideas. "I appeal to anyone", writes Berkeley, "whether it be sense to assert [that] a colour is like something which is invisible" (PHK

§8). Despite his criticism of Malebranche, his theory of divine light is surprisingly close and, as we shall see, it is, for Berkeley, God "in whom we live, and move, and have our being" (§149). God alone is the "pure and clear light who enlightens every one" (§147).

BERKELEY

Subjectivism and immaterialism

Berkeley's idealism can be termed "subjectivist" in that he seems to argue that the existence of things is dependent on the subjective experience of *particular* perceiving minds. The "ideas" that Berkeley is concerned with are ideas in people's minds (although there is a significant exception to this, as we shall see). In this sense his use of the term "idea" is perhaps closer to contemporary common-sense usage than those philosophers who have taken a less subjectivist position with respect to Ideas. This position is not always consistently held to, however, as we shall see. Most of all what Berkeley wishes to do is to deny the existence of matter, the rejection of which, he believes, is enough to overthrow atheism. In particular, he wishes to deny that the reality of things lies in their extended material embodiment independent of the mind's perception of them. According Berkeley, "those things [we] immediately perceive are the real things" and "the things immediately perceived are ideas which exist only in the mind" (GBW II.262).

Nominalist or realist with respect to ideas

We shall see that there appears to be some ambivalence for Berkeley about the metaphysical status of these Ideas. At certain points it seems clear that he is a nominalist with respect to ideas. He insists on the existence of particular things alone, although those things are mental entities not material objects. So things have their reality as "ideas" in the minds of creatures with the capacity for perception, but those "ideas" exist only in those particular minds – *not* as abstract universal forms. The reality of the quality of a thing resides, then, in a particular mind naming that quality. Berkeley denies the existence of abstract universal forms because he is concerned that if he admits their existence then they might appear to be independent of particular minds, and his philosophy is designed specifically to deny any such mind independence. At other points, however, Berkeley attributes an eternal existence to ideas in the "mind of God" (GBW II.232). We must look to see how these two positions are compatible.

IDEALISM

Against scepticism

Berkeley develops all of the key arguments, with which we are familiar, in two key texts: *The Principles of Human Knowledge* and *Three Dialogues Between Hylas and Philonous*. Roughly the same thesis can be found in the two texts.

In the first of the *Three Dialogues*, we find the core of the famous critique of "material substance", and of the mind-independent existence of things. First, however, Berkeley wishes to dispose of the accusation that he is a sceptic. Nothing could be further from the truth, he insists. The sceptic "doubts everything" (GBW II.173), and he argues that this involves a permanent suspension of judgement between affirmation and negation. Berkeley's position is a clear negation of "material substance" and mind-independent things, so his position is not that of a sceptic at all. Indeed, he believes that scepticism actually arises from a belief in the mind-independent reality of things. Surely, he says, what is real is what we experience. If we believe that the reality of a thing is independent of our experience of it then we are bound to be led into a state of doubt about its ultimate existence (this argument appears throughout the dialogues, but perhaps most clearly on GBW II.229–30). So, he claims, his philosophy is, in part, designed to overcome scepticism.

Sensible and non-sensible things

Three Dialogues discusses the nature of the reality of those things of which we are aware through our senses. Berkeley begins, then, with a clarification of what is meant by "sensible things". He makes it clear that "sensible things" do not include "notions of God, virtue, truth" – these might be "signified and suggested to the mind by sensible marks" – but it is only the marks themselves that are truly "sensible things" (GBW II.174).

At various points, of course, Berkeley will have to respond to the possible counter to his arguments that even supposing we only perceive sensible things, those sensible things must have a cause, and that cause is the real material thing, which exists independently of our perception and gives rise to it. In preparation for his attack on materialism he asks whether we ever really perceive the causes of sensible things. He concludes that we do not. One example given is that one part of the sky may look to our sense to be a different colour from another part of the sky. Our reason tells us that there must be a cause for this. But we discover that this cause is not, itself, a sensible thing. "In like manner, though I hear a variety of sounds, yet I cannot be said to hear the causes of those sounds" (*ibid.*). "The deducing therefore of causes or occasions from effects and appearances, which alone are perceived by sense, entirely relates to reason" (II.175). So here we have a formulation of the division between sense and reason that will make its way into Kant's own account. Causes are, for Berkeley, not, themselves, "sensible things"; they are "deduced" by "reason". Berkeley asserts, then, that *"sensible things are those only which are immediately perceived by sense"* (*ibid.*).

Mind

Russell argues that one of the key weaknesses of Berkeley's idealism is that while attributing reality to mind it never provides a satisfactory account of mind or of what is "mental" (1967a: 626). His references to mind are few and rather lacking in detail. In *Three Dialogues* he writes, "The mind, spirit, or soul is that indivisible unextended thing that thinks, acts and perceives". He also says that mind is "no idea, nor like an idea" for the obvious reason that he wants it to be the precondition for ideas – and, as he himself says, one idea cannot be the precondition, or cause, of other ideas (GBW II.231). Like Descartes, he insists that mind as a substance has more certainty of existence than matter because each spirit, soul or mind knows itself directly. We shall see, also, that he believes that, on this basis, we can infer that we, as spirits, exist in a state of dependency on something other than ourselves. Since he holds that nothing exists but spirit, this thing on which we are dependent can only be a superior spirit. He says that the existence of a spiritual substance is further demonstrated by the fact that "I myself am not my ideas", although he provides no detailed demonstration of this (II.233). Elsewhere he admits that ideas cannot really be "in" the mind because, as we saw above, he also claims that mind is "unextended". He claims legitimacy in using the language of extension, with respect to the mind, because it is conventional to do so but insists that we should not misunderstand his use of the term "in". He does not explain how we *should* understand it though, nor does he ever fully elaborate the relationship between mind and idea.

Secondary qualities

What, though, is a sensible "thing"? Berkeley asserts that "It seems … that if you take away sensible qualities, there remains nothing sensible … sensible things therefore are nothing else but so many sensible qualities or combinations of sensible qualities" (GBW II.175). Already, then, even before the core of the argument has taken place, the *substantial* subject of predication has been removed by Berkeley. The "sensible thing" is to be understood solely as an aggregate of sensible "qualities", or predicates, with no underlying substance.

If the sensible thing within perception is merely an aggregate of sensible qualities, what of the "reality" of the thing? The question now to be decided is whether the "reality of a sensible thing consists in being perceived" or whether its existence is separate from that perception (*ibid.*). Since he believes that he has already established that there is nothing to the thing but an aggregate of sensible qualities, he believes he is justified in answering the question of independent existence merely by reference to such qualities.

Consequently, there follows a discussion of whether heat can be considered to have an existence independent of some sensation, in some mind, of that heat. He produces a number of arguments to deny heat's existence independent of mindful sensation. First, he says, heat is a kind of pain, and since, clearly, only those things capable of sense and perception are capable of experiencing pain, so heat (as a form of pain) is dependent for its existence on such sense and perception. He adds the famous argument that if one were to have one cold hand and one hot hand and plunge them into water at an intermediate temperature the water would feel cold to one hand and hot to the other, so how could the heat possibly be, in any sense, "in" the water? What is the "real" heat of the water? He points out that when we are pricked by a pin we do not insist that the sensation we feel is somehow "in" the pin, so why do we continue to insist that the heat that we feel is somehow "in" the fire? We might respond that what we really believe is that the pin has some quality (sharpness perhaps) that can cause the sensation we feel, and that the fire, similarly, has some quality of heat that causes the sensation we feel. Berkeley believes that he has already disposed of this argument, however, since he insists that we never perceive causes. Consequently such causes do not have any real existence within the world of sensory perception. In conclusion, then, he states that "'there is no body in nature really hot", and that "there is no such thing as intense real heat" (GBW II.177).

To be clear, then, Berkeley insists that material substance is not endowed with the kind of "sense and perception" that could make it the "subject of pain" (II.176). Since, he says, there is no separation between the sensation of heat and that of pain, they are not two separate perceptions, therefore *heat is not to be found in material objects, it only has reality in the perception of a minded being.* This is the case for all of the aggregated qualities that make up sensible things.

Reinforcing this point, Berkeley points to a number of other examples. Of taste he points out that "divers persons perceive different tastes in the same food … how could this be if the taste was something really inherent in the food?" (II.180). Similarly, he says, smells are relative to a perceiving being rather than in the "substance" because some animals like to eat what we perceive as "filth and ordure" (II.181). There then follows a discussion of sound. The character Hylas initially claims a distinction between "sound as it is perceived by us, and as it is in itself", a similar distinction to that which we shall later find in Kant. However, it is clear that Berkeley is not at all happy to grant the "in itself" any kind of reality whatever. When his character Hylas suggests that "real" sound "in itself" is a vibratory motion in the air, Berkeley makes fun of this. It suggests, he says, that "real sound may possibly be *seen* or *felt* but never *heard*". He says that this is clearly "contrary to nature and the truth of things" (II.182).

He goes on to ask whether the colours we see in things are really "in" them, the first example being that of apparently coloured clouds. It is decided that the colours we see in clouds are not really "in" them on "closer" inspection. But then he points out that even those things that are directly before us can be inspected more "closely" with a microscope to reveal that their colours are only "apparently" in them (II.184). It is concluded that "all colours are equally apparent, and … none of those which we perceive are really inherent in any outward object" (II.185). If the colour were inherent in the body then it could only change if there were some change in the body, but since it changes from use of instruments, different kinds of eyes, different distances and perspectives, different light and so on, colour cannot be "in" the thing; it must derive its reality from sensible perception. But if colours are not "in" things, might they be "in" the light, then, and might light be a "corporeal substance"? This is followed by a quite astonishing claim. Berkeley points out that even according to this account the light must "shake" the optic nerve in order to create a "sensation" of a colour in the "mind". The colour, then, has "no existence without the mind". Yet the whole reality of that physiology as a *material* cause of perceptions is, of course, called into question by his philosophy.

As with the problem of sound, there is a discussion of colours as perceived, and as they are "in themselves". As is already evident, Berkeley will not entertain any such distinction. He again makes fun of the idea that the colours that we see are not the "real" colours, but that the "real" colours are invisible and can never be seen (II.184).

Primary qualities

Berkeley concludes, then, that all "secondary qualities" are mind dependent (GBW II.199–200). But what of primary qualities? Primary qualities are understood to be "extension, figure, solidity, gravity, motion, and rest". The character Hylas points out that many philosophers make this distinction between primary and secondary qualities, and, while agreeing that the secondary qualities are mind dependent, they maintain the reality of matter on the basis of primary qualities. As we have seen, he is almost certainly referring to Descartes here. So the question now is whether "*extension* and *figure* are inherent in external unthinking substances" (II.188).

Here Berkeley parts company entirely with the Cartesian tradition. He entirely, and very clearly, denies the independent existence of extended material bodies. With respect to extension he says that as we move closer to or recede from an object it changes in scale (II.189). If we look at an object it may seem smooth in figure: if we look through a microscope it will seem rough and angular. This, he says, is comparable to the water felt to be cold by one hand and hot by the other. The quality cannot be in the object (*ibid.*). The discussion moves on to "motion". He says that a motion cannot be both "swift" and "slow". Yet, he says, time is measured by the "succession of ideas in our minds". So where ideas succeed one another at different speeds in different minds things appear to have different speeds of motion (II.190). So again, the primary quality of motion appears to be mind dependent. He then looks at "solidity". "Hardness" or "resistance" are, again, "relative to our senses", he claims. He appeals here, as elsewhere, to the phenomenology of animals: "what seems hard to one animal may appear soft to another" (II.191). Philonous explains that the only real distinction between primary and secondary qualities is that the latter are related more directly to pleasure and pain, so it is more obvious that they are mind dependent. In fact, however, they are all equally mind dependent. *There is no real mind-independent world of material bodies at all* (II.194). Again and again Berkeley makes this point that "those things immediately perceived are ideas, and ideas cannot exist without the mind", and, therefore, that "those things ... immediately perceived are the real things" (II.230, 262).

In addition to breaking with Descartes' division between secondary qualities and extended bodies, he also explicitly distances himself from Malebranche. He writes:

> I shall not ... be surprised if some men imagine that I run into the enthusiasm of Malebranche, though in truth I am very remote from it. He builds on the most abstract general ideas, which I entirely disclaim. He asserts an absolute external world, which I deny. He maintains that we are deceived by the senses and know not the real natures or the true forms and figures of extended beings; of all which I hold the direct contrary. So that, upon the whole, there are no principles more fundamentally opposite than his and mine. (II.214)

Two important elements of Berkeley's philosophy are evident in this critique: the rejection of "abstract general ideas"; and the denial of the "absoluteness" or "in itselfness" of an external world. Since we have already explored Berkeley's critique of things existing in themselves, we turn now to discuss his critique of abstract universals.

The critique of abstract universals

Berkeley argues that comparative concepts such as "large" and "small", "fast" and "slow", have been shown to be mind dependent, but what if behind these comparative perceptions lies some "absolute extension" and "absolute motion"? Even if there are no extended material bodies, what if there is a universal extension and universal motion that are independent of particular minds?

Philonous replies that "it is a universally received maxim that *everything which exists is particular*. How then can motion in general, or extension in general, exist in any corporeal substance?" (GBW II.192). He is here denying the mind-independent existence of abstract universals on the grounds of a "universally received maxim". This seems to make clear the nominalist character of his idealism. A thing (that which alone exists) is made a "hot" thing by our naming it "hot" in accordance in sense experience. We can see this nominalism at work elsewhere when he says that, strictly speaking, we do not see the same thing that we touch, or smell. What we do is gather "ideas" (here meaning merely particular experiences of quality) together under one name. This is how we create the impression of a unified object through a combination via imagination that takes place within mind. Here, as elsewhere, Berkeley anticipates much of what Kant will later elaborate.

It appears at first sight, then, that Berkeley's idealism, at this point, is quite different from that of idealists who are realists with respect to universals such as Plato, Plotinus or, as we shall see, Hegel or Whitehead.[3] It seems that Berkeley wants to claim that extension or motion "in general" would be an idea independent of perception, and nothing exists independently of perception. So not only is he denying the existence of matter, but it also appears that he is denying the reality of universals. He makes this even more explicit in his denial of "pure intellect" and its "spiritual objects" such as "*virtue, reason, God*" (II.194). Is this really the case?

He goes on to clarify his position further by arguing that it is, in practice, impossible to separate motion in general or extension in general from specific cases of "fast" and "slow", "large" and "small". He says that just because we can speak of "motion", or mathematicians can make calculations with respect to some abstract motion, this does not mean that I can "form the idea of it in my mind exclusive of body" (II.193). So Berkeley's claim is that we can only form ideas in our minds as aggregates of qualities that we call bodies. These bodies are not material substances, but real phenomena indissociable from their being perceived. Because the primary qualities, then, are always part of such bodies, and so cannot be conceived independently of things with secondary qualities, so the arguments against the mind-independent existence of secondary qualities count also for the primary qualities.

There would appear to be no doubting Berkeley's purpose here. We encounter this denial of abstract universals on a number of occasions:

> If you can frame in your thoughts a distinct abstract idea of motion or extension divested of all these sensible modes as swift and slow, great and small, round and square and the like, which are acknowledged to exist only in the mind, I will then yield the point you contend for. But if you cannot, it will be unreasonable on your side to insist any longer upon what you have no notion of. (*Ibid.*)

He adds to this the comment that "since I cannot frame abstract ideas at all, it is plain, I cannot frame them by the help of 'pure intellect', whatsoever faculty you understand by these words" (II.193–4). We shall return to this question of realism with respect to the Idea in due course.

Proper objects, common objects and the role of the imagination

In the third *Dialogue*, Philonous, through an example of a red cherry, distinguishes between the various sensible impressions of said cherry and their aggregation – the "body" – which the mind unites. The unifying act, which enables us to refer to an object as "this cherry", is performed by the imagination. "A cherry", he claims, "is not a being distinct from sensations; a cherry, I say, is nothing but a congeries of sensible impressions, or ideas perceived by various senses: which ideas are united into one thing (or have one name given to them) by the mind" (GBW II.249). As Robert Muehlmann (1992) shows, for Berkeley, objects can be divided into two classes: "proper objects", which are the immediate objects of sense – the congeries of sensible impressions outlined above; and "common objects", which are formed by minds' imaginative powers (cherries, apples, houses and animal bodies). "It is important to note", Muehlmann writes, "that imaginative here does not mean fictitious, but rather, image involving, thus underscoring the ideational nature of thought – including sense perception, forming images (whether fictitious or memorial) and conceiving – about the natural world" (*ibid.*: 213). Following Descartes, the ideas are the "forms" of our thought, which we, in an almost Malebranchian way, unite through the faculty of the imagination. The way in which the imagination forms these bodies from the basic ideas of sense transmitted to us via our "five sense modalities" is determined by our habits gained through past experience, inferences that we learn from birth and eventually make rapidly and unconsciously.

In his copy of Berkeley's *Principles*, Leibniz wrote: "There is much here that is correct and close to my own view. But it is expressed paradoxically.

For it is not necessary to say that matter is nothing, but it is sufficient to say that it is a phenomenon, like the rainbow" (AG 307). Leibniz and Berkeley are in fact even closer here than this note suggests. Both believe that a body is the formation of a perceiving mind, which, on perceiving the vast complexity of sensual data, aggregates this data into singular unified perceptions. The difference, of course, is that corresponding to the perceptions of Leibniz is a vast infinity of monads, which these perceptions express, while for Berkeley, as we shall see, the perceptions are of the ideas of sense produced by God, drawn from his eternal archetype.

Private psychological fields

Whitehead points out that the kind of doctrine advocated by Berkeley, and developed in certain aspects by Hume, can lead to a conception of things in which the entirety of reality is confined to "private psychological fields". Among many problems created by this, he writes that:

> This modern doctrine raises a great difficulty in the interpretation of modern science. For all exact observation is made in these private psychological fields. It is then no use talking about instruments and laboratories and physical energy. What is really being observed are narrow bands of colour-sensa in the private psychological space of colour-vision. The impressions of sensation which collectively form this entirely private experience "arise in the soul from unknown causes". The spectroscope is a myth, the radiant energy is a myth, the observer's eye is a myth, the observer's brain is a myth, and the observer's record of his experiment on a sheet of paper is a myth. When, some months later, he reads his notes to a learned society, he has a new visual experience of black marks on a white background in a new private psychological field. And again, these experiences arise in his soul "from unknown causes". It is merely "custom" which leads him to connect his earlier with his later experiences. (PR 326)

These comments concerning problems associated with interpretation of scientific data can, of course, apply to any claimed experience of "reality". What Whitehead is pointing to is the constant threat of collapse into nihilistic solipsism inherent in Berkeley's brand of idealism.

How, then, is Berkeley to defend against a complete collapse of reality? It seems clear that if there is any shared reality, for Berkeley, it is not a consequence of some independently existing things, but rather must be a consequence of some commonality of the functioning of all minds. This, as we shall see, seems to lay the philosophical ground for Kant's categories and the rest of the *a priori* conditions for the experience enjoyed by all finite rational beings. How, though, does Berkeley establish this commonality of minds?

The mind of God

How can things have any stable reality if they are mind dependent for their existence? Again and again Berkeley rejects, of course, the argument that the stable reality of things lies separately from the mind's perception of them. How could this be so, he asks: what would be the relationship between the "real" thing and the perception? As we have seen, he denies that it could be causal – or, at any rate, that we could have any knowledge of such a causal relationship – since we do not experience the causes of our sense perceptions, but only the sense perceptions themselves. He denies that it could be one of similarity, since how could something that is "insensible" be in any way like something that is "sensible" (GBW II.206).

Furthermore, he insists that it is the belief that the reality of things lies outside the mind that leads to nihilistic scepticism. This is because, as he has demonstrated, we can know nothing of that which lies outside the mind, so if we believe that reality is dependent on its subsistence independent of mind, we shall, inevitably, end up doubting reality altogether. The only alternative to such scepticism is to accept that the reality of things is mind dependent. Nothing can exist outside all minds: "that any immediate object of the senses, that is, any idea or combination of ideas, should exist in an unthinking substance, or exterior to all minds, is in itself an evident contradiction" (II.195).

But, he says, when I look around me I see "[h]ow exquisitely are all things suited, as well to their particular ends as to constitute apposite parts of the whole!" When I look out at the universe and observe that "neither sense nor imagination are big enough to comprehend the boundless extent with all its glittering furniture", I know that it is not I that is the author of all reality (II.210–11). Perhaps more importantly it is clear that while my opening of my eyes is an act of positive volition, the sense perception that follows is not determined by my will. Perception is consequent on an act of volition, such as drawing in breath to smell a flower. But whether or not the sensation follows the act of volition is not determined by the volition; it is "passive" in this respect. Berkeley says "*seeing* consists in perceiving light and colours", not in "opening and turning the eyes" (II.197). But if my perception of colours is "passive", where do these colours come from?

> It is evident that the things I perceive are my own ideas, and that no idea can exist unless it be in a mind. Nor is it less plain that these ideas or things by me perceived, either themselves or their archetypes, exist independently of my mind; since I know myself not to be their author, it being out of my power to determine at pleasure what particular ideas I shall be affected by. (II.214)

So, if reality is mind dependent, but it is not my mind that is the source of this reality, then what is? Of the reality of things he ultimately concludes:

> Seeing they depend not on my thought and have an existence distinct from being perceived by me, there must be some other mind wherein they exist ... Sensible things do really exist, and if they do really exist, they are necessarily perceived by an infinite mind. Therefore there is an infinite mind, or God. (II.212)

Nature, science, dreams and illusions

It is, therefore, the ideas of things in the mind of God that provides stability and order to things. It is God's will that these ideas should appear in the individual mind as they do. God determines that they should appear constantly, and consistently, in certain orders and with certain connections. It is this order and connection that we call nature. Because of God, ideas change according to the "fixed order of nature", which provides the "constancy and truth of things" (GBW II.258).

Science, then, is simply a process of observing and reasoning about the "connection of ideas" (II.243). When I look through a microscope I do not see an independently existing material object. I have a quite different experience from that of looking without the microscope. These are not two different experiences of the same external object. Rather, I simply learn to connect these experiences (ideas) in a particular way, and refer to this collection of ideas as a single object. This is what knowledge of nature consists in. Berkeley, in any case, has a very low opinion of the mechanical materialism that dominated the physical sciences of his time. He mocks the scientists for their inability to "comprehend how any one body should move another", nor can they "reach the mechanical prediction of any one animal or vegetable body", nor in any way account for colours, sounds, smells, tastes and the like by the laws of motion. He contrasts this inability of supposed laws governing inert matter to account for anything with the power of God as an "active" spirit (II.217). The cause of thought, he writes, could never be an inert insensible matter; the cause of thought could only be an active spirit – God. And

God has no need of matter as an instrument for implanting his ideas into our minds. He can do it directly, without any pointless mediation (II.214). The rules of the "exhibition" of things to us are the "laws of nature" determined by God (II.231).

It is by virtue of God, also, that we can distinguish between the reality of things perceived and the unreality of things imagined or dreamed. Berkeley argues that products of our imagination are "faint and indistinct", and have an "entire dependence on the will". In contrast, the "ideas perceived by sense, that is real things, are more vivid and clear, and being imprinted on the mind by a spirit distinct from us, have not the like dependence on our will". We can also see that dreams are "dim, irregular and confused" and that they are not "connected" with the rest of our lives (II.235). When we make mistaken judgements about our experiences, these are not really mistakes about independently existing material objects but are about the succession of ideas that we should expect to manifest themselves in our minds. When I see a stick in water and it seems crooked, I should expect – on the basis of past experience of my ideas – that, when the stick is pulled from the water, it will turn out to be straight. The illusion lies in a miscalculation of the ideas that will follow one another as a consequence of God's patterning of ideas to form nature.

Eternal ideas

At this point, in contrast to his apparent earlier nominalism, Berkeley begins to seem decidedly Platonic. The ideas of things are, he writes, all present in the mind of God: "God knew all things from eternity" so that things always had existence in the "Divine intellect" (GBW II.253). The world is eternal in God, so "creation", the emergence of the temporal order of nature, is something that happens only for finite beings. He writes that "the several parts of the world became gradually perceivable to finite spirits endowed with proper faculties". He even says that "created beings might begin to exist in the mind of other created intelligences beside men" (II.252). He says that "external archetypes" are provided by "that mind which comprehends all things" (II.248). He goes on to write that there is a "twofold state of things, the one ectypal or nature, the other archetypal and eternal. The former was created in time; the latter existed from everlasting in the mind of God" (II.254). Ideas subsist in an eternal mind of God, who then manifests these ideas as nature in the minds of finite beings, thus echoing Plato's account of time as a "moving image of eternity" (*Ti.* 37d).

Berkeley points out that the material substance theory makes the reality of things "extrinsic to the mind of God", whereas, of course, his immaterialism makes all of reality immanent to the mind of God. From this point of view

Berkeley's idealism, as well as being Neoplatonic, looks decidedly pantheistic and panpsychic.

This appears to lie in some tension with Berkeley's earlier proclaimed nominalism, where he states that *"it is a universally received maxim that 'everything which exists is particular'"* (II.192). How does the "twofold state of things" – in which there exist both those things that are "ectypal" or "particular" *and* those that are "archetypal" or "eternal" – sit next to the claim that there exist only particulars? We can make sense of this only on the basis of the distinction, set out above in the Introduction, between "abstract universals" (as discussed by medieval philosophy) and the Idea as causal or genetic, as we have found it in idealisms from Plato and Neoplatonism onwards. We must not model the Idea in terms of the abstract universal. Berkeley rejects the abstract universal, but, for all of his strictures about the particular being the only existent, has a realist conception of the Idea as genetic archetype in the mind of God.

THE PHENOMENOLOGY OF ANIMALS AND THE ROLE OF THE BRAIN

Another difficulty arises, however, in relation to one of the most interesting strategies used by Berkeley. Throughout this demonstration of the mind-dependent character of sensible things, he often appeals to the cognitive capacities of other animals. For example, he points out that different animals have different capacities for sight. These are determined, he thinks, by their "use in preserving their bodies from injuries", and are relative to their scale, form and needs. He thinks it likely, therefore, that they see different colours in things than us (GBW II.185). In his discussion of primary qualities, he again appeals to the experience of animals. He says that "their senses were bestowed upon animals for their preservation and well being in life", just like those of men, and that they must relate to "bodies which are capable of harming them". He considers, for example, microscopic creatures and how they must perceive a quite different scale of things, so that "what you can hardly discern will to another extremely minute animal appear as some huge mountain" (II.189–90). We have here a hint of an embodied phenomenology, and an attempt to account for the bodily determination of perception. This is the kind of thing that would be taken much further in the twentieth century by, for example, Maurice Merleau-Ponty (2003), the ethologist Jacob von Uexküll (1957) and, more recently, the neurophilosopher Andy Clarke (2001).

The problem with this is that, as we have seen, he insists that organic bodies are not independently existent, but are themselves products of the imaginative activity of the mind. This must include the bodies to which he is appealing in this phenomenology of animals. A good example of this is the discussion of the role of the brain. It is suggested by the character Hylas that the brain might be a cause of our sense perceptions and, therefore, something outside, and prior to, such experience. However, at this point, Berkeley insists that the brain itself is a sensible thing, like other sensible things. It is simply an "idea" in the mind. How could one such idea in the mind cause the other ideas in the mind, he asks? And how, in any case, could the "motion of nerves" be a cause of something as different in kind as experience in the mind? He concludes that it does not make sense either logically or empirically, and that, therefore, the brain cannot be a cause of experience.

I think we find another manifestation of this confusion in the way Berkeley tries to address the problem of how we, as finite spirits, are to be distinguished from God as infinite spirit. He says that we are limited and dependent spirits – and that "our perceptions are connected with corporeal motions" (unlike God). Then, as though he has temporarily forgotten himself, he goes on to quickly state that, of course, these "corporeal motions" are just more ideas connected to one another. Why, then, one might ask, did he mention them at all (GBW II.241)?

There seems, here, to be a tension within Berkeley's line of argument. Either animal bodies, including their brains, have the power to determine the nature of their perception, in which case they must have an independent reality prior to that perception (a bodily "*a priori*"), or they have no such reality, in which case they cannot be determinant of the nature of perception in the way that Berkeley clearly wants them to be at an earlier stage in the dialogues. This tension would come to characterize many future attempts to base idealism on an account of cognitive capacities.

Although there are many problems and tensions within Berkeley's arguments, his thought had a very significant impact and influence on the further development of idealist thought. As we shall see, this was nowhere more the case than in the problems explored by Immanuel Kant.

Phenomenalized Platonism: Ideas and the Forms of thought

At the beginning of Chapter 3, we made the claim that the important move Descartes made was not to invent idealism but rather to phenomenalize idealism: to invent a form of Platonism that refers strictly to the production of phenomena from Ideas in the *cogito*. Throughout Chapters 3 and 4 we have shown that the four early modern philosophers whom we have examined all engage in such a phenomenalized idealism, but all from their own unique position.

For Descartes, Ideas are the very "forms of our thoughts". They are the innate archetypes that exist in our mind awaiting to be triggered by the right signals read from extension. For Malebranche, the "Ideas" are the exclusive possession of God's understanding; they are the archetypes from which he created the external world and in which we participate every time we perceive. Leibniz and Berkeley both criticize abstract universals while at the same time defending a Platonism of eternal archetypes. The key point for both philosophers is that if something does not exist "in a mind", then it does not exist at all,[4] and they develop an "immaterialist" metaphysics from this axiom. Like Descartes, Leibniz sees the universal forms of God reproduced in every single perceptive substance, or monad. Our conscious ideas are the products of the combined powers of these universal simple forms. The basic forms are infinite in number and far simpler than Locke's "simple ideas"; for Leibniz, just as the colour green comes from a mixture of blue and yellow, all colours, as well as other ideas considered by Locke as simple, such as "warmth", can be regarded as "simple ideas", and only further analysis will reveal a great variety of divisions within them. The created monads differ from the primitive monad, God, in that only in God do the forms exist in their pure unlimited power. The extent to which these forms are limited in each monad is what primarily differentiates each monad from each other and provides each monad with different phenomenal experiences. Each monad shares the divine essence of God but in its own particular way.

Berkeley's idealism is perhaps closer to Malebranche than either Descartes or Leibniz in that the eternal archetypes exist exclusively in the mind of God. As we have seen, Berkeley denies the existence of abstract universals, but develops a theory of eternal archetypes. The difference seems to be that he believes that the former can exist entirely independently of mind, while the latter cannot. Berkeley writes:

> I have no objection against calling the Ideas in the mind of God archetypes of ours. But I object against those archetypes by philosophers supposed to be real things, and to have an absolute rational existence distinct from their being perceived by any mind whatsoever. (GBW II.19)

And "[Y]ou [may] suppose an external archetype on my principles; external, I mean, to your own mind; though indeed it must be supposed to exist in that mind which comprehends all things" (II.248). Like Leibniz, Berkeley believes that all ideas must have a concrete existence. They can never be merely abstract: "the things I perceive must have an existence, they or their archetypes, out of my mind; but being ideas, neither they nor their archetypes can exist otherwise than in their understanding" (II.240). God's mind is the locus of Ideas, which makes up the very "nature of things". We need not infer from Berkeley's polemic against "abstract ideas" that he rejects any form of

Platonic idealism. As Anita Fritz notes, this attack is really "an attack on the process of abstraction as represented by Locke or as represented in many of the later and lesser scholastic treatises … the unique particulars of perception cannot yield 'abstract' ideas" (1954: 564). For Berkeley, it is from the Platonic eternal archetype of God's understanding that we are provided with the particular *immediate* "ideas of sense" as the *forms* of our thought from which we *mediately* produce bodies via the imagination. The eternal is the ground of our temporal existence.

5. IMMANUEL KANT: COGNITION, FREEDOM AND TELEOLOGY

THE IDEAS OF REASON, THE CATEGORIES OF UNDERSTANDING AND THE FORMS OF INTUITION IN THE *CRITIQUE OF PURE REASON*

If we ask what use Kant had for the Idea in the first *Critique* then we can provide at least two answers. One of these would assert that in fact the Idea plays a very restricted role. It arises primarily in the Transcendental Dialectic, which itself appears to be a text aimed at demarcating clearly where the limits of reason lie, criticizing those who have stepped beyond these limits, and pointing out why they are wrong to do so (CPR A293–704/B349–732).

In this context, Kant states that there are, in fact, only three true Ideas of reason. These are the Soul, the World and God. Kant says that they are regulatory principles. They help to focus and organize the thought and activity of finite rational beings. They are not, however, possible objects of experience in themselves. We cannot have "knowledge" of these principles in the same way that we can have empirical knowledge of parts of our "internal" and "external" experience. Indeed, we must not think of them as normal empirical objects at all. To the extent that they are objects in any sense, they are, for the purposes of the reasoning subject, what he calls "unconditioned" objects. That is, they do not depend on anything other than themselves for their existence; they are self-subsistent totalities. Theoretical reason, however, always involves making sense of things by developing an understanding of their conditions. Consequently these Ideas of reason cannot, by definition, be "understood" in any normal sense. As objects of knowledge they always remain transcendental aspirations, forever unreachable. They are like unreachable goals that we, nevertheless, need to imagine if we are to organize our experience, thoughts, knowledge and judgements.

So they are real, they have real effects, but they are not objects that we can interrogate as we would other objects. Before we can begin to make sense of this properly we have to look at the rest of Kant's system in the first *Critique*.

We said that there are two possible answers to the question of the role of the Idea for Kant. Either we can take Kant literally and focus only on the restricted role of the Ideas of reason, or, from a second point of view, almost everything that Kant writes in the first *Critique* concerns Ideas. His core question is: what are the *a priori* conditions of our experience and knowledge of the empirical world? What must first be in place, lying in wait, in order that the disorganized flood of fragmentary sensory data, to which our bodies are subject, can be turned into true "experience", thought and knowledge? The ultimate, "unconditioned", regulatory "Ideas of reason" just mentioned (and to which we shall return) lie at the termination of a long and complex process of formative construction of experience. Each stage along the way adds further *form* to experience. As such, it is arguable that all of this construction concerns the Idea in the broader sense in which we have used the concept.

In order to account for this construction, Kant is interested in what he calls "*a priori* synthesis" (CPR B13–19, A25–39/B40–56). *A priori* synthesis must be contrasted with *a posteriori* synthesis. The latter is the conceptual joining of heterogeneous things in the context of experience. Experience tells me that the heating of water to one hundred degrees Celsius and a phase change from liquid to vapour are linked – this is a synthesis subsequent to experience – and so *a posteriori*. Kant is interested, however, in the existence of syntheses that are themselves *conditions* for the existence of experience itself – syntheses that necessarily come prior to experience – and so are *a priori* syntheses.

Intuition

The first stage in this *a priori* construction is the synthetic assembly of a manifold of diverse sensory traces according to the rules of assembly of the faculty of intuition, or sensibility (CPR A17–49/B31–73). Various aspects of the object are derived from diverse and heterogeneous sensory systems, yet these traces are experienced as aspects of a unified object. There must, therefore, be a mechanism of synthetic assembly of these diverse traces, and this mechanism is an *a priori* condition of all experience. This is now a commonplace of contemporary cognitive neuroscience, but Kant was perhaps the first to enquire into the nature of the mechanisms whereby this assembly takes place.

Most important to the assembly of the object within the manifold of sensory traces is the *form* of space (A22–30/B37–45). From the point of view of common sense, it is, at first, hard to credit the great philosopher with the notion that space and time are not independent existents, but figments of our cognitive apparatus. So it is worth looking at precisely what he says here.

> Space does not represent any property of things in themselves, nor does it represent them in their relation to one another. That is to say, space does not represent any determination that attaches to the objects themselves, and which remains even when abstraction has been made of all the subjective conditions of intuition.
> (A26/B42)

Space is not, then, an absolute extension, independent of human experience, an eternal container of independent objects. Rather, he says: "Space is nothing but the *form* of all appearances of outer sense. It is the subjective condition of sensibility, under which alone outer intuition is possible for us" (A26/B42).

Space is simply the capacity to experience externality. I can only experience "outsideness" in terms of a space in which I can exist as an object alongside other objects, objects that are not within me. This "outsideness", then, is simply a *"form" of experience*. This form, is, however, universal to all human experience. It is, therefore, says Kant, empirically real. All experience of the object has the form of space in common. It would be a mistake to see in this some kind of cognitive relativism. Space is not relative in any sense; it is universal to all experience – a universal form. There is, however, no space independent of experience, within which objects beyond experience subsist, such that experience can *correspond* in a more or less accurate degree to that absolute space and its objects. The way that Kant puts this is to say that space is *empirically* real but not *transcendentally* real. To emphasize the *a priori* character of space he writes:

> [T]he receptivity of the subject, its capacity to be affected by objects, must necessarily precede all intuitions of these objects, it can readily be understood how the form of all appearances can be given prior to all actual perceptions, and so exist in the mind *a priori*.
> (A26/B42)

The synthesis of external sensibility within the form of space is not the only kind of synthesis that takes place through the faculty of intuition however. There is also the synthesis of internal sensibility through the form of time (A30–41/B46–58). Again, he writes that: "Time is not something which exists of itself, or which inheres in things as an objective determination, and it does not, therefore, remain when abstraction is made of all subjective conditions of its intuition" (B49). Rather, time is the experience of temporal succession *of* my experiences. Time is not an absolute extension independent of experience, but, rather, the capacity to have experiences, as a temporal succession, within a temporal dimension. Time is, then, simply another *"form" of experience*, the form of experience of internal sensibility. "Time is nothing but the *form* of inner sense, that is, of the intuition of ourselves and of our inner state. It cannot be a determination of outer appearances; it has to do neither with shape nor position, but with the relation of representations in our inner state" (A33/B49, emphasis added).

Descartes, Berkeley and Hume had insisted that our experience of the "outside" world was unavoidably less certain than our experience of our own selves and the operation of our own internal mental processes. Kant, in contrast, sees that, in fact, both are equally certain experiences, distinguished only by their form, rather than by some substantial heterogeneity. These forms, of time and space, are *a priori* conditions of the empirical existence of time and space within experience. Consequently, these forms cannot, themselves, be entities within empirical time and space since they logically precede the latter. They are, therefore, eternal and universal forms. This forms the basis for Kant's restored certainty with respect to the object, an empirical realism. But what kind of realism, and at what cost?

Empirical realism and the transcendental idealism

For Kant, we must distinguish between two objects, and two realities, with the utmost clarity. These are the domains of the empirical and the transcendental. The former we can know with absolute certainty; the latter we never can, although we can evidently contemplate its possible existence.

We can know empirical reality with certainty precisely because it is the realm of our experience. The object within that realm is the empirical object. When we "know" the empirical object, what we "know" is a construct conforming to the form-providing mechanisms of our cognitive faculties: the forms of time and space provided by intuition (and, as we shall see, the forms of the categories provided by the understanding). These *a priori* structures (ideas in all but name) are what provide the form that the empirical object has in our experience. The truth of our apprehension of reality becomes not, then, a question of our representation *corresponding* to an object external to it, but rather a question of that object being produced in a form that is coherent with these formal structures of cognition. *The empirical laws of nature, governing the relations between objects in the realm of empirical reality, are, thus, the laws of this formal structure of cognition.* A vital question, then, might be: what exactly is the status of this formal structure of cognition? This is a question we shall return to.

So, what prevents this system becoming identical to that of Berkeley or Descartes? Why is this not the most extreme sceptical subjectivism? First, unlike Berkeley, Kant never denies the existence of a reality external to the empirical realm of representational experience. He simply insists on two rules with respect to it: (a) we cannot know it directly; and (b) correspondence between our representations and this hypothetical "outside" should not, therefore, be imagined to be the basis for truth or knowledge. The former he believes leads to what he calls "transcendental realism", a position that sceptics such as Descartes and Hume have shown to be unsustainable. The latter, which was also adopted by Descartes and Hume, leads to a hopeless, and entirely unnecessary, sceptical nihilism.

So there is a reality external to the empirical or phenomenal. This is the reality of the noumenon, the realm of the transcendental object (CPR A235–60/B294–315). Kant says that we must retain this transcendental realm – our empirical experiences are, somehow, experiences *of* that transcendental object – but we can never know in what respect this "*of*" pertains, only that it does. We must then focus our attention, with respect to truth and knowledge, on the realm of the empirical. The latter we know with certainty, and so we can be "realists" with respect to it. We can be, simultaneously, "transcendental idealists" and "empirical realists". Empirical reality is taken inside the structure of the reasoning subject. Consequently, the cost of Kant's empirical realism is a fundamental dualism. This is a dualism of an unknowable transcendental–noumenal matter, and a knowable phenomenal–empirical realm of the Idea.

It could be argued that it is a mistake to see in this a metaphysics; Kant is concerned with only one thing – the conditions of human knowledge. Consequently, it is argued, this is all epistemology: an insistence that we must forget the thing-in-itself, and focus instead on the limits of knowledge. Is this a fair assessment? This is a question we shall return to.

We have seen, then, what Kant believes to be the *a priori* conditions for the synthesis of objects and subjects in space and time. There is a huge difference, however, between a capacity to *experience* unified objects and subjects in space and time, and having *knowledge* of those objects and subjective experiences. How do we come to know and judge with respect to the synthetic products of the sensibility?

The understanding

In the Transcendental Analytic, Kant lays out for us the workings of the faculty that produces knowledge of things so that we can understand the world (CPR A50–130/B74–169). According to Kant, we produce knowledge of objects through concepts. These concepts are generated through the application to objects (previously constructed by the faculty of intuition or sensibility) of a framework of *a priori* categories. What appears is something similar to the Aristotelian table of categories (A80/B106). Aristotle had, from Kant's point of view, made a mistake in including space and time within the categories. They are sensible, not intelligible, forms, says Kant. He demonstrates this in the Transcendental Aesthetic, in a metaphysical exposition, in which he shows that space and time are perceptions, rather than concepts, because concepts contain particulars "under" them, not "in" them, in contrast to space and time.

The primitive *a priori* categories that we apply in order to create conceptual understanding are:

- *Quantity.* This includes all knowledge of unity, plurality and totality.
- *Quality of relation.* This includes all knowledge of reality, of inherence and subsistence, of negation, of substance and accident, of limitation of causality and dependence (cause and effect), and of community (reciprocity between agent and patient).
- *Modality.* This includes all knowledge of possibility, of impossibility, of existence, of non-existence, of necessity, and of contingency (A80/B106).

Of these categories, he writes, "we are entitled to call these representations pure concepts of the understanding, and to regard them as applying *a priori* to objects" (A79/B105).

These categories are, then, the *a priori* possession of the intellect. They are universal forms of all cognition, but they are "empty" forms. To produce experience, they must be filled by objects of intuition. "In the absence of intuition all our knowledge is without objects, and therefore remains entirely empty" (A62/B87). But how does this synthesis of perceptual intuitions within categories come about? How can a synthesis of such heterogeneous elements take place, such that empirical objects can be known in experience? The answer is that space and time mediate between the categories and perceptual intuitions. They can do this because they are both *a priori* and sensuous. This mediation Kant calls the "transcendental schematism of the pure intellect". This "schematism", then, is generated by the operation of space and time in relation to quantity, quality of relation and modality (A137–47/B176–87).

Producing unity of experience among all these operations is a very special form of experience, a particular "act" of thought. This is the act of "I think". The "I think" is not, as Descartes had believed, proof of the existence of a thinking substance; rather, it is, again, a *form* that thought can take in order to provide unity and continuity of experience. Kant calls this form "the transcendental unity of apperception" (A106–10/B131–42). When we experience features of an object as belonging to that object, we do so not because objects really have such groups of qualities but, rather, by virtue of the unifying power of the cognitive process. As Kant puts it:

> It holds good even if the judgment is itself empirical, and therefore contingent, as, for example, in the judgment, "Bodies are heavy". I do not here assert that these representations *necessarily* belong *to one another* in the empirical intuition, but that they belong to one another *in virtue of the necessary unity* of apperception in the synthesis of intuitions. (B142)

So now we have a number of *a priori* syntheses that provide universal forms of intuition, together with universal forms of understanding. The universal and eternal (extra-temporal) character of the categories is guaranteed by the fact that time and space are themselves *a priori* forms only of empirical experience, so cannot be forms of the other *a priori conditions* of experience. The categories are conditions of experience, not part of experience, so necessarily lie outside of time and space.

Realist or nominalist?

The employment of an apparently Aristotelian table of categories raises the question of Kant's relative allegiance to Plato versus Aristotle. This is an extremely complex question. However, a few immediate conclusions can be drawn. It is difficult to see how Kant's categories could be conceived in a nominalist light given that they are explicitly deemed to be *a priori*. They preexist any particular experience of an object. They are not simply the "names" given to groups of objects. They are not simply names for "sets" of objects that reflect their similarities. They are the ontological conditions of empirical objects *per se*. We can see, then, that there remains a strong current of Platonic idealism here.

However, of course, we must remember that the empirical object is no longer what it once was. Kant has relocated empirical reality to the internal structures of the rational subject. Paradoxically, this very relocation provides the intellectual conditions for a powerful strain of post-Kantian nominalist thinking, especially if it is combined with an overemphasis on Kant's account of freedom and practical reason. Only a small change of emphasis is necessary. Suppose we interpret Kant's cognitive synthesis as licence to argue that "the empirical object is whatever we name it as", rather than "the empirical object is whatever the rational cognitive faculties synthesize it as". Suppose, further, that the construction of the object is deemed to be socially, politically and economically determined. The conditions for the nominalist tendencies within epistemology, ethics, political philosophy and the "social sciences" are set.

IDEALISM

The Ideas of reason

There is, then, an act of mind (a form of our understanding) that Kant calls the "I think". But we must not begin to imagine that beneath that act lies an immaterial thinking substance that is the origin of the "I think": that which we often refer to as soul (or mind). Once we do so – and thereby begin to interrogate this entity's nature and origins through the categories of the understanding – then we fall into error. We need the *Idea* of the soul, but we cannot understand or know the soul.

Second, there is a form of organization of our understanding that seeks to find the causes of things, and the effects of things. Again, this is a very useful form for organizing our thoughts. If, however, we imagine an entity that is the unconditioned totality of all causes and effects to the furthest extents of time and space – an entity we call the "world" (cosmos, universe, etc.) – and we begin to interrogate the nature and origin of this unconditioned totality, then we fall into error. Since time and space are internal forms of intuition, not transcendentally external forms, the notion of exploring the furthest bounds of space and time is, for Kant, a confusion.

Third, there is a form of organization of our understanding that seeks to find unity, purpose and meaning in all objects of thought (be they empirical objects or not). Again, this is an essential formal organization of our thoughts, but no more than that. We should not imagine that there is an unconditioned unity of all existence, reality and thought outside our thoughts, and try to turn our faculty of understanding on to this unconditioned unity as though it were an object itself. In particular, when we imagine God as an entity that is the perfect unconditioned cause and unity of being and reality, and we try to prove God's existence through the methods we would use for exploration of empirical reality, we fall into error.

Here is how Kant puts this point:

> All transcendental ideas can therefore be arranged in three classes, the *first* containing the absolute (unconditioned) *unity* of the *thinking subject*, the *second* the absolute *unity of the series of conditions of appearance*, the *third* the absolute *unity of the condition of all objects of thought in general*.
> ... Pure reason thus furnishes the idea for a transcendental doctrine of the soul (*psychologia rationalis*), for a transcendental science of the world (*cosmologia rationalis*), and, finally, for a transcendental knowledge of God (*theologia transzendentalis*). The understanding is not in a position to yield even the mere project of any one of these sciences. (CPR A334–5/B391–2)

These Ideas are, then, like "attractors" of thought.[1] They drive thought on to organize more and more of experience. And there is a sense in which we have to imagine the possibility of a complete knowledge of these ideas for more limited thought to have any meaning. But that knowledge of the unconditioned absolute is forever beyond reach. Such an idea can never be determinate, then; it is, rather, infinitely determinable. This notion of an infinitely determinable, regulative and productive idea, is the germ that lies behind Deleuze's more recent development of the notion of the "problem-idea" (1994: 168–221).[2]

Kant's refutations of idealism

Having said all this, some commentators will point out that Kant is careful to distinguish himself from various forms of philosophical idealism, and that he in fact uses a fair amount of effort criticizing idealism, especially in the "Critique of the Fourth Paralogism of Transcendental Psychology" from the first edition (CPR A367–80) and the "Refutation of Idealism" in the second (B274–9). It is clear, however, that in these texts he is criticizing a particular type of idealism.

In these texts, Kant defines "idealism" as a certain kind of scepticism that involves the claim that our perception of "outer" objects must be uncertain because we have to infer their existence as the cause of our own perceptions. Effects may have more than one cause, so our experiences may be caused by mechanisms within ourselves giving rise to the illusion of external objects. We cannot, therefore, be sure of the existence of outer objects. Along with this scepticism regarding externality goes a belief that we have certainty concerning our inner sense: the "I think". He has in mind, then, mainly Descartes and Hume. As regards Berkeley, Kant does not really hit the target here since Berkeley explicitly denies this distinction between our ideas of things and independently existing "outer" objects or causes.

He asserts that those who believe this are transcendental realists and empirical idealists. They are transcendental realists with respect to the object since they insist that the reality of the object lies in the thing-in-itself. Since we can have no direct knowledge of this we cannot be certain of the object at all. They thus fall into scepticism and empirical idealism.

He describes himself, in contrast, as a transcendental idealist, and empirical realist, for whom the reality of the object lies in its "presentation" in experience. The appearance of an object in space and time is, already, the appearance of a construct, since space and time are themselves the forms of intuition, not transcendental externality. Since the empirical reality of the objects *is* its existence as appearance (representation), we are as certain of the existence of such objects as we are of our own mental operations. Inner and outer sense are equally certain; inner and outer things-in-themselves are equally inaccessible, and irrelevant from the point of view of empiricism.

So, to return to some earlier points, there are two meanings of "outside": empirical and transcendental. We must not mix them up. Things in space are empirically external, not transcendentally external.

The type of idealist dealt with in these texts is just one kind of idealist that Kant ultimately opposes, however. Descartes, Berkeley and Hume he refers to as sceptical idealists, because they state that we can never be sure of the existence of real objects independent of our experience because such existence can never be proved.[3] As we have seen, Kant's answer to these sceptical idealists is that they are looking in the wrong place for the empirically real object. Kant also distinguishes another type of idealist: what he calls the dogmatic idealist. "The *dogmatic idealist* would be one who *denies* the existence of matter, the *sceptical idealist* one who *doubts* its existence, because holding it to be incapable of proof" (A377). The dogmatic idealist denies existence of matter altogether because it is self-contradictory. Here he may be thinking of Leibniz and Berkeley. All his criticism of idealism in the "Critique of the Fourth Paralogism", and the "Refutation of Idealism", concerns sceptical idealism, however. As we have seen, while Kant deals with their scepticism, none of it prevents Kant himself from being an idealist, even if he does seek to differentiate *his* idealism from that of others.

Cognition and "critique"

Kant is, then, among other things, the philosopher who, properly speaking, founds cognitive science as we know it today. His point of departure is the ancient world of metaphysics, but the world he delves ever more deeply into is the modern world of cognition and the brain. In the course of this journey he never leaves metaphysics behind, just as contemporary neuroscientists have been drawn ever more deeply into Kantian and Cartesian metaphysical paradox. For the first time ever, though, he asks: how can this manifold of diverse and heterogeneous sensory impression be bound into a unity, into an object world? Varied frequency electromagnetic radiation, varied frequency sound vibration, airborne chemical messengers, pressure contacts: how can I ever know that a smell, and a vision, and a feel, and a sound, the presence of which are derived from entirely different and organizationally heterogeneous parts of a body, are of the selfsame "object", in an object world, structured by dimensions of time and space? How, indeed, can I know that there can be such a thing as an object so that this experience can subsequently come about? As the ordering of the sentence implies, this knowledge – of the possibility of a unity of experience in an object – must be something that I "know" prior to experience itself. It must be, a "synthetic *a priori*". The bulk of Kant's effort is then devoted to an account of the *a priori*. We must possess those cognitive structuring faculties, prior to any kind of experience, in order for experience of an object world to be possible at all. How does our brain manufacture an experience? Two hundred years later, these are precisely the questions that now form the core of the cognitive neuroscience research programme.

Ironically (given the scientific standing of the cognitive science programme), another major legacy of the cognitive constructivism of the *Critique of Pure Reason* has been the ontological nominalism and epistemological relativism that characterized much of the late twentieth century and, in particular, the "critical" and constructionist social sciences. Once Kant opened up the question of the determination of experience, the whole area was ripe for various forms of exploration. If experience is determined by *a priori* cognitive structures, then what if those structures are, themselves, determined by factors outside themselves? Such questions came to dominate the intellectual history of the twentieth century in a variety of forms. Many of these were explicitly "critical", with the term here implying not just the demarcation of the limits of human knowledge, but critique of the social and political determination of reality and our knowledge of it.

DUTY AND THE IDEA OF FREEDOM: PURE PRACTICAL REASON

For Kant, there is more than one domain for the application of reason. Reason is applied not only to the problem of *judging* what is true and false, but also to the problem of *deciding* what one should do in the world. This is the theme of Kant's works in the area of practical philosophy. This includes, most importantly, *The Groundwork of the Metaphysics of Morals*, and the *Critique of Practical Reason*.

What is the role of the Idea in relation to this problem of practical activity? I think that we can, again, reasonably say that it is pervasive throughout Kant's writing. The ground for pure practical reason is provided by freedom, and the categorical imperative. Freedom and the will are linked in *a priori* synthesis, as a condition of the categorical imperative. Such *a priori* synthesis is, in the Kantian system, the very definition of the eternal, universal, unconditioned and form-giving.

Desire: the imperative

For Kant, the problem of decision, of practical reason, arises within the faculty of desire. His objective is, he says, that:

> the *a priori* principles of two faculties of the mind, the faculty of cognition and that of desire, would be found and determined as to the conditions, extent, and limits of their use, and thus a sure foundation be laid for a scientific system of philosophy, both theoretic and practical. (Ak. V.12)

The faculty of desire is that faculty which motivates me to act in the world. It is the faculty lying behind all practical activity. Kant points out that there are two very different conditions under which we make such choices to act. These are the two conditions under which practical reason operates. Both of these are conditions in which we find within ourselves an "imperative" to act, a form of desire. This is something that seems like an internal command to act. The source of this imperative we shall return to, to explore further. But the imperative itself can appear in two *forms*. First, this faculty of desire may motivate me towards the achievement of certain *ends*. If I have a practical capability to set alongside this desire for certain ends, then I am able to transform my desires into decisions and action. This practical capability requires a prescription for action given certain circumstances: *if* I wish to reduce my carbon footprint, *then* I should insulate my home more effectively. Second, the internal imperative may come in an unconditional form: I *ought* to reduce my carbon footprint. The former, instrumental and conditional form of command is a "hypothetical imperative", and, as he puts it, "hypothetical imperatives … contain mere precepts of skill" (Ak. V.20). The latter, unconditional form of command is a "categorical imperative". While the hypothetical imperative forms the domain of instrumental decision-making, the categorical imperative forms the domain of moral choice. This, he says, is choice determined by "a rule characterised by 'ought', which expresses the objective necessitation of the action, and signifies that if reason completely determined the will, the action would inevitably take place according to this rule" (Ak. V.20). We can see easily how the mechanics of a hypothetical imperative can be informed by knowledge gained in the domain of empirical experience. Pure theoretical reason, through the production of empirical knowledge, constantly feeds into the formulation of such hypothetical imperatives.

Two questions are outstanding at this point, however: (a) what is the source of the imperative desire in the first place?; and (b) what could form a rational basis for the second kind of imperative to act? What could be the basis for this "categorical imperative"?

Will

The source of this command to act is, says Kant, the very ground of the faculty of desire itself: it is the *will*. This, of course, begs the question of the will itself. From where does this issue? The will comes in two forms. Sometimes, it seems, the will is the vehicle of impulses, of the animal self. The will is captured by the conditions and objects of experience, and wills only animal inclinations, impulses, instincts. But humanity raises itself up from the condition of the animal will by becoming self-legislating. The human will can form its own laws of decision, quite separate from the inclinations, impulses and instincts of animal existence. The human will can, then, be conditioned by itself alone, and take on the form of a *free*, rational, will. "The will is conceived as a faculty of determining oneself to action *in accordance with the conception of certain laws*. And such a faculty can be found only in rational beings" (Ak. IV.427).

Here we find a form of causality that lies outside the deterministic causal chains of nature: a causality of self-given laws. To obey a self-made moral command is to do one's *duty*, but in doing such duty one is, paradoxically, most autonomous and free. Freedom, then, is a *form* of the will: "With this faculty, transcendental *freedom* is also established" (Ak. V.3). It is because this form of practical decision-making issues from an unconditioned free will that it is called *pure* practical reason.

Freedom: the noumenon

This free form of the will must be real, says Kant, because it is an *a priori* condition of the categorical imperative. Nevertheless, such freedom is, by definition, unknowable. The moment we try to understand a decision (someone else's or our own) it becomes a part of our empirical experience, and as such our understanding imposes upon it the deterministic framework common to all such understanding of experience. This is why free will has its ground in the noumenon, where determinacy and causality have no place. It is only from the domain of the noumenon that such a causeless cause is possible. Kant describes the "paradoxical demand to regard oneself *qua* subject of freedom as a noumenon, and at the same time from the point of view of physical nature as a phenomenon in one's own empirical consciousness" (Ak. V.6). This all seems to suggest a great deal more "knowledge" (or at least "thinkability") of the noumenal domain than Kant was willing to allow in the *Critique of Pure Reason*. It also still leaves open the problem of the rational basis for such moral self-legislation. Supposing our will can be free, how is this freedom exercised? How do we *form* our self-made rational laws of conduct?

Duty, freedom and the categorical imperative

According to Kant, we cannot decide what is a moral action by looking at the ends or consequences. Such consequentialist reasoning is flawed by the fact that desirable ends can easily be the accidental outcome of malevolent motivation, and vice versa. So utilitarianism can never provide a sound moral philosophy. The only possible basis for moral virtue lies in the nature of the will itself. Morality requires a "good will": a will that conforms to its self-legislated duty.

> [T]he moral law is an *imperative*, which commands categorically, because the law is unconditioned; the relation of such a will to this law is *dependence* under the name of *obligation*, which implies a *constraint* to an action, though only by reason and its objective law; and this action is called *duty*. (Ak. V.32)

This is not an invitation to make up whatever rules we prefer for ourselves, and then follow them. Kant insists that while the will is autonomous in its self-legislation, this autonomy manifests itself not in following arbitrary personal inclination (such appetites and inclinations he terms "pathological", since they could never be the basis for universal maxims), but in following the dictates of reason in formulating the maxims according to which we shall act. Moral duty is possible: "only, when reason of itself determines the will (not as the servant of the inclination), is it really a *higher* desire to which that which is pathologically determined is subordinate" (V.24–5). And, reason being precisely what is common to all "rational beings", we shall all freely come to the same conclusions regarding which maxims it is our duty to follow. According to Kant the moral maxims followed by pure practical reason do not issue from subjective inclination at all. They are entirely objective, universal and eternal.

So, this is an autonomy that must, inevitably, issue in conformity to a common, universal categorical imperative. Kant's freedom, then, is a freedom to exercise one's duty to conform to a universal moral law of reason. Freedom must always be linked to the categorical imperative through an *a priori* synthesis with the will. A very paradoxical freedom indeed (at least to a twenty-first-century eye). Whenever we do what our inclination tells us and thereby fail to conform to the categorical imperative, we are, by definition, unfree, since our will has been captured by the pathological seductions of animal impulse. We have failed to judge rationally, and instead been dragged along by a corrupt desire.

What, then, is the basis for the *form* of the rational maxims to which we shall conform? To begin with, Kant says that "I am never to act otherwise than so *that I could also will that my maxim should become a univer-*

sal law" (IV.402). Would we will, for example, that a maxim that we follow be "implanted in us as such by natural instinct" (IV.423)? And, returning to the theme of the "good will", he says, "an absolutely good will is that whose maxim can always include itself regarded as a universal law" (IV.447).

Kant points out that there are many forms of human activity that are formed by maxims which could not possibly be willed to become universal laws. All these forms of activity are, then, at some level, amoral. There are several possible reasons for this. To make the maxim according to which we act into a universal natural law of decision-making might result in incoherence or contradiction. For example, could I universalize a maxim according to which I may deceive others? It is arguable that under the universalization of such a maxim, nobody would any longer believe anyone else at all, and so the very possibility of deceit could not exist. Consequently, such a maxim is self-contradictory. Indeed, it could be argued that the opposite maxim can, and must, be universalized if the use of language as communicative medium is to be possible at all.[4] To be truthful is, therefore, a "perfect duty", according to Kant. Alternatively, the maxim, if made into a universal law, might result in circumstances that no rational being would possibly will. For example, it is not incoherent to will that uncharitable behaviour should become universal since it is possible to imagine a world in which no charitable behaviour existed. However, there are always possible circumstances in which I might need such charity myself, such that an uncharitable world could not be desirable for any rational being, and I, therefore, could not possibly will it as a universal law. It is perfectly possible, however, to conceive of universalization of the opposite maxim: of the imperative to conduct oneself charitably. To be charitable is, therefore, what Kant calls an "imperfect duty". He marks the distinction between the two kinds of duty in the following way: "*Perfect* duties are usually understood to be those which can be enforced by external law; *imperfect*, those which cannot be enforced. They are also called respectively *determinate* and *indeterminate*, *officia juris* and *officia virtutis*" (IV.421 n.). Kant also makes distinctions between duties to oneself (such as the duty not to commit suicide) and duties to others (such as the duty not to kill).

Moral categories

Kant develops a broad typology of duty and a system of categories similar to that associated with faculty of understanding. He provides a table of categories that, beyond the categorical imperative itself, provide the form of moral judgements. These categories directly parallel the categories of understanding that provide the form of cognition. What is clear, then, is Kant's conviction that, as with cognition, moral actions and judgements have eternal and universal form. To briefly address, again, the question of nominalism or realism with respect to these categories, it is difficult to see how they could be conceived in a nominalist light given that they are explicitly deemed to be *a priori*. As with cognitive categories, they pre-exist any particular instantiation. They are not simply the "names" given to groups of judgements; they are the *ontological conditions of moral judgements*. As such it is arguable (from the point of view of assessing Kant's relationship to idealism) that the forms of practical reason are real Ideas in the broader sense that we outlined at the beginning of the chapter, just as the forms of cognition are.

The difficulty of freedom

The exercise of freedom, for Kant, then, is always a struggle. In order to be free we must impose a will to act as our pure practical reason tells us we ought. This is always in the face of the powerful desires and temptations that threaten to undermine our freedom. We know what is the right way to act, and we are quick to tell others when they have not done so. The most profound temptation, though, is always to make exceptions of ourselves. We know very well when we act wrongly, since our reason tells us clearly that the maxim by which we have acted could not be willed to be universal. We never really believe that our misdeed could be justified by a universal law, despite our protestations. We know the choice is wrong; we simply excuse ourselves and, as slaves to our "pathological" inclinations, become unfree as a result.

The "kingdom of ends"

Kant develops second and third formulations of the categorical imperative, which are really logical elaborations of the first. They further elaborate the objective conditions of pure practical reason. In his second formulation Kant insists that since humanity is the source of the very rationality that makes the categorical imperative possible, it is self-contradictory to use humanity as a means to an end, since, again, we could not will this as a universal maxim. "Now I say that the human being and in general every rational being *exists* as an end in itself, *not merely as a means* to be used by this or that will at its discretion" (Ak. IV.428).

In his final formulation, he says that our maxims must be harmonizable in terms of the conditions that issue from their collective pursuit. We cannot will the universalization of maxims that result in behaviour that leads to the breakdown of society. Our maxims must be harmonizable in what he calls a "kingdom of ends". He describes the aspiration:

> [T]he idea of a pure world of understanding as a system of all intelligences, and to which we ourselves as rational beings belong (although we are likewise on the other side members of the sensible world), this remains always a useful and legitimate idea for the purposes of rational belief .... [T]he noble ideal of a universal kingdom of *ends in themselves* (rational beings), to which we can belong as members then only when we carefully conduct ourselves according to the maxims of freedom as if they were laws of nature. (IV.462–3)

This image of a world of normative consensus built on collective rationality has been enormously attractive for many socially and politically minded neo-Kantians, from Emile Durkheim to Jürgen Habermas and John Rawls. The influence of Kant's practical philosophy goes far beyond the normative alone, however.

Freedom, praxis and reality

At the outset of the *Critique of Practical Reason*, Kant makes a remarkable claim, apparently concerning its relative standing in relation to the *Critique of Pure Reason* and its subject matter:

> Inasmuch as the reality of the concept of freedom is proved by an apodictic law of practical reason, it is the *keystone* of the whole system of pure reason, even the speculative, and all other concepts (those of God and immortality) which, as being mere ideas, remain in it unsupported, now attach themselves to this concept, and by it obtain consistence and objective reality; that is to say, their *possibility* is *proved* by the fact that freedom actually exists, for this idea is revealed by the moral law. (Ak. V.3–4)

The grounding ideas of pure reason are "unsupported", he seems to say, until they are "proved by the fact that freedom actually exists". This appears to establish a hierarchical relationship between the two critiques in which the "practical" is ontologically prioritized. This has provided an invitation for the development of a praxis-oriented idealism stretching through from Fichte to Marx, to the Frankfurt School, to the social constructionists and postmodernists and beyond. Regardless of their many differences, what these thinkers, and a great many others in the history of the human sciences, have in common is their insistence on the *prioritization of the ethico-practical in the active construction of reality*. Without Kant, such "critical" thought would not have been possible. This is a theme we shall investigate further in relation to the work of Fichte.

It is arguable, however, that Kant's third *Critique* provides the clues for a quite different relationship to ontology, one in which *nature*, rather than ethics, takes on a far more prominent role.

THE IDEA OF ABSOLUTE TOTALITY AND SELF-ORGANIZING LIFE IN THE *CRITIQUE OF JUDGEMENT*

The *Critique of Judgement* seems to be concerned with at least three separate problems, all of which emerge as deeply interconnected. First, is it possible to find some bridging principle between the understanding of empirical reality under pure reason on the one hand, and acting and making judgements according to moral imperatives under practical reason on the other? We need this, in part, because we assume the causal efficacy of our choices within the empirical world. "Nature must consequently also be able to be regarded in such a way that in the conformity to law of its form it at least harmonises with the possibility of the ends to be effectuated in it according to the laws of freedom" (Ak. V.176). Without this, our choices would be meaningless. They must have empirical effects. So there must be a bridge between the empirical domain of strict determinism, and the practical domain of free will.

Second, how do we account for the capacity of finite rational beings to make "aesthetic" judgements? Nothing so far in Kant's system does this. Yet for Kant there is nothing irrational about this domain. It is a matter of rational judgement and of judgement according to universal criteria, but how? What, then, are the *a priori* conditions of aesthetic judgement?

Third, how is it possible for us to think of certain aspects of the world in terms of purpose? More specifically, this seems to be the way we think of living organisms. But how, since nothing in the first two critiques seems to provide us with the grounds for doing so? The capacity to conceive of purpose, or finality, in nature is connected with the faculty of judgement, according to Kant: the same faculty that provides the bridge between pure and practical reason. What, then, are the *a priori* conditions of this "teleological" judgement?

And we must ask, what is the role of the Idea in these domains of aesthetics and teleological judgement?

Wholes, purposiveness and the pleasure of judgement

According to Kant both aesthetic judgement and teleological judgement are kinds of judgement that involve thinking of the world in terms of "purpose". Here we mean purpose in a sense roughly analogous to the idea of "function". That is, we are able to think of a thing in terms of the role that it plays within a larger whole. We think in terms of purpose when we make sense of the parts of a living organism in relation to the whole, and when we understand the behaviour of a living organism in relation to its environment. This is teleological judgement, which will be discussed in due course. However, we also think in these terms when we judge an object with respect to its "beauty". At such times, according to Kant, we appreciate the harmonious relations of forms between part and whole. This is the case when we see beauty in nature, or when we see beauty in a work of art. But why would we have such a capacity to enjoy pleasure in our perception of such holistic purposive forms in the first place?

We can begin to answer this question by considering first the relationship between the faculty of understanding, and the idea of the totality of nature. The way we understand the world, as we have seen, is to assemble sense experience into objects and object relations, according to the *a priori* synthetic mechanisms of the intuition, imagination and understanding. The former provide sense data assembled into objects in space and time, the latter provide the scheme of categories and concepts according to which a sensible object may be understood, and the *imagination* mediates between the two, finding the schema according to which this synthesis can come about. Kant tells us that it is the activity of judgement that lies at the heart of this mediating activity of the imagination in finding the basis for such synthesis, and in providing a thirst for understanding in the first place. So what is this "judgement"?

The initial synthesis of understanding provides us merely with discrete segments of "understood" experience: discrete "objects". This is not sufficient to satisfy our thirst for understanding. We continuously move on to attempt to assemble connections between these objects of experience, providing yet more understanding, driven always by the regulative *Idea* of a "whole of nature" to which we aspire. This is the driving force behind scientific discovery. And every time we find ourselves able to understand a little more of our object world, and make such connections between aspects of experience towards the whole, we experience pleasure. We *feel* the falling into place of our ever growing understanding of things. The successful application of categories to sense data, and the subsequent, enlarged, connecting of experience in relation to the idea of a totality of nature, produces this pleasure. This pleasurable feeling of things falling into place in relation to a totality is the faculty of judgement at work within the imagination. Judgement is a *feeling* of pleasure activated by contemplation of totality, functionality or purposiveness. It is this feeling that we experience as the "meaning" of things.

This applies to the interpretation of purposiveness of elements of the totality of nature when it drives the onward march of the understanding, but it also lies behind our assertion of purpose with respect to individual organisms, and aesthetic contemplation of works of art or of nature. We find pleasure in harmony and meaning: we find an absence of pleasure in discord and meaninglessness.[5]

Feeling and creativity

This emphasis on judgement as a feeling signals a significant shift in Kant's focus of attention. In the *Critique of Pure Reason* the focus is on high-level cognitive constructions, and in the *Critique of Practical Reason* it is on a similarly high level of functioning at the level of linguistically expressible normative maxims, but in the *Critique of Judgement* suddenly the focus is shifted to a much more primitive level of functioning: that of feeling. Judgement provides a feeling of how the world is that precedes the higher levels of understanding and reason. As we shall see, in the early twentieth century, Whitehead will attempt to build his system on this Kantian insight.

One thing to add here, with respect to judgement, is that there seems to be a range of fluidity with which the concepts of the understanding may be applied in this process of assembling experience, and in which the faculty of judgement within the imagination may arise. At one end is the application of already established concepts of understanding to experience. This enables more and more of the world to become understandable. Each time another piece of the world is assimilated into this overarching conceptual framework there is pleasure at the felt movement towards "total" understanding. Some sense experiences resist such assimilation, however. This necessitates a more fluid and creative search for new concepts under which experience may be subsumed and understood. Both of these operations involve the faculty of judgement, and the associated inner sense of pleasure. The former kind of judgement is called, by Kant, "determinant judgement"; the latter, more fluid and creative kind, is called "reflective judgement".

> Judgment in general is the faculty of thinking the particular as contained under the universal. If the universal (the rule, principle, or law) is given, then the judgment which subsumes the particular under it is *determinant* …. If, however only the particular is given

> and the universal has to be found for it, then the judgment is simply *reflective*. (Ak. V.179)

It is this latter form of judgement that is involved in aesthetic contemplation and attribution of purpose in general. This is the creative application of judgement. Sometimes it is applied to creative conceptualization, and sometimes to aesthetic contemplation with little or no conceptual content at all. It is an application of judgement filled with potentiality for new forms of understanding. This raises the question of the place in nature of potentiality and creativity in general. Again, this is a theme we shall return to in our discussion of the twentieth-century idealism of Whitehead.

Aesthetics

Kant deals with the question of aesthetic judgement in Part 1 of the *Critique of Judgement* (Ak. V.203–356). As we have seen, within Kant's system, the "power of judgement" at work within "imagination" creates a pleasurable feeling of cognition.

> If we wish to discern whether anything is beautiful or not, we do not refer the representation of it to the Object by means of understanding with a view to cognition, but by means of the imagination (acting perhaps in conjunction with understanding) we refer the representation to the Subject and its feeling of pleasure or displeasure. (V.203)

Intuitions are always drawn into the ever wider scheme of associations generated by the understanding, subject to the overarching idea of the "harmonious whole". Conformity to this idea is what produces the sense of pleasure associated with judgement. This conformity, and associated pleasure, is what it means for something to "make sense". So, it follows that the imagination should be that faculty most closely associated, also, with the pleasures of aesthetic contemplation, because, according to Kant, it is precisely this same pleasurable "inner sense" of judgement, with respect to harmony, that is at work in aesthetics, but set free from the conceptual constraints of the understanding. "The cognitive powers brought into play by this representation are here engaged in a free play, since no definite concept restricts them to a particular rule of cognition" (V.217). Aesthetics arises as a kind of malfunction of the imagination once it is decoupled from understanding (and so from the requirement to conceptualize). Instead, in this decoupled state, it seeks the experience of order, purpose, unity and harmony outside the conceptual schema of the understanding. The power of judgement creates a feeling of pleasure at the playful achievement of this in non-conceptual works of art, or in aesthetic contemplation (rather than understanding) of nature.

By virtue of the combination of the idea of harmonious totality, and the feeling of judgement in relation to this idea, we are able to contemplate pleasurably the whole of nature of which our chunks of experience are parts. We can sense how perfectly adapted the shark is to its natural context, we can see how perfectly it performs its purpose within the system of nature, and as we perceive that perfect harmony of the part–whole relation, we experience, with a pleasurable fascination, the terrible beauty of the shark.

This perfect harmony strikes us as being as it is "'as though" it were designed so: "as though" it were designed, indeed, for us to contemplate it. For Kant *none of this is actually a fact of nature* as it is in itself. It is all a manifestation of the working of the rational faculty of judgement in its never ending search for unity of form under the idea of totality. Always the contemplation of form:

> In painting, sculpture, and in fact in all the formative arts, in architecture and horticulture, so far as fine arts, the *design* is what is essential. Here it is not what gratifies in sensation but merely what pleases by its form, that is the fundamental prerequisite for taste. (V.225)

We can see, then, how judgements of beauty can be rational. These feelings of purposive harmony are not just personal to each of us. They are rational judgements that involve claims to universality. If I claim that something is beautiful, I can be justified in insisting that it is universally so. This is not the same kind of universality as that involved in pure reason because of the shared categories and concepts of understanding, or under practical reason because of the shared categorical imperative. There is no independent categorical basis for beauty. Nevertheless the faculty of judgement, and the underlying idea of "formative purpose in relation to a harmonious whole" is common to all finite rational beings. It is on this basis that Kant believes that universal aesthetic claims are possible. We are all capable of this feeling of pleasure in relation to judgement of part–whole relations, of experiencing the sense of design at work in this, and, therefore, likely to see beauty in the same way as one another.

> This state of *free play* of the cognitive faculties attending a representation by which an object is given must admit of universal communication .... As the subjective universal communicability of the mode of representation in a judgment of taste is to subsist apart

from the presupposition of any definite concept, it can be nothing
else than the mental state present in the free play of imagination
and understanding. (V.217–18)

For example, in my contemplation of music or a painting I perceive an order. This order is not, according to Kant, in the notes of music themselves, or in the paint on the canvas, but in my perception. The faculty of judgement within my imagination produces in me a feeling of harmonious, formative unity. Only rational creatures are capable of such a synthesis. I have grounds, therefore, to assume that my pleasure is common to all creatures such as myself, to the extent that they are rational, of course.

As already stated, in this aesthetic judgement the imagination is freed from understanding and the determinant work of judgement. Often, then, it is entirely free from concepts and sees only non-conceptual forms of order. This is the basis of the neo-Kantian formalist aesthetics, and Kant would have been very excited by abstract expressionism's exploration of entirely non-conceptual form in the twentieth century. Where concepts *are* allowed into such aesthetic contemplation (as in figurative art) they are not used in a determinant manner, says Kant. So the concept of a face, for example, is not applied to the operation of cognizing something *as* a face, but for recognition of a representation of a face within the totality of a work of art. It is the faculty of judgement within the imagination "at play".

The sublime

To judgements of beauty, Kant adds another kind of aesthetic experience. This is the experience of the sublime (Ak. V.244–78). Kant makes the following distinction:

> The beautiful in nature is a question of the form of the object, and this consists in limitation, whereas the sublime is to be found in an object even devoid of form, so far as it immediately involves, or else by its presence provokes a representation of limitlessness, yet with a super-added thought of its totality. (V.244)

Experience of the beautiful form is of a limited form that we can conceive as part of a harmonious whole. The sublime experience, on the other hand, is provoked by sensory experience that cannot be adequately assimilated at all because it overwhelms our capacity to think. Such experience fills us with a sense of sublime awe. This might be a natural object of great scale, or of great danger. Again, we can make aesthetic judgements about such sublime experience. We implicitly assert the universality of our judgements, but how? How can our particular perception of an experience as sublimely unassimilable be universalized? Because, says Kant, the sublimity of the experience is, again, not within the object of contemplation itself, but, rather, it is to be found in the nature of reason.

The object of incomprehensibly great scale provides a kind of visceral, and apparently direct, encounter with the existence of an incomprehensibly vast totality of things. Yet this totality is not really out in the world at all; it is an *Idea* of reason. It is, as we have repeatedly seen, part of the inner workings of finite rationality. Similarly, the object of great danger reminds the subject of the freedom of the will, since it provides an opportunity for a willed encounter with danger, one in which I *will* not retreat despite my fear. Neither form of the sublime is really a reminder of nature itself (whatever that might be), but rather of the superiority of reason over nature. This is inevitable since, of course, it is reason that constitutes the entire experience of nature. The sublime is, in reality, a reminder of the transcendental dominion of reason in the construction of all human experience. As Kant himself puts it:

> In this way external nature is not estimated in our aesthetic judgment as sublime so far as exciting fear, but rather because it challenges our power (one not of nature) to regard as small those things of which we are wont to be solicitous (worldly good, health, and life), and hence to regard its might (to which in these matters we are no doubt subject) as exercising over us and our personality no such rude dominion that we should bow down before it, once the question becomes one of our highest principles and of asserting or forsaking them. Therefore nature is here called sublime merely because it raises the imagination to a presentation of those cases in which the mind can make itself sensible of the appropriate sublimity of the sphere of its own being, even above nature. (V.262)

The sublime experience is merely a reminder of our power to act according to our own maxims of practical reason regardless of the forces of nature ("I will not retreat from great danger because to do so would be cowardly, and cowardice is morally repugnant, and to resist retreat in such circumstances will, therefore, fill me with a feeling of my own power and freedom"). And so, Kant reasserts, again, the dominion of the ethico-practical over nature.

Life

Most interesting of all, however, partly because it is not entirely compatible with conclusions just reached, is Kant's account of teleological judgement with respect to life (Ak. V.359–485).

Kant viewed Isaac Newton's mechanistic materialism as the true categorical structure of empirical reality. Pure reason necessarily functions by providing explanation in terms of efficient causal relationships between discrete material bodies, moving and externally affecting one another in space and time. However, no amount of such mechanical explanation, thought Kant, would ever account for the apparently purposive activity of living organisms. He famously states: "It is utterly impossible for human reason, or for any finite reason qualitatively resembling ours, however much it may surpass it in degree, to hope to understand the generation even of a blade of grass from mere mechanical causes" (V.409–10).

Something about living entities is impervious to such explanation, and so we resort, instead, to teleological explanation. Mechanical materialism relies on the idea that all events have *external* causes that can, in principle, be discovered. Living things are, says Kant, "self-organizing". They appear to have self-causing powers. And, it is certainly arguable (in light of future developments) that here lies the real core of the third *Critique*:

> In such a natural product as this every part is thought as *owing* its presence to the *agency* of all the remaining parts, and also as existing *for the sake of the others* and of the whole, that is as an instrument, or organ. But this is not enough – for it might be an instrument of art, and thus have no more than its general possibility referred to an end. On the contrary the part must be an organ *producing* the other parts – each consequently reciprocally producing the others. No instrument of art can answer to this description, but only the instruments of that nature from whose resources the materials of every instrument are drawn – even the materials for instruments of art. Only under these conditions and upon these terms can such a product be an *organised* and *self-organised being*, and, as such, be called a *physical end*.
> (V.373–4)

This is really a quite extraordinary passage. Recalling what was said about Plotinus and Proclus in previous chapters, what we find here is a Neoplatonic combination of form, final cause and dynamism, articulated in a fashion that provides the schema for many subsequent developments in biology (see ch. 14). He differentiates clearly the application of the power of judgement in aesthetic matters from the question of the organism and its "natural end". Aesthetic objects may be harmonious wholes of differentiated forms, but those forms do not *produce* the whole as organs do the organism. He, equally, distinguishes the self-organizing organism from the machine, which, although it may have functional parts, again does not produce itself. It is this that provides a bridge between the determinism of empirical reality and pure reason, and the free will of practical reason. We are perfectly able to experience self-determining ("free") living entities within an otherwise mechanically determined world because we are able to think in terms of teleological processes. In other words, we see organisms behaving as they do because they have purposes towards which their will is directed. Life, for Kant, seems to be defined by this self-organization, which is equivalent to freedom since it amounts to self-causation. Not only are whole organisms driven by purpose, but so are the organs of which they are composed. Each organ is explained not by means of efficient causality, but by virtue of its purpose within the totality of the organism. He says in words that, as we shall see, would be closely echoed by the biologist Stuart Kauffman over two hundred years later, that "strictly speaking, therefore, the organisation of nature has nothing analogous to any causality known to us" (V.375; see Kauffman 2000: 104).

As with aesthetic pleasure, we find that this experience of the world as composed of purposeful totalities leads to that "inner sense" of pleasure that defines the activity of the faculty of judgement. This is why we search for understanding within a context of purpose or meaning: because we are rewarded with pleasure when we find it.

This was a prescient vision of the meaning of life. But the moment Kant offers this striking vision of the heart of nature, he immediately withdraws it. He allows teleological judgement only extremely limited scope and application. As with all his system, he insists that we must not imagine that these purposes are in any sense part of the real world as it is in itself. Rather, life appears purposive, because that is how we make it appear, and because the pleasure of judgement rewards us for doing so. Moreover, the teleological framework can never be truly part of scientific understanding of the world. It is not a part of the *a priori* constitutive mechanisms of the intuition and understanding. We have an idea that everything has a purpose, and we may deploy this idea to make sense of things, but such purposiveness cannot be truly given in experience; it is a "supersensible principle" (Ak. V.381). Rather, it should be seen, he says, as a *regulative* idea.

> The concept of a thing as intrinsically a physical end is, therefore, not a constitutive conception either of understanding or of reason, but yet it may be used by reflective judgment as a regulative

conception for guiding our investigation of objects of this kind by a remote analogy with our own causality according to ends generally ... (V.374)

So, while the power of judgement is constitutive of our aesthetic feelings of pleasure, it cannot be thought of as a true reflection of nature in any sense. Indeed the only "real" purpose is that which we as free moral actors manifest in our chosen pursuit of duty. Natural purpose is thought only "analogously" to this. He points out that we never really directly experience the apparent purpose at work within an organism as we can our own purpose, and we can never prove decisively that organic life cannot be explained purely in terms of blind mechanical causality. Instead, the role of this teleological judgement with respect to nature, within the imagination, is simply to spur us on to new investigations and understandings – but no more than this. Others would, however, take these themes developed in the third *Critique* and make much more of them. We shall see this with respect to Schelling, Hegel, Whitehead and the idealist sciences.

6. FICHTE AND THE SYSTEM OF FREEDOM

INTRODUCTION

Kant's *Critique of Judgement* convinced his successors that the integration of nature and freedom under a single, consistent system was the most urgent task facing modern philosophy. The manifesto "The First System-Programme of German Idealism" (1796), probably co-authored by Hegel, Hölderlin and Schelling, sets this out. It begins with:

> [A]n Ethics. Since the whole of metaphysics falls for the future within *moral theory* [which] will be nothing less than a complete system of all ideas or of all practical postulates (which is the same thing). The first idea is of course the presentation of *myself* as an absolutely free entity. Along with the free, self-conscious essence, there stands forth – out of nothing – an entire *world*, the one true and thinkable creation out of nothing. Here I shall descend into the realms of physics; the question is this: How must a world be constituted for a moral entity? (Stewart 2002: 110)[1]

This was precisely what Kant had set out, but failed, to achieve, as his immediate successors agreed. It is in light of this failure that Fichte, in his "science of knowing", undertook to unify transcendental philosophy under the "postulate" of free action. Yet Fichte achieved this *ethical determination of the world* at the cost of "descending to physics", and was criticized accordingly by Hegel (1977a) and later by Schelling: "What is … the essence of his [Fichte's] entire understanding of nature? It is that nature must be employed, used, and … exist no further than it is thus employed" (SW VI.17). Fichte cannot properly claim a concept of "nature in itself", since his entire position is that "nature" becomes actual only when posited by a free subject or "I". So nature for him must be the transcendental product of that I. By contrast, Schelling argued for the priority of nature over and to the "I", making it self-positing or active, and the root, therefore, of all activity, including our thinking about it. The philosophical problem of nature therefore divides the beginnings of German idealist philosophy just as it divided Kant's third *Critique*. Yet Fichte's "practical postulate" has proved powerful against more bloodless "first principles", which were vulnerable in any case to criticism by sceptics who sought to limit mere cognizing where *living* was required.

By contrast, the other legacy Kant's successors drew from him was the idea of organization, or the unity constitutive of "all transcendental ideas" (CPR A334/B391). To become a "science", the "complete system of ideas", as the "System-Programme" noted, must fall under a single unity. "The true is the whole" (1977b: 11), Hegel famously wrote, not merely this or that part. Nature may be first in point of time, as Schelling claimed against Fichte, but the true "alpha and omega" (1970b: 19) is the Idea, which is simultaneously the structure and the thinking of being. Logic replaces metaphysics because true being is the Idea, and the truth of the whole is the system of reality actualized in thought.

The German idealist tradition constitutes one of the boldest and most productive seams in the history of philosophy, and its problems and solutions deserve more intensive scrutiny than what some count as our "postmetaphysical" age grudgingly accords it. Even as an exercise in the philosophical imagination, few philosophers offer more than do these early-nineteenth-century idealists. In what follows, we shall trace their understandings of the idea among the debates that drove this vibrant, imaginative contribution to philosophizing at its fullest.

FICHTE: THE FIRST SYSTEM OF FREEDOM

Fichte is the first philosopher of radical freedom,[2] a freedom that usurps the position of ontology as "first philosophy". Yet despite overt repetitions of this thesis by many a philosopher over the past two centuries, he remains less well known than he ought to be, in part because he is viewed merely as a bridge between Kant and Hegel, and in part because his insights tend to be ascribed to his better-known successors. Yet as we shall see, Fichte's brand of idealism is both ubiquitous in subsequent philosophies, and paradigmatic therefore of a particular type of idealism that remains current even now, albeit often misunderstood as "materialism" by virtue of its insistence on the primacy of *practice*.[3] We shall return to these themes in what follows.

Fichte's philosophical career is unusual, in that he devoted his life's work to the establishment, elaboration, revision and popularization of a single philosophical project, to which he gave the name *Wissenschaftslehre* or "science of knowledge".[4] Although this sounds like a synonym for "epistemology", and therefore to belong exclusively to theoretical philosophy, his works on "applied" topics such as *Foundations of Natural Right* (2000b) and *The System of Ethics* (2005a) are each subtitled *According to the Principles of the Wissenschaftslehre*. Fichte's philosophy is inseparably theoretical *and* practical, although ultimately practically determined. Yet it contains a prodigious amount of speculative invention in transforming the details of Kant's understanding of transcendental philosophy into a practical project. The practical works therefore provide excellent entry points to the "grounding principles" of the science of knowing as a whole.

TRANSCENDENTAL MONISM AND THE PROBLEM OF GROUND

Before examining these grounding principles, we shall consider the problems Fichte inherits from the two precursor philosophers he most frequently cites: Spinoza and Kant. Although Fichte sets the two philosophers against one another as the archetypes of dogmatic realism and critical idealism, respectively, it is a mistake to eliminate Spinoza's positive contribution to a philosophy Fichte is happy to describe as "Spinozism made systematic" (1982: 119). To imply that Spinoza's philosophy is *not* systematic may be surprising, since his *Ethics* is famous for its employment of the "geometrical method", and its deductive framework. Fichte's sense of "system", however, like his understanding of "science", is critical. A science possesses "systematic form", he writes, when "all [its] principles are joined together in a single, grounding principle, in which they unite to form a whole" (*ibid.*: 102, trans. mod.).

This principle supports Spinoza's monistic aims while transforming their effect. Spinoza sought to generate a systematic metaphysics on the basis of a *single substance* from which everything can be explained. As a "consistent dogmatism" (Fichte 1982: 117), this system must be complete in itself and possess a systematic form deriving from its grounding principle. While Spinoza uses his system's first principle to explain or to *conceive* the ground of all things as "God-or-nature", Fichte uses his to *demonstrate* the ground of all experience. The critical point flowing from a grounding principle is this: "Whoever can point out the smallest distinction in or with regard to what some philosophical system has posited as its highest principle has refuted that system" (Fichte 2005b: 24).

Although Fichte repeatedly denies that, if consistent, dogmatism can be refuted, stating only and famously that "what sort of philosophy one chooses, depends on what sort of man one is" (1982: 16), he sets his *Wissenschaftslehre* the implicit challenge of explaining more than can his dogmatic opponent, since otherwise the system Fichte himself proposes would be vulnerable to the criticism that, in the *Wissenschaftslehre*, "nature ... *is not there*" (Heidegger 1997: 184).[5] Indeed, having opposed Spinoza's ontology, which he concedes has an "accurate grasp of the concept of being", Fichte claims that "we are only able to speak of a science of being by a misunderstanding, so far as we fail to recall our knowing and thinking thereupon" (W X.3). The very idea of ontology is misbegotten from the first, since the only "being" we know is an artefact of consciousness. Thus Fichte can demonstrate a distinction in the highest concept of Spinoza's system – being *for itself*, and being *for consciousness* – and therefore not simply reject, but *refute* Spinozism.

The victorious Fichte takes the concepts of systematicity and ground from his encounter with Spinoza, and applies them to his encounter with Kant. In return, Fichte superimposes Kantian transcendental concerns on to Spinoza's methodological and metaphysical ones. In consequence, it is as a hybrid of these two sources that the *Wissenschaftslehre* is best conceived, since for Fichte, both seek a *systematic* metaphysics and a viable concept of *ground*. This should not, *contra* Spinoza, be sought in *things*, but in the *acts* by means of which they come to be for us.

The concept of "ground" or principle of sufficient reason, Fichte holds, animates Kant's critical enquiries as much as they do Spinoza's;[6] but while Spinoza locates this in *substance*, Kant fails to ground his system at all. To show this, he applies the same test as to Spinoza: to find unresolved differences in the "highest principle" of a system is to refute it. Fichte has no doubt, in contrast to Spinoza, that no ground is to be found in substance, in *things*, but only in *acts*. If metaphysics no longer asks what things *are in themselves*, but concerns itself instead with the *acts that constitute them as things in the first place*, then philosophy need not be content to interpret or conceive, but must seek instead to *change* them. As he writes, "It is impossible that the world should remain as it is; it must, oh it must become different and better" (1987a: 81).[7]

While Kant himself first asserted the "primacy of pure practical reason" (Ak. V.119–21), he had not consistently followed this through, leaving him with "three absolutes" (Fichte 2005b: 32). According to Fichte, Kant "undertook the investigation of reason or knowledge not in its absolute unity, but as itself already split into diverse branches as theoretical, practical and judging reason" (1997: 3). Kant had not, that is, succeeded in unifying these "diverse branches" in accordance with *reason*, and thus suffered from an inconsistency. For example, consider Kant's claims, in the *Critique of Practical Reason*, that (a) "reason, as the faculty of principles, determines the interest of all the powers of the mind and its own" (Ak. V.119); and (b) that "every interest is ultimately practical, even that of speculative reason being only conditional and reaching perfection only in practical use" (V.121). Taken together, these two assertions mean *either* (i) that reason determines the interest of every power as practical; or (ii) that reason does not determine interest at all, because all interest *is* practical *in itself*. In the first case, Kant is inconsistent in withholding reason from practical determination in general. In the second, the assertion that such and such a thing *is* simply undermines the transcendental method.

Here we have everything necessary to demonstrate that, in its highest or grounding principles, Kant's system "refutes itself" as a system. Nevertheless, for Fichte, Kant had pointed the way forwards. Thus, a further thing to note about the second of the above propositions from the *Critique of Practical Reason* is that it contains the germ of the unification of theoretical and practical reason, that is, of the worlds of nature or sense, and of freedom and the supersensible.

Kant had, of course, sought a unity between the sensible and moral domains in the *Critique of Judgement*, but sought this "uniting ground" *beneath* the dichotomy of nature and reason, therefore in something *subtending* and *external to* reason. Of course, Kant's is a *transcendental* problem, meaning that "nature" is that nature *possible for us*, or the domain of sense experience. But why, then, introduce a "gulf" between them, asks Fichte, if the problematic is indeed a transcendental one? Considered from the perspective of consistency, Kant's proposed solution is that there is a *faculty*, a *Vermögen* or "power" of judgement, capable of combining the presentations of sense with the imperatives of practical reason in a "regulative" manner, and therefore without either the legislative authority enjoyed by speculative reason, or the determination of interests that is the role of practical reason.

Fichte reacts to Kant's proposed solution by asking: what is a "power" that is not active but a mere capacity to act? What, in other words, is a power that *does not* act? On the issue of the reality of forces, Kant is in an awkward position in so far as, in the *Metaphysical Foundations of Natural Science*, he had argued that while he cannot argue that forces are *not* actual, nor can they "be assumed to be actual" (Ak. IV.524). This clarifies some of the difficulties of Kant's "inert power" problem. At any rate, here is what Fichte draws from the problem of inert powers:

> Kant ... first factically discovered the distinction between the sensible and supersensible worlds and then added to his absolute the additional inexplicable quality of linking the two worlds, a move which pushed us back from genetic manifestness into merely factical manifestness. (2005b: 44)

Apart, that is, from the failure to ground the unity of transcendental idealism by bridging the gap between the two worlds, Kant also fails to *generate* the evident or manifest distinction between them. To have fully accounted for the famous "great gulf fixed" (Ak. V.175), Kant ought to have *generated* it rather than merely noting it *as a fact*. Thus, Fichte too will maintain that "intellect and thing ... inhabit two worlds between which there is no bridge" (1982: 17), but he will also *generate* this rupture from the grounding principles of the science of knowledge.

Rather than seek to resolve the relation of reason to nature in terms of a separable ground distant from what it grounds, Fichte will simply consider reason to issue an "unconditioned decree" (1982: 106, trans. mod.): "Reason must create itself" (2005b: 45). Reason therefore *guarantees* the immanence of what it produces, just as Kant's critical philosophy had demanded, as is clear from the following proposition: "The character of rationality consists in the fact that that which acts and that which is acted upon are one and the same" (Fichte 2000b: 3). Instead of powers awaiting activation, Fichte's foundationalism finds its grounding principles in the *acts* of intelligence, from which, as he says "we might be able to derive ... all those laws that explain how there comes to be a world for us. This is what idealism has to demonstrate" (1992: 100).[8] In consequence, the science of knowing will develop an immanent concept of self-creating reason as its absolute. This immanent self-grounding is what the science of knowledge sets out to achieve, and it does so by means of executing those "necessary actions ... that follow from the concept of the rational being" (2000b: 3).

FICHTE'S GROUNDING PRINCIPLES AND THE PRACTICAL IDEAL

Depending on which version of the *Wissenschaftslehre* we examine, it comprises either one, three or five grounding principles. Indeed, late in his career, Fichte himself remains unsure how to count them. Both the unitary and quinternary extremes, however, are modifications of the *Wissenschaftslehre*'s "grounding principles", of which Fichte asserts "there can be no more than three" (1988a: 110). Noting the later increase in their number, we shall nevertheless assume in what follows only the three that form the foundations of the early *Wissenschaftslehre*.

These are *positing, counterpositing* and *limitation*. From their combination, we ground all our knowing, says Fichte. He asks us to examine *what happens* when we reflect on anything at all. The immediate content of reflection is not the object reflected on, but rather the activity of reflecting. This activity, says Fichte, is spontaneous in us, and is a *positing*, but not *by* us. It is, he says, an "act of absolute freedom, and this is a creation out of nothing, an act of producing something that did not exist before, an absolute beginning" (1992: 139). There *is* nothing from which activity emerges, since activity is prior to all beings. Positing is always a positing *of* something – "I do not know without knowing *something*" (2005a: 10) – but no reflection will reveal this positing to be authored by some other thing *behind* it, like a "subject". Fichte therefore criticizes Descartes for assuming that the positing of thinking entails a substantial I, as a "thinking thing", *behind* the thinking. Rather than this *being* or *substance*, there is only this acting, positing and reflecting that becomes my I. When I am intuiting, "I am this intution and simply nothing more, and this intuition itself is I. It is not the case that through this self-positing, something like the existence of the I, as a thing existing independently of consciousness, is brought about" (Fichte 1994: 114). Rather, the empirical I is just this intuiting, while activity in general is transcendental.

We thus derive an extremely illuminating contrast between *being* as "substance" and *activity*, which ramifies throughout Fichte's philosophy, and to which we shall return. The I is not the agent, but the acting itself. Thus, when Fichte asks us to consider how it is that the I appears, the resultant intuition is, he claims, not of a substance or thing, but only of an acting in some determinate form: here, self-reflection. Rather than conclude that there is some *thing* behind the act, Fichte asks us to stick with the evidentness of the intuition, and to deduce what follows from it concerning the nature and constituents of our knowing. The first such deduction concludes: "The intellect, for idealism, is an act" (1982: 21); the second, "I do not know anything … without separating something subjective in me from something objective" (2005a: 10). It is important to note again here that Fichte is a transcendental philosopher, that is, he is not arguing – or does not set out to argue – about the nature of being *in itself*, but rather about being *for consciousness*. Accordingly, "knowledge and being are not separated outside of consciousness and independent of it; instead, they are separated only within consciousness" (*ibid.*: 11).

We should not assume, then, as some of Fichte's contemporaries did, that when he talks of deducing the not-I from the I, he means that reality in itself is a product of mere thought. Fichte sometimes encourages this view, as when he writes that the *Wissenschaftslehre* "furnishes us with a nature as something necessary [that] has to be viewed as independent of us" (1988a: 64). This highlights an ambiguity concerning "necessary somethings": *either* the science of knowing determines what these somethings are, where "are" refers only to their being for consciousness; *or* "are" refers to the whole situation of a thing "being" for consciousness while also exceeding it. In the former case, Fichte's science covers a knowing condemned in advance as necessarily partial; while in the latter case, it is premised on an unresolved dualism rendering it contradictory by his own lights.

As we shall see, Fichte's solution to the epistemological problem of the not-I is finally practical. In epistemological terms, however, the not-I is simply the determination of any particular positing as the content of the positing. We cannot therefore say that the not-I is an "object" or a "world", because "one must first show how it becomes an object and a world" (1992: 82–3). Again we find that Fichte establishes *activity* as the ground of *things*. The appropriate analysis of things is therefore the enquiry into their *genesis*, and is completed by tracing things back to the positings by which they are determined. Ultimately, these positings reduce to the three principles that ground "all possible sciences" (1988a: 107): positing, counterpositing and limitation.

As regards the third grounding principle, Fichte starts with the results of the second: all positing, in so far as it is a positing of *something*, is a *determinate* positing, or a counterpositing of something that is *not-I*. In consequence, the I that is the positing is *limited* by the not-I it posits to a particular or determinate degree. Since the I is activity, the determination of the not-I determines the quantity of activity that makes up reality. Fichte explains:

> The I is *not* posited in the I ... with that measure of reality, wherewith the not-I *is* posited. A measure of reality, i.e., that attributed to the not-I, is abolished within the I. [Both] are posited as divisible in respect of their reality. Only now, in virtue of the concept thus established, can it be said of both that they are *something*.
> (1982: 109)

The terms of Fichte's analysis here are important. He is discussing the not-I, the negation of the I, in terms of mutually limiting quanta of reality so that "the reality of the one eliminates that of the other" (*ibid.*: 122). In other words, what is being limited is the *reality* attaching to quanta of activity as opposed to quanta of being. For Fichte, "the concept of being is ... derived by counterpositing to activity, and hence [is] a merely negative concept" (*ibid.*: 69), or a merely negative quantity of activity, precisely because "to *limit* something is to abolish its reality, not *wholly* but in *part* only, by negation" (*ibid.*: 108).

The third grounding principle therefore returns us to the unresolved opposition between being and activity discussed above. It demonstrates the form of the *limitations* of the I through determinate positing. If I wish to know something concerning nature in general, therefore, my knowing activity is limited, that is to say, in part negated, by a not-I that introduces a determinate quantity of being, that is, of negated activity, into my knowing. It is in this form that for a purely theoretical philosophy – that is, an epistemology or a metaphysics – reality entails a quantity of negated activity on the part of that "in itself" whose existence I posit. For *practical* philosophy, on the other hand, "the infinite I must alone remain" (*ibid.*: 138) in this struggle over the determination of reality. Yet what is this reality? Recall that "being" is derived from the negation of activity, rather than the other way round; since this activity issues primarily, that is, originally, spontaneously, and as free action, from the positing I, then the reality in question is clearly the reality of the positing, that is, of the I itself. Accordingly, therefore, Fichte indicates how the problem of the relation of activity and being is to be resolved:

> The I is posited as a reality, and in that there is reflection on whether it has reality, it is necessarily posited as *something*, as a [determinate] quantum; yet it is posited as all reality, and is thus necessarily posited as an infinite quantity, a quantum exhaustive of reality. (*ibid.*: 241)

Questions concerning reality are therefore *theoretical* ones; but theoretical questions arise from *acts*. Thus Fichte establishes the metaphysics by which the practical reason has primacy over the theoretical. George Seidel explicates the contrast with particular clarity: "*The Ich posits the not-Ich as limited by the Ich* (the 'practical' part); and *The Ich posits itself as limited by the not-Ich* (the 'theoretical part')" (1993: 60). In asking, therefore, "whether the independence of the thing should be sacrificed to the independence of the I, or conversely" (Fichte 1982: 14), the Fichtean responds: as opposed to things, which merely are and remain what they are (*ibid.*: 154) in the "dead persistency ... of matter" (*ibid.*: 119), the I posits itself as an infinite quantum, that is, sets itself as its goal to determine the whole of reality, a goal it *strives* to realize. It is because, in other words, "things" *persist* while the I *strives*, that practical determination, which consists in acts flowing from the grounding principles (positing, counterpositing and limitation), is primary with respect to its limitations derived from the theoretical. Thus, if in the theoretical domain, the I is limited by the not-I of necessity, in the practical, the I is maximally active, but is not conceived merely as the symmetrical limitation of the not-I. Since the latter is derived from the former as its limitation, and so "has reality [only] insofar as the I is passive" (*ibid.*: 130), its supplanting *removes* not simply the determination of the I's activity within the sphere of the I, but *every realization of limitation as such*. Accordingly, the I conceived as "infinite quantum" is, far from being *impossible in reality*, an "Idea of reason", as Kant would express it, that *determines the I to act in accordance with it*.

Yet to conceive of the I as an "infinite quantum" is also a theoretical act. By this means, the I is grounded as "unconditioned" or *absolute*, and it is this I that exerts the authority of reason over my actions after the manner of a categorical imperative that "requires the conformity of the object with itself" (*ibid.*: 230). Thus the categorical imperative, which in Kant supplies a command only for pure practical reason, is shown equally to *command the Copernican revolution* with which Kant's critical philosophy began. Theoretical activity, in other words, is free only at the cost of conformity with this imperative. The conceivability, therefore, of an Absolute, of an I as "infinite quantum" of reality as "a possible object", requires that the I become "*an infinite striving*" (*ibid.*: 231). Since under this command, reason is *unconditioned* by being, it becomes inconsistent if it does not apply this commandment to *all possible being*. Thus, in *Practical Philosophy*, Fichte spells out his conception of "the ideal": "the whole universe ought to be an organised whole; and each infinitesimal part of this universe in turn an organised whole belonging necessarily to that whole" (GA II.3.247, our trans.). In the end, this is how Fichte's theory of the ideal resolves the dualism of freedom and nature: that nature, too, be subject to the same "ought" that determines reason, since otherwise, *reason is set against itself* and the science of knowing fails, as Fichte acknowledges: "I must also *act* in accordance with … necessary thought, otherwise my acting stands in contradiction my thinking – and thus I stand in contradiction with myself" (2000b: 11).

Fichte's major contribution to post-Kantian idealism is to have reconceived the distinction between transcendental theoretical reason and practical reality in terms of being and activity, respectively. Although we could say that theoretical philosophy is doubly determined by the not-I within the I (i.e. the not-I as thought by the I), on the one hand, and by the not (I and not-I) that is nature (and that is not thought by Fichte at all), on the other, Fichte has it that this antinomy for theoretical reason is fundamentally resolved by the unity of reason under the command of the practical ideal. Under it, the determination of reality by quantum of activity is not merely assessed in the abstract terms of theoretical philosophy, but also by means of will in the practical world of ethics and politics. Thus, following on from part III of *The Science of Knowledge*, which deals with the "Foundation of Knowledge of the Practical", Fichte quickly wrote the *Foundations of Natural Right* in 1795–96, and *The System of Ethics* in 1798. Common to both works is an emphasis on the body as the means by which objects are tackled, not as epistemic problems, but as obstacles. *The System of Ethics* accordingly derives the fact of our efficacy in the world from "the natural basis of willing" (Breazeale & Zöller, in Fichte 2005a: xxxii) in a theory of the body's *drives*. As Fichte writes: "Viewed as a principle of efficacy in the world of bodies, I am an articulated body; and the representation of my body is itself nothing but the representation of myself as a cause in the world of bodies" (*ibid.*: 16).

Despite this emphasis on the body in the practical works, as Daniel Breazeale and Günter Zöller write, Fichte "always insists that it is neither nature within us nor nature outside of us that acts when we act, but rather the I as reason" (in *ibid.*: xxxii). In other words, it remains unclear that Fichte can gain theoretical access to the domain of bodies and causes by means of a transcendental philosophy premised on these being derived from a positing I. This being the case, Fichte's account of nature can gain no egress to nature beyond a practical understanding of self-causing organic nature, much as

Kant had conceived this in the *Critique of Judgement*. Promising to complete Kant's transcendental idealism, Fichte ends where he began, asserting that "no human understanding can advance further than that boundary on which Kant, especially in the *Critique of Judgement*, stood, and which he declared to be the final boundary for finite knowing" (1988a: 95).

FICHTE'S RELEVANCE: PRACTICAL REASON AND PHENOMENOLOGY

Fichte is the first philosopher of radical freedom, a freedom that usurps the rights of ontology to "first philosophy", and that drives his entire system. Yet despite overt repetitions of this thesis by many a philosopher over the past two centuries, Fichte's philosophy remains less well known than it ought to be, in part because received wisdom considers his contribution superseded by Hegel's. Yet a specifically Fichtean idealism remains current to this day, albeit often misunderstood as "materialism", owing precisely to its proponents' insistence on the primacy of *practice* (see Rockmore 1980; Ameriks 2000b). Fichte prefigures Marx in his plea for change rather than interpretation: "It is impossible that the world should remain as it is; it must, oh it must become different and better" (1987a: 81).

In the "theoretical" domain, however, Fichte's legacy is also considerable. Following Fichte's coinage of it, the term *Wissenschaftslehre* was subsequently used by Bernard Bolzano for the title of his *Theory of Science: Attempt at a Detailed and in the Main Novel Exposition of Logic*. During a crucial period in Husserl's development of phenomenology, he was introduced to the study of Bolzano's work by his teacher Franz Brentano, demonstrating the ongoing influence of the Fichtean project in the origination of transcendental phenomenology.[9] Husserl himself clearly acknowledges this Fichtean debt in his lectures on "Fichte's ideal of humanity" from 1917, where he presents Fichte's as a "practically directed" but nevertheless "theoretically anchored" philosophy (Husserl 1995: 112). In these lectures, Husserl uses Fichtean reasons for phenomenology's "excluding the natural attitude" (1989: §§27–30), that is, the naive acceptance of the world as existing "on hand" without my conscious intervention. On the contrary, for Husserl as for Fichte, idealism means that "subjectivity is world-creative" (1995: 115). It does not simply create a world of *things*, but also of values, and indeed of an organized system of values. The integration of Kant's dichotomy of theoretical and practical reason therefore constitutes "the only genuine task of philosophy", which consists in "grasping the world as the teleological product of the absolute I" (*ibid.*: 118).

Phenomenologists and Fichteans alike must dispense, therefore, with what Husserl calls "the affect of Being" (*ibid.*: 121), that is, the feeling that there must be some *thing* that acts in order that there be acting at all, in favour of the "history of acts" or "pragmatic history" (Fichte 1982: 198) that constitutes the absolute I. Whereas, for the practically directed Fichte, this "teleological idealism" is satisfied by positing an "infinite chain of goals" for which to strive, an "abiding ought-to-be" as a normative idea (Husserl 1995: 117–19). Yet Fichte's is not only a practical philosophy for Husserl. Properly considered, his "teleological idealism" consists in the theory that the "ultimate ontological ground" of the world is "its *telos*" or goal. Similar accounts of idealism will be found in T. H. Green and, although tempered by a decidedly anti-transcendental naturalism, in Bosanquet.

Recognition of his pioneering role in the techniques and discovery of the objects of phenomenological investigation has been a staple of European Fichte studies since the 1950s:[10] the concept of *Evidenz* or "manifestness" that plays so important a role in Husserl's phenomenology is presented and discussed in Fichte's 1804 lectures. For Husserl, phenomenology is transcendental because it premises its accounts of phenomena on the primacy of intentionality with respect both to reason and to sense experience. Transcendental phenomenology then has as its task the analysis or "reduction" of phenomena to the *intentional object*, or the thing itself being intended by a consciousness. Although Husserl stakes the originality of phenomenological investigation on precisely this procedure, its roots in Fichte's positing are unmistakable since, just as for Husserl, intentionality means "all consciousness is consciousness of an object",[11] so Fichte had claimed that "I do not know without knowing *something*" (2005a: 10).

Of all the phenomenologists, however, it is Heidegger who is most engaged with the idealist legacy, with several books and lecture series on Kant, Hegel, Schelling and Fichte published in his *Gesamtausgabe*.[12] Heidegger reworks a number of concepts, in particular from Schelling, but the similarities between his concept of "projection", as developed in *The Essence of Grounds* (1929) and the Fichtean concept of "designing" from the *System of Ethics* are indeed striking.[13] Further, the assertion that "freedom is the origin of the principle of reason" (Heidegger 1998: 132) demonstrates the Fichtean line followed through in Heidegger's transcendental account of phenomenological ontology.

What most distinguishes Heidegger from Fichte, however, is the markedly contemplative character of the former's philosophy, more pronounced as his career developed. In the latter, the contemplation of contemplation is subjugated, as Aristotle claimed it must be for rational animals, to the practical ends necessitated by freedom. Although Heidegger will describe Schelling's *Philosophical Investigations into the Essence of Human Freedom* as the "summit of Idealism", he elevates this above Fichte's account precisely because Schelling's discussion is overtly concerned with the metaphysics of freedom. Fichte's, meanwhile, is focused on the striving that freedom entails. In this way, Fichte is also inherited by existentialist philosophy, from Kierkegaard to Sartre.

Indeed, of the idealists, it is Fichte who is present each time the practical is defined as (a) primary to and (b) determining of either (i) the theoretical domain or (ii) reality. Hence the Platonic theme of the "good beyond being", with which Heidegger signals his essential agreement, brings Levinas ultimately to the conclusion that ethics should replace metaphysics as what Aristotle termed "first philosophy".

Levinas's essay "Ethics as First Philosophy" (1989) begins by characterizing the background against which he makes this proposal. Since Aristotle, he writes, first philosophy has been identified with the knowing of being or of things (*ibid*.: 76). This already makes knowing into what Levinas memorably characterizes as "the *psyche* or pneumatic force of thought" (*ibid*.: 77), and as such brings it close to exactly the intuiting of the actions of consciousness by consciousness that forms the ground of Fichte's science. Investigating not the grounds, but the cost of this certainty, Levinas notes that "the priority of A = A …, this sovereignty or freedom of the human I" (*ibid*.: 81) raises an ethical question concerning this I. This question, Levinas argues, is "the question of all philosophy. Not 'Why being rather than nothing?', but how being justifies itself" (*ibid*.: 86). If, that is, it is the I's freedom that is established by the science of knowing, this is a freedom to know and thus to master the entire "order of things" that is ontology (*ibid*.: 84). A mastery of all by I is either solipsistic or it usurps every possible position of another as its own. Thus the I, "at the height of its unconditional identity confesses that it is hateful. … I begin to ask myself if my being is justified, if the *Da* [there] of my *Dasein* [*being-there* or *existence*] is not already the usurpation of someone else's place" (*ibid*.: 85).

Although Levinas's project is conceived against the priority of knowing in Husserl's phenomenology, like the latter, his reasoning reaffirms the same Fichtean lineage. While Husserl, however, clearly distinguishes between the absolute I and the empirical Is into which it is split, Levinas here elides that difference, making the "unconditional identity" of A = A into the conditioned identity of particular Is, defined as such by opposition to others of the same kind. As Fichte puts it, to think of myself as an individual, "I must also think of myself as determined in a realm of rational beings outside myself" (1988a: 409). Thus Fichte shares with Levinas the overall project of the priority of ethics over ontology, but in terms of free as opposed to constrained actions rather than of justification. Interestingly, while Husserl (1995: 120) overtly compares Fichte to Plato on the grounds that both assert the priority of the good over being, Levinas effectively introduces an ethical contrast between being and knowing that forms no part of the Platonic tradition. While it belongs to that tradition to assert the supremacy of the ethical, Levinas's distinction removes him from it on principles whose derivation from Fichtean idealism is barely concealed.

7. IDEALIST PHILOSOPHY OF NATURE: F. W. J. SCHELLING

Despite monographs on him by philosophers such as Martin Heidegger, Karl Jaspers and Jürgen Habermas, and more recently by Manfred Frank and Slavoj Žižek, F. W. J. Schelling's work remains largely unknown. Part of the reason for this stems from Hegel's criticism that Schelling "conducted his philosophical education in public" (1970a: vol. 20, 421), that is, developed no fixed or final system. In consequence, philosophers tend to follow Nicolai Hartmann's (1923–29) account of Schelling, and Fichte before him, as incomplete Hegels (Kroner 1921–24), and not therefore as presenting a philosophy worth studying on its own terms. Even the post-1950s "boom" in Schelling scholarship, although it disputes Hartmann's conclusion, tacitly accepts Hegel's by dividing Schelling's work into roughly five periods, a division that really only Heidegger resists. These periods are: Fichtean (1794–97); philosophy of nature (1797–1800); identity philosophy (1800–1807); the philosophy of freedom (1809–27); and the positive philosophy (1830–54).

Heidegger's 1936 Schelling lectures begin by accepting the mutability of Schelling's thought that Hegel notes, but dispute that these diverse expressions express correspondingly different philosophical positions.

> When Schelling's name is mentioned, people like to point out that this thinker constantly changed his standpoint, and one often designates this as a lack in character. But the truth is that there was seldom a thinker who fought so passionately ever since his earliest periods for his one and unique standpoint. (Heidegger 1985: 6)

Even when it is accepted that Schelling offered "one ... unique standpoint", the question of what it might be remains controversial. To prepare the ground for answering this question, we shall briefly assess each of the periods ascribed to Schelling's philosophical labours.

THE FICHTEAN PERIOD

Schelling's earliest published works, the essay "On the Possibility of a Form for all Philosophy" (1794) and *Of the I as the Principle of Philosophy or on the Unconditioned in Human Knowledge* (1795), appear at first glance to follow Fichtean lines. The first announces its interest in the question of formalism and systematicity in philosophy, a question Fichte and others had inherited from Kant's division of propositions into their analytic and synthetic forms. Much impressed by Fichte's 1794 *Concerning the Concept of the Wissenschaftslehre*, Schelling followed that work's pursuit of a scientific philosophy, one that would, as a "science of all sciences" (1975: 23), unite in turn the special sciences that rest on its foundations. Kant's division, Schelling argues, cannot provide the primary form of all thought, which must contain both its analytic and synthetic forms. A third primary form must therefore be composed from the two that issue from it, much as Kant claimed resulted from considering the tripartite forms into which the categories of the understanding divide (CPR B110–11). The form in question therefore consists of a posited, its antithesis and the combination of the two, which collectively form the content of all knowing. Although this form was already familiar from Fichte, Schelling adds to it an emphasis that will become important later: rather than making *positing* the act from which knowing derives, as does Fichte, Schelling insists that the form at issue is that of "being unconditionally posited as such" (1975: 22). While Fichte makes any and all reference to *being* into an index of dogmatic rather than critical philosophy, Schelling's first published essay already moves into *ontological* territory.

The same emphasis on *the* unconditioned is evident in *Of the I*:

> "To condition [*bedingen*]" means the act by which something becomes a *thing* [*ein Ding*], "conditioned [*bedingt*]", what has been *made* into a thing …. The unconditioned [*das Unbedingte*] cannot therefore lie in the thing as such, nor even in what can become a thing …, but only in what simply cannot become a thing i.e. if there is an absolute I, in the absolute I alone.   (1980: 74)

Schelling's point is not only the Fichtean one that the I is not a thing, but also that *there is an unconditioned*, and it is in pursuit of this that *Of the I* is conceived.

This agenda becomes clearer still in Schelling's final work of the Fichtean period, entitled *Treatise Explicatory of the Idealism in the* Science of Knowledge (1797). The Kantian conception of critical philosophy as engaged only in the analysis of concepts has become, Schelling complains, an end in itself for certain philosophers, who no longer note the merely preparatory status of the critical project with regard to the metaphysics that was to follow it. Properly understood, rather than segregating reality (the "thing-in-itself") from our knowledge, Kantian philosophy sought to re-establish the insuperable reality of the Idea following Plato. Schelling therefore lays considerable stress on Kant's account of the "*nature* of our cognition",[1] rather than on its *limitations*. Kant's enterprise *must* therefore be conceived, if it is "to prove internally cohesive" (Schelling 1994a: 84), as describing the reality of the idea.[2] The *Treatise* begins to establish this account of real-idealism by demonstrating the coincidence of Kant's and Plato's accounts of how reason limits the unlimited, making a synthesis of the two in grasping what is. For Schelling, idealist principles entail the "correspondence of object and representation, of being and cognition" (*ibid.*: 77), leading to the profoundly anti-Fichtean conclusion that the true principle of philosophy lies "outside of consciousness" (*ibid.*: 131).

Clearly Schelling's so-called Fichtean period is Fichtean *to the extent that* the latter's philosophical innovations form the linchpin for Schelling's critical analyses of the form and possibility of a true philosophical idealism. To describe early Schelling as Fichtean in the sense that he uncritically accepts and promotes the latter's philosophical agenda would therefore be false. This being the case, we are now in a position to appreciate the problem to which Schelling's next so-called phase, the philosophy of nature, is proposed as a solution.

THE PHILOSOPHY OF NATURE

Schelling's philosophy of nature comprises three major books (1988, 2003, 2010) and the essays published in the *Journal of Speculative Physics* and *New Journal of Speculative Physics* (1800–1802) and the *Annals of Scientific Medicine* (1806). Yet it persists throughout the period of the identity philosophy, the first manifesto of which, the *Presentation of My System of Philosophy*, appeared in the *Journal of Speculative Physics* in 1801, and Schelling was still contributing to it as late as 1844. For this reason, its importance is not restricted to the period bearing its name, nor, as we shall see, to Schelling's philosophy alone.

The problem to which the philosophy of nature proposes solutions is the one Schelling's earliest essays establish: the proper constitution of idealist philosophy. The philosophy of nature, Schelling writes, is the "physical explanation of idealism" (SW IV.76). An idealist philosophy, that is, a philosophy that sets out not merely to explain this or that, but to address itself unconditionally to the unconditioned, can exclude nothing from its remit. In terms of its recent history, however, Schelling finds that it is precisely when addressing nature that his precursors Kant and Fichte are most restricted. For Kant, nature is the totality of appearances, while for Fichte, it is the not-I that limits the I. Yet intelligence cannot be regarded as something separate from nature, as different in kind from it, without condemning idealism to dualism. Schelling's *System of Transcendental Idealism* thus states: "Anything whose conditions simply cannot be given in nature, must be absolutely impossible" (1978: 186). Therefore, the philosophy of nature must proceed on the naturalistic assumption that intelligence, the I, is a product of nature. Rather than a subjectively restricted reason giving the law to appearances, nature "is its own lawgiver" (2003: 17). This means that the reason expressed after nature's production of intelligence is not different in kind from the laws nature gives itself, so that the science of reason, or idealism, necessarily has nature's production of it as its remit. According to the *Ideas for a Philosophy of Nature*, therefore:

> what we want is not that Nature should coincide with the laws of our mind *by chance* ..., but that *she herself*, necessarily and originally, should not only express, but even *realize*, the laws of our mind, and that she is, and is called, Nature only insofar as she does so. (1988: 41–2)

Where Schelling has nature realize mind, Hegel's (1977a) differentiation of Schelling's philosophy from Fichte's presents the philosophy of nature as being incomplete without a separate transcendental philosophy. Only when combined, Hegel argues, do they form the system of reason. While Schelling does indeed argue that both are necessary, he also argues that mind is a product of nature, in a manner Hegel ultimately rejects: "There is an idealism of nature, and an idealism of the I. To me, the former is the original, and the *latter* the derivative" (SW IV.84).

This order of derivation demonstrates that nature and the I are not simply related as complementary aspects of *reason*, but rather as producer and product. From Fichte, Schelling takes the supplanting of being by activity, but an activity rooted in nature rather than the I. The resultant ontology of powers accordingly naturalizes the grounding principles of the *Wissenschaftslehre*, so that nature produces and limits, forming a basic "antithesis of forces" in the production of things. So when Schelling postulates the "identity of the dynamic and the transcendental" (1978: 91), this neither warrants the reduction of forces to acts of an I (Fichte), nor their equivalence (Hegel), precisely because the productive relation of nature to intelligence is irreversible: "it is not because there is thinking that there is being, but rather because there is being that there is thinking" (SW XIII.161n.). No conscious "I" can even in principle retrospect all its conditions of production, since consciousness depends not only on its production as such (second product), but also on a something (first product) of which it is conscious. "Self-consciousness", as Schelling pithily puts it, "is the lamp of the whole system of knowledge, but casts its light ahead only, not behind" (1978: 18). This is an important indicator of the post-Kantian character of Schelling's philosophy. Where Kant considers the conditions under which knowledge is possible to be *transcendental* conditions, Schelling asks "How is transcendental philosophy possible?", and answers that something knowable is a precondition of all knowing. Rather than ignoring the transcendental, as Kant suggests previous philosophy had, Schelling naturalizes it, asserting the "identity of the transcendental and the dynamic" (1978: 91): "a phenomenon is dynamically explained", Schelling writes, when it is explained "from the original conditions of the construction of matter" (SW IV.76).

The irreversible relation, whether between what was there to know and the knowing of it, or between forces and products, remains crucial throughout Schelling's philosophy as a whole. With it, Schelling attempts to organize what he calls a *Stufenfolge* or "sequence of stages" running from the construction of matter to the production of concepts. The construction of organized matter is always the starting point of philosophical enquiry, which reaches its conclusion only when a phenomenon has been explained in accordance with the basic unit of nature: the antithesis of forces on the basis of which the "self-construction of matter" arises (SW IV.4).[3] Schelling variously calls forces "the only primitives in nature", and their antitheses the "dynamic process" (*ibid.*), the "seed of a universal world-organisation" or simply the "world soul" (2010: 114). This raises two questions: why *more than one* force; and what are forces?

Taking these questions in order, if there were only one force, then nothing would counteract it, and it would therefore run immediately to an infinite extent and "with infinite speed". As he puts the point in the *First Outline of a System of the Philosophy of Nature*:

> One can imagine one original power, infinite in itself, radiating out in all directions from a central point, but which, unless a counteracting (retarding) activity gives its expansion a finite speed, does not remain for one moment at any one point in space, and thus leaves it empty. (2003: 17)

Of course, *imagined* points are no more real than imagined forces; but *should there be forces at all*, then there must be more than one. What then *are* forces?

Schelling claims, following Kant, that "*real antithesis* is possible only between things *of one kind and common origin*" (2010: 117). A transcendental wind, that is, cannot drive a real sailing boat. Where, then, there is antithesis, there is only one nature. Since all of nature produces, according to Schelling, by antithetical forces, antithesis is always actual, and antithesis of forces therefore universal. So far, we can say that the conceptual construction of forces is internally consistent, and that a pair of antithetical forces being given, they must be of the same kind. *On the World Soul* begins with the presentation of the "first force of nature", noting first that nature's productivity is empirically *observable* not merely in the fact of its products, but especially in phenomena such as *light*, which we know, Schelling acknowledges, "only in its propagation", rather than, for example, as a material body (*ibid.*: 96). Since the propagation of light is observable and is not a thing but an activity or force, it can be inferred that not only is light the phenomenon of a force, but also that it is opposed by another, since otherwise it would not be visible at all: "If the originally positive force were infinite, it would lie entirely beyond the limits of all *possible perception*. Restricted by the opposing force, it becomes a *finite magnitude* – it begins to be an object of perception, or manifests itself in *phenomena*" (*ibid.*). Thus in all phenomena we find this "original duplicity" or "bifurcation" (*ibid.*: 107): manifest propagation and restriction, that is, a real antithesis evident as *motion*. Without such antithesis, light's motion would not be possible, and would still not be possible unless the forces that counteract one another are of the same nature or kind. Assuming, therefore, light to be a material process, it must follow that all matter is homogeneous, and at the same time phenomenally heterogeneous, since no phenomena would be possible at all without opposing forces, demonstrating the necessity of real antithesis in and as the condition of the empirically observable phenomena of nature. Nor, finally, is real antithesis ever absolute, since this would entail that each force in the antithesis be the *absolute* negation of its opposite; yet no such absolute negation is found. Rather, since each force "admits of an infinity of possible degrees, none of which is absolute" (*ibid.*: 101), all multiplicity in nature emerges from the restriction of finite force by finite force.

Forces, however, are not themselves phenomena, but "conceal themselves behind" them (*ibid.*: 96). We cannot consider the phenomena generated by this process to be "unreal" in the sense that they are "merely conceptual", since to be so generated, they must be of the same kind as the forces that generate them. Thus, Schelling concludes (*ibid.*: 114), "the phenomenon of every force is therefore a matter". It is this that led Jaspers to note that, for Schelling, the activity of forces or motion is "not the *object* of thought ..., but rather the *matter* of thought" (1955: 77–8). From this, it follows not only that there are forces wherever there is matter, but also that there is no difference in kind between matter and force, or between appearance and production.

While nature bifurcates without end, therefore, the "dynamic philosophy" advances "original forces" as a *limit* concept and a necessary presupposition for all natural science (Schelling 2010: 101). Schelling's dynamic philosophy of nature therefore provides a systematic attempt to think the entirety of nature from the perspective of its production; not as a thing or as a collection of material bodies, but rather as a continuous process, a production self-generated by its own, constant bifurcation.

THE IDENTITY PHILOSOPHY

"Original forces" form a limit *concept* in the sense that, in so far as they are thinkable, they constitute the identity thought in all nature's productions. Thinking is not, therefore, different in kind from other natural productions, since if it were, reality could not be thought at all, and no natural science would be possible; but thought does differ in its powers, not least in so far as it is that production whereby the entirety of what is can be thought, at the limit, in its identity. Thus "identity" becomes a principle of philosophy for Schelling.

While identity had been a problem that had focused Schelling's attention throughout the philosophy of nature, the return of the problem of the system, with which Schelling's philosophizing had begun, to centre stage marks the emergence of the philosophy of identity. This return occurs in the *System of Transcendental Idealism* (1800). Held by many to be the first complete statement of his philosophy, distinguishing it both from Kant's incomplete transcendental idealism and from Fichte's practicist solution to that incompleteness, the *System* is also held to be a preliminary attempt to resolve the same problems as would Hegel's *Phenomenology of Spirit*, seven years later:[4] that is, to overcome the dichotomy of subject and object. As cashed out, since Descartes, in terms of mind and nature, this dichotomy, Schelling is concerned to demonstrate, is parasitic upon an "absolute identity of the subjective and the objective, which we call nature, and which in its highest potentiality is again nothing but self-consciousness" (1978: 17).

The *System*'s purpose is to demonstrate this identity in its development through self-consciousness. The antithesis between subject and object we are left with is not therefore between items of a different kind, but rather between the core elements or "organizing principle" (2010: 96) of nature: between *product* and *production*. In the *System*, the identity of product and production is first and only realized for self-consciousness in art, where the productivity of the artist and the product that emerges from it are inseparable. This differs greatly from the project of Hegel's *Phenomenology*, whose goal it is to "recollect" the forms adopted by consciousness that lead to "Absolute Knowing, or Spirit that knows itself as Spirit" (Hegel 1977b: 493). If the *Phenomenology*'s path begins and ends with the self-knowing of Spirit, the *System*'s is to show that consciousness bears within itself the antithesis of product and productivity from which it emerges in the first place. Whereas for Hegel Spirit can recollect its entire history, for Schelling this is structurally impossible, since the productivity from which self-consciousness emerges cannot be included *in* that self-consciousness. Schelling's initial conception of identity, then, is dynamic.

It is after the *System* that Schelling worked most closely with Hegel, and for that reason, the identity philosophy holds weight, among scholars of Schelling, of Hegel and of German idealism in general, disproportionate to its difference from what preceded it. Schelling unequivocally states in the retrospective preface to the *Philosophical Investigations into the Essence of Human Freedom* (1809) that he "has confined himself wholly to investigations in the philosophy of nature" (2006: 4). This claim is strengthened even by the fact that the "manifesto" for the identity philosophy, the *Presentation of my System of Philosophy* (1801) appeared in the *Journal of Speculative Physics*. Its major statement, the posthumously published *System of Philosophy in General and the Philosophy of Nature in Particular* (1804), devotes two-thirds of its compass to the latter field. In order to assess Schelling's "system of identity"[5] in its actual relation to the philosophy of nature, we must extract what we think of as being recognizably Hegelian in it.

Schelling held the Chair of Philosophy at the University of Jena and was instrumental in securing Hegel a position there, for which the latter delivered his dissertation "On the Orbits of the Planets" in 1801. In the same year, Hegel published *The Difference between Fichte's and Schelling's System of Philosophy*. The two philosophers then co-edited the *Critical Journal of Philosophy*, which ran for three issues from 1802 to 1803. It is Schelling's identity philosophy that Hegel would make his own, coining for it the "speculative" formula "the identity of identity and non-identity" (Hegel 1977a: 156). There, Hegel uses the principle of identity to systematize the relations between the transcendental and natural philosophies as they inform Schelling's work. While transcendental philosophy covers the domain of the "subjective subject-object", the philosophy of nature covers the "objective subject-object". Together they constitute the identity of subject and object. We have already noted that this misconstrues Schelling since it eliminates the order of production in the philosophy of nature. For Hegel, however, it is because the two basic sciences form a single system of philosophy that it has the absolute Idea as its principle.

Schelling's *Presentation* formulates the precise sense in which identity is absolute: "*Everything that is, is absolute identity itself*" (2001: 352). Identity, in other words, is what everything *is* "in itself". If it is identity at all, it can never, in any way, differ from itself. Why, however, does this make identity "everything that is"? Accepting the hypothesis, we might answer that were identity different from what it is not, it would not be absolute, but only relative to what it is not; therefore if identity is absolute, it must be everything that is. Yet Schelling argues differently: "Absolute identity is the unique thing that absolutely *is* or is *in itself*; so everything is in itself only to the extent that it is absolute identity itself, and to the extent that it is not absolute identity itself, it is simply not *in itself*" (2001: 352). Being-in-itself is self-identical, while being not-in-itself differs from it. In other words, the *unique* Absolute is identical in everything that is: whatever is, is self-identical because being is one. It follows that: (a) all cognition of identity is the *self*-cognition of identity (if it were not, then identity could not be cognized in itself); and (b) "the self-cognising of absolute identity in its identity is infinite" (*ibid*.: 355). If infinite, it leaves nothing out, so that "absolute identity is ... the universe itself" (*ibid*.: 359). This is why the "identity system" entails rather than replaces the philosophy of nature: "we understand by *nature* absolute identity first and foremost to the extent that ... absolute identity exists" (SW IV.203).

It is because nature is thus identical to the idea that cognition of identity is cognition of the Absolute. Identity is *in itself* everything, that is, the universe, including the ideas that have it as their object and that form part of it, or the Idea's comprehension, its knowing embrace, of the infinite. To explain the great diversity of natural phenomena, Schelling reverts to the *World Soul*'s argument that real antithesis is possible only between things of the same nature. This nature is *power*, which is "the essence of absolute identity" and "the ground of reality" (2001: 371). The universe is "being", differentiated only by degree, because differences are "differences in power, but not in essence" (1994a: 192). Particular "things" are only differentiated "powers" of this absolute identity. Since there can exist only *quantitative* differences, the theory of powers expresses these quantitative differences as relative proportions of different powers, differing both among themselves and from the Absolute. As one scholar puts it, the powers provide a "general expression of finitude", since any quantitative difference from the Absolute must be finite, while the only thing that "exists in the form of all the powers" (Tilliette 1992: vol. I, 331) is absolute identity, which is infinite.

There is also, however, a causal dimension to the theory of powers, which Schelling calls "the immanent cause of reality" (2001: 371). "$A = B$" provides a formula for them since, whatever the powers at issue, their relative proportion expresses a becoming. The finite nature of each power, that is, entails a transition. By their nature, powers are, as Schelling writes, "truly primal concepts" (SW XII.61). They are the "differential determinations" (Tilliette 1992: vol. I, 331) of being (absolute identity) and therefore "originary" of what becomes (quantitative differences, factors of the Absolute).

Thus Schelling's identity philosophy adds a final element to complete his portrait of the Platonic Idea, as what is "in itself" (Schelling) or is "itself by itself" (Plato): powers are the "immanent cause of reality" (Schelling 2001:

137

371), or what Whitehead calls the "Immanent Law" (1933: 154ff.), by which approximations, always lower in power than what absolutely is, come into existence and form the becomings in which nature consists. The Idea is no longer limited, as Schelling complains it was by Kant, to the moral dimension, but, in keeping with his early investigations of Plato's cosmology (Schelling 1994c), now embraces nature as factors of the Absolute or approximations of infinite identity. To consider the Absolute or identity in the form Hegel imputes to Schelling, as the systematic whole of reason, thus obscures the Platonic dimension that had, from the very first, been present in Schelling's philosophy.

Having achieved this Platonic synthesis, Schelling next turns to the problem of freedom. He will find this in the "restless sea of becoming" constituted by his theorization of Platonic powers so that, rather than locating the ground of freedom elsewhere than in the ground of being, the root of the former lies precisely in the latter, in the ceaseless becomings of nature. This is why *Philosophical Investigations into the Essence of Human Freedom* is followed by *Ages of the World*, the "real basis of which", according to one commentator, "is modern geology" (Sandkühler 1984b: 21). We shall conclude this section, therefore, with the final element of Schelling's naturalism and his return from this to the problem of "systems".

FREEDOM, SYSTEM AND WORLD: THEMES FROM SCHELLING'S LATE PHILOSOPHY

In 1809, fifteen years after his first publication, Schelling wrote the last major work he would publish during his lifetime. The *Philosophical Investigations into the Essence of Human Freedom*, according to Heidegger, "attains the summit of the metaphysics of German Idealism" (1985: 165).

The elements that compose Schelling's philosophy up to this point are: the search for a principle of philosophy; a naturalistic Absolute; powers; and the problem of system or the "principle of organization" (2010: 96). The *Philosophical Inquiries* brings all these concerns to a head, investigating the alleged incompatibility between freedom and system (2006: 9). Many hold that, therefore, the *Inquiries* rejects the very idea of systematic philosophy, but as we shall see, this is not the case. The basis of the claim lies in the *Inquiries*' introduction of the concept of the "unruly" (*das Regelose*), or "the incomprehensible base of reality in things, the indivisible remainder, that … cannot be resolved into reason" (*ibid.*: 29). At issue, then, is the role of this irreducible chaos in systematization, not the elimination of the latter in the interests of the former. *Prima facie*, therefore, it would be a mistake to suggest that the *Inquiries* amount to a watershed in terms of a "systematic" early Schelling and a "post-systematic" or existential later one. Yet Schelling was the first to declare that "will is primal being" (*ibid.*: 21) and thus paved the way for the philosophies of will presented by Schopenhauer, Nietzsche, Freud and, latterly, Žižek.

Beginning by repeating an ancient version of the principle of identity, that "like is recognized by like" (*ibid.*: 10), and presenting this work as the first to treat of "the ideal part of philosophy" (*ibid.*: 4), there is evident continuity between it and Schelling's preceding work. In particular, the philosophy of nature continues to play a major role in this account of an *ontology* of freedom: the "root of freedom", he writes, "is recognised in the independent ground of nature" (*ibid.*: 39). Moreover, maintaining his early (1994c) contrast of Kant and Plato, he constantly references the Platonic and Neoplatonist account of evil as deriving "from primal nature" (2006: 41, trans. mod.). In offering such an account, the *Inquiries* is clearly rejecting the Kantian view that freedom and morality arise from reason alone, purified of all "pathological" or physical influence. It also replaces a rationalist with an "irrationalist" account of freedom, grounded, however, in nature. The unruly that cannot be resolved into reason is precisely the *origin* of evil, and therefore of freedom. Evil is not something to be explained away, as the traditional problem of evil tried to, but rather the necessary basis of freedom that is itself prior to reason. The *Inquiries* therefore makes two basic claims: (a) that freedom is prior to reason, and cannot be "resolved into it" because (b) nature is prior to reason.

In the context of modern discussions of the basis of morality – the rules of our behaviour or deliberations on it – as lying in reason, Schelling takes a naturalistic or "ethical" path that owes most to the ancients, enquiring into the *essence and character* of a freedom that exercises, and is exercised by, humans. The ethical dimension of the question of freedom therefore necessarily opens on to its metaphysical dimension. This is why Schelling asserts that the "point of view which is fully adequate to the task to be undertaken here can only be developed from the fundamental principles of a true philosophy of nature" (*ibid.*: 26–7). If, then, "will is primal being" (*ibid.*: 21), this does not mean that a *human* will ultimately determines what is, so that ethics becomes first philosophy, as Fichteans maintain; rather, it means that freedom lies in the ground of all existence. Accordingly, the essence of human freedom – of a freedom that actually exists in human actions – lies not in humanity at all, but in primal being or nature.

The *Inquiries* follows the distinction, first made in the *Presentation*, "between being insofar as it exists and being insofar as it is merely the ground of existence" (*ibid.*: 27). In the *Presentation*, the ground of existence itself exists only in so far as it grounds actual existents, just as existents exist only in so far as they are grounded. Yet if everything that exists does so in so far as there is a ground of its existence, then if ground itself exists, it must in turn have a ground of its existence, so that a vicious regress ensues. Alternatively, if there is no ground for the existence of ground, there are no grounds for existence at all.

This is known as the principle of sufficient reason, or, in German, *Satz vom Grundes*. Since *Grund* means both "reason" and "ground", the principle asserts that there is both a reason and a ground for everything that exists. Hence, according to Leibniz's formulation of it in the *Principles of Nature and Grace* §7 (G VI.602; AG 209–10), the principle of sufficient reason bridges the domains both of physics and metaphysics, both of actual existents and of reason itself.

In developing this problem, Schelling draws attention to the *antecedence* of ground to grounded. Thus absolute identity in so far as it exists is *nature*, but for that reason cannot exist in itself. The *Inquiries* therefore makes what is prior to ground into the solution of the problem not of the nature of ground, but of the nature of antecedence, as Schelling writes: "The being of the ground, as of that which exists, can only be that which comes *before* all ground, thus, the absolute considered merely in itself, the unground" (2006: 68–9). It is the being of this unground that "cannot be resolved into reason", because it precedes and therefore *is not* reason. As the "unruly", therefore, that "still lies in the ground" (*ibid*.: 29), it is that from which reason derives. It is not, however, simply a principle of "unreason", but also an account of nature, as Schelling argues:

> The abyss [*Abgrund*] of forces into which we gaze here opens up with the single question: in the *first* construction of our Earth, what can have been the ground of the fact that no genesis of new individuals is possible upon it, otherwise than under the condition of antithetical powers? (2003: 230 n., trans. mod.)

This "unruly" element, the *Un*-ground or "*Abgrund*" is the chaos of forces *prior to* organization, teeming with maximally plastic life and inchoate will. In consequence, it acts *not only* in human freedom, but at the origins of all organization, all systems. Schelling's task now becomes to explain how this is possible, how "the world came to be caught in the nets of reason" (1972: 222). This became the project Schelling called the *Ages of the World* or *Weltalter*.

Schelling began the *Weltalter* proper in 1810, had corrected but not returned to his publisher three typeset drafts of that part of it entitled "The Past" by 1815, but did not stop working on it until the lectures entitled *System of the Weltalter* of 1827–28. The first sketches of this "incomplete masterpiece" (Tilliette 2007: 75) are, however, given in the *Inquiries*' narration "of the ground active in nature" from "initial creation" through serial crises to the "emergence of I-hood" and "the end of the present time" (Schelling 2006: 44–7). Many commentators, therefore, call this Schelling's "historical philosophy".[6] Historical it undoubtedly is, but not such as could consider "nature and history to be utterly distinct", as Karl August Eschenmayer remarked in his review of the *Inquiries* (SW VIII.146). Rather, following conclusions established in an early essay on the philosophy of history, Schelling argues that all history is natural history, but one that "would think nature in its freedom as it evolves along all possible paths in accordance with an original organization" (SW I.469). The *Weltalter* therefore establishes the parameters of the philosophical natural history it proposes: "Now, after long wandering, science has once again become the recollection of nature and of its former being one with it. ... Barely had the first step in uniting philosophy with nature been taken, than the great age of the physical had to be acknowledged" (Schelling 1946: 8–9).

A science "at one" with nature would not merely describe what nature *is*, but also and importantly, via the recognition of its "great age", how it came to be. Its ambition, according to Schelling, is to become a "co-science of creation" (2000: xxxvi, trans. mod.): a philosophy of creation *and* created. The *Weltalter* proposes nothing less than a philosophical cosmogony, a science of the emergence of the universe, of the grounding of grounds, to encompass all existence. Small wonder that even after two decades it remained unfinished.

The first problem for this philosophical cosmogony is the past, the problem *par excellence* of natural history. As philosophers or naturalists, in investigating "the great age of the physical":

> We see a series of times in which one always follows another and the following always covers over the foregoing; nothing original ever shows itself, a mass of strata laid one upon the other; the labour of centuries must be stripped away, in order finally to reach the ground. (1946: 12)

Although this seems to hold out the prospect of an ultimate or "final" ground, it is a central thesis of the *Weltalter*'s "system of times" (*ibid.*: 11) that the past is "eternal" (2000: 39). Schelling calls it an "abyss [*Abgrund*] for thought" (1946: 218) because the attempt to render the entirety of the past into a conscious present, to make *creation* wholly and entirely into the *created*, must always encounter the basic fact of the "before" and the "after". The "prior" of grounds is the "unground", which "cannot be resolved into reason", which is why "nothing original ever shows itself" (*ibid.*: 12); there is always something prior to what actually exists. The *Weltalter*'s cosmogony does not, therefore, attain to a "final" or ultimate ground, precisely because creation cannot retrace its own prehistory.

Schelling casts the problem of creation in terms of the emergence of order from disorder. Order and form are not original; rather, "the unruly was brought to order" (2006: 29), echoing the Platonic cosmology from which his studies began (1994c). It follows that no system can be internally consistent and universal. This is why time, for the *Weltalter*, does not form a simple series running uninterruptedly from past to future, but rather a production of separate systems. For this reason, Schelling's lectures of the same period, especially "On the Nature of Philosophy as Science", develop the concept of "asystasy" in which "human knowing" results:

> The thought or the striving to discover a system of human knowing or, put differently and better, to view human knowing collated in one system, naturally presupposes that originally and of itself it does not comprise a system, that it is therefore an *asystaton*, a non-collation, a conflict. (1997: 210)

Against this *asystasy* he sets the pre-human world. To the question, "To what extent is a system ever possible?", Schelling responds:

> [L]ong before man decided to create a system, there already existed one, that of the cosmos. Hence our proper task consists in discovering that system. ... At the same time, it is impossible to uncover the true system in its *empirical* totality, which would require the knowledge of all, even the most discrete, links.
> (1994a: 197)

The cosmos is already a system whose sheer scale (its "empirical totality") precludes human knowing from encompassing it. The possibility of system is given at the same time as its "incompleteness" condition, which applies because it is not possible that the product exceed the resources involved in its production. This was already indicated in the discussion of epistemological systems, the source of which cannot be sought in systems, since this issues in the same regress we encountered in the problem of ground. Only an "asystasia" that precedes system as its "external ground" (1997: 215) can supply a solution. As external to the system, however, it renders the system necessarily exclusive. Thus, as Jaspers notes, "Schelling even thinks the present failure of every exclusive system ... systematically" (1955: 150). Yet Schelling continues to argue that any system of human cognition, however, necessarily confronts nature as its precedent. As he puts it in a late work, "it is not because there is thinking that there is being, but rather because there is being then there is thinking" (2007: 203n.).

If the *Inquiries* emphasizes the irreducible chaos in any system, the *Weltalter* concerns chaos as the source of systems. Schelling invests considerable subsequent effort in the problem of antecedence and production, of "*prius*" and "*posterius*". Enquiries into the ground of all things do not reveal solid ground at all, but only chaotic beginning. It is this *production of order from the unruly*, "that force of beginning ..., the primordial seed of visible nature, out of which nature developed in the succession of age" (2000: 30–31) that Schelling's philosophy explores, from his *Timaeus* studies to the philosophy of nature, from the production-by-differentiation of the in-itself or Absolute to the irreducible chaos at the core of systems and their exteriors, and from the *prius* or beginning to the *posterius* or "system of the world" (1994a: 197). That he explores this *genetically* stems from his repeated demonstrations that nature as genesis cannot be thought as substance, but only as powers. Even in his late philosophy, powers retain the sense they held in the philosophy of nature: "The precedent always consists in the consequent according to potency; this law has been effected by the philosophy of nature in particular in greater extent and constancy" (SW XI.376).

Otherwise called by Schelling a "generative dialectic", and because it is grounded in nature as creation, the theory of production is that "unique standpoint" that Heidegger (1985: 6) argued Schelling struggled repeatedly to make plain: the force of beginning that precedes thinking, the chaos that precedes order, gives rise to systems that have their basis in asystasy – in the non-system formed by their totality that seeks in vain to approximate the world-system that gave rise to it and which is grounded in turn in chaos. Hegel's objection to Schelling that he never had a single system turns out to be a necessary consequence of that "unique standpoint". At root, this standpoint is the same one he pursued from the first, namely, to provide a "physical explanation of idealism" (SW IV.76). It is to Schelling that we owe a consistently naturalistic idealism, based on extending nature to the idea rather than reducing it to nature. This is because nature and the idea work in accordance with powers, making an essential contribution to the metaphysics of powers followed up by Whitehead (see ch. 13) and contemporary metaphysics. The exploration of the origins of order, whose conceptual structure Schelling set out throughout his career, has acquired a particular urgency in the natural sciences (see chs 14–15) in recent years, demanding a philosophical treatment whose outlines Schelling already provides.

8. HEGEL AND HEGELIANISM: MIND, NATURE AND LOGIC

G. W. F. Hegel's philosophical achievement is staggering to all who encounter it. Much of his current renown is premised on a normative, non-metaphysical account of Hegel pioneered in the mid-1970s by Klaus Hartmann (1976) and Charles Taylor (1975), and extended by Terry Pinkard (1994), Robert Pippin (1989) and the Pittsburgh neo-Hegelians. Since the normative account of Hegel has recently become predominant, we shall discuss it as an important aspect of contemporary idealism (see ch. 15). The complexity of Hegel's philosophy supports many accounts that dispute the normative consensus, particularly as regards the philosophy of nature and the logic. Since in this book we are concerned to demonstrate that idealism is not incompatible with naturalism, we shall lay particular stress on his philosophy of nature, within the context and framework Hegel himself sets down in his mature work. By following that framework, we shall attempt to clarify the relations between the Idea, Nature and Spirit that form the three parts of Hegel's *Encyclopaedia of the Philosophical Sciences*.

LOGIC AND THE DIALECTIC

In the *Encyclopaedia Logic*, Hegel defines the ambit of that science not as an abstract formalism, but rather as "the science of *things* grasped in *thoughts*". Accordingly, the "*concept* of things … cannot consist in determinations … alien and external to things. [This is because] thinking things over leads to what is *universal* in them, but the universal is itself one of the moments of the Concept" (1991: 56). Although highly condensed, two things are immediately clear. First, for Hegel's "objective idealism", concepts are not alien to things. Concepts are the ways in which things are determined, and since these are not unique to this or that particular, these real determinations of particulars are themselves universal. The concept is the real universal in a particular, whose particularity is consequently the ideal element of the concept. Hence "the proposition that the finite is ideal constitutes idealism" (1969: 154) because the finite is a particular element of the real abstracted from it. Idealism then, as Hegel conceives it, does not reject realism; rather, it preserves "the reality of finite content" (*ibid*.: 156) as extending beyond it. The very essence of abstraction consists in what it is abstracted from, that is, the universal. What, then, is a universal?

Frederick Beiser (2005: 55–7) argues that in Hegel, concepts such as Spirit, the Absolute and the Infinite are universals. Universals are "first in order of explanation" while particulars are "first in order of being". Emphasizing Hegel's Aristotelianism, universals, Beiser continues, provide the *telos*, the reason or purpose, of things but come into existence only through them. Yet Hegel disputes the criterion of priority, and thus argues that it is the Idea (*Idee*) that is the *alpha* and *omega* of the whole (1970b: 19), that is, the "concrete universal" (1991: 254). The universal self-divides into particulars just as nature self-divides into species. Yet neither species nor particulars "are" independently of the universal or of nature. On this account, it is the Idea that is first in order of being and of explanation, just as it is the Idea to which, at the end of the *Encyclopaedia Logic*, we return, although "this return is an advance" (*ibid*.: 307).

The other thing we learn from the passage cited concerns precisely the nature of this "advance". In that the universal is one of the "moments of the Concept", it is clear that the "*telos*" Beiser identifies entails *movement*, becoming or transition. That the Concept has "moments" in the order of its explication is one of Hegel's important philosophical innovations. Yet these moments are themselves "inseparable" from the Concept, which is the "concrete universal" in which these moments inhere (*ibid*.: 241). For this reason, Hegel calls the Idea "a process", emphasizing the "there and back" movement or "immanent dialectic" (*ibid*.: 290) between Concept and externality, subjectivity and objectivity, that makes up the Idea.

Nor are these moments separable from the things of which they are the determinations, since if they were, they would not be the concepts expressed in those things. For Hegel, therefore, there is only one concrete universal, which he calls the Idea or "the absolute unity of Concept and objectivity" (*ibid*.: 286). As a consequence of this real or objective idealism, therefore, *logic cannot be separated from ontology* for Hegel; it is "the science of things grasped in thought", where both thing and thought are real moments of the Idea.

Accordingly, the *formal* account of concepts and relations is not the form exclusive to the Concept, but also an account of the "natural necessity to take shape" (1977a: 194) evident throughout objective reality. The system of logic is not given merely as a form to be followed in our reasoning, but rather emerges from the fabric of reality itself *as it progresses* or *returns to the universal*. In logic, therefore, as in organic Nature, the formal is always conjoint with the final. Logic comes first in the *Encyclopaedia*, before Nature and Spirit, and Nature is only treated late in the *Science of Logic* precisely to demonstrate the forms of the universal derived in the earlier parts of these works in terms of the objects of their later parts. Thus the *Science of Logic* closes with the Absolute Idea, while the last sections of the *Encyclopaedia*, having moved from anthropology through phenomenology and psychology to law, morality, ethics and the state, address absolute Spirit (*Geist*).

Hegel's logic therefore attempts to demonstrate two things. First, it is progressive, carrying content across propositions, and combining propositions into reasoned accounts or *logoi*. Second, it is formally recursive, with the movement of reason in things repeated in the concept before returning to the absolute Idea or "concrete universal".

Indeed, the progressivity of Hegel's logic can already be inferred from the inseparability of formal from final causes: the form of a thing is inseparable from its purpose or function. Since the function of any proposition of logic is to contribute to the truth, and since "the true is the whole" (1977b: 11), the "ascent to the whole" governs the procedure of reason.

In *The Difference between Fichte's and Schelling's System of Philosophy*, Hegel already qualifies what he calls "the speculative proposition", namely, the proposition that asserts the "identity of identity and non-identity" as "the Absolute itself" (1977a: 156), invoking one of the most notorious aspects of Hegel's dialectic: the role of contradiction. The contradiction at issue here consists in the assertion of an identity of "identity and non-identity". Either there is identity, or there is non-identity, we will be apt to say, invoking the law of non-contradiction. Yet in reality there is both identity and non-identity, or identity and difference, so if philosophy has as its remit the complete, systematic and non-exclusive logic of the Absolute, it must include both identity and non-identity. In other words, that formal systems may not tolerate contradictions without inconsistency points to the one-sidedness of such systems, for contradictions do in fact occur when reason engages reality. The Absolute, then, contains both, and logic is charged with developing this accommodation. In fact, by invoking the dichotomy of the formal and the real, we have already begun such an accommodation, since clearly reality involves both formal and real elements; otherwise put, the merely formal is an abstraction from the whole whose truth it is the business of philosophy to articulate in reason. What cannot be acknowledged by what Hegel calls the Understanding (*Verstand*) is anything on the far side of a dichotomy, since the Understanding, which analyses and then recombines, has abstraction and one-sided formalism built into it. Reason (*Vernunft*), however, is not so constrained, since it articulates these real dichotomies and the reasons for them in their identity with (i.e. in their indifference from) the whole or Absolute that is their real element.

To summarize, logic articulates each perspective of the Understanding, in so far as each such has been "abstracted" from the whole; from this, the Understanding is inevitably driven to oppose or contradict this perspective with another, which Reason then speculatively combines. Reason, finally, does not *eliminate* or deny the actuality of contradictions or dichotomies, but rather raises them from the level of parts and partiality to the whole where they are maintained as parts thereof. The *telos* of logic is therefore to realize the whole with which Reason is identical.

As regards the recursive element in Hegel's logic, this derives in part from the fact that logical form itself is extant in particulars, the antitheses of particulars one to another, and their combination into the form of greater universality. We saw this in Hegel's account of the universal that is in things, and that is in turn an element or moment of the Concept. In other words, what seems whole turns out to be partial, and even the whole emerging from it is in turn part of a larger one. To the question "Which is part and which whole?", when asked of anything finite, the answer must always be "part in this respect, whole in this"; it is only when asked of the Absolute that these contraries are evident in their identity.

Once again, we see how vital contradiction is to the system, providing it with its developmental motor. The repeated movement from abstraction to contradiction to universal evinces what Hegel calls "dialectical form": determination, negation, sublation. "These three sides", Hegel says:

> do not constitute three *parts* of the Logic, but are *moments of everything logically real*; i.e., of every concept or of everything true in general. All of them together can be put under the first moment, that *of the understanding*; and in this way they can be kept separate from each other, but then they are not considered in their truth.
> (1991: 125)

Once again Hegel emphasizes the recursive element: if the moments of the dialectic are considered under the first moment alone, they are all separate and yet are moments of the logic as such, and thus all connected. Thought in this manner, not only does the Understanding not progress beyond the contradictory account of each moment as separate and connected, but it also fails to articulate the truth of the whole, the absolute Idea, that it is logic's purpose to supply.

By contrast, once the Idea has thus been articulated as universal, it has acquired a subjective side. That is, it is not only conscious of its universality (it is so only in particulars) but *thinks itself*, in which form the logic, the living soul of the system, acts throughout. This becomes the domain of Spirit or Mind, which, since it forms the basis of much contemporary engagement with Hegel, will be addressed in Chapter 15. But it also has an objective side, in the forms from which it is articulated: Nature. Just as it is at this point that the *Encyclopaedia Logic* gives onto the *Philosophy of Nature*, so we turn to Hegel's organic idea and its legacy.

THE ORGANIC PHILOSOPHY OF NATURE

Of primary importance for Hegel, and other Romantic and absolute idealist thinkers, was the establishment of a philosophy of nature to address perceived problems associated with the mechanistic worldview that had emerged throughout the scientific revolution and Enlightenment. This latter worldview understood the universe to be a series of contingent interactions between inert material bodies (atoms, corpuscles, etc.), which could be characterized by general laws governing such interactions. Such interactions were, indeed still are in classical mechanics, understood to take place within a vessel of space and time. These mechanical interactions can be understood locally in terms of their antecedent (or "efficient") causes alone. Importantly, such interactions are understood to be entirely "external"; that is, the bodies themselves are not conceived, in this kind of thinking, to have internal characteristics that could effect and be effected by interactions with other bodies. The "idea" of a totality of such external cause-and-effect relationships between otherwise inert bodies (a universe, or cosmos) was left in abeyance by most scientists, and, as we have seen, explicitly ruled out as an object of rational contemplation by the transcendental idealism of Kant.

As we have already seen, for Kant the *Idea* of a totality (of all causes and effects) is a necessary "regulative ideal" for the faculty of understanding to do its work in assigning efficient causes to segments of our experience. However, reason must not overreach itself in the belief that this totality (the world or cosmos) has a reality beyond our cognitive constructions, or that the understanding can, therefore, really capture this totality in some sense. The "reality" of this idea of totality lies only in its function within the human cognitive apparatus. There is no deeper metaphysical basis to this assumption; it simply regulates our activity (as an always "out of reach" aspiration) as rational empirical scientists.

Romanticism and the later phase of German idealism (so called "absolute" idealism) explicitly rejected this limited mechanistic philosophy of nature. Instead, they insisted not on the primacy of individual efficient causation, but on the systemic totality of the universe. First, *the unified totality is real, not simply a regulative ideal*. Second, entities should be understood not only in terms of efficient causality, but also in terms of the role they play in larger systems: that is, in terms of the "purpose" or "function" they have in relation to the "end" (final cause) of systems of which they are an integral part.

We have seen that Kant argued that we assign "teleological" reasons for things and accepted that apparently "self-organizing" entities could not be reduced to mechanisms of efficient causality. However, he insisted that this attribution of unified organization driven by purpose was, again, simply a capacity of the cognitive apparatus: a capacity associated with the "faculty of judgement". And this capacity, he argued, again, was merely regulative.

Kant, as Beiser points out, also anticipated the generalization of the teleological principle to the cosmos as a whole. Only five pages on from his astonishing definition of self-organization he writes: "this concept necessarily leads to the idea of the whole of nature as a system in accordance with the rule of ends" (Ak. V.379). Yet the moment he offers the possibility of a fully organic philosophy of nature, transcendental constraints compel him to withdraw it, concluding that it is simply a means whereby we regulate the way we see and make sense of things, not something that can be determined as in nature itself.

The German idealists took the contrary position. They insisted that the "real" organic interconnection, functionality and totality of nature is an *a priori* constitutive prerequisite for the existence of reasoning creatures that can think in terms of purposes. As Beiser writes, "Hegel affirmed, and Kant denied, that we have reason to assume that nature really is an organism" (2005: 98) . Nevertheless, Hegel himself praises Kant for his insight into the role of the Idea in nature as the final cause of the cosmic organism:

> The Idea that is all-embracing even with respect to content is set up by Kant as the postulated harmony between nature (or necessity) and the purpose of freedom; i.e., as the final purpose of the world thought as realised. ... But the *presence* of living organisations and of artistic beauty shows the *actuality of the Ideal* even for the senses and intuition. That is why Kant's reflections about these objects were well adapted to introduce consciousness to the grasping and thinking of the *concrete* Idea.   (Hegel 1991: 102)

This kind of explanation was not new; it had been an integral part of Aristotelian and Neoplatonist metaphysics. As Ernst Cassirer puts the case:

> The Aristotelian entelechy thus signifies the fulfilment sought earlier in the Socratic *eidos* and the Platonic Idea. The question of how the particular stands in relation to the universal, how it

> differs from it and how it is identical, is answered for Aristotle in the idea of the end; for by this idea we immediately grasp how every individual event is joined to the whole and is conditioned and brought forth by a comprehensive whole. (1981: 277)

Aristotle had called such purposes "final causes". According to the principle of final causes, for example, if we wish to understand a seed then we have to understand it as part of a system. This system exists spatially but also temporally (indeed space and time are constituted by such natural systems). It is a system that gives rise, "finally", to a tree. The seed only "makes sense" in relation to the tree. The system we call the "life of a tree" provides the "purpose", "sense" or "function" of the seed. It is, somehow, part of a system that is the unfolding of a tree. The tree is, somehow, embedded *in* the seed.

But how can the tree be in the seed, without us being reduced to the absurd idea of some miniature tree homunculus? This was one of the great mysteries of ancient philosophy, and one that preoccupied the idealists and Romantics also. Somehow the tree must be in the seed as a real "activity". It is this real activity that we might think of as the Idea *grasped* or *conceived* as the tree. In this kind of philosophical idealism, then, the Idea is the real arrangement of things that gives the universe its form by virtue of final causes (cf. Hegel 1991: 279–80). We shall see also, then, that realized final cause, and Idea fully unfolded and "grasped" (*begreift*) are, in this context, consonant with what we often refer to as "organization".

For Hegel, the grasping of the Idea in things is the "Concept" (*Begriff*, sometimes translated as "notion") of things. He says: "The animal is intrinsically the most lucid existence in Nature, but it is the hardest to comprehend since its nature is the speculative Notion [*Begriff*]. For, although this nature is a sensuous existence, it must nevertheless be grasped in the Notion" (1970b: 358). Now, if the seed (or animal) is caused to be what it is by virtue of the Idea manifest in the tree, this is only so in so far as the tree is caused to exist in relation to the planet, which is in turn what it is in relation to the cosmos. Ultimately, the absolute idealists thought, the universe, like the tree, must have a final unfolding that makes sense of all its parts (both spatially and temporally). So just as the seed makes sense, or has a purpose, in relation to the Idea as such (manifest in the tree), every part of the universe makes sense, or has a purpose, in relation to the final unfolding of the universe, or nature as such: "the Idea that is, is Nature" (1991: 307). This is the meaning of the "Absolute" Idea, and why Hegel's is an "absolute idealism". The Absolute is the final and total manifestation of the Idea in relation to which everything else has its purpose, sense or function. According to Hegel, this absolute idealism is a realism with respect to the Idea because the very existence of nature as a *whole* is manifest in each living organism:

> This idealism which recognizes the Idea throughout the whole of Nature is at the same time realism, for the Concept [*Begriff*] of the organism is the Idea as reality, even though in other respects the individuals correspond only to one moment of the Concept. What philosophy recognizes in the real, the sensuous world, is simply the Concept. (1970b: 358–9, trans. mod.)

The point of departure in our understanding of nature, Hegel argues, must be to understand the overall Idea or principle of organization of things as a totality. Only then do we see how particular elements play their role in this organization, as moments in the Concept. Philosophy re-cognizes the Concept as the real world of sense, and idealism raises it to its reality in the Idea. Conversely, reasoning from part to whole, every particular has moments of the Concept it includes. Thus, the moments of the Concept of "animal organism" are the nervous system, the circulatory system and the digestive system (*ibid.*: 359). Each system is itself a totality, or it would not operate systematically; but each also has as its medium the animal totality; and each animal the organic domain in general. Real particulars therefore show the same structural complexity at the lowest level of their organization as they show in turn with respect to the total organization whose moments they are.

It is important, however, to understand the difference between the Idea and the Concept in Hegel's "conceptual [*begreifend*] treatment of Nature" (*ibid.*: 6, trans. mod.). Whereas natural particulars are moments in this conceptual treatment, Nature as such "exists", says Hegel, as "externality … in relation to the Idea" (*ibid.*: 14). Because the organization of the Idea does not stop with Nature, the real must return to the Idea in the form of Spirit. Nature is "external" in that nature is the Idea that has not yet become conscious of itself as such. As the Idea does become conscious of itself, so Nature becomes Spirit. This movement from Nature to Spirit ("externality" to internality) occurs logically by means of dialectic. Thus, just as the *Logic* concludes with the transition to Nature, the *Philosophy of Nature* concludes with the Individual, the highest stage prior to the system's transition to Spirit. "The aim of these lectures", Hegel writes, "[h]as been to give a picture of Nature in order to subdue this Proteus: to find in this externality only the mirror of ourselves, to see in Nature a free reflex of Spirit" (*ibid.*: 445).

While it is ultimately in the domain of Spirit that Nature finds its moment as transitional between Logic and Spirit, Hegel has already acknowledged that nature's externality to the Idea does not rob it of its reality. In consequence, we may continue to regard Hegel's "conceptual treatment" as offering specific terms for an idealist engagement with Nature. That, for instance, we may understand things in terms of their role in a broader scheme of things, even in the absence of direct empirical confirmation, is not, of course, a method entirely foreign to science. Hegel is not suggesting anything very outlandish here. We shall see this confirmed when we meet further interrogation of the problem of organization by contemporary science in later chapters.

GOD AND NATURE

For the Romantics and idealists the absolute Idea has theological connotations. While the determination of the form of reality by eternal and paradigmatic Ideas is derived ultimately from Plato, the notion that God is coextensive with the total system of the universe was derived from Spinoza. For him, "God" and "Nature" are identical. Rather than being some external "super-natural" intelligence, God is immanently Nature, and vice versa. Many of the thinkers in question were explicit Spinozists, and early disputes that acted as precursors for the idealist movement centred around F. H. Jacobi's forensically critical study of that philosopher.[1] The absolute idealists, and Hegel in particular, took the step of making the Spinozist God identical with the Idea. God is the totality, and therefore explains everything within it.[2]

The question remaining for Hegel was: what *shape* might the Idea itself have? Hegel's account of "shape" is a vital element of the *Phenomenology*, which charts the progress of consciousness through its various shapes or forms until it reaches its "final shape … Spirit knowing itself in the shape of Spirit" (1977b: 485). Yet that the Idea itself might have a final shape, regardless of its scrutability, is difficult to conceive. Supposing there were a final state (the totality of nature's equivalent of the fully grown tree) which provides the teleological purpose (final cause) of everything that constitutes the passing time and space of history (natural and social): what would it be? This is a question we shall return to.

Nothing, therefore, in the theological connotations of the absolute Idea makes idealism either anti-rationalist or anti-science. The idealists simply assert that reason and science must be understood in relation to an organic (as opposed to mechanistic) philosophy of nature, of the kind just described. And, as Beiser points out, Hegel was careful to make clear that the purpose of nature was not to be understood anthropocentrically, as some kind of supreme intentionality:

> Hegel insists that this concept does not involve intentionality, the attribution of will or self-conscious agency to a living thing. To state that a natural object serves a purpose is not to hold that there is some intention behind its creation, still less that there is some concealed intention within the object itself. Rather, all that it

> means is that the object serves a function, that it plays an essential role in the structure of the organism. (Beiser 2005: 102)

In other words, as we indicated earlier, if purpose is to be understood as "function", then the Idea, in relation to which purpose stands, is, in fact, another word for "organization". An important point to note, then, is that much of contemporary science is, therefore, implicitly idealist. Any domain of science that asserts the existence of systems, and/or uses the language of "functionality" and "organization", in order to explain the existence of components of those systems, is idealist in character. This would include much of biology, systems theory, cybernetics, complex systems theory, ecology, population theory and so on (we shall be exploring this directly in Chapter 14). It would also include the social and psychological sciences, where they rely on functional or systemic explanation, and theories of organization.

THE GERMAN ROMANTIC MOVEMENT AND RATIONALIST MYSTICISM

But how was the Idea of the "whole" to be grasped at all? We can already see in this the shadow of the mysticism that was undoubtedly a part of the Romantic movement that formed the broader context for the development of absolute idealism.[3] It is important not to misunderstand this mysticism though. Mysticism is often thought of as an insistence that the universe is not, ultimately, intelligible by means of rational scientific methods, because of the "irrationality" of the universe. This is absolutely not the position of the Romantics though. For them the world is perfectly rational. Like Neoplatonists such as Plotinus, though, they see the universe as governed by a Platonic order of ideas, which subsists in the eternal domain of pure ideas (objective ideas as already described) or "Intellect" (this is the divine, eternal "Intellect" not that of ordinary mortals). But many Romantic idealists, like Plotinus before them, argued that this eternal domain was not directly amenable to human "understanding". It is not that the universe itself is irrational, but more that its reason or structure is not amenable to being "thought" by human understanding. Normal scientific thinking cannot get at it, at least not directly, for reasons we saw Schelling describe in Chapter 7.

Of course, many of the Romantics were even more convinced of the inaccessibility of the Absolute by their Kantian inheritance. As we have seen, for Kant, the faculty of "understanding" is not good at contemplating totalities. Its job is to chop up experience into pieces and apply "concepts" to it in order to construct and understand the world in terms of discrete objects. Far from contemplating the totality, it chops up experience into discrete objects and then links them back together, bit by bit, through efficient causation.

Scientific reasoning, according to Kant, is driven by this faculty of "understanding", and so science cannot easily deal with totalities and systems.

Many of the Romantics disagreed with Kant's view of the relationship between nature and rational mind. They insisted that human subjects are not the creators of reality; rather, they are the expressions of the system of nature of which they are a part. However, they agreed with Kant that analytical scientific understanding is not capable of apprehending and contemplating the totality of nature, the Idea or Absolute. So, how can we get at this totality? If not by thought, they said, then by "intuition". We must rely on a more immediate intuitive encounter with the reason that is manifest in the totality of nature. In this, again, they inherited directly the Platonic mysticism of Plotinus: a mysticism directed, not towards the non-rational, but precisely towards "contemplation" (intuition) of the Absolute, unified source of the divine rational Intellect.

Hegel, ultimately, parted company with the Romantics here. Early in his thinking he too had toyed with such mysticism, but ultimately came to believe that it was possible to "think" the Absolute, but that we must employ thinking faculties other than the "understanding"; or, at least, the understanding must rise to a higher level. He affirmed precisely what Kant had denied as possible – to think the unconditioned:

> It is true that it [philosophy] does, initially, have its objects in common with religion. Both of them have the *truth* in the highest sense of the word as their object, for both hold that *God* and *God alone* is the truth. Both of them also go on to deal with the realm of the finite, with *nature* and the *human spirit* and their relation to each other and to God as to their truth. (1991: 24)

But what kind of thinking could lead "Spirit" from fragmented analytical understanding, to a rational self-consciousness of the purposeful unity of multiplicity in the Idea?

DIALECTICAL LOGIC WITHIN NATURE

How can the "unfolding" of a system guided by final causes proceed? As we have already seen, Hegel believed that underlying the unfolding of the Idea must be a fundamental logic at the heart of nature. If there were no such logic then we would have to conclude that the unfolding of nature were irrational, a position rejected out of hand by the Romantics and absolute idealists.[4] This logic must, then, be detectable in all of the manifestations of nature: in organic systems, in the peculiarly human part of nature we call "history" and in the growing self-consciousness of nature that we call "mind". "Dialectic", he writes:

> is the genuine nature that properly belongs to the determinations of the understanding, to things, and to the finite in general. ... The dialectic ... is the *immanent* transcending, in which the one-sidedness and restrictedness of the determinations of the understanding displays itself as what it is, i.e., as their negation. ... Hence the Dialectical constitutes the moving soul of scientific progression, and it is the principle through which alone *immanent coherence and necessity* enter into the content of science. (1991: 128)

This dialectic logic passes through the phases of unity, multiplicity and unity in multiplicity. Organic systems, for example, proceed from single cells, to multiplicities of cells, to a differentiated but unified system of many cells: an *organism*. Human societies, similarly, proceed from small, isolated, social groups, to multiplicities of groups, to differentiated but functionally unified divisions of labour.

Reason as manifested in thought also passes through such phases, and this is the key to understanding the purpose of philosophy with respect to the Idea that guides it, along with everything else. As Kant had pointed out, the faculty of understanding takes nature and breaks it into apparently independent parts, parts that it then connects. Hegel argues that the "contradictions" of parts that are apparently independent (and yet not really independent at all) cause the understanding to rise to the higher level of the whole, and see the parts as connected parts determined by the organization of a genuinely unconditioned whole: from unity, to multiplicity, to unity in multiplicity. Hegel turns Kant's antinomy, with respect to parts and wholes, into the dialectical movement of *reason immanent to nature*. All of nature, according to Hegel, proceeds according to this logic. Here, then, we begin to get our first sense of what the Idea of Nature might look like. The Idea must be the "unity in multiplicity" of the totality of nature.[5]

NATURALISM, SUBSTANCE MONISM, INTER-SUBJECTIVITY AND SPIRIT IN ITS RELATION TO NATURE

As we can already begin to see, absolute idealism was a direct challenge to the dualism of the Cartesian early modern period, to the philosophy of the subject that arose from it, and to the epistemological problems derived from it. Whole generations had struggled and failed to provide a convincing philosophical account of how subject and object could be connected. How could there be a relation between the physical world and knowledge of the physical world in the (non-physical) mind?

Kant thought he had solved the problem by making the world of empirical objects a "construct" of the human cognitive apparatus. There was no problem of linkage between the object and the subject, because the object was, he said, simply a construction of the cognitive "faculties" of "rational" subjects. All that "objectivity" means to a Kantian is that we share an "object" world by virtue of the cognitive similarities that we share as "rational beings". As we have seen, this created all kinds of new problems. The idealists who followed Kant were acutely aware of these. Their solution was, in a sense, the reverse of Kant's. They insisted, like Spinoza, that there can only be one substance, and that the material and the mental must both be manifestations of a single more fundamental substance. This single substance, said Hegel, is the Idea. Both matter and mind are functional attributes of the unfolding of the total system that is the Idea.

> Philosophy must therefore comprehend mind as a necessary development of the eternal Idea and must let the science of mind, as constituted by its particular parts, unfold itself entirely from its Notion. Just as in the living organism generally, everything is already contained in an ideal manner, in the germ and is brought forth by the germ itself, not by an alien power, so too must all the particular forms of living mind grow out of its Notion as from their germs. (1971: 5)

This has important implications for how we think about mind and the self. No longer can we think of a self-subsistent entity; if mindedness is just as much an attribute of the Idea as are material objects, then mind and the self must also be understood in systemic terms. German Romanticism and idealism provides a "decentred" account of subjectivity. Following Fichte, Hegel is quite explicit about the fact that subjectivity is always "inter-subjectivity": it is always relational; a mind's focus of experience from the context of which we are an expression. In particular, argued Hegel, this context is a processes of mutual recognition. "Self-consciousness exists in and for itself when, and by the fact that, it so exists for another; that is, it exists only in being acknowledged …. The detailed exposition of the Notion of this spiritual unity in its duplication will present us with the process of Recognition" (1977b: 111). Hegel proceeds to detail the dialectical movement according to which this "process of recognition" occurs. It is arguable, in this context, that contemporary theories of decentred subjectivity (postmodern, neo-Freudian, structuralist, etc.), particularly those that emphasize a dynamic relation between "self" and "other", are, in this sense, offshoots of Hegelian idealism.

This "context" of which the mind is an expression is not just the context of other subjects; it is the context of nature. Mental events are not separate from nature; they are nature's "highest expression". As Beiser puts it:

> If nature is an organism, [as Hegel] argues, then it follows that there is no distinction in kind but only one of degree between the mental and the physical, the subjective and the objective, the ideal and the real. They are simply different degrees of organisation and development of a single living force, which is found everywhere within nature ... The mental is simply the highest degree of organisation and development of the living powers of the body.
> (Beiser 2005: 106)

The progressive unfolding of the Idea was, or will have been, according to Hegel, identical with the coming to self-consciousness of being in its entirety; yet what does this mean? We are now in a position to develop further our understanding of the Idea. We have seen that for Hegel the unfolding of the Idea manifests itself in the unfolding of purposive organic systems, and in the unfolding of nature's consciousness of itself. Hegel solves the problem of the duality of mind and body by making them both manifestations of the Idea itself. Nature and Spirit are inextricably bound up in the Idea. And, indeed, this is what makes science and philosophy of nature possible. He says:

> [W]e think natural objects. Intelligence familiarizes itself with things, not of course in their sensuous existence, but by thinking them and positing their content in itself; and in, so to speak, adding form, universality .... This universal aspect of things is not something subjective, something belonging to us: rather is it, in contrast to the transient phenomenon, the noumenon, the true, objective, actual nature of things themselves, like the Platonic Ideas, which are not somewhere afar off in the beyond, but exist in individual things as their substantive genera. (1970b: 9)

So we see that, through the logic of the dialectic, the emergence of rational mind immanent to nature proceeds by increasing analytical understanding, which breaks up experience into a multiplicity of conceptually defined elements (as Kant described in the first *Critique*), and then proceeds towards an integration of this multiplicity into a totality (the ultimate work of reason), such that the whole system of the world eventually becomes conscious of itself as a unified system. This unfolding of the self-consciousness of nature is the unfolding of "Spirit". The "unity in multiplicity" of nature, therefore, will be characterized by a full coming into being of the self-consciousness of nature in its entirety.

> This unity of intelligence and intuition, of the inwardness of Spirit and its relation to externality, must be, not the beginning but the goal, not an intermediate, but a resultant unity ... man must have eaten of the tree of the knowledge of good and evil and must have gone through the labour and activity of thought in order to become what he is, having overcome this separation between himself and Nature. (1970b: 9)

And furthermore:

> From our point of view mind has for its *presupposition* Nature, of which it is the truth, and for that reason its *absolute prius*. In this truth Nature is vanished, and mind has resulted as the "Idea" entered on possession of itself. Here the subject and object of the Idea are one – either is the intelligent unity. (1971: 8)

This, then, is what the Idea, finally, looks like.

9. BRITISH ABSOLUTE IDEALISM: FROM GREEN TO BRADLEY

In this chapter and the following two we shall investigate the importance of the "neo-Hegelian" movement in British philosophy, which flourished from the late nineteenth century before dying down significantly[1] by the mid-twentieth century. After briefly summarizing the journey of Hegelian philosophy from Germany to England, we shall provide a discussion of six of the most important theorists of this period. This discussion will attempt to present the core metaphysical ideas of each philosopher for two reasons. First, this material is less well known than, for example, their ethical and political philosophy (see Boucher & Vincent 2000); second, this material will make it clear that "refutations" of idealism, however influential, are wide of the mark indeed.

The problems that emerge from British idealist philosophy are certainly heterogeneous, but there is one set of issues to which we shall pay particular attention. These issues revolve around the twin constraints of holism and monism. Pursuing these, for instance, leads Bradley famously to deny the reality of relations, since partiality is necessarily mere appearance. Monism therefore entailed, for Bradley, the elimination of particularity. For J. M. E. McTaggart, on the other hand, it entailed precisely the converse, to demonstrate which the philosopher undertook to correct Hegel. In general terms, this is a problem about the relation of wholes to their parts, and whether, without some form of negativity, parts are not necessarily eliminated from monistic and holistic metaphysical systems.

ABSOLUTE BEGINNINGS: BRITISH IDEALISM AND THE SECRET OF HEGEL

In the first few decades of the nineteenth century, British philosophy was highly insular and had been viciously criticized for its lack of contribution to European research. Writing in 1828, Victor Cousin claimed that for the past fifty years no great work of metaphysics had been published in Britain (see Muirhead 1927). Indeed it was not until 1855, twenty-four years after his death, that Hegel's philosophy began to be translated and published in English (see Sloman & Wallon 1855). The journey of Hegel's philosophy from Germany to Britain was extremely slow and by the time it came to be fully appreciated by the British audience, interest in Hegel's philosophy in his own country was beginning to decline. Ferrier was probably the first important British idealist philosopher to have some grasp on Hegel, but as he readily admitted, his understanding was limited: "With peaks here and there more lucent than the sun, his intervals are filled with a sea of darkness, unnavigable by the aid of any compass, and an atmosphere or rather vacuum in which no human intellect can breathe" (Ferrier 1854: 54). No intelligible word, Ferrier claimed, had been written either by or about Hegel.

Arguably, the first intelligible word to be written about Hegel would appear twelve years after Ferrier's proclamation, in 1865, the year after his death, by James Hutchinson Stirling. While living in Germany in the 1850s, Stirling became attracted to Hegel through his reputation as the "deepest and darkest of all philosophers" (Muirhead 1927). In 1857, despite being trained in medicine, Stirling decided to move back to Britain to work on Hegel's philosophy and spent the next eight years, working twelve hours a day, producing the era-defining *The Secret of Hegel* (1865). This book is the historical starting point for the proliferation of British Hegelian idealisms that were to follow. So what is the secret of Hegel? The secret, Stirling argued, is the union that Hegel calls the "concrete notion":

> The conditions of a concrete, and of every concrete, are two opposites: in other words Hegel came to see that there exists no concrete which consists not of two antagonistic characters, where at the same time, strangely, somehow the one is not only through the other but actually is the other. (1865: 139)

Stirling made it clear that we must not consider the Absolute to be the unthinkable, since the Absolute is the object of all thought.

> Thought when it asked why an apple fell sought the Absolute and found it – at least so far as outer matter is concerned. Thought, when, in Socrates, it interrogated many particular virtues for the one universal virtue, sought the Absolute. Thought in Hume when it asked the reason of our ascription of effects to causes sought the Absolute and, if he did not find it, he put others on the way to find it. What since the beginning of time, what in any corner of the earth has philosophy, has thinking ever considered but the Absolute? (*Ibid.*: 139–40)

Stirling considered Hegel's philosophy to be the culmination of Kant's critical project, uniting sense and the understanding, renouncing Kant's unknowable Absolute and transforming his "halting" idealism into an absolute idealism.

After Ferrier and Stirling, a third name deserves mention for the key role in introducing German philosophy to Britain: T. H. Green. According to Rudolf Metz, "It was with Green and not before him, that German idealism really began its mission on Anglo-Saxon soil" (1938: 268).

GREEN AND THE ETERNAL CONSCIOUSNESS

Green's metaphysics of the eternal consciousness is, as Peter Nicholson has recently written, "the heart of his philosophy, which supplies the life-blood of the individual's intellectual and moral activity" (2006: 158). The aim of Green's metaphysics, which grounds his ethical system, is to show that there *cannot* be a science of man but that there *can* be a metaphysics of freedom, since it is provable that man's free will is outside the system of mechanical causes. Green shared the views of those across the continent that British empiricism had reached a dead end. German idealism was so important for Green because in the works of Fichte, Kant and Hegel he believed he could see a fertile source capable of leading us away from this sterility. His system is explicitly a synthesis of the Kantian and Hegelian philosophies and he believed that Hegel's metaphysics must be "recreated" by first returning to Kant. From Kant, Green takes the famous dictum "the understanding makes nature" (2003: 15), but with Hegel, he rejects the distinction between the phenomena and the noumena, instead postulating the existence of an "Eternal Consciousness", which is the ground of all reality and through which we as finite souls are united. Implicitly, underlying Green's system is a distinct Aristotelianism, where form and matter are essential to an adequate conception of substance. Even when Green professes his Hegelianism or Kantianism this is always through Aristotelian lenses.

Green's aim in book I of his *Prolegomena to Ethics* is to show that the answer to the question "Can the knowledge of nature be itself a part or product of nature, in the sense of nature in which it is said to be an object of knowledge?" (*ibid.*: 129) is no. The first step is to show that reality is fundamentally "relational". If we attempt to define matter by making a list of all its necessary qualities but abstract from this list all relations, such as "relations between facts in the way of feeling, or between objects that we present to ourselves as sources of feeling" (*ibid.*: 13), we shall be left with nothing. Similarly, motion is nothing under such an abstraction. Abstracted from all relations, motion reduces to a composition of different positions of a body from which, as Zeno's paradoxes showed, motion itself can never arise. Green takes as an axiom the fact that something must explain these relations and argues that this something cannot be produced by the bodies themselves given that without relations these bodies could have no prior existence. If there is to be regularity and order to nature as we experience it then there must be an "organizer" for nature, a "something" outside the order of nature that makes such an order possible. *Mere* sensations are as incapable of relationless reality as are motion and matter. We can arrive at the idea of a "mere" sensation by a process of abstraction but such an abstraction does not lead us towards a fact. A sensation that has not been determined by thought or the character of a previous sensation is, strictly speaking, nothing at all. It can present to consciousness no reality. Our conscious world and the physical world must be strictly relational.

Modern philosophy accepts, Green claims, that we can know nothing except for phenomena. To anything unrelated to consciousness, we are necessarily blind. Therefore, there must be a subject to produce any object. It is at this point that Green begins to ask whether Kant's dictum that the "understanding makes nature" should not be given a wider scope than Kant himself allowed it:

> If nothing can enter into knowledge that is unrelated to consciousness; if relation to a subject is necessary to make an object, so that an object which no consciousness presented itself would not be an object at all; it is difficult to see how the principle of unity, through which the phenomena become the connected system called the world of experience, can be found elsewhere than in consciousness. (*Ibid.*: 15)

It is essential to Green's metaphysics of freedom that consciousness lies outside the network of physical mechanical causes and he argues that the fact that consciousness is aware of a series of natural events as a series is proof enough that this consciousness cannot be part of that very series. He argues that if consciousness were merely the "result" of such a series then at best it could "supervene" on this series at a particular stage, but if this were the case then it would not be aware of the series as a series. If it is to be thus aware, it must be *equally* present at every stage of the succession and cannot change while the series itself changes. Green freely acknowledges that this argument is easy to criticize. Granted, the natural series we are presently aware of could not have produced that conscious awareness; but could an earlier natural series not have produced it so that it is now in existence ready to be aware of the current natural series? For Green, this merely postpones the problem and brings us to a more serious issue. If we are to call the "natural series of events" a "cause" of consciousness then it must be able to satisfy certain conditions in order to count as a cause. Green claims that to be a cause a thing must (a) be able to "explain its effect", that is, be "equivalent to the conditions into which the effect may be analysed" or (b) at the very least be that to which "experience testifies as the uniform antecedent of the effect" (*ibid.*: 22). It fails as (a) because it contains none of the ingredients that could give rise to consciousness. There is nothing in matter that is "consciousness like" that could count as the condition for the production of consciousness. It also fails because (b) it is impossible to experience matter as antecedent to consciousness since without consciousness experience is impossible. So when we claim that consciousness is the result of natural causes we have things the wrong way round. In order for us to experience a natural series of events there must be, prior to this process of change, a consciousness that does not change, because without a singular unchanging reference point, no relations of before or after, here or there, are intelligible. Our "understanding", then, in the Kantian sense, makes nature what it is for consciousness, which is the only nature there could be. Similarly, without an unchanging consciousness, we would experience no world whatsoever.

Green will argue that there is an "eternal system of related elements" that forms the "really real" and that this system can be "related with endless diversity" (*ibid.*: 19). The key difference between the "eternal consciousness" and our own is that it is the former that is the organizer that provides us with the eternal, unchanging, really real order of nature, while our own consciousness reports this order in its own diversified way depending on its own individual perspective. The distinction between "fact" and "fancy", for Green, depends on whether the relations we have perceived can be combined with the true eternal order of nature. All feelings are real feelings and the false claim that we can have "unreal" feelings is one of the problems that, as we shall see below, led the empiricists and Kant into error. Green asks us to consider a train driver who perceives a signal incorrectly; imagine that this driver believes that the signal shows "go" when in fact it shows "stop". The feeling the driver has of this sign showing "go" is just as "real" as the feeling of the true signal "stop"; it is just that the system of relations "between combinations of moving particles on the one side and his visual organs on the other, between the present state of the latter and certain determining conditions" (*ibid.*: 17) do not correspond with the true order of relations. A "matter of fact", then, is one that is always the same order of relations, that is, it corresponds with the eternal system of relations rather than merely the contingent relations of individual consciousness. What the signal "really showed" at that moment in time is eternal and will never change, it is part of the unalterable system of relations. Whether or not the train driver had the correct perception depends on whether or not it agrees with those relations, but his perception was still a real experience even though it does not agree with the true system.

Green argues that the claim that the perceptions of the mind are "opposed to the real" undermines the importance of the work of the understanding and, concurrently, introduces an apparent difficulty, or even contradiction, into our perceptions. For if our perceptions are not "real" then they are merely privations, they can have no qualities, but as our perceptions *do* have qualities *and* relations, we cannot legitimately say that they are not real. In fact they are just as real as anything else. It is important, then, for Green, that any attempt to define what is real by what is unreal is doomed to failure. With a quick wink to Kant, Green claims: "The 'mere idea' of a hundred thalers … is no doubt quite different from the possession of them, not because it is unreal, but because the relations which form the real nature of the idea are different from those which form the real nature of the possession" (*ibid.*: 28).

After having shown that the distinction between the real and the unreal is invalid and having attempted to prove that an unalterable system of relations is presumed by the very claim that there can be "matters of fact", Green asks: "What is implied in there being such a single, all-inclusive, system of relations? or, What is the condition of its possibility?" (*ibid.*: 31). And as he does this, he is edging towards his own version of the "Absolute Idea", that is, the eternal consciousness. Essentially Green's argument is that in order to have a system of relations – a many in one – there must be something to "unify" this "manifold". As discussed above, he denies that this unification can be the product of singular things because without relations singular things are nothing. The unity of the manifold depends on an ontologically distinct unifier, which is the primary ground for singular things. Green argues that the very agency that does this primary unifying is analogous to our own understanding and the process by which the "manifold" of the physical world becomes a "many-in-one" is a process analogous to how our phenomena become a "unified" series of events. Green is stretching Kant's "synthetic unity of apperception" from the phenomena to the noumena, simultaneously undermining the distinction between the two. Green argues that Kant's distinction is a distinction between form and matter: the phenomenal world is the world of form, the relations of experience, while the noumenal is the unknown relationless matter about which we can say nothing. Green's problem with this thesis is that he believes it sets up two separate worlds that exist in a position of negation. In order that both worlds exist, both must be subject to processes of determination but the processes for both worlds are heterogeneous, therefore:

> [T]he conception of a universe is a delusive one. Man weaves a web of his own and calls it a universe; but if the principle of this universe is neither one with, nor dependent on, that of things-in-themselves, there is in truth no universe at all, nor does there seem

to be any reason why there should not be any number of such independent creations. We have asserted the unity of the world of our experience only to transfer that world to a larger chaos.
(*Ibid.*: 45)

Any relationship of dependency the phenomenal could have on the noumenal world is blocked by its disparate nature. Furthermore, correspondence would rely on relations and all relations between the phenomena and the thing-in-itself are also blocked. We are left with an "unaccountable residuum". Our world becomes less than an illusion because we lack any criteria for differentiating fact from fancy. In the earlier example of the train driver, there could be no objective standard to test whether or not the driver saw the signal correctly or incorrectly, for beyond our subjective phenomenal experience we have no way of establishing objective fact. All possible routes to truth are blocked. Green therefore argues that there is no need to postulate such an unaccountable residuum and that we should rather understand the organizing principle in nature as analogous to the organizing principle in our own consciousness. He writes:

> There could be no such thing as time if there were not a self-consciousness which is not in time. As little could there be a relation of objects as outside each other, or in space, if they were not equally related to a subject which they are not outside; a subject of which outsideness to anything is not a possible attribute; which by its synthetic action constitutes that relation, but is not itself determined by it. (*Ibid.*: 59)

Green's conclusion here is that "nature in its reality, or in order to be what it is, implies a principle which is not natural" (*ibid.*: 61). It is important here to note, as Peter Hylton does, that "while Green's philosophy is consciously anti-materialistic, it is not crudely so" (1990: 35). In fact to call it anti-materialistic at all is perhaps to go too far. Green's main point is that atomistic materialism presents us with an account of nature that is at best an abstraction. Most seriously it is an abstraction that cannot account for the processes it intends to explain. It can tell us that there are laws of nature, but how such a world of disparate material objects could achieve such incredible regularity is left a mystery. Green's conclusion is that in order for such regularity to occur there must be a principle in nature, a "spiritual" organizer that produces such regularity. This is the eternal system of relations that cannot be a product of nature because without the system of relations nature could not exist. Therefore, there must be a self-organizing "spiritual" principle. However, we would be wrong to understand the spiritual principle and the natural world in separation; this is not a dualism of nature and spirit. Green claims that if it were not for all of the connotations wrapped up with the term "nature", it could be used to refer to both the spiritual principle and the natural world. To imagine either in separation would be to put forward a fatally flawed abstraction. The distinction between "spirit" and "nature" is really, for Green, the Aristotelian distinction between form (spirit) and matter (nature); just as, "matter" and "'form" are inseparable for Aristotle, so too for Green's "manifold" and "unifying principle".

> Apart from the unifying principle the manifold would be nothing at all, and in its self-distinction from that world the unifying principle takes its character from it; or, rather, it is in distinguishing itself from the world that it gives itself its character, which therefore but for the world it would not have. (2003: 86–7)

When we perceive an object in nature, such as a flower, we perceive a certain number of its determinate relations; we do not see the whole because we are finite and the eternal system of relations is infinite. As everything is part of this network, to see the flower in its completeness would be to see the whole world, spiritual and natural, in its entirety. The extent to which our own "understanding makes nature" is the extent to which our own consciousness interprets the relations; our individual experience and training will mean that we perceive objects in very different ways. My experience of the flower will differ substantially from that of the botanist. The objective fact for both of us is the same but the botanist will perceive a far greater number of the relations than I will. For both of us, the understanding plays an active role fusing our various sensory experiences of the object together and providing us with our own presentation of the flower. It is a mental assemblage formed by a consciousness "in time", which, Green believes, as discussed above, must be outside time in order to possess such a power:

> The presentation of the sensation, again, as of a fact related to other experience, is in like manner an event …. Yet the content of the presentation, the perception of this or that object, depends on the presence of that which in occurrence is past, as a fact united in one consciousness with the fact of the sensation now occurring; or rather, if the perception is one of what we call a developed mind, on numberless connected acts of such uniting consciousness, to which limits can no more be set than they can to the range of experience, and which yield the conception of a world revealed in the sensation. The agent of this neutralization of time can as little, it would seem, be itself subject to conditions in time as the con-

stituents of the resulting whole, the facts united into consciousness into the nature of the perceived object, are before or after each other. (*Ibid.*: 76)

The Hegelian element to Green's metaphysics is that the eternal consciousness, which is the self-organizing principle at the heart of his system, gradually realizes itself through the "society" of finite individuals. Our experience can be considered in one of two ways, which are not distinct but rather two ways of looking at the same thing: (a) as a series of modifications of our sensibility, that is, how our experienced world changes as a succession through time; and (b) as our consciousness of this succession, which is in itself outside this temporal succession. First, it is the series of phenomenal events and, second, it is the knowledge of such a succession. It is the difference between "perception" on the one hand and "conception" on the other. Green writes: "What we call our mental history is not a history of this consciousness, which in itself can have no history, but a history of the process by which the animal organism becomes its vehicle" (*ibid.*: 78). At the same time this consciousness is gradually becoming a vehicle for the eternal consciousness. It is through the animal organism that the eternal consciousness realizes itself and it is in this sense that the eternal consciousness and the finite consciousnesses form a unity. The knowledge that we strive to attain exists as part of the eternal consciousness, primarily as part of the eternal unchanging order of relations, and as we learn we attain true knowledge of this Absolute: "the attainment of knowledge is only explicable as a reproduction of itself, in the human soul, by the consciousness for which the cosmos of related facts exists – a reproduction of itself, in which it uses the sentient life of the soul as its organ" (*ibid.*: 83). Just like in the system of nature and our sensations, in this system of facts that constitutes knowledge, the facts cannot exist separately and distinct from one another; they too require a single uniting organizing principle, that is, the eternal consciousness.

Since consciousness exists in a sense "outside" time and becomes conscious of time, becoming and history by being itself outside time, human beings are "free causes" and thus capable of ethical actions. We distinguish ourselves as "selves" and by doing so exert our power as free causes. This is the result of the dual nature of our conscious activity: on the one side we perceive owing to the functions of our organic body and brain, but on the other side we are able to understand this activity as a historical series because we consciously perceive such a series outside of time. This is why, for Green, ethics is possible.

F. H. BRADLEY: APPEARANCE AND REALITY

F. H. Bradley was arguably the most respected and important of all the British idealist philosophers. His extraordinary work *Appearance and Reality* is an attempt to argue for the existence of a non-relational harmonious Absolute, *a priori* through a critique of relations, and *a posteriori* through our knowledge of immediate experience. While for Green relations are the foundation and the ground for the possibility of all reality, for Bradley, relations are merely appearance and do not possess the hallmark of the really real.

Bradley opens his *Appearance and Reality* by stressing the importance of the distinction between primary and secondary qualities: a distinction that, he claims, is essential for an adequate metaphysics. For Bradley, it is primary qualities alone that are truly real and secondary qualities are mere appearance. Secondary qualities such as colour, sound and heat are relative to the observer and so cannot be objectively real. However, the error of materialism has been to deny secondary qualities altogether, so that we are unable to talk about reality sensibly. Without secondary qualities we have no way of talking about primary qualities as we can only talk about extension as related to some organ, and thus far he agrees with Green. While secondary qualities are mere appearance, Bradley argues, the primary qualities cannot stand on their own. Appearances exist, he claims, and to deny this is nonsense; but these appearances and relations are a "beggarly show" of the truly real. Throughout the first book of *Appearance and Reality*, "Appearance", Bradley goes through a list of categories said to be essential for our phenomenal experience of reality and shows how these categories can only be appearance and not true reality. The proof of this relies on his denial of relations.

Relations and qualities are inseparable. Nowhere can you find a quality without a relation or vice versa. "Diversity without relation", Bradley tells us, "seems a word without meaning" (1930: 24). However, he also points out that relations and qualities combined lead to almost as much confusion. Two qualities together must be related; otherwise they are nothing. Yet, in order for a relation to connect two qualities, this relation itself must be truly something; otherwise it could have no function. It must be ontologically distinct from the quality. Again, if the relation is itself something it must be related to the two qualities, and for this we require two new relations. We will then need further relations to connect these new relations, and so on to infinity. Since our understanding of relations leads us towards an infinite regress, we can conclude that relations cannot be classed as fully real, and must therefore be mere appearance.

Bradley next assesses space and time, arguing that these too must be mere appearances and not reality. For space to be space it must consist of extended parts – spaces – which, in order to be anything substantial, must be related together; however, as we have seen, the theory of relations leads us into immediate contradictions. Bradley then assesses the Leibnizian theory that space is nothing but relations, which he rejects as absolute nonsense; if the parts that make up space are not spaces, then the result is not space. Time suffers from the same problem: Time "is a relation – and, on the other side, it is not a relation; and it is, again, incapable of being anything beyond a relation" (*ibid.*: 33). If time is merely a relation between singular units (moments) that have no duration of their own then the whole cannot possess duration. Duration cannot emerge from non-duration; if duration does belong to time and the individual units possess duration they cease to be units and become one. Again on Parmenidean bases, Bradley argues that the One cannot be said to possess duration so time is "helplessly dissolved" (*ibid.*: 34).

Following this, Bradley's critique takes a "practical" turn, focusing on what Kant, and Fichte after him, had identified as the centre of experience: the self. Instead of directly targeting either, Bradley tells us that he had heard somewhere a rumour that the final resting place for reality may well be the self: the one place capable of bringing order to the chaos outlined above. Whenever we try to characterize what the "self" is, we cannot deny that it in some sense exists; we all experience a self. However, Bradley asks us to examine exactly what this self is; the best definition of the self perhaps is that it is our habitual dispositions and internal contents. Bradley's problem with this definition emerges from the fact that these properties are not merely internal. The outward environment is just as essential to our "self" as our internal activities. Take the individual away from their friends, family and normal habitats and you will change their self beyond recognition. Thus, overturning Kant's "Copernican Revolution", Bradley argues that there is no essential self, since our physical and psychical elements change so much that to try to define where our essential characteristics end and our accidents begin is "a riddle without an answer" (*ibid.*: 68). "Personal" identity is merely a contingent and mutable collation of internal and external elements. For Bradley, there are no elements of the self that are eternally fixed and thus the self is too ambiguous and contradictory an entity for any concrete reality to be founded on.

> In whatever way the self is taken, it will prove to be appearance. It cannot, if finite, maintain itself against external relations. For these will enter its essence and so ruin its independency … The self is no doubt the highest form of experience which we have, but, for all that, is not a true form. It does not give us the facts as they are in reality; and, as it gives them, they are appearance, appearance and error.   (*Ibid.*: 103)

This is a momentous conclusion in that it dispels the commonly held view that all idealism is subjective idealism. It does so, moreover, at the cost of the Copernican Revolution Kant had inaugurated, which furnished the practical grounds for all subsequent philosophies of finitude. We shall return to this below. This does not, however, entail that the grounds of possible experience are similarly eliminated. Rather, it entails that the "self" is not the necessary condition of experience, as Kant had maintained, but rather an accident thereof.

In *Appearance and Reality*'s second book, "Reality", Bradley aims towards positive knowledge of the truly real. His criterion for ultimate reality, the Absolute, is that it must be free from contradictions. The validity of this criterion is proved by the fact that any attempt to argue anything contrary must assume the truth of the non-contradictory Absolute in order to begin. To doubt the harmonious Absolute, Bradley argues, is a logical impossibility. The real then possesses all of experience in harmony. Bradley expresses his panpsychist idealism explicitly when he claims that the true characteristic of the Absolute is that it is sentient experience.

> Find any piece of existence, take up anything that any one could possibly call a fact, or could in any sense assert to have being, and then judge if it does not consist in sentient experience. Try to discover any sense in which you can still continue to speak of it, when all perception and feeling have been removed; or point out any fragment of its matter, any aspect of its being which is not derived from and is not still relative to this source. When the experiment is made strictly, I can myself conceive of nothing else than the experienced. Anything, in no sense felt or perceived, becomes to me quite unmeaning. (*Ibid.*: 127–8)

Bradley is certainly not arguing here for any form of solipsism such that it would make reality a single subject's experience, for this would be to repeat the errors of the theories of self outlined above.[2] Reality is the one Absolute that *is* sentience; "it will hence be a single and all-inclusive experience which embraces every partial diversity in concord" (*ibid.*: 129).

Bradley continues his arguments for the insufficiency of appearance and concurrently the truth of the Absolute by asserting the existence of two sides of every observed existent: first, there is the "that", an existent; and second, the "what", the existent's content, its predicates. The ideas we form of an existent depend necessarily on our ideas of its "what", which must be torn loose from its "that"; without such a process thought would be able to make no distinctions at all. The predicates are a dissection of reality and could never possibly show the full reality of the predicated existent. This is because true reality must be free from all relations and thus there can be no true plurality in the unity of the Absolute, as such, we can never know the truth of any existent without knowing the entirety of the Absolute, a simple impossibility for finite consciousness. Thought, in order to be thought, must maintain the dualism between the "that" and the "what", for to transcend this dualism would be for finite consciousness to access the truth of the Absolute at the cost of thought itself. Bradley's commitment to this dualism ultimately undoes the Parmenidean heritage, therefore. The relational form is the essential foundation for thought but it must be remembered that it brings us towards appearance and not ultimate reality.

For Bradley, nature, *qua* the sum-total of individual things, is the product of finite sentience. The physical, unrelated to a finite sentient being, is not a possible actuality. He argues that when we widen our view of what sentience consists of there seems to be no reason why all of nature should not be in relation to some form of finite sentience. Our brains, which we do not perceive, may always be monitored by some faculty of sense of which we are not aware. The same is true of mountains and the other aspects of physicality that seem to precede human existence. Ultimately, it must be remembered that as corporeal, nature is created by finite sentience; it is just another aspect of the phenomenal world that is appearance and not reality. The body, being a part of the physicality of nature, obviously suffers this same fate. The sharp difference between Green and Bradley should here be apparent. For Green, materialism is a reductivist doctrine that discusses "abstractions" from the really real, but the "matter" that the materialists admit, he does not deny. The key point for Green is that matter requires an ontologically distinct organizing principle, his version of the Absolute, the eternal consciousness. However, Bradley is more straightforwardly anti-materialist. Matter is a beggarly show of the really real and it is "created" by *finite* sentience. Nature *is* real for Green while for Bradley it is mere appearance.

Bradley even goes as far as denying the reality of the soul, even if he maintains that it is far less unreal than the physical. It is a transcendental construction that somehow manages to maintain a form of "sameness" while continuing in time. The soul "transcends" the present, but as a consequence its "what" is a distorted version of its "that" and thus is riddled with inconsistency. This is made worse by the circularity of the fact that thought is produced by souls, which are at the same time made by thought. Also, the body depends on the thought of finite souls for its own creation. When discussing the relation between the body and the soul, Bradley claims that it is important to recognize that the physical body and the psychical soul form a causal unity that cannot be understood in separation. Thoughts do not cause other thoughts independent of the causal influence of bodies and the effectual influence on bodies and vice versa.

> The soul is never mere soul, and the body, as soon as ever the soul has emerged, is no longer bare body. And, when this is understood, we may assent to the physical origin of mind. But we must remember that the material cause of the soul will never be the whole cause. Matter is a phenomenal isolation of one aspect of reality. (*Ibid.*: 299)

With the idea of "aspects of reality", Bradley demonstrates his refusal to allow the productions of finite intellect be the ground of reality-as-appearance. So understood, matter is an isolated aspect of reality to the degree that it is corporeal and graspable by finite intellect or sense experience. The sensible qualities that we perceive are divergent from even those of our nearest neighbour; however, this is all to do with the "degrees of the absolute". The further from absolute reality we are, the more the qualities we perceive are the result of our idealized abstractions; if we were to rise to the heights of the Absolute then all variety would be transformed into the harmony of the One. Bradley's doctrine of degrees, which he claims is highly indebted to Hegel, is essential for an understanding of his Absolute. Bradley's Absolute has no degrees; it includes all and is completely harmonious. Truth and error also depend on the doctrine of degrees; nothing in appearance is absolutely true or absolutely false, but is a relative mixture of truth and falsity depending on how close or far the thing in question is from the Absolute. The more false a thing is, the more it is in need of redistribution in the Absolute, but all can be redistributed and dissolved into harmony. There is nothing that is absolute error. The Absolute is, and is nothing but, all of its appearances, which taken by themselves can only lead to contradiction; it is super-abundant so that all of the internal contradictions of the different elements of appearances are resolved. It has no history and never changes, yet it contains all the multiple histories that make up appearance. It makes no sense to say that the Absolute progresses as it has no seasons. Bradley, like Leibniz, defends a "best of all possible worlds hypothesis"; while there is much pain in our world, he believes that ultimately pleasure outweighs the pain and again pleasure and pain are resolved in the Absolute.

Finally, it is important to stress the importance that Bradley places on the "felt background" of all experience or *immediate experience* (Bradley uses feeling and immediate experience interchangeably). All finite experience depends on a felt background in which the opposition between self and not-self has not yet been formed. It is the self's connection with the whole of reality. It is this *feeling* that provides us with a "positive idea of non-relational unity" (*ibid.*: 470). While there is never a stage when experience is only immediate, immediate experience is never fully transcended; it always remains. Returning to the critique of relations, Bradley argues that our knowledge of objects is incomplete and any attempt to fulfil our knowledge with completion by its relations obviously leads to contradictions. No matter how all-inclusive this relational knowledge becomes, it is not complete until it is an "idea of a positive non-distinguished non-relational whole, which contains more than the object and in the end contains all that we experience" (1909: 62). This is our knowledge of immediate experience: the felt background that may never be transcended. Finite experience emerges from immediate experience and breaks up through its own imperfection as a finite centre; inner unrest gives birth to the self and the ego, both of which are never fully separated from the wider whole.

One of the most unsatisfactory elements of Bradley's discussion is that he cannot tell us how or why the finite souls are created from the Absolute and he cannot explain why or how the body and the soul are connected. He simply informs us that it is inexplicable and that the whole investigation would be hopeless. This is because both the soul and the bodies are not full realities: they are abstractions from the Absolute and as such they are filled with contradictions that make further exploration into their essence an impossible task, leaving us only to catalogue their appearances in "immediate experience" or "feeling". Bradley accepts the impossibility of a full system of metaphysics and claims that his knowledge of the Absolute must remain "miserably incomplete".

Bradley's metaphysics produces some alarming ethical consequences. Along with causality, time, space, nature and so on, he argues that goodness, religion and God (if he exists at all) must be mere appearance and not full reality. The Absolute is not a moral entity, so to ascribe to it moral characteristics such as "goodness" would be a grave error; there is nothing good or bad in the complete harmony of the Absolute. Like truth and falsity, good and bad are relative characteristics that are dissolved. Religion, too, is fiercely critiqued: "The man who has passed, however little, behind the scenes of the religious life, must have had his moments of revolt. He must have been forced to doubt if the bloody source of so many open crimes, the parent of such inward pollution can possibly be good" (1930: 393). Both religion and morality can only be stages of the good, and goodness is as contradictory as every other element of appearance. Either God can be merely an aspect of the Absolute, and as a consequence hardly worthy of the name God at all, or his existence is nullified completely. The Absolute is not God and while A. E. Taylor (1925) claimed that Bradley was an intensely religious man, this sense of religiousness never appears in *Appearance and Reality*. The only faith in Bradley's metaphysics is a faith in logic. The obvious critique of Bradley is that this presents us with an ethically dangerous vision of the world: one in which the pains and the sufferings of existence are brushed under the carpet of the harmonious Absolute. Bradley had already prepared his response to the moralist critique and argued that morality must not dictate to metaphysics without being prepared to listen to its response. If Green's metaphysics was constructed as prolegomena for a system of ethics, Bradley's system is a pure metaphysics and has no other goal. Metaphysical arguments must be regarded as good metaphysically, regardless of whether or not the ethics they seem to imply are satisfactory. Metaphysics is not and ought never to be ethics' handmaiden, but provides the problematics from which an ethics must be derived. This is what Bradley means when he argues that, "it is a moral duty to be non-moral" (1930: 386). He is not arguing that we must give up the virtuous life; he is arguing that Ethics must listen to Metaphysics before it proscribes its morality. While it is possible that Bradley's arguments may have frightening consequences for the ethicist, it cannot be for this reason alone that we choose to reject his arguments, nor can it furnish the ground for their refutation.

However, accepting Bradley's premises does not necessarily entail denying the existence of the good, as the contemporary idealist philosopher John Leslie argues (see ch. 15). Taking a staunchly Platonic line, Leslie argues that the virtue of the good is to exist, so that existence itself is good. Rather than eliminating the ethical, Leslie's programme therefore transforms the good from a differentiating predicate of individual actions or character into an ontological category: accordingly, evil is non-existence. For many, such revaluations invite scepticism; for others, the only possible ethics must be grounded in nature or in being, as they are, for example, in the work of Alistair MacIntyre and Alain Badiou. For others, such a grounding is delusional since we cannot reach behind the fact of our own finite existence, so that an "ethics of finitude" must precede and determine our metaphysics. The investigation of these alternatives is one of the most important of idealism's philosophical bequests.

10. PERSONAL IDEALISM: FROM WARD TO MCTAGGART

HEGEL AND PERSONALITY: FROM ABSOLUTE TO PERSONAL IDEALISM

Andrew Seth Pringle-Pattison[1] was the co-editor, with R. B. Haldane, of *Essays in Philosophical Criticism* (Seth & Haldane 1883), one of the foundational texts for Hegelian absolute idealism in British philosophy. Yet, four years later he would publish *Hegelianism and Personality*, an objection to absolutism on the grounds that it presents an insufficient treatment of the personal, thus giving birth to personal idealism. Pringle-Pattison claimed that the unification of consciousness in a single self was the radical error of both Hegelianism and the allied English doctrine of absolute idealism: "I have a centre of my own – a will of my own – which no one shares with me or can share, a centre which I maintain even in my dealings with God himself" (1887: 217).

Despite introducing personal idealism, Pringle-Pattison would distance himself from subsequent personal idealists, such as Ward and McTaggart, whom he regarded as putting *too much* emphasis on the personal and eventually putting God at risk. For Pringle-Pattison, reality must still be considered as a single rational whole. Nature, man and God form an organic whole, and none of these factors can be considered in isolation. Individual personalities are still incarnations of the Absolute, which, in turn, is God's eternal manifestation. Pringle-Pattison's views are perhaps better seen as a "halfway" house between absolute and personal idealism, which G. Watts Cunningham (1933) called "Personalistic Absolutism".

Personal idealism is an important, under-studied part of the history of British philosophy and was important for the development of emergentism, in the work of Conwy Lloyd Morgan and Samuel Alexander, as well as for process philosophy in Whitehead, George Santayana and George Herbert Mead. The first personal idealist we shall examine is James Ward.

JAMES WARD: THE REALM OF NATURE AND THE REALM OF ENDS

James Ward was trained as a scientist, published numerous articles on psychology (as well as several *Encyclopaedia Britannica* articles) but most of all he was a philosopher. He was particularly troubled by the relation between science and religion and was very critical of the epistemology of naturalism. Ward was also troubled by the tendency of psychology to be subjugated to physiology and his work on psychology was an attempt to separate the two. He stressed the importance of maintaining the distinction between inter-subjective public experience and private individual consciousness and argued that it was the latter that should be the subject matter for psychology. Central to Ward's notion of psychology was the idea of activity, which he believed was the fundamental principle underlying all experience. While the notion of activity was being introduced into psychology through Alexander Bain's work on physiological brain processes, Ward's main influence was Leibniz and his monads. His method was to start from that which he believed we are: *conative, cognitive subjects* in a world that consists of nothing other than an indefinite number of such subjects. As A. H. Murray (1937) points out, Ward's psychology is actually closer to phenomenology, except that Ward's phenomenology is not the be all and end all of his philosophy, but rather the starting point for his investigations into metaphysics.

Ward was highly critical of naturalism, but we would be wrong to interpret Ward as an anti-naturalist as Bradley was. Naturalism, for Ward, is the form of philosophy practised by scientists and epistemologists who present the mechanistic worldview as an exhaustive account of reality. Mechanism leads towards a philosophical agnosticism. Ward was well trained in science and was not critical of science *per se*, but rather of the tendency of scientists to stretch beyond the jurisdiction of their discipline and to make excessive philosophical claims without properly examining the epistemology that underlies those claims. The problem with the mechanist worldview is that it is only a partial view of reality; it presents us with a world of inert particles devoid of free agency. However, when we observe the world of history we become aware of a very different side of existence:

> The individuals of the historical world have characteristics the diametrical opposites of all this. They remember the past, they anticipate the future, and have thus a sense of their own identity – an identity, however, which would mean nothing if it were but the stark dead permanence of the physical atom, whose ceaseless motions are externally determined, but which itself does nothing and suffers nothing. (Ward 1927: 240)

Using Leibniz's distinction between the truths of reason and the truths of fact, Ward tells us that we must see that the truths of history are the real truths of fact, while the truths of science are only truths of reason. Of course, these truths of reason are undeniably important, but they must not be confused with the truths of fact necessary to make claims for an all-inclusive cosmology. Mechanism's undeniable appeal is its ability to bring knowledge under the simplicity of mathematical forms, which some may argue are as close as we can get to the intuitions of the deity; however, this perspective is somewhat limited. Human experience, for instance, expresses much more than mere mathematical relations: "while it is impossible from the standpoint of Nature to reach Spirit, it is only from the standpoint of Spirit that Nature can be understood: in a word we take the universe to be spiritual – a realm of ends" (1911: 431). Ward's Hegelian historicism leads him to an alternative worldview: not Hegel's Absolute, but rather Leibniz's monadology. In agreement with Leibniz, he believed that the *kinematics* of the mechanists must be grounded by a metaphysics, a spiritualist *dynamics*.

Ward (1915: v) labelled his philosophy a "spiritualistic monism" in order to place his work in opposition to materialist monism; however, a more appropriate title, that would emphasize the differences between his own position and absolutism, would be "spiritualistic monadism". Ward rejects absolute idealism for its picture of a static universe and its failure to understand activity as the essential condition for all of reality: he sees no reason why the "realm of ends" should be out of time. The interaction of finite centres, which Bradley admits in his system as only appearances, are in fact the fundamental constituents of reality. For Ward, the absolutism of Green and Bradley was reached by a process of anti-sensationalist abstraction just as severely limited as that of the naturalists. Bradley's approach to the Absolute through pure thought was, according to Ward, merely a form of logical sophistry. He argued that the empirical must come first in our philosophical investigations and the first true fact of all experience is that subjective existence is always related to an objective "Other". To be a subject without relation to the Other is to not be a subject at all. As there is no way to transcend this dualism, Bradley's Absolute, in which all plurality disappears, must, by his own strictures, be a myth and not reality.

The primacy of activity combined with the inescapable subject–object dualism of experience led Ward to develop a form of Leibnizian monadism: the world must be composed of what he referred to as "conative agents", that is, a plurality of substances endowed with activity and purposive aim. Determinate agents come first and our world emerges from their action and interaction. Each conative individual perseveres to conserve its own being as well as aiming towards betterment; in addition each individual monad is unique. The diversity and constant change observable in our world are the result of the effort of each monad striving for existence, and contingency emerges from the monads' cross-purpose interactions. Ward's monadology differs from Leibniz's in that he discards the doctrine of pre-established harmony but allows the monads windows in recompense. Novelty emerges from the interaction of monads not from the pre-programming of God. The "background-independence" of the monadological framework means that there can be no laws prior to the monads themselves. The only law determining a monad's behaviour is its individual appetition. A monad's original spontaneity is governed by its mutual interaction with every other monad and consequently temporary habits are formed. This means that the laws of nature that physicists seek must merely be the statistical averages of habits formed by monadic interactions. Ward claims that while the statistician is aware of the deviations underneath his aggregates, the physicist is blind to this fact and treats his abstractions as if they are realities.

In the exposition of his metaphysical system, Ward quotes Tennyson's "one far off divine event to which the whole creation moves"; it is important to note that by this he simply means that the community of monads is lured by progress – the Platonic "Idea of the Good". He is certainly not arguing that the whole of reality has been written out in advance and that the world is gradually unfolding towards a final perfection. Such talk is for him "reprehensible". While Leibniz's monadic world was an unfolding of God's pre-established harmony, in Ward's monadology progress and novelty emerge through epigenesis. His appeal to epigenesis means that he is critical of any talk of "potential" and argues that reality is entirely actuality. Real contingency is absolutely essential for progress and novelty. The new, Ward claims, is always the result of a creative synthesis. Ward's knowledge of biology means that his work is informed by examples from the sciences, which he uses to back up his arguments. Accordingly, in order to highlight the contingency inherent in evolution, he tells us that:

> The feathers of the bird are homologous to, i.e. genetically connected with, the lizard's scales: The subsequent modification of those attached to the wings and tail so as to subserve flight has no connexion with the original functions of feathers as a dermal covering, which remains their sole function for the most part. It is just to the coincidence of their plasticity with the new conditions of nascent bird life that their development is to be attributed.
>
> (1911: 83)

One of the key reasons why mechanism is such a poor description of our world is that it is necessarily reversible and thus cannot account for the chance occurrences that suddenly and unpredictably change the course of history.

While mechanism can be reversed, life and experience can never be. Creative synthesis produces actualities that are far more than the sum of their parts. Holding on to both the principle of continuity and the principle of creative synthesis means that we have a far better method of explanation than mechanism.

Ward's monadism is an objective continuum of individual yet interrelated monads that differentiate and develop both through their own appetitions and their relations with other monads. Monads vary greatly in their degree of development, and Ward appeals to Leibniz's distinction between confused and distinct perceptions to describe this development. At the lowest level, a monad in its most confused state will merely strive for a purely egoistic preservation; however, certain monads through their interrelations and strivings will obtain higher levels of perception and therefore possess and control larger areas of the environment. The reciprocal relationships formed through processes of evolution lead to higher-grade monadic perceptions and differentiations. As biology can account for the evolution of our bodies, sociology can account for the evolution of our human reason. It is the epigenetic result of "inter-subjective" intercourse.

Despite Ward's claim that human nature is continuous with animal nature, he highlights human nature as supposedly the height of all progress. Monads start as purely egoistic and it is only in human nature, he claims, that we get the real possibility of altruism. In *The Realm of Ends* he recalls learning the truth of the animal kingdom at an early age when he witnessed his three pet rabbits merrily prancing around seconds before being killed and devoured by a snake, which showed not the slightest remorse for having just murdered his childhood pets. The law of the animal kingdom is that "might is right": the guiding principle of natural selection. At the human level we have the possibility of justice or what he presciently calls "rational selection", which operates at the level of species: the possibility of a community of inter-subjective values is not available to non-human animals. Kant's distinction between judgements of perception and judgements proper is key here. Judgements of perception are the judgements that are as close as possible to being individual and as far away as possible from inter-subjectivity. The judgements made by very young children and lower animals are Ward's examples. Proper judgement is the result of inter-subjective intercourse and social development is dependent on this process from the former to the latter. For Ward, this is the Hegelian[2] "progress" from nature to spirit.

Ward's Hegelianism is most overt in his discussions of social development. He argues that we can think of society as an organism with an objective mind. This objective mind is not a transcendent $n + 1$, functioning over and above its individual members, but rather "the informing spirit immanent in the whole" (1911: 121). It is through the unity of society's contributing members that the individuals are able to rise to a higher state of reason, a higher unity. Acknowledging that a given social organism may be far from fully developed, he remains optimistic that the tendency towards betterment characteristic of each monad will result in a gradual progress of reason, through which we may become masters of our own fate, overcome our egoistic impulses and look towards the accomplishment of perfection, whereby a Kantian accord of the wills of the many and of the one will arise.

While his own philosophy could reasonably be called pluralistic, Ward claimed that the pluralist perspective was incomplete and would achieve adequacy only if completed by a theism. The problem is that without theism, a pluralist cosmology is merely a totality and can never be a unity. However, the definite progress that Ward believes evolution has shown must be seen as the unified aim of the universe towards the Idea of the Good. Ward's God, then, is at the same time immanent to the world and also its transcendent creator who has limited himself by creating the world. He is both the creative Idea and the medium through which the monads interact. Critically it could be argued that Ward has created another Absolute as ground and merely repeated the absolutists, yet he argues: "If God is the ground of the world at all he is its ground always as an active, living, interested, Spirit, not as a merely everlasting, changeless and indifferent centre, round which it simply whirls" (*ibid.*: 447). Ward's monadology is at all times undeniably Hegelian: the Absolute is not the beginning and end, as in Bradley's metaphysics, but, rather than rejected, it becomes teleological, securing advance by the inachievability of its perfectability.

While Ward considers his philosophy to belong to the empiricist tradition, it is highly speculative, combining empiricist epistemology with Leibnizian–Hegelian–Platonic metaphysics. That the world is gradually progressing towards the Idea of the Good is always liable to empirical counter-examples: rationality leads equally to civilized and barbaric consequences, to social creativity and the destruction of nature. Accordingly, Ward's theism may seem little more than an inexcusable *deus ex machina* thrown in at the end of his cosmology to try to make ends meet. Yet his is neither the first nor last to attempt this. Ward's work is a fascinating conjunction of biology and sociology, of Platonism and science, and his concerns are each indicative of paths taken by earlier and later idealists. His work on creative synthesis and the irreversibility of contingent events could serve as focal points for much current philosophical and scientific research. Not an anti-naturalist in the contemporary sense, Ward would find himself in agreement with many of the non-reductive naturalists of today.

JOHN MCTAGGART ELLIS MCTAGGART: LOVE AND THE C-SERIES OF TIME

In certain respects John McTaggart Ellis McTaggart[3] was closer to Bradley than to either Ward or Pringle-Pattison. McTaggart held a very high opinion of Bradley and doubted whether any of the professed Hegelians understood the "secret of Hegel" as well as he did. Like Bradley, McTaggart denied the reality of time and the physical basis of sense experience, defending an eternal Absolute. Yet he differed from Bradley on two major points: the reality of the individual and the reality of relations. McTaggart classified himself as a personal idealist against Hegel's failure to emphasize the "individuality of the individual" (1901: 4), which, McTaggart argues, is one of the major problems of his cosmology since individuality is properly consequent on his logic. Notwithstanding this criticism, McTaggart wrote three important but unconventional works on Hegel's philosophy. His *Studies in the Hegelian Dialectic* (1896) argued that while Hegel's logic is extremely valuable, his application of that logic is not. In consequence, *Studies in Hegelian Cosmology* (1901) attempts to repair the flaws in these applications and to argue for conclusions he claimed must follow from Hegel's logic, particularly as concern the theory of the absolute Idea.

McTaggart argues that differentiation and multiplicity are much more important to Hegel's Absolute than is usually acknowledged. Eternal spirit must be eternally differentiated into finite selves. The very meaning of the unity of the absolute Idea is its differentiation into a plurality and the very meaning of the plurality is its combination into unity. Neither unity nor individuality is subordinate to the other; both are *for* the other. As the Absolute is timeless, perfect and made up of finite selves, no self could ever perish as this would break from the unity of the absolute and change its entire formation. McTaggart was critical of the personal idealists, who argued that the self was an emergent property. Thus, reviewing Pringle-Pattison's *The Idea of Immortality* (1922), he argued that such a view "would suggest the self is an activity of the body, and that the brain produces thought as the liver produces bile – which would be materialism without a thin disguise" (McTaggart 1923: 222). Rather, McTaggart places the self at the apex of his metaphysical system. The self is not an attribute of the Absolute but rather *is* the Absolute in its connection with every other immortal self.

McTaggart's personal idealism presents the Absolute as the organic interdependent community of selves, but the Absolute itself, he argued vehemently, is not personal. It must be addressed as an "it" and certainly not a "he". While the Absolute is the organic unity of a cosmic society of selves, this does not make it a person: "Moreover, if the Absolute is to be called a person because it is a spiritual unity, then every College, every goose-club, every gang of thieves, must also be called a person" (1901: 86). This is also one of McTaggart's reasons for his atheism. If the Absolute is not personal, then there is no place for the existence of the omnipresent God of traditional theism.

McTaggart's *magnum opus*, *The Nature of Existence* (1921, 1927), was the culmination of his life's work and the rational defence for his metaphysics of mysticism. It is an extremely dense and tightly woven logical work. He was critical of the inductive method, and his own method is largely *a priori*; however, he does begin his investigation from two appeals to perception, which he defends on the basis that both conclusions can be established from any singular perception. First, he establishes that "something exists", claiming that the attempt to assert that something does not exist is self-refuting. From any single perception, then, we can be sure of existence.[4] Second, McTaggart argues that there is a whole that is differentiated into a plurality of parts. While this could be proved *a priori*, it can again be proved by a single perception, which immediately perceives that things must have qualities as well as existence in order to be perceivable at all. Whatever possesses qualities also non-possesses numerous qualities and McTaggart argues that non-possession is also positive in that it continues to add to our knowledge of the particular substance. A circle is not a square and not a bird, and so forth. It is owing to the positive nature of non-possession that McTaggart is able to argue that every existent possesses as many qualities as there are positive qualities.

After qualities, relations must also exist. While, as we have seen, Bradley famously denied the reality of relations, McTaggart sides with Green in their favour. In an ontology of plural substances, relations are essential. Even in a solipsist universe where only I exist there would still be relations; I could neither love nor hate myself without relations. I cannot doubt relations without there being a relation between myself – the doubter – and my doubt. McTaggart claims that the main reason for the denial of relations is the claim that there is nowhere for relations to exist. The reason why this argument is invalid is because it treats relations as if they were qualities and assumes they would behave in the same way. When relations cannot behave in this way, it leads some to assume that they do not therefore exist. Relations, McTaggart argues, do not exist "in" substances in the same way that qualities do, but "between"[5] qualities. He argues that this conclusion is undeniably valid owing to the impossibility of stating anything without at once asserting the reality of both qualities and relations. Substance, quality and relation are all indispensable for McTaggart's account of existence.

From this theory of qualities and relations, McTaggart argues that there can be no two substances that possess exactly the same characteristics.[6] This argument is very similar to Leibniz's principle of the "identity of indiscernibles" but differs in that for Leibniz every substance must differ through its qualities, while McTaggart sees no reason why substances must necessarily possess different qualities; what is essential is that the *relations* differ. He could walk through Princess Sophie's garden, find two leaves alike, yet not disprove the principle owing to the differences in the two otherwise identical leaves' relations. McTaggart also took issue with the name of Leibniz's principle, claiming that it was misleading. The principle does not discuss identical indiscernibles but rather diverse dissimilars, so that the principle would be better called "the dissimilarity of the diverse". Given the dissimilarity of the diverse every property must have both an "exclusive description" and a "sufficient description". Exclusive description merely highlights the identifiable quality that isolates the substance from any other, for example "the father of Henry VIII" is an exclusive description of "Henry VII", while "the father of a sovereign" would be only a description and not an exclusive one. A sufficient description is a description that refers to the substance alone in purely general terms without using any proper names. The use of the name "Henry VIII" means that it cannot be a sufficient description. Fingerprints, as Geach (1979) notes, would be a clear example of any human being's "sufficient description". Every substance must have both an exclusive description and a sufficient description because an exclusive description alone would lead to infinite regress, having always to refer to additional entities. Since exclusive descriptions lead to regress, it is sufficient descriptions that are essential. A particular must be capable of a sufficient description without recourse to a vicious regress otherwise it could not exist at all. It is worth quoting McTaggart's defence of the importance of sufficient description in full:

> A must be dissimilar to all other substances. The possibility of this depends on the existence of B, and the existence of B depends on its dissimilarity from all other substances. And this depends on the existence of C, and this on its dissimilarity to all other substances, and so on. If this series is infinite, it is vicious. For starting from the existence of A, each earlier term requires all the later terms, and therefore requires that the series should be completed, which it cannot be. If, therefore, the series is infinite, A cannot be dissimilar to all other substances – cannot, in other words, have an exclusive description – and so cannot exist. Therefore, if A does exist, the series cannot be infinite. And if the series is not infinite, A has a sufficient description. Every substance, therefore, must have a sufficient description. (1921: 108)[7]

The many dissimilar existents that make up McTaggart's ontology are all connected into a single unity: the universe. It is clear that there must be a single substance of which all others are part, and the principle of the dissimilarity of the diverse can be used to prove that there can be only one universe. For if there were two, they would possess the same content and could not be given a sufficient description. The universe is the sufficient description of the one substance of which all others are a part. This universe is an organic unity, in which all of its parts are essential to the whole. The relations that exist between substances are of two kinds: "intrinsic" and "extrinsic". Intrinsic "determinations" exist whenever there is a necessary connection between two substances. If there is always an X whenever there is a Y, then X and Y are related by intrinsic determination. If Y and X were not necessarily related then they would be contingently determined. However, in McTaggart's ontology every substance is related to every other through the process of "extrinsic determination", as all substances are related owing to the unity of the whole. If the nature of any substance changed it would change the nature of its relations to its surrounding substances, which would in turn change the relations of every other substance and change the whole.[8] All substances and their characteristics are bound together, through extrinsic determination, into what he calls a single, "block universe". The key objection to this type of "block" universe, he argues, is that it would be unpleasant and destructive to morality, reducing contingency to nothing. To this McTaggart responds without concern: "We have only to note that, if the absence of contingency is an evil, it is an evil which is inevitable and universal" (*ibid.*: 155).

McTaggart's block universe is necessarily one in which there can be no simple substances, that is, substances that are parts without being wholes. Every substance has content, a multiplicity of characteristics. This can be easily demonstrated by an object's existence in time. My pen possesses a different system of relations with every passing moment owing to its existence in temporal succession and the changes due to extrinsic determination. Even if time is not real, as McTaggart famously argues it is not, the appearance of time does in fact exist, so changes in relation are real even if time ultimately is not. He argues that even though Leibniz claimed that monads were simple substances, he did in fact reject simple substances. A monad's perceptions are its parts and these perceptions are of every other monad perceiving the world. A monad, then, is as far from simple as can possibly be.

McTaggart's denial of simple substances puts his theory at risk of infinite regress: "If every substance has parts, then every substance has an unending series of sets of parts, then each part in any set will be a substance which has parts, and the parts of the parts will form a fresh set of parts of the original whole" (*ibid.*: 183). This is undeniably an infinite series, but infinite series are not necessarily vicious, and McTaggart attempts to show that this is not a vicious regress through his theory of primary wholes and determining correspondence. In order to prevent the regress from being vicious there must be, in the universe, a primary substance and its primary parts, the rest of the universe being the result of their correspondence. The finite series that contains parts of the primary whole enter into relations of determining correspondence,[9] which intrinsically determine the existence of the infinite secondary characteristics that emerge from the relations to each other formed by the primary parts. *A*'s characteristics *B* and *C* perceive both themselves (*BB* & *CC*) and each other (*BC* & *CB*) which then form *BBC*, *CCB*, *BCB* and *CBC* and so on to infinity. The sufficient descriptions of the primary wholes are determined by their relations to each other, which imply sufficient descriptions of their emergent members without including them. The emergence of new qualities and relations is infinite but a regress is avoided owing to the possibility of a sufficient description of each new member.

After, in volume 1 of *The Nature of Existence*, McTaggart has established, for the most part deductively, what must exist, volume 2 introduces the empirical and investigates the divergence between what appears and what is actually real. He develops his destructive arguments for the denial of time and matter and argues for the probability that what exists ultimately is a community of spirits.

McTaggart's denial of time is the most famous element of his metaphysics and continues to this day to be the starting point of all discussions regarding the metaphysics of time. He starts his discussion by arguing that there are two series of time that must be essential to time if time is real. First there is the set of temporal positions, which run from the past, to the present and to the future. This is the A-series. In the A-series an event will first be in the future, will then become present and finally will become part of the past. In addition to this series it is necessary that there be a second set – the B-series – in which events are earlier or later than each other in temporal succession without reference to the present. This series is permanent. The Second World War will have always occurred after the First World War and this will never change. According to McTaggart we never observe any event in time without it involving both series. Despite the permanent nature of the B-series, it is dependent on the A-series and without the A-series time could not exist. No movement could ever occur in the B-series alone as its events are temporally static. They are earlier or later, but they do not change.

McTaggart uses the example of the death of Queen Anne to illustrate this point. The fact of the death of Queen Anne does not change, and at the very final moment in time it would still be the death of Queen Anne. The only one respect in which there has been change in the event of the death of Queen Anne is that: "It was once an event in the far future. It became an event in the nearer future. At last it was present. Then it became past, and will always remain past, though every moment it becomes further and further past" (1927: 13). Therefore, the only reason that the death of Queen Anne has been an event in time is because of its existence in the A-series. If the A-series is real then even the past changes, because the past is constantly travelling further and further away from the present, but without the A-series, nothing would change at all.[10]

The B-series depends on the A-series and cannot exist without it, for the categories of the B-series – "earlier" and "later" – depend on temporality that exists only if the A-series exists. If the A-series turns out not to be real then the B-series cannot be real either and time must not exist. McTaggart then goes on to prove the unreality of the A-series and thus the unreality of time.

Past, present and future are not qualities but rather relations, and if anything can be called any of the three then it must be something outside the time-series connected to it through its relation. Past, present and future are necessarily incompatible terms and an event cannot be past and present, or past and future and so on without undermining the whole meaning of the individual terms. The contradiction of the A-series becomes apparent when we realize that every event possesses all three relations: it is future, it will be present and then will become past. McTaggart writes that obviously the critic of his argument will argue that by stating this argument the solution is immediately apparent: *it is*, *it will be* and *it will become* are the essential terms here – an event is all three successively *not* simultaneously. However, and this is the crux of the argument, this gives birth to a vicious regress, because it assumes the A-series in order to account for the A-series. We are arguing that X will be Y at a moment of future time, X will be Y at a moment of present time and then Y at a moment of past time, but this "moment" is itself part of the temporal series that is future, will be present and will become past. We must then assume another A-series to account for the A-series we have already introduced to account for the original temporal succession. This regress must then go on to infinity.

> The attribution of the characteristics past, present and future to the terms of any series leads to a contradiction, unless it is specified that they have them successively. This means, as we have seen, that they have them in relation to terms specified as past, present and future. These again, to avoid a like contradiction, must in turn be specified as past, present, and future. And, since, this continues infinitely, the first set of terms never escapes from contradiction at all. (1927: 22)

McTaggart then claims he has disproved the reality of the A-series and consequently the B-series. However, he does not deny that what appears as time is a real series. The series we really perceive is the C-series, which contains all the reality we observe; however, it does not contain the realities in temporal succession. We never perceive the C-series, but we can infer its existence from our misperceptions of its elements as a B-series. He claims, thus, that this puts his argument in line with Hegel who argued that the time-series was a distorted reflection of something real at the heart of the true timeless Absolute.

After denying the reality of time, McTaggart goes on to prove that matter too must be appearance and not reality. Matter is an illusion because it fails the test of determining correspondence as outlined above. To be fundamental to reality, matter must be analysable in terms of a primary whole containing a series of primary parts that correspond to each other, from which the rest of reality emerges; but what could these primary parts be? McTaggart first explores non-spatial qualities such as colour. Let us imagine one primary part, *red*, in correspondence with another, *blue*. If they corresponded with each other their relationship would entail that they would be both red and blue, which is contradictory, as the mixture would result in neither. The problem would be similar for any other quality and the problem is further exacerbated when we consider the combination of different types of qualities. For example, how could different flavours relate to different colours? Introducing non-spatial qualities as primary parts cannot possibly work. Spatial qualities such as size and shape are equally contradictory because they always relate to their position to the whole, and as substance is infinitely divisible, the whole is an infinite series. The sufficient description of a primary spatial part would be impossible without a description of a last term of a series that has no last term. The only option for spatial sufficient description is that it would have to be described by its relation to non-spatial qualities and, as we have already established, these cannot be the primary parts from which reality emerges.

McTaggart's denial of matter leads him to the conclusion that the only substance capable of meeting the requirements for both sufficient description and determining correspondence is spirit. He defines spirit as that quality which contains the content of selves, and the content of selves is perceptions. Like Bradley, he denies the possibility of any form of experience not involving a self. He also denies the fundamental reality of matter, so selves cannot emerge from matter; selves must therefore be fundamental. All of the primary parts of the primary whole must be selves: selves capable of perceiving each other's perceptions.[11] Each self is capable of a unique perception of each other self and each of the parts of each other self. *A* perceives *B*, *B* perceives *B*, and *C* perceives *B*, but owing to the differences in the intensity or tone of each perception, each perception can be unique to the percipient. Therefore, these unique perceptions are capable of bringing forth sufficient descriptions of each percipient self. These perceptions also bring forth novel perceptions *AB*, *BB*, *BC*, which can then be perceived by the percipients bringing forth further novel perceptions *AAB*, *BBB*, *BCC*, and so on to infinity. The parts of the percipients, the primary parts of the primary whole, are perceptions that can then bring forth further series of parts within parts and the series is capable of extending towards infinity. It therefore enacts determining correspondence. McTaggart accepts that this is not positive proof of the reality of spirit; there could be another possible substance of which as yet we know nothing and this substance may be capable of producing reality through the process of determining correspondence. However, as we currently have no knowledge of any other possible substance, he can assume that spirit is the ultimate reality. Unlike matter, then, spirit is logically capable of existence, if its parts are nothing except perceptions.

In our present experience we are only capable of perceiving other selves indirectly; McTaggart assumes that given the conclusions above, in absolute reality percipients would be able to perceive each other directly. This direct knowledge of others, he argues, would be emotional in tone and the only emotion present would be love. This is the crux of McTaggart's work, and it is the point towards which the whole of the complex logical architecture in *The Nature of Existence* has been aiming. For McTaggart, the truth of the Absolute is love: the intense, passionate liking for other selves.

> When *B* loves *C*, he feels that he is connected with him by a bond of peculiar strength and intimacy – a bond stronger and more intimate than any other by which two selves can be joined. In present experience, as we said above, our knowledge of any other self is never perception, and is reached through double mediation. Yet there are times when the intimacy of the relation in love is felt to be scarcely less than the intimacy of a man's relation with his own self. (1927: 150–51)

This love in the Absolute would be of incredible intensity as the life of every percipient would be dependent on its love towards others and its love from other percipients. There is nothing outside this love and therefore love is supreme in its power.

The distinction between the absolute reality and the reality of everyday appearance returns us to McTaggart's discussion of time in which the appearance of the B-series is really the C-series misperceived as existing in time. Our erroneous perceptions of this series lead us to believe in the temporal and infer the existence of matter. The fundamental nature of the B-series is its transitive asymmetrical relation from earlier to later and this directly corresponds to what McTaggart believes is the fundamental nature of the C-series: a similar asymmetrical relation that moves from inclusive to more inclusive. All of our perceptions are included in the C-series and the amount of error involved in our perceptions depends on the position of our perception in this series. The final term in the C-series will be all-inclusive, it will be infinite rather than finite and will be free from the errors of erroneous perception.

> The last stage of the *C* series of any self is at the same point in the *C* series with the last stage of the *C* series of all other selves, and so of the *C* series of the universe as a whole. And therefore, *sub specie temporis*, the last stage of the *B* series of any self is at the last point of time of the *B* series of every other self, and so of the *B* series of the universe as a whole. There is no time which is later than the last stage in the life of any self, and therefore the last term in the life of every self does not end. (*Ibid.*: 374)

The final stage of the C-series is infinite, eternal and unbounded, and a state of great good. The most important fact about the future, McTaggart claims, is that this state of infinite goodness must one day be reached. Unlike Ward, he does not argue that we witness consistent progress; rather, we perceive constant oscillations between good and bad, happiness and unhappiness, but what he does argue is that this evil is only passing and there is a future where it will exist no more (*ibid.*: 479). This future is the future of the goodness of love. This future cannot be reached alone but only through the harmony of all other selves; it can be reached as a united community or not at all.

> We should find ourselves in a world composed of nothing but individuals like ourselves. With these individuals we should have been brought into the closest of all relations, we should see them, each of them, to be rational and righteous. And we should know that in and through these individuals our own highest aims and ends were realised. What else does it come down to? To know another person thoroughly, to know that he conforms to my highest standards, to feel that through him the end of my own life is realised – is this anything but love? (1901: 260)

11. NATURALIST IDEALISM: BERNARD BOSANQUET

BERNARD BOSANQUET AND SPECULATIVE PHILOSOPHY

The philosophy of Bernard Bosanquet suffers from the assumption that his is merely a pale imitation of the Bradleyan metaphysics of which he was an acknowledged disciple. Even on those rare occasions when this assumption is challenged, and Bosanquet's differences from Bradley are pursued,[1] the differences in question emphasize Bosanquet's ethical and political concerns, and thus falsely elevate the self to the summit of his metaphysics. In part, it is this ethicist interpretation of Bosanquet's contribution to philosophy – a perspective he condemns as "one sided" (1921: 100–101) – that is responsible for the continuing renown of his *The Philosophical Theory of the State* (1923b), which is generally considered his most significant philosophical work. Ethical concerns are certainly not alien to Bosanquet's philosophy. His Gifford Lectures for 1912, *The Value and Destiny of the Individual* (1923a), for example, are expressly concerned with the finite individual in the "vale of soul-moulding". Yet soul-moulding must be understood as following from the "bodily basis of mind" and the evolutionary adaptations forced upon it, as theorized in his Gifford Lectures of the previous year, *The Principle of Individuality and Value* (1912). It is in this work that Bosanquet's primary philosophical concerns are worked out, and his differences from Bradley made most clear, especially as regards the philosophy of nature and the "bodily basis of mind" (1912: 160–61), on the one hand, and the reality of appearances, on the other. It is, however, in *The Meeting of Extremes* (1921) that Bosanquet best characterizes his philosophy as the union of realism and idealism that he calls *speculative philosophy*. In this regard, as we shall see, Bosanquet is closer to Ward or Whitehead's "realist idealism" than to Bradley. In what follows, we shall therefore elaborate the character of Bosanquet's speculative philosophy by concentrating equally on its naturalism and its underpinning idealist metaphysics.

PHILOSOPHY OF NATURE

As we have seen Bradley considers nature to be appearance, and, to that extent, not reality. His arguments are effectively directed against any account of nature that "fall[s] outside of all mind" (1930: 231). Bosanquet, by contrast, is an insistent naturalist: "What governs thought and finds utterance in its coherence is, as I hold, simply the nature of things" (1921: 176); everything positive in mind is drawn from nature (1912: 367). He criticizes Bradley's conception of metaphysics as solely discursive,[2] because it refuses to allow for thought as part of the reality it describes. As Bradley writes, "You are led to take the physical world as a mere adjective of my body, and you find that my body, on the other hand, is not one whit more substantival" (1930: 236). On this basis, thought would have to remain ultimately external to reality and, moreover, to a *physical being*, the reality of which the consistent Bradleyan would have to deny. Hence Bosanquet's response: "the nature of external objects is continuous with that of the stuff of mind, and is physical, i.e. has variations relative to those of other objects, as well as psychical" (1911: vol. 2, 309).

Where, then, Bosanquet joins Bradley in criticizing any conception of "nature as mere externality", it is not externality to mind, but rather to system, to organization, that Bosanquet rejects. Accordingly, Bradley's critical conception of nature as it falls outside mind reflects a particular conception of nature for which the concept "externality" plays a vital role. That conception of nature in which it is thought as externality with respect to organization is *mechanism*: "With the externality of Nature is bound up the conception of Mechanism. The essence of it is that the world consists of elements, complete in themselves, and yet determined in relation to elements beyond them" (Bosanquet 1912: 73). Bosanquet's response is not to deny the reality of externality. Indeed, going somewhat against the grain of British Hegelianism, he invokes Hegel in support of the necessity of externality: "Matter, the externality of things to things, was to Hegel, for example, a necessary way of being in which one great characteristic of the universe found its indispensable expression" (Bosanquet 1913: 9).

That externality's rights are guaranteed means that, unlike Bradley, Bosanquet has no need to deny any ascription of real existence to a physical universe exceeding finite mind's capacity to perceive it; mountain formation is beyond any percipient's capacity to witness, but is nonetheless a real and necessary process. Nor, however, does this mean that Bosanquet is prepared to conclude his entire philosophy of nature with the mechanical externality of element to element. As we noted, mechanism consists in the thesis that there are self-enclosed elements that are "*yet* determined in relation to elements beyond them"; the fact of such determining relations demonstrates that nature consists in arrangements or organizations of such elements. How these organizations come about is the work of natural selection: "For us natural selection means the operation of a realm of externality in modelling its responsive centre, and thereby coming alive itself in a partial individuality which represents it" (1923a: 75).

In summary, as Clifford Barrett notes, Bosanquet not only refuses "to reduce the physical world to nothing more than objects or contents or states of any conscious mind", but adds to this the evolutionary dimension whereby "human knowers … com[e] late in the evolutionary development, and … depend upon an environment external to their own existence, and upon their own highly organized physical bodies" (1933: 423–4).

Mind is not, therefore, alien to nature, but arises from the complex nature of physical bodies. Bosanquet's realism is clear from his insistence on "the bodily basis of mind" (1912: 160–61),[3] that is, the nervous system; but his idealism is evident from his thesis that mind has as its function the focusing of the world into unity: "Mind has nothing of its own but the active form of totality; everything positive it draws from Nature" (*ibid*.: 367). The question is whether this form of totality is imposed on the real world as something alien to it, or whether it is the totality *of* that world. This is a question concerning the real nature of coherence, on the one hand, and the meaning of the law of non-contradiction, on the other.

LOGIC AND REALITY IN SPECULATIVE PHILOSOPHY

Bosanquet shared with the realist philosophers of his time,[4] especially Samuel Alexander,[5] the denial of the unreality of appearances. While for the realists this amounted "to order man and mind to their proper place among *the world of finite things*"(Bosanquet 1921: vi), according to a "minimum" conception of thought's contribution to that reality, for Bosanquet himself it meant that the reality that is the totality of *all* there is includes thought at its maximum (see Bosanquet 1917a). While he was therefore fond of citing Hegel's dictum that "the true is the whole" (1977b: 10; cf. Bosanquet 1912: 43ff.; 1913: 24), he disagreed with Hegel that what made all genuine philosophy into idealism was the "ideality of the finite" (Hegel 1991: 152): "It is a mistake to treat the finite world, or pain, or evil, as an illusion. To the question whether they are real or are not real, the answer must be, as to all questions of this type, that *everything is real, so long as you do not take it for more than it is*" (Bosanquet 1912: 240, emphasis added).

From idealism, therefore, Bosanquet retained the truth of the whole; as applied to realism, this meant not that the "world of finite things" was, *qua* finite, illusion, but that finite things were real in so far as they left their mark on that whole. This is a difficult position to maintain, since if the reality of finites is affirmed, then either the whole is itself a finite part, in which case it is not a whole at all; or it is the whole, in which case not a part. Yet this scruple is disingenuous, according to Bosanquet, since it affirms that reality is what is composed of everything that is, and as such *forms a unity and a totality*. It is the task, therefore, of speculative philosophy to unify realist parts and idealist wholes. Bosanquet's hypothesis is that this task is fulfilled by a proper understanding of logic.

Logical systems all assign a crucial role to the law of non-contradiction, which Aristotle called "the most certain of all principles": "It is impossible for the same attribute at once to belong and not to belong to the same thing and in the same relation" (*Metaph.* 1005b). Bosanquet, however, draws his account of the "law of contradiction" from Plato's *Republic* 524b–c, where Socrates is examining the capacity for sensible versus rational discrimination. Can sight report whether a finger is large or small, or touch whether an object is hard or soft, heavy or light? "It is probably in this sort of case that the mind calls in reason and thought and tries to investigate whether one object has been reported to it or two" (Bosanquet 1912: 224).[6]

The difference between Aristotle's and Plato's accounts is that where in the former contradictions are found only among predicates, in the latter, contradiction is a test of the unity of subjects. To Bosanquet, therefore, the law of contradiction serves at once to distinguish finite features of the real world, but also supplies a "test of universality": "The test of universality … is not the number of subjects which share a common predicate, but rather … the number of predicates that can be attached to a single subject" (1912: 39–40). The law of contradiction is not therefore a bare logical rule concerning well-formed propositions, but rather a means of investigating reality, and of allotting to each element of it its proper place in the whole: "There are places for all predicates; and when all predicates are in their places, none of them is contrary to any other" (*ibid.*: 225). In the end, contradiction functions as an organizing principle that produces variation and difference. It cannot be denied, however, that contradictory attribution in the Aristotelian sense does in fact occur. When it does, it attests to what Bosanquet calls the uniting of predicates "on an inadequate basis of distinction" (*ibid.*), that is, on the basis of a failure in identifying real differences, and the consequent construction of flawed systems: "Contradiction, then, we suggest, is not a dead fact about certain predicates; it is an imperfection in the organisation of systems" (*ibid.*: 225).

Accordingly, Bosanquet's logic is *mereological*, that is, concerned with part–whole relations. The law of contradiction identifies real differences and organizes them in accordance with the "one true individual real" (1911: vol. 2, 259). Accordingly, "non-contradiction … is the principle of individuality"

(1923a: 76) in two senses: the one individual real, and the finite individuals that compose it. What matters in the composition of the whole is the systematic range of organization, that is, the degree to which the whole is organized with respect to its parts.

The logical means by which this is achieved is called by Bosanquet "inference". Again, rather than the rules of inference that logic is held to catalogue, Bosanquet means by inference the *systematization of differents*. The forms we commonly consider as exhausting the character of inference – from premises to a conclusion, or from observations to generalizations – are in fact restricted cases of a more general type: "Inference ... includes every operation by which knowledge extends itself" (1920: 2); inference, that is, relates the parts from which it begins to wholes of increasingly greater scale. Note that Bosanquet gives no criteria as to when this is finally achieved; rather, the law of contradiction provides an index of where knowledge is *required* to extend beyond the finite particulars on which it is focused.

Take a particular case of inductive inference. It is usually held that inference works by generalizing from repeated instances of the same: a certain number of blue cats will suffice to support the rule that "all cats are blue". This, says Bosanquet, is in fact incapable of producing new knowledge, and can at best manage tautology. If, as Henri Bergson argues, "the function of intelligence is to bind the same to the same" (cited Bosanquet 1911: vol. 2, 174), the product of intelligence is the invariant unity of that particular, rather than the systematic interconnection of the whole. If we observe any actual science, however, such as embryology, the function of intelligence is quite different to Bergson's claim. We have instead, writes Bosanquet:

> the plain fact that it is the essential character of intelligence to bind different to different in binding same to same .... The universality or generality, which is the aim of such a process ..., is not measured by millions of repeated instances, but by depth and complexity of insight into a sub-system of the world. (1927: 69)

The logic of actual science is therefore to find laws of variation, or, as Bosanquet puts it, "every universal nexus tends to continue itself inventively in new matter" (*ibid*.: 72). Instead of repeating identical instances, from which a law is supposed to emerge that will give us new knowledge, inference has as its essential function to inventively organize the passage from different to different, as revealed by the law of contradiction.

Bosanquet's logic is in part, therefore, a formalized response to the "minimalist" agenda of the realists with respect to thought, since it integrates thought into the world of which it forms part. It is also a protest against the impoverished state of logic[7] that, as Hegel notes, consists in cataloguing syllogistic figures as if they were "sixty odd species of parrot" (1969: 682; cited in Bosanquet 1911: vol. 1, 1). Fundamentally, however, it is the view that logic carves reality at the joints that Bosanquet in particular, and the idealists in general, were interested in. Rather than the investigation of valid propositional forms, logic has the larger task of undertaking a "direct investigation of the real". Rather than investigating epistemology, or "the nature of knowledge apart from the reality", the speculative logician must condemn "as irrational *ab initio* the doubt and the inquiry whether knowledge is still possible" (1917a: 6). Rather than denying that judgements or propositions assert the existence of their referents, as do Kant and Frege, Bosanquet argues that "thought involves existence in proportion to its coherence with the world" (1921: 81). It is to the world, or maximal nature, that we now return.

THE LOGIC OF THE WORLD

Since logic is concerned with the coherence of thought *as a dimension of reality*, it is inseparable from metaphysics, as Bosanquet attests in an early essay: "The general science of reality cannot be distinguished from the science of knowledge. Reality is the connection with the whole, and logic is the science of this connection in general" (1883: 74). Accordingly, far from being positioned as an observer outside but looking on to a "transcendent world – a block universe – fixed in itself as an object without life or activity" (1921: 1), thought about the world takes place within that world, teeming with life and activity. If logic is a dimension of reality, it must be subject to the same laws as the reality it systematizes. Thus, "what governs thought and finds utterance in its coherence is, as I hold, simply the nature of things" (1921: 176). In answer to the inevitable question, "What then *is* the nature of things?", Bosanquet borrows a term from Darwin to characterize the logician's task, as investigating the "morphology of knowledge" (1911), in referring to logical forms as adaptive owing to selection pressures from reality. In arguing for this naturalistic account of logical form and development, Bosanquet is unusually relying not on a representational account of knowledge of nature, but rather on a productive account of nature as an agent in shaping or moulding cognition.[8]

Bosanquet is therefore concerned to resolve the problematic relation of mechanism to teleology bequeathed us by Kant's treatment of it. The *Critique of Judgement* left the relation between these two kinds of "causality" as a divide between nature and reason, with the latter as the seat and source of purposes, and the former as insuperably mechanical. Bosanquet calls this the "received account", culminating in an opposition "between purposiveness and mechanism" (1912: 74) he holds ultimately untenable; it is precisely because nature is conceived as an externality set against the inward that we end up with a conception of a mechanical nature to which reason is alien (*ibid.*: 73).

Rather than proclaiming mechanism wrong in principle, Bosanquet protests against an inadequately conceived mechanism. He is adamant that in thinking, "the formed mechanism of the brain is our instrument throughout" (*ibid.*: 202) and that "neural process … gives the physical response or the course of brain change" (*ibid.*: 213). Despite the general antipathy to mechanistic explanation amongst idealist philosophers, Bosanquet holds that mind is impossible without it. Mechanism holds "that the world consists of elements, complete in themselves, and yet determined in relation to elements beyond them" (*ibid.*: 73). Elements are always "relatively" determined in so far as they are inconceivable without relatedness to one another, which relatedness is given in the form of "determinate reactions according to law" (*ibid.*: 162). That elements are always elements of a system formed in accordance with physicochemical laws means that *there are no extra-systemic elements*, and this fact of the systematic combination of elements demonstrates that combination into larger wholes amounts to an immanent law governing elements, a law Bosanquet calls "purpose": "The purpose of the whole, after all, simply is the whole, put together as it must be put together if it is not to contradict itself and the context of experience" (*ibid.*: 162).

For Bosanquet, therefore, unlike Kant, there is no explanatory gulf between mechanical nature and conceived or rational purpose, since the latter is revealed as immanent in combination, in system. Accordingly, "everything goes to show that … consciousness should not be regarded as the source of teleology, but as itself a manifestation, falling within wider manifestations, of the immanent individuality of the real" (*ibid.*: 152). Rather than following the subjective idealist route of making reality subject to mind's teleological governance, Bosanquet concludes his investigation of Kant's antithesis by naturalizing teleology: "We have seen that teleological wholes are inevitably constituted by what may fairly be called mechanical relations, that is to say, a determinate relativity of part to part in the light of the whole" (*ibid.*: 161).

In terms of the nervous system as the bodily basis or mechanical relations from which mind arises, the "determinate relativity of part to part in the light of the whole" reformulates the antithesis of mechanism and teleology. Rejecting the notion that the cortical process – the brain – alone should be considered as the physical basis of mind, since an isolated cortical process would be incapable, in the end, of coordinated thought, expression or activity, Bosanquet insists that it is the "whole nervous system, not merely cortical process" (*ibid.*: 200) from which mind derives. Nor in turn can this system be isolated, for it must be adapted to the "externality" or "Nature" to which it adapts, and of which it is a part. Thus, "our *whole* world is at work in every remodelling of itself" (*ibid.*: 202), including the production and exercise of mind, which is not the source, but the product, of a teleology immanent in combination: "According to the conception here advocated, mind is not so much a something, a unit, exercising guidance upon matter, as the fact of self-guidance of that world which appears as matter when that reaches a certain level of organisation" (*ibid.*: 193–4).

Here we see the basis of Bosanquet's favoured philosophical union, comprising Hegel and Darwin, citations from whom open his *Logic* (1911: vol. 1, 1). In common with Darwin, Bosanquet holds that "it is the world, the environment, which is responsible for the respective differences between the forms of organic evolution" (1912: 150). The agent, that is, that "moulds mind", is nature (*ibid.*: 202). Nor, however, is Hegel abandoned. Rather, Bosanquet's contention is that Hegel's is in effect a natural philosophy of logical form, based not on Linnaeus and his classificatory systems, but on *organism*: "Metaphysic … would show that finite minds which for Logic sustain the universe, are ultimately organs moulded by it and through which it sustains itself. Both points of view are true, and it is the test of a philosophy to succeed in combining them" (1911: vol. 2, 316).

Organic forms develop in accordance with the systematic relations between different, functionally adapted parts. If finite organisms, meanwhile, are *possible* in a given environment, then the latter plays as much of a role in forming the organism and enabling it to continue as the organism does in maintaining itself. Thus, between mind and mechanism, there is a relation between whole and part that strives to unite them. Using the spatial terminology of mechanical materialism, Bosanquet writes, "Mind, so far as it can be in space, is nervous system; nervous system, focussed in this nisus towards unity …, is finite mind" (1912: 219). The purpose of finite mind is, therefore, to focus the whole of a reality that exceeds it. Of this reality, Mind is a "supervenient perfection" (*ibid.*: 202) precisely because it aims at, but cannot be, this whole.

Now it may be objected that Bosanquet wholly misinterprets evolutionary theory as aiming at "perfection". Indeed, at times Bosanquet writes as though the realization of mind is nature's ultimate achievement, a kind of "end of natural history" in parallel with Hegel's Prussian state in the early nineteenth century or with Fukuyama's global economic liberalism at the end of the twentieth. Were this what he maintained, it would amount to holding that evolution is directed towards the realization of a single, perfect species, that is, that it is teleological overall, rather than an ongoing process of adaptation. In short, this objection would amount to saying that Bosanquet naturalizes teleology at the cost of evolution.

We should not think this, however, in terms of the "natural prejudice" (*ibid.*: 125) premised on the "analogy of the finite contriver … compelled, because finite, to exercise selection within the universe", but to which "particular class of creatures" there can be no question of ascribing "ultimate value" as the agent of selection, nor an "end unsupported" by nature and "the entirety of what is". Accordingly, purpose cannot be assessed on the basis of finite want, but exists only where there is "objectiveness of selection" (*ibid.*: 138). Since such selection operates both in "finite mind and also mechanical nature" (*ibid.*: 146), however, purpose must be conceived as universal, in two senses: first, it is "everywhere, e.g. throughout the inorganic world, and consequently nowhere *par excellence*"; and second, *it is to the concrete universal* that purpose belongs – "so-called purpose is really at every point of the whole" (ibid.: 194), or the individual at a maximal point of comprehensiveness.

It is worth pausing here, with the introduction of the "concrete universal".[9] The idea is essentially that particulars are not other than such universals, but elements of them, so that particulars form, with universals, the "plastic unity of an inclusive system" (Bosanquet 1924: 62). Particulars, moreover, are not indivisible or atomic; each has "internal diversity of content" (Bradley 1922: 187), making it a concrete universal in turn. We cannot, therefore, understand this universal in the familiar terms of the medievally sourced problem of universals, which, as Sprigge (1983: 11) presents it, tells us of "the possible forms particulars assume", but rather in terms of the complex internal and external organizations that form particulars and that they form in turn. It is such facts of organization that the concrete universal expresses, rather than possibilities of predication. Since therefore there are many concrete universals, each is involved in all up to the maximum degree of concrete universality which in Hegel is the Concept (1991: 241), while Bosanquet calls it simply "world" or "cosmos" (1912: 37). In either case, it is the complex medium of all particularity expressed in particulars as its microcosm.

Hence the anti-subjectivist implications of Bosanquet's notions of "individual" as the seat of purpose and "perfection" as its goal. To conceive of purpose as having an end to which means are subordinated is part and parcel of the subjectivist, anthropocentric prejudice that attaches purpose only to a particular, supplying its wants or remedying its deficiencies. Subjectivism in teleology transforms it into *perfectibility* and *progressism*, politically popular doctrines that Bosanquet criticizes for their one-sidedness (1921: 185–7). By contrast, the perfection in question, being of the whole – the *complete*[10] – rather than the part, is there from the outset, but its fuller realization is stunted and segregated precisely by the ascription of purpose to the "poor work" of "subjective selection" (1912: 138). Accordingly, "it is intolerable that Nature, through which alone spirit attains incarnation, should be treated as a directionless material" (*ibid.*: 133–4), because in selection it is precisely *not* the particular creature or consciousness that is active, but rather *the world*, the self-maintaining individual or environment. In conclusion, then, "a teleology cannot be ultimate; it can express nothing but a necessity for change *founded upon a whole which constitutes the situation to be modified*" (*ibid.*: 16, emphasis added). Bosanquet's is a protest, therefore, against conceiving nature as merely external and mechanical, as "directionless matter", and against conceiving subjective, finite mind or consciousness as the sole bearer of purposes or plans, which results from a one-sided reading of Kant, but which Bosanquet finds in Dreisch's vitalist "entelechies" (*ibid.*: 195) and in Ward's, Bergson's and Bradley's ultimate segregation of organic from inorganic natures (*ibid.*: 134). Nor is nature inert and directionless, "fixed in itself as an object without life or activity" (1921: 2); nor thought something extraneous to that nature; rather, a mind without content, a bare consciousness, is for Bosanquet the abstraction. Not only does "the nature of things … govern thought", but thought is a "supervenient perfection", because in it nature "finds utterance in its coherence" (*ibid.*: 176).

CONCLUSION

Having established the biological basis of Bosanquet's speculative philosophy of nature, however, even a reader sympathetic to the claim that idealism does not deny the existence of a mind-independent nature may wonder in what respect a realism premised on structures constitutes an idealism at all, rather than a subspecies of realism. Like his contemporary Whitehead, Bosanquet himself remains uneasy about ascribing to his position the term "idealism":

> While it is true that the "modern" or "neo" idealist insists upon thought – actual thinking – as the creator, condition, and only genuine type of reality, it is to be borne in mind that there is another idealism, or at any rate a philosophical position, which might equally well claim the title of speculative philosophy which, rejected by the neo-idealist, might well appeal for support to the neo-realist. (Bosanquet 1921: 1–2)

A "speculative philosophy" accommodates realism's rejection of mind-dependence alongside what we might call idealism's *inflationary* ontology. Whereas a "physical realism", as Bosanquet (1913: 11) calls it, committed to the real existence of physical simples (atoms, elements, particles, etc.), each with a unique spatiotemporal location, finds in higher levels of organization only rearrangements of parts, and therefore pursues a reductionist or *deflationary* strategy that ascribes reality only to the parts, the speculative philosopher acknowledges as real *everything that occurs*, on the grounds that a consistent realism cannot withdraw reality from any phenomenon, event or relation. Both realist and speculative philosophy "demand a place and being and value ... for all that sense-perception has to give us" (Bosanquet 1921: 7), because they share the view that there is a mind-independent reality. Realism grants only epistemic value to those sense-perceptions as corroborating what there is, whereas speculative idealism finds those perceptions a place *as part of* reality, and as transcending their finite nature in the direction of that reality. In this respect, Bosanquet's philosophy investigates a single problem: "knowledge of the union which the mind has with the whole of nature" (1912: 235).

12. CRITICISMS AND PERSISTENT MISCONCEPTIONS OF IDEALISM

In a 1994 review of Nicholas Rescher's *System of Pragmatic Idealism* entitled "Idealism *contra* Idealism", the late T. L. S. Sprigge criticizes his author for insufficiently differentiating between realism and idealism. In so doing, Sprigge is continuing a debate that reached a peak of intensity in the 1930s, but which began in response to Moore's "Refutation of Idealism" (1903). Moore had sharply distinguished between a general or "ordinary" realism (*ibid*.: 434)[1] and the "spiritualist" or "theological" Berkeleyan account he identified with idealism. The equation "idealism = Berkeleyanism" remained strong enough throughout the twentieth century for Burnyeat (1982) to use it to deny that any ancient philosophy might correspond to what is called "idealism". That there was a debate until the 1930s concerning its adequacy, however, demonstrates that Moore's equation cannot be regarded as an uncontroversial characterization of idealist philosophy. In fact, from the outset Moore's "Refutation" is fraught with interpretational problems. He gives three definitions of idealism at the start of his article, successively increasing in focus. All three, however, are problematic and insufficient to encapsulate the vast range of idealisms dominant in his day.

Moore's first definition is: "[Idealism] is certainly meant to assert (1) that the universe is very different from what it seems, and (2) that it has quite a large number of properties which it does not seem to have" (1903: 433). This first definition is exceptionally broad. What is perhaps most remarkable about it is that the one philosopher whose work this definition of idealism does not encapsulate is that philosopher whose doctrine *"esse is percipi"* Moore is attempting to refute. Berkeley's phenomenalism is an extreme empirical *realism*. As Wilson (1999d: 307) notes, "[Berkeley] construed the appearances of ordinary sense experience – the purple skies, 'wild but sweet notes of the birds,' fragrant blooms, and warm sunshine – as *the real world*". Berkeley's sensory realism and antithetical status in regards to the definition given above is exemplified clearly in his third *Dialogue*:

> I am of vulgar cast, simple enough to believe my senses, and leave things as I find them. To be plain, it is my opinion that the real things are those very things I see, and feel, and perceive by my senses. These I know; and, finding they answer all the necessities and purposes of life, have no reason to be solicitous about any other unknown beings ... It is likewise my opinion that colours and other sensible qualities are on the objects. I cannot for the life of me help thinking that snow is white and fire is hot. You indeed, who by *snow* and *fire* mean certain external, unperceived, unperceiving substances, are in the right to deny whiteness or heat to be affections, inherent in *them*. But I, who understands by those words the things I see and feel, am obliged to think like other folks. (GBW II.229–30)

Moore was not alone in considering Berkeley an illusionist: Kant makes similar accusations in his first *Critique*. Nevertheless, both philosophers are in error and miss the importance of Berkeley's sensory realism.

Moore's second, more focused, definition of the idealist philosopher claims that an idealist is one who upholds the doctrine that "the whole universe ... is in some sense conscious ... it has what we recognise in ourselves as the *higher* forms of consciousness" (1903: 433). Moore is claiming here that for the idealist a mountain is conscious in the same way that you or he is conscious. It may well be possible to find an idealist philosopher who holds this view but at this point in the book we hope to have given enough evidence to prove that this is far from an inclusive view of the idealist position. A philosopher such as James Ward, whom we have discussed above, claimed on numerous occasions that reality is inherently spiritual *but* he does not mean by this that mountains share with humans the ability to enjoy conscious reflective experiences. What Ward is arguing is that the dualism between mechanist materialism, on the one hand, and thought or "spirit", on the other, cannot be maintained. The mechanist's conception of inert matter, Ward argues at length in the two volumes of his *Naturalism and Agnosticism*, is explanatorily insufficient. We need a conception of objective reality that is powerful, active and dynamic, that is, that possesses the qualities that have, since the Cartesian rejection of scholasticism, been confined to thought alone. Reality should be conceived of as one type of substance, which is powerful and of which our consciousness is a high degree. It must be emphasized that just because Ward argues consciousness is not different in its substantial being to rocks, that does not mean he believes rocks can entertain conscious thoughts.

After stating his second definition, Moore claims that he does not intend to show that reality is not in fact spiritual – he hopes it is; rather, he merely aims to show that the idealist has no reason to believe that it is.[2] He intends to do this by refuting a single premise, which he believes all idealists rely on. This is Moore's final definition of idealism: all its adherents rely on the premise "*esse* is *percipi*" – "That wherever you can truly predicate *esse* you can truly predicate *percipi*" (1903: 436). Moore believes that if this premise is refuted then it follows that all idealist philosophies crumble with no sufficient ground on which to erect a stable foundation. The mistake that the idealists all make, Moore argues, is to fail to understand that perception and the object of a perception are distinct in the same way that we can conceive of two different colours as distinct. Idealist philosophers have failed to develop a distinct conception of consciousness and understand how it differs from material reality: "They have not been able to hold *it* and *blue* before their minds and to compare them in the same way in which they compare *blue* and *green*" (*ibid*.: 450). The failure of the idealists then, for Moore, is a failure to adequately distinguish between subject and object. Once this is recognized, epistemic Kantian and Berkeleyan problems are immediately extinguished.

> There is, therefore, no question of how we are to "get outside the circle of our own ideas and sensations". Merely to have a sensation is already to *be* outside that circle. It is to know something which is truly and really *not* a part of *my* experience, as anything which I can ever know. (*Ibid*.: 451)

Moore's attempts at refutation continue by, contrary to Descartes, an equivalence of the "*cogito*" with the evidence of an external reality. If we reject that the perception of an external reality is enough evidence for a real "out there" then we must reject that we exist at all, for the perception of our existence is equivalent to the perception of external existence. Therefore, either (a) we accept that matter exists as well as spirit or (b) we fall into absolute scepticism: "All other suppositions", Moore concludes, "– the Agnostic's that something, at all events, does exist, as much as the Idealist's, that spirit does – are, if we have no reason for believing in matter, as baseless as the grossest superstitions" (*ibid*.: 453).

What Moore has failed to see in his attempted refutation of Berkeley's doctrine is that he in fact gets Berkeley the wrong way round and thus he is blind to the true reasons for Berkeley's speculations. Moore interprets Berkeley as a sceptic who has not gone far enough and should recognize that in fact his scepticism leads not only to the denial of matter but also to the denial of all reality. However, Berkeley is in fact a *common-sense realist* who follows this common-sense realism as far as it will go. If we are to trust our perceptions, why trust these senses only partially? In fact, Berkeley saw his idealism as a defence against the scepticism that may emerge from the Lockean distinction between primary and secondary qualities. If we deny that secondary qualities exist because they vary in appearance to different observers then this same reasoning could easily be extended to primary qualities. One object may seem circular to one but uneven and angular to another. If this is the case, then on the grounds of the scepticism towards the one, scepticism towards the other must follow. However, Berkeley's reasons for his extreme empirical realism are developed in response to a deeper problem, a target that Moore, had he wanted to refute idealism adequately, should have addressed. For Berkeley, as for numerous idealist philosophers, admitting a real distinction between matter and spirit leads ultimately to an insoluble problem regarding causation. If mechanist matter is inert and lifeless then how can it cause the phenomena that make up our consciousness? How do objects possessing primary qualities causally result in the production of secondary qualities if these qualities are different in kind? "What connexion is there between a motion in the nerves, and the sensations of sound or colour in the mind? Or how is it possible these should be the effect of that?" (GBW II.310).[3] It is a problem of causation that inspires Berkeley's idealism, not a failure to conceive a difference between a subject and object. Berkeley has considered such a philosophy and finds all the scientific explanations available equally unable to explain such a causal process. In sum, this problem is the legacy of Cartesian dualism and if Moore wanted to truly refute idealism he would have needed to find a way out of this minefield. Moore demands that we must accept the existence of two distinct types of substance, "spirit" and "matter", but offers us no causal explanation and thus at the end of the article we have no more reason to reject idealism than we did at the start.

Berkeley's ontology, which is undeniably problematic, is not the only logical result of a critique of mechanism, and many idealists maintained this critique of mechanism without postulating that the distinction between subject and object be erased (even Berkeley maintained the distinction between subject and the archetype for the subject's perceptions, his key argument being that all things/ideas must exist in some mind, either finite or infinite). In the philosophies of Ward and Bosanquet there certainly is a distinction between subject and object, but this distinction is not so great as to necessitate a difference of substance. In *The Distinction between Mind and its Objects*, Bosanquet crisply advances an example of such an idealism, providing an insider's account of the then current philosophical idealism he calls "the speculative movement", which:

> entirely dismissed and ignored that primary doubt, so often ascribed to Idealism, as to the direct apprehension and real existence of external nature. Matter, the externality of things to things, was to Hegel, for example, a necessary way of being in which one

great characteristic of the universe found its indispensable expression. (Bosanquet 1913: 9)

Philosophers who rejected the equation, therefore, of idealism and Berkeleyanism – among whom Bosanquet cites Hegel, Green, Edward Caird and William Wallace as idealists who "have always accepted external nature as an existent feature and characteristic of the universe" (1917a: 12) – became in consequence, it was held, indistinguishable from those "properly called realists", that is, "[a]ll who thus believe that existence is far wider than experience – that objects exist in and for themselves, apart from our experiencing of them" (Pratt, quoted in Barrett 1933: 428).

The problem for these idealists is made clearer by Bosanquet, who encouraged the equation "idealism = maximum realism",[4] or even "empiricism on a grand scale" (1921: 182), and who further characterizes realists as those who: "believe in physical objects as existents ..., existents which are in themselves what they are, and are not affected in their nature as existents by perception or cognition, but exist just the same whether there is awareness of them or not" (*ibid.*: 130–31). While the contrast of realism with the Moore–Burnyeat version of idealism becomes clear in these passages, those who, like Bosanquet, reject this Berkeleyan position as inadequate to characterize idealist philosophy must therefore become *physicalists* or *naturalists* and, therefore, the implication runs, not idealists at all.

While Moore's attack proved decisive for the post-idealist generations of philosophers, starting with Russell, and was therefore a landmark essay, there is in it, as indeed there is in Russell and in Frege, an overt Platonism. Moore, for instance, insists on the difference between "yellow itself" and "yellow object" on the grounds that the former cannot be yellow, while the latter cannot not be yellow (1903: 442), and calls the rejection of the equivalence between sensation and thought "the true view" (*ibid.*: 437). From "On Sense and Reference" (1892) to "Thought" (1918–19), we find Frege clearly expressing his Platonism. "Comments on *On Sense and Reference*" (1892), for example, explicitly acknowledges that his assertion that the *Bedeutung* of all propositions is "the True (as the True)" entails that "thought and Being are the same" (Frege 2000c: 174) in exactly the manner of Parmenides. Throughout his career, Frege remains concerned to argue, as he puts it in a 1906 letter to Edmund Husserl, that "Thoughts are not mental entities, and thinking is not an inner generation of such entities but the grasping of thoughts which are already present objectively" (2000a: 302). And in "Thought" he repeats the fundamental Platonic proposition concerning the difference between the sensible and the intelligible: "The thought, in itself imperceptible to the sense, gets clothed in the perceptible garb of a sentence, and thereby we are enabled to grasp it" (2000d: 329). No wonder that Frege's editor Michael Beaney notes that "securing objectivism without Platonism is arguably the central problem that Frege's work poses" (in Frege 2000a: 36). Yet in attempting to thus secure it, he is fighting what Russell called the "incurably Platonic" nature of logic (1962: 54). What this widespread Platonism warns us against, therefore, is reducing Moore's interest in the problem of idealism to the refutation of Berkeleyanism. What he contests is, if *esse* is *percipi* characterizes idealism, then it is an inconsistent and therefore a meaningless philosophy; therefore this Berkeleyan mantra *cannot* characterize a consistent idealism. Accordingly, he praises "the main service of the philosophic school, to which *modern* Idealists belong, [which is] that they have insisted on distinguishing 'sensation' and 'thought' and on emphasising the importance of the latter" (Moore 1903: 437, emphasis added). Of course, the claim that Platonism is idealism at all has been widely contested, not least because Platonism is also an extreme realism, in the sense that it ascribes objective reality to the objects of thought in so far as they are thinkable. So Moore's is a refutation of idealism as such if, and only if, idealism is identical with the rejection of any and all realism.

Yet the very idea that Platonism *could* be an idealism was of course challenged by Burnyeat on the grounds that no thesis that "everything is in some substantial sense mental or spiritual" was impossible in antiquity. What both Moore and Burnyeat have in common, and the closed net they cast over idealism throughout English-language philosophy in the twentieth century, is the twofold thesis that (a) idealism asserts the existence only of mind-dependent reality; and (b) such a reality is *immaterial*. Immaterialist sensationalism, then, would be the more literal understanding of what Moore sets out to distinguish from the "true", that is Platonic, view and what Burnyeat sets out to salvage Platonism from. The most telling element in both, however, which Burnyeat makes more fully clear, is that idealism is thus defined as *negating* the materiality of the physical world. In consequence of this dependence on negation, immaterialist sensationalism is, as an ontology, a self-refuting monism, true only, as Burnyeat uses Plato to show, of the sense organ that reports "this white, here now" (1982: 13). As we have seen, this is not in fact a position maintained by many philosophers, regardless of whether they call themselves idealists.

Ultimately, the view Burnyeat, like Moore, sets out to defend against immaterialist sensationalism (and why did Burnyeat, in the 1980s, regard this as a view worth refuting – again?) is realism, and Plato's contribution to this view. It is a realism that is profoundly *epistemological*, and Burnyeat characterizes it as the lesson ancient philosophy has to teach the moderns: "The characteristic worry, from Parmenides onwards, is not how the mind can be in touch with anything at all, but how it can fail to be" (Burnyeat 1982: 19). As we have seen, such a view lies at the core of Bosanquet's justification of speculative philosophy, although he sources it not only from Plato,[5] but also from Spinoza. On its own, then, realism is insufficient to differentiate idealist philosophers from Platonists, so that both Moore and Burnyeat fail to save the Platonic legacy from idealism.

In common, however, with their impoverished understanding of idealism, they also operate with an etiolatedly *epistemological* realism, as shown by Burnyeat's interjection above, and the devotion of section III of his essay to an argument against scepticism. Bosanquet, by contrast, shows how such a realism *entails* speculation as a philosophical method, on the grounds that if wrong, this will be demonstrated by the nature of reality, and not by a merely formal or methodological constraint on knowledge acquisition and its reasons. In other words, Bosanquet's realism is ontological, and, like Frege, he includes, among things that are, the thoughts that form part of that reality. If reality affects knowability, the common target of Moore, Bosanquet and Burnyeat should be Kant, not Berkeley.

Among British idealist philosophers of the turn of the twentieth century, it was Bradley who was, in fact, Moore's target. As an idealist committed to the insuperability and inexhaustibility of "experience", surely Bradley must confirm the accuracy of the Moore–Burnyeat equation? As we have seen, he does not, not only because of his claim that "our standard is Reality" (Bradley 1930: 332), but also because he rejects even the idea that thought might be identified with reality. "Can thought", Bradley asks in the Appendix to the second edition of *Appearance and Reality*, "however complete, be the same as reality, the same altogether, I mean, and with no difference between them? This is a question to which I could never give an affirmative reply" (*ibid.*: 492).

This is one sense in which Idealism cannot simply be conceived as the contrary of realism: both agree that reality exceeds acts of finite mind, as Bosanquet says expressly: "The body of reality is not a dead transcendent block, limited once and for all, *because it is beyond the immediacy of our mental life*" (1921: 2, emphasis added). Yet there is another sense in which the two are not contraries: the role of nature in idealist philosophy in general. We have already noted that the difference between Schelling and Hegel, on the one hand, and Fichte, on the other, consists precisely in the role of nature in their respective systems. For Schelling, "anything whose conditions simply cannot be given in nature, must be absolutely impossible" (1978: 186); the place of nature in Hegel's system remains hotly debated to this day, but his *Encyclopaedia of the Philosophical Sciences* confirms that, at the very least, it enjoys a "central" role. For Fichte, by contrast, nature is what the I must minimize in order to maximize freedom. Any philosophy that investigates "what is" at all, let alone nature as such, is condemned by Fichte as "dogmatism", while only a critical philosophy properly completed, namely, the "science of knowledge", can enhance the quantity of freedom in the world. For the British idealists, too, the position of nature is a crucial determinant of their positions. Once again, Barrett provides a useful account of the idealists' conception of nature:

> By its structure quite as much as by its material, or substance, the world is what it is, and it is this structure, in all its various complex manifestations, which demands explanation. No view of reality is adequate which is not capable of comprehending within itself all that the manifestations of reality disclose to us. (1933: 428)

This "structural realism" is distinguished from naturalism in so far as the latter grants "universal application to the categories and postulates of mechanistic explanation" (*ibid*.). This mechanical naturalism, that is, begins not with structure, but with basic constituents – atoms – and their motions. As Kant puts it, "When we consider a material whole as being ... a product of its parts and of their forces and powers for combining on their own ..., then our presentation is of a whole produced mechanically" (Ak. V.408). In consequence, (a) mechanical naturalism is quite unable to explain organism or the emergence of structure in general, and (b) there are other ways of conceiving a material whole, that is, as *organized*.

If those philosophies criticized by idealists as "realist" share the principles of mechanical naturalism, then the difference between these two philosophical movements lies not in the assertion or denial of a mind-independent reality, but rather concerns the basic character of *nature*. Whereas the realist starts from atoms and builds up, the idealist starts from structure and builds down. This is not a "top-down/bottom-up" distinction such as we find in philosophy of science textbooks, which is an *epistemological* or *methodological* concern; the difference is instead a difference at the level of *ontology*. To the question "Which comes first – structure or element?", the mechanical naturalist will reply "element", "particle" or "atom"; but the *objective* idealist will reply "structure" or "the whole". Neither, by that token, reject realism concerning mind-independent reality. Moreover, since structure is intelligible, mind is no longer conceived as an external spectator of a passive and inert nature, but rather located "squarely within the world [as] an organically functioning part of its total organisation" (Barrett 1933: 425). Because "organization" therefore takes the place of "atom" in the objective idealist's conception of nature, such a naturalism will tend to emphasize the priority of organism or organization[6] among nature's products.

That Bosanquet, for instance, was an antitype to the Moorean idealist is acknowledged directly by McTaggart, who, commenting on *The Principle of Individuality and Value* (1912), wrote that "almost every word Dr Bosanquet has written about the relations between mind and matter in this chapter might have been written by a complete materialist" (McTaggart 1912: 422).

Paradigmatic of this perspective are statements such as the following, which rejects the basic tenets of the Moore–Burnyeat characterization of idealism as Berkeleyanism: "*You* do not make the world; *it* communicates your nature to you, though in receiving this you are an active organ of the world itself" (Bosanquet 1921: 3).

In a passage that offers a foretaste of the combination of information science with molecular biology common since the last quarter of the twentieth century,[7] Bosanquet envisages a world that, in communicating, forms the "nature" of its organs, forging an *organic* metaphysics in two senses. First, in so far as natures arise from a communicating world, this provides a generative account of nature, corresponding to the Aristotelian conception of nature or *physis* as "genesis" (*Metaph.* 1014b16ff.). Second, in so far as the natures so communicated belong to the world, they are *the world's* organs, turning the world into an organization or, what amounts to the same thing for Bosanquet, an "individual". For these reasons, "biologism" is a better descriptor of Bosanquet's metaphysics than McTaggart's "materialism". It is further evident in the citations with which Bosanquet's *Logic* (1911) begins – the one from Darwin, and the other from Hegel – and in the subtitle of that work, *The Morphology of Knowledge*. It is worth remarking that the combination of idealist metaphysics and evolutionary biology demonstrates that the strong connection between idealism, the philosophy of nature and the natural sciences that we find in the German idealists is continued by Bosanquet and, as we shall see, Whitehead.[8]

13. ACTUAL OCCASIONS AND ETERNAL OBJECTS: THE PROCESS METAPHYSICS OF ALFRED NORTH WHITEHEAD

For Alfred North Whitehead, the idea (or "eternal object", as he would have it) finds its place within a "process philosophy" that he calls "the philosophy of organism" (in *Process and Reality*). His emphasis on systemic unity, on final causation and on the reality of the idea can all be compared directly to the inheritance of German speculative idealism. In his assertion of the fundamental indeterminacy of the event (or "actual occasion", as he terms it), and of the ontological generality of "decision" in that context, he revives, also, the broader German idealist (and Romantic) concern with the relation between freedom and nature. Unlike the German idealists, however, Whitehead attempts to solve the problem by placing freedom, and creativity, at the heart of every "atomic" component of nature.

PROCESS

What does the term "process" mean for Whitehead? He gives an account of the connectedness of things, and of the nature of change and transformation. However, there is something very strange in his account of these things, certainly in terms of our normal common-sense conception of change, because while Whitehead is interested in change, there is a profound sense in which, for him, no *thing* ever actually changes, and, moreover, that spatial extension, in a mechanical, Newtonian sense, does not exist either. "The baseless metaphysical doctrine of 'undifferentiated endurance' is a subordinate derivative from the misapprehension of the proper character of the extensive scheme" (PR 77).

So what kind of "process" emerges from this denial of "undifferentiated endurance"?

CONTEXT

It helps if we approach Whitehead's philosophy from the point of view of some of the apparently intractable disputes, because these are Whitehead's own targets. This would include the apparent problem of the relation between mind and matter. Like the speculative idealists, Whitehead aims to eliminate this problem, along with related problems. He does so by arguing that it is a consequence of a fundamental mistake made early in the history of Western metaphysics by Aristotle. Here we need to recap a number of well-known themes for the sake of clearly stating where Whitehead's own position lies.

From Whitehead's point of view, Aristotle's mistake is to argue that existence must be understood as composed of basic "substance" or "substances" to which "accidental" things occur. This is expressed in a subject–predicate logic, which itself draws from the common grammatical structure of European languages. What our languages seem to express is that there are things in our universe that retain a consistent identity over time. This would include selves, species, planets, bodies, rocks and any other apparently persistent, or enduring, entity. The passage of time consists of happenings occurring *to* these persistent entities. These happenings are not essential to the things themselves, however, and do not change the underlying substance of the things to which they happen. So a self or a species might incur a certain range of variation over time (thoughts/experiences or mutations respectively), but the variation does not change the underlying identity of the self or species; if it did then, by definition, it would no longer be the same self or species. So we have persistent things or substances – to which accidental occurrences (accidental because they are not essential to the substance) happen.

Metaphysics comes to be defined, then, by a search for the basis of persistent substances and the accidental things that happen to them. So the disputes about nominalism and realism, dualism or monism, mind, spirit and matter are, to a large extent, structured by disputes about the nature of these substances and accidents. Even if we can discover what the basic substances are that compose the universe, we are still left with the problem of the accidental forms. If we have some basic substance(s), how do all the huge variety of forms we see get into those basic substances? As we have seen, this a problem that has produced innumerable varieties of idealism. One of the important philosophical positions that we have tried to highlight at various points is that philosophical idealism is, very often, not really characterized (as is commonly held) by the position that reality is produced by the thoughts that people have, but, rather, that reality is produced by the form giving power of the Idea. While the subjectivist interpretation has had considerable purchase, especially in its early modern and neo-Kantian forms, it was not, we have argued, what Plato or Hegel had in mind.[1] The kind of questions that often seem to interest these philosophers are: how does form get into the world, how do we recognize forms when they get there, and how does the emergence of forms relate to the passage of time? If there are basic substances, like matter, why don't they stay homogeneous, formless and empty for eternity? Where do the differences, patterns and regularities come from, and where do the changes in such forms come from?[2] This, arguably, is why materialism and idealism never truly escape one another, because materialism always needs to explain how matter gets to be formed, and idealism often (at least until Whitehead) searches for substances into which the Idea (the form) can enter.

Another contextual factor that is worth noting is the state of the physical sciences at the time of Whitehead's writing. Newtonian mechanical materialism is rooted in this conviction that the existence of the universe is expressed through the distinction between persistent substances and their accidental forms. In the Newtonian universe we find persistent bodies, subject to accidental forces, in a vessel of persistent space (common to all bodies), set against the time of a cosmological clock common to all bodies and events in this common and persistent space. Early modern Cartesian idealists, as we have seen, sought to add accidental qualities to this picture of material bodies through ideas in the substance of mind. Einstein's relativistic revolution at the beginning of the twentieth century obliterated this picture. Time, space, rigid bodies, and their qualities became relativized. There was to be no common space, no common cosmological clock, and therefore no commonly identifiable passage of forms through persistent substance. All such matters are always relative to particular frames of reference, and such frames of reference diverge, potentially infinitely, depending on their relative motions (Einstein 1954).[3] The question "What is really happening here and now?" does not have a sensible answer to which everyone in the universe – regardless of their mass, position, relative velocity, and acceleration – could subscribe.

Whitehead was, like Einstein, a mathematician. He was, with Russell,[4] the author of the three-volume *Principia Mathematica* (Whitehead & Russell 1910, 1912, 1913). Whitehead knew full well the implications of Einstein's revolution. The philosophical logic of substance and accident (subject predication) was no longer tenable as a metaphysics befitting the physical universe described by Einstein's mathematics and the theories of relativity. Whitehead's philosophy of organism can, in large part, be understood as an attempt to provide a metaphysics appropriate to relativity (1926: 142–60).[5] He was also fully aware of early developments in quantum mechanics, and, again, sought to provide a metaphysical system commensurate with these developments (*ibid.*: 161–71). The consequence of this had to be a complete break with Aristotelian "substance and accident" metaphysics.

FROM SUBSTANCE TO EVENT: IDEALIST ATOMISM

So the first key metaphysical claim for Whitehead is that persistent substance does not exist. This removal of substance, thought Whitehead, would solve many of the ongoing disputes in metaphysics. There is no mind nor matter, in general, either. Wherever we think that we see a persistent, or enduring, entity or subject, what we actually see is a huge collection of much smaller entities, none of which have any significant temporal persistence. Time is, he says, "atomic" (PR 61).

When I use a name to refer to what I believe to be a single person who endures through time (but having different thoughts, actions and experiences along the way), the name is really an umbrella under which I place all the much smaller entities that actually make up what I imagine to be a single person. And, indeed, this is the case for everything in the universe. In particular, when I use the term "matter" there is no underlying substance to which I refer. Instead the term is an umbrella concept for every little thing and occurrence that there has ever been. Whitehead points out that these umbrella terms are, then, in fact, abstractions from many individual events: "There is an error; but it is merely the accidental error of mistaking the abstract for the concrete. It is an example of what I will call the 'Fallacy of Misplaced Concreteness'" (1926: 64). Along with those who assert the existence of persistent mind and matter, the thinkers that he is, seemingly, most critical of here, are those ("nominalist" thinkers) who assert that the fundamental things in reality are the "concrete" particulars that we see around us: chairs, tables, buses, people and so on. These are not the fundamental parts of reality at all; they are products of abstraction. So, if there are no persistent things or substances, what does exist? What exists are what he calls "actual entities" or "actual occasions":

> "Actual entities" – also termed "actual occasions" – are the final real things of which the world is made up. There is no going behind actual entities to find anything more real. They differ among themselves: God is an actual entity, and so is the most trivial puff of existence in far-off empty space. (PR 18)

These are the "atomic" events that make up the spatial extension and temporal passage of existence: "the ultimate metaphysical truth is atomism. The creatures are atomic" (PR 35). Additionally, as dictated by relativity, there is no single frame of reference for time, but "creative advance" of many "societies" of actual occasions: "In these lectures ... 'creative advance' is not to be construed in the sense of a uniquely serial advance" (PR 48).

To put this another way, there is "no continuity of becoming", as successfully demonstrated by Zeno, but a "becoming of continuity" (PR 35), indeed, of a multiplicity of continuities. The actual occasions that constitute these continuities are individual "organisms" of varying scales, all of which have a developmental process from birth through concrescence to perishing. They are the *only* things that do *actually* exist. This actuality does not exhaust the whole of reality though. There are other entities immanent to actual occasions, which have a real existence as *potentia*, and which express themselves through the actual existence of actual entities.

Whitehead calls his metaphysics an "atomic philosophy" then, because actual occasions are the true atoms of existence. Existence is process and actual occasions are the atoms of this process, each having no significant temporal endurance. They emerge or concresce over a tiny, and indivisible, period.[6] This period of concrescence within an actual occasion he calls the "duration" of the actual occasion. At the very moment that they concretize into existence, however, actual occasions perish: existence is a "perpetual perishing" (PR 60). So this duration is the time the atom of existence takes to reach its moment of "satisfaction" at the end of its process of concrescence. And it is the passage from one concrescent actual occasion to another that composes the apparent persistence of things in the world: the "becoming of continuity". This is why the appearance of a persistent "concrete" thing, or substance, is actually an abstraction from a process containing many actual occasions.

CREATIVITY

What is the character of this process of constant emergence, concrescence and perishing of atomic events? Its most profound character is creativity. The universe is creative.

> "Creativity" is another rendering of the Aristotelian "matter", and of the modern "neutral stuff." But it is divested of the notion of passive receptivity, either of "form" or of external relations; it is the pure notion of the activity conditioned by the objective immortality of the actual world – a world which is never the same twice.
> (PR 31)

What does this mean? The first thing it means is that the universe is not entirely and mechanically deterministic. As we know, Whitehead, along with every other competent mathematician and physicist of the twentieth century, rejected Newtonian mechanics. The loss of faith in determinacy in general has been more reluctant, but evident. We see it in the rise to prominence of realist interpretations of the probabilistic field theory of quantum mechanics, in developments within idealist biology (as we shall see in Chapter 14), and in the parallel rise of complex systems theory. Indeed Ilya Prigogine wrote a book concerned with *The End of Certainty,* as he sees it, in all these areas (Prigogine 1997). As Prigogine has been at pains to point out all along, with a loss of determinacy comes an arrow of time. The deterministic mechanism of Newton and Laplace defines a universe in which the future is as clear and determinate as the past. Past and future are indistinguishable as a fixed continuum of mechanically determined events. Conversely, the removal of certainty creates an asymmetry between past and future. The past appears, for Whitehead, as an ever accumulating foundation of the "given": that which provides the ever changing potential for what can possibly happen, while the future remains ripe with potential, but always undecided. What, then, is "given"?

THE "GIVEN" WORLD

Every real "decision", at every level from the subatomic to the cosmological scale (neutrinos decide, molecules decide, organic cells decide, organs decide, organisms decide, ecosystems decide, planets decide, galaxies decide), is always made in the context of a "given" world: "creativity is always found under conditions, and described as conditioned" (PR 31).

The past constitutes the given world which the current moment (actual occasion) *prehends* as the raw potential for its own coming into existence. It is the past that provides the given "potential" from which the present moment selects or decides. The past actual occasion becomes the object of prehension of the new actual occasion. And by virtue of its entering into all future actualities, as "given", it gains "objective immortality". "This function of creatures, that they constitute the shifting character of creativity, is here termed the 'objective immortality' of actual entities" (PR 32).

What we always prehend is the past. This is self-evident when we look out into space and a photon enters our eye from a star that died millennia ago. We see the distant past at that moment. But the same is, in fact, true of every perception. Nothing passes instantaneously. The passage of information is absolutely limited by the speed of light. It is only ever possible to perceive the past. At the very moment of an occasion's becoming an object for another occasion in the present moment, it perishes to become the past, giving way to the new concrescence of the new present. As such every past occasion enters into the constitution of every future concrescence as an element of potentiality.

Whitehead does not provide us with preconstituted subjects that *have* perceptions or prehensions of a world that is separate from them. This process of prehension *is* the process of concrescence of the actual occasion. You are made out of your prehensions, and those of the billions of actual occasions subsumed by your body as a whole.[7]

Whitehead also reworks relativistic time in this context. After Einstein (1954: 25–7), there can be no sense in which events can be held to be contemporaneous according to an absolute cosmological clock. So what does it mean to say of one event that it is contemporaneous with another? Whitehead provides a fully relativistic account of temporal relations entirely in terms of the constitution of actual occasions. For Whitehead, actual occasion A precedes actual occasion B if, and only if, A can enter into the constitution of B by virtue of the "ingressions" of A and the "prehensions" of B. If A and B cannot enter into one another's constitution then they are, by definition, contemporaneous: "so far as physical relations are concerned, contemporary events happen in *causal* independence of each other" (PR 61). Of this comment Whitehead says in a footnote, "This principle lies on the surface of the fundamental Einsteinian formula for the physical continuum" (PR 61n.). Elsewhere he says, in more Whiteheadian terms, that "Actual entities are called 'contemporary' when neither belongs to the 'given' actual world defined by the other" (PR 66).

ETERNAL OBJECTS

Yet if the past occasion has indeed perished to become the "given", how can it enter into the present, and the future? It does so as *potential form*. Whatever appears to be a persistent entity is in fact a chain, or what Whitehead calls a "society", of actual occasions, one following and prehending another. The apparent endurance of objects is a consequence of the passing of a form from one occasion to the next. What passes from one moment to the next is not substance, but the overall organization of the entity. The entity is created entirely anew in each moment, and it is the organization that ensures this repeated "self-causation". This is a theme that we shall see re-emerging in late-twentieth-century idealist biology (see ch. 14). The forms making up the organization, that is, passed on from occasion to occasion, Whitehead terms "eternal objects". They are understood in clearly Platonic terms:

> [B]y stating my belief that the train of thought in these lectures is Platonic ... I mean that if we had to render Plato's general point of view with the least changes made necessary by the intervening two thousand years of human experience in social organization, in aesthetic attainments, in science, and in religion, we should have to set about the construction of a philosophy of organism.

> In such a philosophy the actualities constituting the process of the world are conceived as exemplifying the ingression (or "participation") of other things which constitute the potentialities of definiteness for any actual existence. The things which are temporal arise by their participation in the things which are eternal. The two sets are mediated by a thing which combines the actuality of what is temporal with the timelessness of what is potential.
> (PR 39–40)

Whitehead's Platonic idealism could hardly be more clearly expressed. These eternal objects are to be understood as Platonic Forms or Ideas,[8] and actual occasions are the things that "mediate" between the "things which are temporal" and the Ideas "which are eternal". Actual occasions are the means for the actual "realization" of eternal Ideas. "If the term 'eternal objects' is disliked, the term 'potentials' would be suitable. The eternal objects are pure potentials of the universe; and the actual entities differ from each other in their realization of potentials" (PR 149).

Eternal objects must have active formative force if there is to be any passage of form from one event to another: in other words, if there is to be any efficient causation. This active force Whitehead refers to as "ingression":

> [A]n eternal object can be described only in terms of its potentiality for "ingression" into the becoming of actual entities; and … its analysis only discloses other eternal objects. It is pure potential. The term "ingression" refers to the particular mode in which the potentiality of an eternal object is realized in a particular actual entity, contributing to the definiteness of that actual entity.
> (PR 23)

The process of concrescence within the actual occasion is, therefore, characterized by the passage from "indeterminacy" to "determinacy" via decision:

> Actual occasions in their "formal" constitutions are devoid of all indetermination. Potentiality has passed into realization. They are complete and determinate matter of fact, devoid of all indecision … But eternal objects … involve in their own natures indecision. They are, like all entities, potentials for the process of becoming.
> (PR 29)

Michael Epperson has devoted an excellent study to a step-by-step comparison of Whitehead's account of this transition from pure potentiality to actuality, with the same transition as found in the decoherence account of the collapse of the wave function in quantum mechanics. The parallels are astonishing, and suggest that behind Whitehead's metaphysics lies a substantial groundwork of mathematical reasoning (Epperson 2004).

REALISM WITH RESPECT TO UNIVERSALS

The emphasis on the reality of the actual occasion does initially appear to have nominalist implications, but only if we make the mistake of conceiving of the actual occasion as a concrete particular. The above account of the reality of eternal objects and real potentialities makes clear, however, that this would be a mistake. The actual occasion is the "mediating" means by which the reality of eternal pure potentia makes the transition to the reality of temporally and spatially extended objects. *Actual occasions are the means for the constitution of concrete particulars, not the concrete particulars themselves.* When Whitehead tells us that actual occasions are the only "reality", what he clearly means to tell us is that actual occasions are the only means to generate "actuality". Eternal objects are not "actual" unless they have been actualized through an actual occasion. They are, however, perfectly "real". Indeed, they may continue to exist and to be "real" while never being actualized at all, so long as they remain as a potential for actualization within our world. Whitehead is a realist with respect to the Idea as pure potential.

FEELING

So, this is what we are: societies of actual occasions, societies in which Ideas are passed on from one occasion to another with constant variation and mutation of form. This passing on, and mutation, of form is the "ingression" of "eternal objects". Each actual occasion "prehends" the eternal objects emerging from the given conditions of past occasions.

What is the raw character of prehension: of the current actual occasion's assimilation of the past as object? Here, Whitehead puts a great deal of distance between himself and Kant. It certainly is not thought, consciousness or concept that characterizes raw prehension. These are very far along in the process of concrescence: very "late achievements".

> The organic philosophy holds that consciousness only arises in a late derivative phase of complex integrations ... (i) Consciousness is a subjective form arising in the higher phases of concrescence. (ii) Consciousness primarily illuminates the higher phase in which it arises, and only illuminates earlier phases derivatively, as they

> remain components in the higher phase. (iii) It follows that the order of dawning, clearly and distinctly, in consciousness is not the order of metaphysical priority. (PR 162)

The early and raw state of prehension is not consciousness, but "feeling".

> Feelings are variously specialized operations, effecting a transition into subjectivity. They replace the "neutral stuff" of certain realistic philosophers. (PR 40–41)

> The philosophy of organism aspires to construct a critique of pure feeling, in the philosophical position in which Kant put his *Critique of Pure Reason.* (PR 113)

The actual occasion does not first "think of" or "conceive of" the object. The object is first "felt". This feeling of the world is directly connected with the world and senses the past as causally efficacious on the present, but (in contrast to Descartes' and Leibniz's demands for the "clear and distinct") such feeling is vague and indistinct. The felt eternal objects are always and everywhere present as potential within the given; we "feel" the potential in the world.

VALUE, PURPOSE AND DECISION

This indistinct, felt, potential must, then, be turned into something actual.[9] Potentia are, therefore, foregrounded or backgrounded in particular occasions. In Whitehead's terminology they are "positively" or "negatively" prehended. The currently concrescent occasion has to decide which of the eternal objects present in the given are to be foregrounded as relevant for characterizing that which is given within the new concrescence of actuality. What potential will be actualized? Which present potential will be actualized, and which will not, is the subject of a "decision" regarding relevance or value: what is relevant to the present actual occasion. What we take to be the "meaning" of things, then, is just a subset of nature's wider category of "relevance".[10] Whitehead says "The four stages constitutive of an actual entity ... can be named, datum, process, satisfaction, decision" (PR 150–51).

This is not merely the valuation and decision of conscious human agents, but those of every "atom" of nature. The progressive concrescence of every actual occasion involves an elimination of some feelings of form as irrelevant, and a heightening of others as relevant through valuation. This is how the feeling of the object becomes a conception of the object, and becomes part of a "proposition" that aligns real potentialities to become actualized. This is how the "subjective pole" of the actual occasion then processes potentiality to become the actuality of itself as a subject-become-object or "superject". One might ask: relevant for what? It is relevant for what Whitehead variously refers to as "lure", "appetition", "subjective aim" or "final cause" of the actual occasion.

> The determinate unity of an actual entity is bound together by the final causation towards an ideal progressively defined ... According to this account, efficient causation expresses the transition from actual entity to actual entity; and final causation expresses the internal process whereby the actual entity becomes itself.
> (PR 150)

Here we see, then, Whitehead's solution to the relation between freedom and nature. He inserts freedom into the core of every atom of nature's existence. Indeed, it is arguable that he inserts the whole Kantian schema inside each actual occasion, and then links these actual occasions together into the fabric of nature. Nature, then, becomes purposive by virtue of the insertion of a subjective aim (and a complete Kantian cognitive apparatus) into each actual occasion. All discrimination and decision in organisms is derived from organic purposiveness. All such purposiveness (including even my purposive activity in quenching my thirst) is derived from cosmic purposiveness: the system as a whole. The actual occasion is brought into being by a combination of "efficient causation" (the ingression of eternal objects) and "final causation" – determinacy and purposiveness respectively (as we find in Kant and Hegel) – through which a selection of relevant influences occurs. As we feel the world (internally and externally) "all physical experience is accompanied by an appetite for, or against, its continuance" (PR 32). The actual occasion, therefore, passes through a process of "conceptual valuation" of the eternal objects available to it by virtue of its actual predecessors. It is this conceptual valuation that will provide form of thought (if there is any), body and action.

Each moment of existence is conditioned by the potentiality provided by a given past and strives towards satisfaction of its own creative aim through conceptual valuation. However, this is a selection of influences, a series of decisions that, as for Hegel, are, ultimately, tailored towards the achievement of cosmic purpose.

EXPERIENCE

So each actual occasion in the universe is a subject in the sense that it is an experiencer of the past of the world as object. Every causal relation is efficacious by virtue of it being an experience *by* the present *of* the past. Each actual occasion passes from subject to become object in the sense that it becomes an objective, and immortal, potential for the experience of future actual occasions; it makes a transition from subject to "superject". The universe is entirely experience of feeling – made superject. "Apart from experience", says Whitehead, "there is nothing". Human experience is just a tiny subset of experience in general: the experience of the rock, of the neutrino, of the planet, of the star.

Actual occasions prehend one another not only linearly or temporally but also laterally or spatially. The potential giving rise to myself as present actual occasion is given first by my experience of myself as past actual occasions ("my past self") – "the most primitive perception is 'feeling the body as functioning'", says Whitehead (1929: 112); and then, second, by my experience of the surrounding actual occasions that also provide potential for my present and future existences. I am, in this way, cognizant of myself and my surrounding world. Indeed, this is how worlds are, reciprocally, constituted. This mutually constitutive prehension can be compared to what later idealist biologists such as Humberto Maturana and Francisco Varela would term "cognition", as we shall see (see ch. 14). Each actual occasion becomes itself through its prehension, cognition or experience of the past actual occasion in its "society", and its cognition of other, surrounding, actual occasions. Such integration of actual occasions, through "experience", Whitehead refers to as a "nexus" of actual occasions. An organic body is a nexus of organs, which are in turn nexus of cells. A social system is, in Whitehead's terms, such a nexus. The universe is entirely connected temporally by "societies" and spatially by "nexus", all mediated by experience. This means that, as with the absolute idealists, the relation between the whole and each part is entirely reciprocal, systemic and interpenetrating. As Whitehead says, "the continuum is present in each actual entity, and each actual entity pervades the continuum" (PR 67).

Whitehead's pan-experientalism returns the power of decision, creativity and freedom to the world (following the brief interlude of Newtonian mechanical determinacy), but with a further Copernican revolution: this time one that removes the experience, "meaning", decision and creativity of the human from the centre of things, and places them in nature's own experience and creativity. Conscious human decision is an abstraction of many millions of unconscious decisions subsumed by the human occasion. The human decision, in turn, is subsumed by social, ecological, planetary and cosmological decisions, and finally by the decision and creativity of the cosmic organism itself – God.

> [B]y the principle of relativity there can only be one non-derivative actuality, unbounded by its prehensions of an actual world. Such a primordial superject of creativity achieves, in its unity of satis-

faction, the complete conceptual valuation of all eternal objects. This is the ultimate, basic adjustment of the togetherness of eternal objects on which creative order depends. It is the conceptual adjustment of all appetites in the form of aversions and adversions. It constitutes the meaning of relevance. (PR 32)

14. SELF-ORGANIZATION: THE IDEA IN LATE-TWENTIETH-CENTURY SCIENCE

In this chapter we intend to demonstrate the importance of metaphysical idealism to contemporary science. The point of this chapter is not that the scientists we discuss are unusual in their adoption of an idealist metaphysics. On the contrary, our point is that, far from being antithetical to scientific thinking and discovery, philosophical idealism is essential to science.

In the opening chapters we saw ancient idealism emerge in response to the identity of thought and being set out by Parmenides. We set out the possibility of a "one-world" interpretation of Plato's Ideas in which the Idea is understood in terms of causality (rather than mimesis): a final, rather than efficient, causality, of course. We saw a Plato for whom there are many such genetic Ideas, which are in complex and hierarchical participation with one another: Ideas that emerge through reciprocal relations of difference (negation). We saw a Neoplatonic tradition emerging through the further systematization of this picture, together with the development of an asymmetrical ontology of genetic powers: the Idea manifested in actuality through the medium of difference in powers. Arguably, we shall find all these ingredients in the account of idealist science that follows. We shall find the Idea (as final cause) manifest most strongly in the concept of "*organization*" (as well as "system", and "function").[1] We shall find the development of an ontology of difference, of asymmetrical powers, in the "*far-from-equilibrium*" conceptual apparatus. We shall find the interrogation of the identity of thought and being in the elaboration of the concepts of "*cognition*" (including subordinate concepts such as "measurement", "recording" and "semantics"). It seems that at one point we are even given a glimpse of the kind of mathematical order by means of which the Idea (organization) produces, simultaneously, body and mentality. We shall see the influence of Kant's teleological judgement most obviously. But it is arguable that this work has its foundations very deep within the idealist tradition indeed. We shall see powerful connections to the work of Leibniz, Hegel, Whitehead and others.

We could have chosen our examples from mathematics, chemistry or the various developments in contemporary physics and cosmology that have such idealist characteristics.[2] We have chosen to provide some examples from contemporary biology, however. We have done so because, as we shall see, such work connects directly to Kant's own concerns with respect to the organization of life in the *Critique of Judgement*. There we saw the development of the Idea as a lure to the "self-organization" of life. We followed this thought as it developed in Hegel's organic philosophy, and on to Whitehead's philosophy of organism. We have argued that it is part of a persistent engagement, by idealism, with nature that goes back to the earliest responses to Parmenides. Now we see its manifestation at the heart of contemporary sciences of life.

MATURANA AND VARELA: AUTOPOIETIC LIFE

Autopoiesis and the Idea

Humberto Maturana and Francisco Varela's essay "Autopoiesis: The Organisation of the Living" was first published in 1972. In his preface to the English edition of the essay, Stafford Beer provides a one-page account of the historical origins of the scientific method, in which Plato's "synthetic method" is progressively undermined by an "analytical" mode of thought deriving from Aristotle, and built on by the "categorisation that took hold of medieval scholasticism". Even the seeming "revolt of rationalism" resulted, he says, through "methodical doubt", "mechanism", "dualism" and "more categorization" in "denying relation altogether" . The "revolt of the empiricists", which "began from the nature of understanding about the environment", resulted, paradoxically, through scepticism, in the "bizarre outcome, whereby it was the empiricists who denied the very existence of the empirical world". Relation remained, for the empiricists, only as "relation between mental events". As Beer nicely puts it, "the system 'out there', which we call nature, had been annihilated in the process". This "system" goes on to find its new place, as he says, within Kant's various cognitive faculties. It is this tendency that he blames for the fragmentation of academic knowledge and communities, and the incapacity of science and scientists to recognize the fact that the ultimate test of the viability of scientific knowledge must be its commensurability and unifiability *as* knowledge *of* a unitary nature, produced *by* a unitary nature (in Maturana & Varela 1980a: 63). In contrast to this fragmented and anti-realist tendency, he says, Maturana and Varela state that "our purpose is to understand the organization of living systems in relation to their unitary character" (*ibid*.: 63–5). This could be a line taken directly from Hegel's philosophy of nature where he attempts to describe precisely the same organization of the "[t]he whole, as structure completely developed into a self-subsistent individual" (Hegel 1970b: 373).

Unity

The very first sentence of Maturana and Varela's essay states that "A universe comes into being when a space is severed into two. A unity is defined. The description, invention and manipulation of unities is at the base of all scientific enquiry" (1980b: 73). What concerns them, as for other idealists, is, they say, the seeming "autonomy" of living systems. A core aspect of this "autonomy", as they see it, is the fact that such systems are able to produce "diversity" or "variation" while, simultaneously, maintaining "identity". This, of course, is a problem that has haunted the whole history of metaphysical speculation. How can a thing remain the thing that it is, while undergoing many "accidental" transformations that do not seem to change its underlying "identity"? Does this mean that the qualities or properties of a thing are entirely separate from its identity, or that some of its properties are essential to its identity while others are not? Is there an underlying "essence" to each thing that cannot be changed by any sequence of "accidental" variations in quality? Is there an underlying "substance" to actuality that ensures that each real thing has the quality of "being" regardless of its accidental transformations? Or is identity, as Whitehead suggests, not a matter of substance or essence at all? Is it, instead, a consequence of the passing on of "eternal objects" (Ideas) and of the "objective immortality" of the past within the present and the future? This problem of essence versus accident is even more profound among the living than the non-living, since it appears that one of the qualities of the "autonomous" living entity is an *active* preservation of that underlying identity.

Evolutionary theory, Maturana and Varela admit, has unlocked the key to understanding the diversity of life, but "its emphasis on diversity, reproduction, and the species in order to explain the dynamics of change has obscured the necessity of looking at the autonomous nature of living entities for the understanding of the biological phenomenology" (*ibid.*: 75). It is this that leads them towards the exploration of "living systems in their unitary character".

Autopoietic "machines", "organization" and Platonic idealism

At this point we require some clarification of terminology. Maturana and Varela state that their approach will be "mechanistic". This language bodes ill for an understanding of their theory in idealist terms. However, it is evident that there is a semantic confusion here. Their definition of "mechanistic" explanation is simply that "no forces or principles will be adduced which are not found in the physical universe" (1980b: 75). This clearly does not mean, however, that they rule out the existence of non-material components of this "physical universe", since they state that they are not interested in the properties of physical "components" of systems – but in "processes and relations between processes realized through components". They make a clear distinction between the particular physical instantiation of a system, and the system itself (as a multiply instantiable blueprint). The latter they refer to as the *organization*, and the former as the *structure*. This organization can always be, potentially, actualized with different components, in a different place and time. They state that "a given machine can be realized in many different manners" (*ibid*.: 77).

Their supposed "mechanism" involves, then, organized unities or systems, and they include, as part of their "physical universe", multiply realizable *organizational* ordering principles. What Maturana and Varela refer to as an "organization" is an Idea in the Platonic sense. In referring to organisms as "machines" they mean to distinguish their account from, as they see it, the evils of Aristotelian "vitalism", in which "living systems [are endowed] with a non-material purposeful driving component" (*ibid*.: 74). As we shall see, it is doubtful that they succeed in producing an account of life devoid of such "purposeful driving component[s]"; nevertheless, this seems to be their motive in introducing the, arguably misplaced and misleading, language of mechanism into their, otherwise perfectly organic, philosophy.

The "domain of description"

Maturana and Varela end their introduction by asking, "What is the organization of living systems, what kind of machines are they, and how is their phenomenology, including reproduction and evolution, determined by their unitary organization?" (1980b: 75). The term "machine" might best be replaced with a more neutral term such as "entity" throughout, for the reasons described above. Why the use of the Kantian language of "phenomenology" though? They say of a living thing that:

> [I]t is central to distinguish in it what pertains to the system as constitutive of its phenomenology from what pertains to our domain of description, and hence to our interactions with it ... notions arising in the domain of description do not pertain to the constitutive organization of the unity (phenomenon) to be explained. (*Ibid*.)

The "real" organized entity is here claimed to be "constitutive" of *its* own "phenomenology", which, in turn, is distinguished from *our* "domain of description" (which, presumably, is constituted by our own phenomenology – and, by implication, our own organization). On the surface this looks straightforwardly Kantian. We shall unpack this in due course when we encounter Maturana and Varela's account of cognition. Ignoring, for the moment, various apparent terminological confusions, what arises in Maturana and Varela's system is a distinction between:

(a) the *organized* living entity in nature;
(b) the *"phenomenology"* of the organized living entity;
(c) the interactive system between ourselves as cognizing entities and the objects of our cognition and manipulation (in this case both self and object are living systems);
(d) our own accounts within the *"domain of description"* of the object entity as they arise from the interactive system in (c);
(e) Maturana and Varela's own account of the *autopoietic* existence of the living entity in nature as it "really is", stripped of "that which pertains to our domain of description" (*ibid.*).

The "domain of description" referred to in (d), we can only assume, is that which Stafford Beer refers to, in the preface, as "analytic" in character: the multiple, partial, reduction of the entity into component parts of a heterogeneous variety (chemical, mechanical, electrical, psychological, behavioural), and partial reconstruction in terms of such components for the purpose of "description". This is a process that is, as Maturana and Varela explain, always guided by our placing of the entity to be described into a context of usage, utility or purpose related to ourselves (What does this thing do for me, how does is relate to my purposes, what is its role in my environment of action?). In contrast the autopoietic systems theory referred to in (e) will provide an account of "what pertains to the system" itself "in terms of relations, not of component properties" (*ibid.*: 75–6). *Thus the distinction between (d) and (e) parallels precisely the same distinction that we find between Kant's "understanding" and "teleological judgement", and Hegel's "understanding" and "dialectical reason"* (see chs 5 and 8).

Like Hegel, and unlike Kant, Maturana and Varela are quite convinced of the capacity of the human intellect, in principle, to grasp the autopoietic reality of life; they state emphatically that "autopoiesis is necessary and sufficient to characterise the organization of living systems" (*ibid.*: 82). A living entity can never be characterized by enumerating characteristics (reproduction, evolution, metabolism, etc.), but can only be properly characterized as a *self-producing organizational unity*. Furthermore, they mock the suggestion that life is impervious to our intellect, and insist, in a direct contradiction to Kant's strictures about the futility of trying to understand "even a blade of grass", that "[t]he beauty of life is not a gift of its inaccessibility to our understanding" (*ibid.*: 83). Since they clearly believe that our experience of the object of observation (including the autopoietic organism) is always a prisoner of the domain of description, it is necessary to ask how they, or we, can have access to knowledge of the autopoietic reality of life beyond the domain of description. This was the question that caused Kant to retreat into a claim that our teleological judgement is based not on experience but on mere analogy. It was, subsequently, the question that forced Hegel to invent dialectical logic. No obvious answer to the problem is forthcoming from Maturana and Varela, although we must presume that they have in mind some form of transcendental deduction. At any rate, it is evident that it is to the idealist tradition that one would have to look for answers to such a question.

Purpose

Maturana and Varela often elide two conceptions of purpose (as, of course, does Kant). They understand the concept of purpose primarily in terms of the use to which an entity can be put, beyond itself. The purpose of a machine is not intrinsic to the machine itself, but is a product of the "domain in which the machine operates" (1980b: 77). The machines that we ourselves make, we make for a purpose, and so legitimately understand them in terms of that purpose. When we think of living entities in nature in terms of such purposes, however, we are only doing so in order to "call into play the imagination of the listener and reduce the explanatory task in the effort of conveying to him the organization of a particular machine" (*ibid.*: 78). However, this "should not lead us to believe that purpose, or aim, or function, are constitutive properties of the machine … such notions are intrinsic to the domain of observation and cannot be used to characterize any particular type of machine organization" (*ibid.*). This seems, on the surface, to be a straightforward Kantian denial of the applicability of teleological judgement to nature, in anything other than a metaphorical sense (see ch. 5). Nature seems to be designed according to purpose, but this is just part of our way of looking at things, says Kant. But there is more than one sense in which "purpose" finds its way into Maturana and Varela's discussion. Besides this "purpose" connoting active design there is a further conception of purpose as the playing of a role within a "unitary" system: what we might otherwise call a "function". This is "purpose" *internal* to the autopoietic entity itself. It is difficult to see how one could speak of systemic "unities" without taking such a conception of "purpose" quite literally rather than metaphorically.

Components really *do* have purposes within such systems. Since Maturana and Varela have committed themselves at the outset to the elaboration of a theory of living entities in terms of their "unitary organization", and the assertion that these "organizations" are real things, it is difficult to see how they could escape the, literal, inclusion of this kind of "purpose" in their account. The *organization* is what provides an explanation for the parts rather than the other way around. *The parts are as they are because of the "purposes" imposed on them by the organization.*

Nevertheless, they insist that accounts given in terms of purpose lie in the "domain of description" only. We place, or imagine, such entities within a context in which we can understand them as purposeful or useful. Autopoietic organization itself should be conceived only in terms of relations between parts, which ensure that particular states will lead, mechanically, to other states (*ibid.*: 86).[3] Indeed, they insist that even the concept of "development" lies in the domain of description. We should not understand ontogeny in terms of transition "from an incomplete (embryonic) state to a more complete or final one (adult)", but rather as a "becoming of a system" from one state of unity to another state of unity by virtue of efficient causation (*ibid.*: 87). Their Kantian critical impulses are clear, then, on this score. But, apart from the difficulty of making sense out of the "becoming" of an always already complete system, their insistence on the reality of the organization, independently of its physical instantiations, seems radically incompatible with this mechanistic materialism. Either they must abandon the Platonic–Hegelian realism with respect to the "organization" (Idea), or they must abandon the Kantian aversion to the reality of teleology and teleonomy. The latter abandonment, we would argue, is far more in keeping with the rest of their project.

Self-production

Here, then, is Maturana and Varela's initial definition of an autopoietic entity:

> An autopoietic machine is a machine organized (defined as a unity) as a network of processes of production (transformation and destruction) of components that produces the components which: (i) through their interactions and transformations continuously regenerate and realize the network of processes (relations) that produce them; and (ii) constitute it (the machine) as a concrete unity in the space in which they (the components) exist by specifying the topological domain of its realization as such a network. (1980b: 79)

It is a "network of processes of production" that produces "components", which themselves "realize" the "network of processes". The existence of these components consists only in their specification of the "topological domain" in which the "network" will, on this occasion, be "realized". To reiterate, the "network of processes of production", otherwise known as the "organization", is what primarily exists. It is what provides an explanation for the existence of the autopoietic entity. While processes of efficient causation can be empirically traced throughout such an entity, the asserted reality of the "organization" as the determining factor implies, we would suggest, that the ultimate determinant is not efficient causation, but something more akin to a Hegelian final causation or teleology.

Processes and relations of production

This "network of processes of production" is not engaged in a once-and-for-all production, but a continuous production of itself. It is realized through an "endless turnover of components". As Maturana and Varela put it, "if the processes stop, the relations of production vanish; as a result for a machine to be autopoietic, its defining relations of production must be continuously regenerated by the components which they produce" (1980b: 79). This is a conception very closely allied to Whitehead's "society" of "actual occasions" (see ch. 13). In precisely the same way, the autopoietic entity must be actualized anew at every moment. At this point it is again worth asking whether the authors' strictures against teleology and teleonomy are compatible, in any meaningful sense, with such a language of "production". How can "relations of production" be a meaningful determinant in the dynamics of the autopoietic entity unless they are explicitly directed at the production of *something*, which is their end or final cause? One might go as far as to say that "production" is an inherently teleological concept. The *purpose* of the relations of production is clearly the reproduction of the entity.

Autopoiesis and autonomy

Maturana and Varela make a distinction between "autopoietic machines" and "allopoietic machines". A living organism is an example of the former, while a motorcar or a computer or a machine in a factory is an example of the latter. What makes autopoietic machines distinctive, as we have seen, is that their production process is simultaneously determined by, and directed towards production of, their own organization. All productive processes are subordinated to this objective (an autopoietic entity may include some allopoietic processes so long as they are consistent with, and subordinate to, self-production). All other machines are allopoietic. That is, their productive processes are directed towards the production of something other than themselves. It is this direction of productive process towards self-production that Maturana and Varela view as definitive of autonomy. This is what it is to be autonomous – to be self-producing. Perhaps, even, as Kant clearly suspected, it is what it means to be free. But while Kant could not conceive of how anything could be really self-producing within nature, Maturana and Varela's biology is concerned with precisely that problem.

Far from equilibrium systems

It is worth saying a little more here about the contrast between autopoiesis and allopoiesis. Of course, most allopoietic machines have no self-reproductive or self-repair systems whatsoever, and, over time, lose their organization in the process of producing something other than themselves (they corrode, decay, wear, etc.). The second law of thermodynamics determines that they are inevitable victims of entropy. Autopoietic machines, therefore, are, as later complex systems theorists would point out, apparently, negentropic machines. According to Ilya Prigogine and Isabelle Stengers, and later thinkers, this local negentropy is achieved by ensuring that the machine exists within an environment of permanent energetic disequilibrium. Autopoietic systems are what complex systems theorists would call "far from equilibrium systems" (Prigogine & Stengers 1984).[4] It is here that we find direct parallels with the asymmetrical powers ontology that we saw, initially, emerge with the Neoplatonists.

Autopoietic systems must "feed" on energy differentia[5] in order to ensure the constant flux of process, within which the endless rebuilding of the system is possible. They are "organizationally closed" but materially and energetically "open". The organism must metabolize food and oxygen in order to fuel its constant process of self-production (autopoiesis). The overarching disequilibrium is that between the temperature of the surface of the Sun and that of the Earth. This ensures a constant passage of energy between the two, which in turn ensures constant energy disequilibria at the Earth's surface. It is within these streams of energy dissipation that autopoietic systems are able to produce negentropic effects. As autopoietic systems produce more autopoietic systems, as well as themselves, we see a local build of organizational complexity (at an overall cost of loss of energy or information at the cosmic level – according to conventional thermodynamics). The Neoplatonic account of an "emanation" from an undifferentiated maximum power, to more complex and differentiated hypostases, via a structuring Intellect of

Ideas (organization), is manifest in this disequilibrium between the Sun and the Earth. This iterative account of the autopoietic system, first published in 1972, formed, then, a prototype for the proliferation of theories of far-from-equilibrium self-organization within complex systems theory over the following decades. Prigogine would later refer to such systems, in general, as "dissipative structures" (Prigogine & Stengers 1984). All of these theories have a similar idealist metaphysical character.[6]

Essence and accident

Autopoietic entities, while focused on reproduction of their organization relations, are, evidently, subject to perturbations from the environment. They will "undergo internal structural changes which compensate these perturbations" (Maturana & Varela 1980b: 81). However, regardless of the extent of such changes, they "maintain constant certain relations between components" (*ibid*.). There is a distinction, then, for Maturana and Varela, between: (a) those organizational relations that define the "individuality" and "identity" of the particular entity in question; and (b) other features of the entity that may derive from its interaction with its environment ("perturbations"), but which are not aspects of the organization proper (and which do not interfere with that organization). I might accumulate new memories, for example, as a consequence of perturbations by the environment. These memories do not fundamentally undermine my organic organization though. I do not change to a different species, or suddenly die.

We might observe in this distinction something like the Aristotelian distinction between essence and accident. The essence of an autopoietic entity lies in those organizational relations that are directed exclusively towards the self-reproduction of the entity in question. These relations define what Maturana and Varela refer to as the "individuality" of the entity (*ibid*.: 87). Without these basic relations the entity in question would disappear. All autopoietic entities must, therefore, have mechanisms (membranes, digestion, immunity, etc.) for ensuring permeable boundary maintenance such that, while other alterations may occur, these basic *organizational* relations remain undisturbed. All other accumulated features beyond those basic organization relations are, in Aristotelian terms, "accidental".

An end in itself

This leads to another interesting feature of the autopoietic entity, in contrast to the allopoietic. An autopoietic entity may be deployed for allopoietic purposes. Any animal, plant or person may be used instrumentally by another. It will be conceived, then, in terms of input and output, just like any other allopoietic machine ("what do I have to do with this 'machine' to get it to do what I want?"). The using "observer" will, in these circumstances, conceive of the entity being used, within the "domain of description". The underlying autopoietic organization of the entity will be invisible from this point of view. Maturana and Varela therefore make the point that from the point of view of autopoiesis *per se*, the entity has no "inputs and outputs" (1980b: 81). *It is its own input and output.*

This recalls Kant's strictures regarding the importance of treating the human being as an end in herself. While Kant defends this on the basis of a universal moral maxim, Maturana and Varela, astonishingly, seem to insist that it is, in fact, an epistemological necessity. It is the condition of true knowledge of the nature of autopoietic life in-itself. In a sense Kant was correct to argue that moral and cognitive reasoning are intertwined, but this is because avoidance of instrumental thinking is necessary in order to see that life *really is* its own end.

The absolute organization?

In their account of autopoietic machines, Maturana and Varela make a telling point regarding the boundaries of such machines. It has long been a tenet of cybernetic theory that all such machines reproduce themselves, and maintain certain aspects of themselves constant through the mechanism of feedback. Such feedback produces homeostatic effects.[7] Autopoietic living entities are a mass of such feedback loops. According to Maturana and Varela:

> [A]ll feedback is internal to them. If one says that there is a machine M, in which there is a feedback loop through the environment so that the effects of its output affect its input, one is in fact talking about a larger machine M' which includes the environment and the feedback loop in its defining organisation. (1980b: 78)

But, of course, every living entity is embedded in multiple systems into which it feeds output modulated directly by its inputs (a predator hunting its prey, a parent caring for its young, two people conversing). What I say and do is modulated by what I experience. Indeed, it is difficult to imagine any kind of organic output that does not have, at some point, a dual aspect as input, and vice versa. This seems, inevitably, to make social systems and ecosystems into autopoietic systems. It is difficult to see, as Stafford Beer points out, how one can avoid the conclusion that "human societies are biological systems" (1980a:

233

70). This unitary, organic, logic (a dialectical logic), extends onwards and outwards to the organic totality of the entire universe. In successively dissolving each living thing into a wider system of which it is a part, Maturana and Varela find themselves in the company of Plotinus, Hegel and Whitehead yet again.

Cognition, life, reality

Maturana says, in his introduction to the two key essays in *Autopoiesis and Cognition*, that as a young biologist in the late 1950s and early 1960s, the two questions that constantly plagued him were: what remains "invariant" in all living entities, and what is perception? We have seen something of his answer to the first of these questions, but what of the second? What are experience, perception, cognition, mentality? A number of interesting claims emerge:

(a) There is no representation in cognition. Neither we, nor any other organism, extract information from a pre-given world and "represent" it to ourselves.
(b) Cognition, then, is not *of* a world; rather (as for Berkeley, Kant, Hegel and Whitehead in slightly different ways), cognition "*brings forth a world*" (Maturana & Varela 1998: 26)
(c) Cognition is, therefore, coextensive with life. To live is to experience – again, echoing many earlier idealists.
(d) Cognition runs far wider than mere "thought". All living entities engage in cognition. Cognition is possible even in the absence of a brain or nervous system.

Maturana's early work was on the neurobiology of colour perception. He says that in the early days he followed an epistemological model according to which "reality [is] external to the animal and independent of it (not determined by it), which it could perceive" (Maturana & Varela 1980a: xiv). Perception, in this model, is a matter of extracting "information" from a pre-given object world, and "representing" that reality within the animal's perceptual "space". Over time, however, he found that this model simply was not viable. He could not consistently map environmental stimuli to neurological activity. It simply was not the case, he says, that, for example, "red" mapped to a simple range of electromagnetic frequencies. It could be triggered by a vast range of environmental conditions. He decided that "a different approach" was required. He asks, "What if, instead of attempting to correlate the activity of the retina with the physical stimuli external to the organism, we did otherwise, and tried to correlate the activity of the retina with the color experience of the subject?" (*ibid*.: xv). In other words, henceforth the "external world" would function, in relation to an autopoietic entity, merely as a "trigger" (via "perturbation") to perception. The external world would not, however, "specify" the precise structural changes that would take place in the cognizing entity. This specification would, instead, be a function of the organization of the autopoietic entity itself.

Within the theory of autopoiesis, this is what "choice" (even, perhaps, freedom) amounts to. The brain and nervous system are "organizationally closed". The retention of organization is the primary objective of the organism. But, in order to retain its organization, the entity must respond or adapt to its environment or "medium". It must have a capacity for plasticity of structure, even though only structural changes that are compatible with this organizational closure are possible. Therefore, the organizationally closed brain and nervous system must "specify" or "choose" how the entity should structurally "adapt" in response to the perturbation in question. The influence of Kantianism is, again, evident here. This linking of the autopoietic entity to the entity's medium such that it can produce structural modulations enabling successful adaptation to that environment, from moment to moment, is known as "structural coupling" (Maturana & Varela 1980a, 1998; Varela *et al*. 1993; Maturana & Poerksen 2004).

This structural adaptation or "coupling", under autonomous specification, *is* cognition. In a very Parmenidean move,[8] they argue that cognition is identical with every single physical modulation and activity of the organism in response to its environment, as specified by the organization of the entity itself. Not all structural changes are cognitive. For example, damage to the organism is a structural change, but one that takes place outside the organizational specification of the organism; the organism has not "chosen"; such damage defies the organism's autonomy.

Cognition, *mental activity, is immanent to all of life,* at every level of its self-organization, then. As Maturana puts it "the question: 'How does the organism obtain information about its environment?' [is] changed to: 'How does it happen that the organism has the structure that permits it to operate adequately in the medium in which it exists?" (Maturana & Varela 1980a: xvi). No longer is the organism (autopoietic entity) attempting to extract information from an environment from which it is separated by an epistemological gulf. Instead the organism modulates its structure, in harmony with the structure of its "medium", in a way that is specified by the organization of the organism itself, such that the organization can persist. Returning to Parmenides, thought, one might say, is identical with the being of an organic universe.

So, to "know" something new is to endure a change in structure. To change in structure is to "do something". To know is to act: "knowing is effective action" (Maturana & Varela 1998: 29). All knowing is action and accumulation of structural change. As a consequence, there is, over time, gradual structural change at the level of the individual organism and the species. While organization is preserved, adaptations are added to generate diversity of structure around that organization. This specification of structural change by the organization itself is what permits both phylogenetic and ontogenetic "drift" in structure while organization is preserved.[9]

Phenomenology or the philosophy of organism

In a book written specifically on the cognitive and epistemological dimensions of autopoiesis, Maturana and Varela state that "knowing cannot be taken as though there were 'facts' or objects out there that we grasp and store in our head". Rather, "*every act of knowing brings forth a world*" (1998: 25–6). The implication that understanding brings forth empirical nature recalls Kant's *Critique of Pure Reason*. And in a sentence that might have come from many of the idealists that we have studied, right back to Parmenides, they say there is an "*unbroken coincidence of our being, our doing, and our knowing*" (ibid.: 25).

This can, of course, be taken in two directions. On the one hand, it could be taken into the domain of phenomenology. Knowledge of the world is always from the perspective of the specifications of our particular organization. Our organization, as Kant insists, determines our phenomenology (recall this assertion by Maturana and Varela at the outset of this chapter). Here we are in some danger of the appearance of solipsism and isolation from nature. Maturana and Varela themselves are clearly aware of this danger; they humorously depict their "epistemological Odyssey: sailing between the Scylla monster of representation and the Charybdis whirlpool of solipsism" (1998: 134). On the other hand, with Hegel and Whitehead (perhaps even Parmenides and Plotinus), we can conceive of cognition as immanent to all of nature. There is no question of being trapped inside an organizationally determined phenomenology, because the organizational specification of the structural modifications of each autopoietic entity is precisely what specifies the structure of the actual world. Mind is not in an inner phenomenological space of some kind; it, along with all other aspects of life, is specified by the *organization* of the natural world. This is what it means to take the assertion that there is an "unbroken coincidence of our being, our doing, and our knowing" seriously. In fact, Maturana and Varela never fully make this leap into the latter kind of idealism. It is implicated in all their work but they slip constantly into a Kantian dualism and phenomenology despite all the inherent difficulties of that position, especially for scientists such as themselves.[10]

Part of the problem for Maturana and Varela is that they create too clear a distinction between the reproduction of the organization proper, and the creation and reproduction of other structural features of the organism. Cognition is restricted to the latter. The reproduction of the organization is simply taken as given. But what is the organism doing when reproducing its own organization if not cognizing itself? This is one of Whitehead's key points. Experience *is* the process whereby the enduring entity reproduces itself from actual occasion to actual occasion. The first given fact that the new actual occasion of an organism's existence "prehends"[11] is the last occasion. How do I know how to be myself at this moment if not by knowing the last moment of myself? This is how I reproduce my organization.

Furthermore, and to reinforce the point, autopoietic entities provide one another's "medium". Each entity is modulating its structure in response to the perturbations of other entities as well as its own organization. What emerges are higher and higher levels of organization, each of which are preservative of themselves *as* organizations. So the structural coupling *between* autopoietic entities becomes part of the "relations of production" of higher-level autopoietic organization (societies, ecosystems, etc.). Organizational reproduction and structural coupling cannot be cleanly separated in the way Maturana and Varela claim. In a science focused on the "unitary" entity, *all* structural modulations are aspects of the organization.

Conclusion

Maturana and Varela provide, in the theory of autopoiesis and cognition, an excellent example of the power of idealism in science. The theorization of the primacy of organization and relation as definitive of a self-organizing totality is very similar to that of Hegelian idealism. The account of the process of self-production itself is highly reminiscent of Whitehead's organic philosophy, as is the theory of structural coupling. Organization is, in their account, a universal existent that can be instantiated in many particular actualities, to which it bears a relation of final cause. The Platonic idealism here is evident.

The account of organizational closure, and the complete specification of structural modulation by the organization, are overplayed. This threatens to result in, at best, Kantian or phenomenological constructivism, and, at worst, completely nihilistic solipsism. But it need not be so. The boundary between organization and structural modulation need not be so tight, nor specification so entirely unidirectional. In Whitehead's version of this process, the organization of a past actual occasion is a given for the present. The present must "prehend" this in order to produce itself, preserving identity over time. But this passage of organization from actual occasion to actual occasion occurs along with prehension of the entire environment *other* than the organization.

To put this another way, the environment cannot simply be a "trigger" to structural modulations. Some form must pass from the environment to the autopoietic entity. The organization does not simply "specify" whatever modulations it prefers without any reference to the form of the environment. It has, as Maturana and Varela themselves state, to create structural modulations that facilitate "adaptation". Clearly all structural modulations (cognitions) have to be compatible with the maintenance of organization, and the organization has to ensure this (through its "choices" or "decisions"); organisms do not normally vanish or disintegrate as a consequence of their cognitions. This does not mean, however, that the internal organization of the individual organism entirely specifies the form of cognition. It does not. Indeed, if it did, then such structural modulation would be useless for purposes of adaptation since it would be entirely self-referential. Each autopoietic entity must modulate its structure as part of a larger autopoietic entity of which it is, in turn, a part. All such modulations must, ultimately, harmonize at whatever level of autopoietic unity we wish to examine. The logical (Hegelian) implication of autopoietic idealism is that the "autonomous" specifications of autopoietic organizations are entirely constrained by the organization of an autopoietic universe. Our own organization *has* to constrain us to experience things as they necessarily are. Even for Maturana and Varela, it seems, only God really has autonomy.

STUART KAUFFMAN: "ORDER FOR FREE"

Stuart Kauffman places a quotation on the dedication page of his book *Investigations*:[12]

> An organized being is then not a mere machine, for that has merely *moving* power, but it possesses in itself *formative* power of a self-propagating kind which it communicates to its materials though they have it not of themselves; it organizes them, in fact, and this cannot be explained by the mere mechanical faculty of motion.

The quotation is from Kant's *Critique of Judgement*. Kauffman's biology is not merely implicitly idealist; the book is an *explicit* attempt to provide a scientific grounding for Kant's teleological judgement, not as analogy, but as the real organization of nature. This is driven by Kauffman's suspicion that "the way Newton, Einstein and Bohr taught us to do science may be incomplete" (2000: ix).

Kauffman's particular brand of complex systems biology first came to broad attention in the early 1990s in his books *The Origins of Order: Self-Organisation and Selection in Evolution* (1993) and *At Home in the Universe: The Search for Laws of Complexity* (1995). We shall be focusing mainly on the more recent *Investigations*, however, in which many of the themes of the first two books are reiterated, together with some broader philosophical speculation. Kauffman's work bears close comparison to much of the idealism that has been outlined in this book, in quite sophisticated form. It is, therefore, worth looking at his ideas in some detail.

Autocatalysis, self-production, catalytic tasks/purposes

Take 10,000 buttons, Kauffman says, and begin to join two at a time together with threads. Gradually the ratio of threads to buttons increases. At first, small clusters appear, then an exponential rise in size of clusters follows, and then, suddenly, at a particular "critical ratio" of buttons to connections, there is a phase transition to giant clusters. Kauffman believes that there are such phase transitions to "giant connected components in chemical reactions". This, he claims, is one of the factors leading to what he calls "autocatalytic sets" (2000: 35–7).

He suggests that we take some chemical substrates that react together to form a product. The rate of reaction will be proportional to the concentration of the substrates. As the concentration of product increases, a reverse reaction will begin to produce the original substrates. The overall conversion of the original substrate into product will slow as the substrate concentration diminishes, and the product concentration increases. Eventually the conversion will stop as the two reactions balance one another out. This is the point of chemical equilibrium for this closed reaction. All chemical reactions tend towards this point. However, if we "open the system" by continuously adding substrate, and removing product, we can keep the reaction going for ever as we maintain it in the "far-from-equilibrium" domain. This is the domain that is of interest – because it is the domain of dissipative structures, autopoietic entities, and life in general. Organisms feed on matter and energy, and expel waste in order to remain far from equilibrium (*ibid.*: 40).

In a complex environment there will be many substrates; they will react to produce many more chemical species; these, in turn, will react with one another and the original substrate to produce yet more species; and so on. These substrates and product species will, in a far-from-equilibrium environment, constitute a "reaction network". Kauffman asks, what happens if we catalyse some of the reactions in the reaction network? As we catalyse more and more of the reactions, eventually there is, as with the buttons and threads, a rapid transition to a "giant cluster" of catalysed reactions. As we add matter it will tend to flow into this "cluster". The cluster will act as an "attractor", drawing matter and energy into itself. We see this notion of "attractors" throughout Kauffman's work. It is a theme common to the whole area of complex systems theory. However, as we shall see, Kauffman is very clear about the independent universal existence, and determining effects, of organizational attractors. They are real entities that are not substantial in themselves, but which give rise to the organization found in apparently substantial entities. This is a strong idealist theme throughout his work.

When the substrates, and products, within a catalysed far-from-equilibrium reaction also act as catalysts for some of the reactions in this far-from-equilibrium reaction process, then we have what Kauffman calls an "autocatalytic set". When *all* the reactions that need to be catalysed can be catalysed by chemicals within the set, then the set has "catalytic closure". The set has become self-reproducing and organizationally autonomous in the sense described by Maturana and Varela. Kauffman says:

> [T]his holism is not mystical; it is instead an objective, observable property of a collectively autocatalytic set of molecules ... The radical new view of life that I adhere to is that life is based on collectively autocatalytic sets of molecules ... And more, as I shall suggest below, the emergence of collectively autocatalytic sets of molecules is not improbable but becomes almost inevitable in sufficiently diverse chemical reaction networks. (*Ibid.*: 32)

The catalytic closure of a set, then, is a quality not of any particular interaction, but of the set as a *unity*. Again, Kauffman's account of life seems to have the hallmarks of idealist science.

These autocatalytic sets constitute self-reproducing molecular systems. They self-assemble suddenly and spontaneously when chemical substrate conditions reach an optimum point, because of the (non-linear) phase transition characteristics associated with increasing connectivity: "life is an expected, emergent property of complex chemical reaction networks" (*ibid.*: 33). Catalysis is, he says, "ubiquitous". Effectively entire complex organisms are composed of many such autocatalytic sets: self-reproducing and regulating, far-from-equilibrium, molecular transformation processes.[13]

Why should autocatalysis occur? Kauffman shows that chemical diversity inevitably increases in any system unless there are mechanisms to limit it. As diversity increases, "the reaction graph becomes pregnant with the possibility of autocatalysis" (*ibid.*: 45). Once it is established, as we have seen, chemical "food" is drawn into the catalytic network "species"; autocatalysis acts as final cause.

Kauffman argues that, because the autocatalytic set is a self-producing unity, it is appropriate to conceive of molecules as performing "catalytic tasks" within the set. He says that "The molecules carry out the tasks, the tasks coordinate, or organize, the processes among the molecules" and that "the closure of the catalytic tasks … achieves a coordination or organization, of the flow of matter and energy into the autocatalytic system". And this language of "tasks" (purposes) is not merely analogy: "this closure in catalytic task space is a new concept with real physical meaning … and any free living cell, achieves catalytic closure" (*ibid.*: 62). Kauffman seems to be quite clear, then, that the language of "tasks" is perfectly appropriate within this context. Molecules, and their activity, within the autocatalytic network really can be accounted for in terms of their *purpose*. Hegel would have been proud of such a discovery.[14]

Autonomous agents, measurement and work cycles

Self-reproducing autocatalytic sets are molecular examples of what Kauffman calls "autonomous agents". The definition of an autonomous agent is something that is self-reproducing and does a "thermodynamic work cycle" (Kauffman 2000: 8). A thermodynamic work cycle is what a steam engine or internal combustion engine does repeatedly. The transfer of thermal energy is utilized to generate organized work: a "constrained release of energy". Overall the amount of entropy in the universe may have increased, but locally some new order has been produced: the order of the work generated by the constrained release of energy. A steam engine, going through repeated work cycles, drives a factory full of looms weaving fabric. The fabric production is a patterning, ordering; it is locally negentropic. In autonomous agents the work cycle is an integral part of the self-reproduction of the autonomous agent itself; the negentropy produced is the negentropy of the autonomous agent – its own organization. Kauffman is using the term "autonomous agent", then, where Maturana and Varela would refer to "autopoiesis".

Autonomous agents are "necessarily … non-equilibrium systems", as described above. He says there is "no agency at equilibrium" (*ibid.*: 68).[15] As Neoplatonism suggested, disequilibrium appears to provide the conditions necessary for the apparent purposiveness of autonomous agents. Work cycles are cycles around a reaction network facilitated by a system being open to constant external input of energy and food that drive it far from equilibrium, and this ensures the continuation of the reaction cycle. The reaction cycle *is* the entity in question. An organic cell is a series of linked reaction cycles driven by disequilibrium (asymmetrical powers).

The various positions in the work cycle are "states" in what is referred to as the "state space" of the system (the total of states that the system is theoretically capable of occupying given all its components and all the various combinations of those components). We shall see later that the system has to be "constrained" so that it oscillates predictably around the particular states that make up the work cycle. Without constraint such systems would disintegrate into a chaotic series of states within the, much larger, overall potential state space of the system.[16]

How is the far-from-equilibrium environment maintained? Metabolism has to link exergonic chemical reactions (which release energy) to endergonic reactions (which require energy). "Living cells link endergonic and exergonic reactions in order to build up high concentrations of molecular species" to drive the concentration of those species above their "equilibrium concentrations" (*ibid.*: 67). This is what enables far-from-equilibrium dynamics to continue. Autonomous agents are defined by their capacity to "measure" the environment in order to detect energy slopes or differentia[17] that can ensure this *metabolic process*. This "measurement" is cognitive and is a "purpose" of the agent.

Kauffman writes:

> I have a hunch ... that the coherent organization of the construction of sets of constraints on the release of energy which constitutes the work by which agents build further constraints on the release of energy that in due course literally build a second copy of the agent itself, is a new concept, the proper formulation of which will be a proper concept of "organization". (*Ibid.*: 72)[18]

By "copies of themselves", here, he refers not to the agent's cell division, but to "its ongoing construction of itself". It builds a "rough copy of itself" from moment to moment. This provides an account of self-production very similar to that of Maturana and Varela, and with strong echoes of Whitehead's "actual occasions". Mathematical modelling of the internal organizational determination of this autocatalytic self-reproduction of an autonomous agent is possible using differential equations. The equations model the changing concentrations of chemical components of the system as functions of one another (*ibid.*: 69).[19]

His autonomous agents, he believes, are (as with Maturana and Varela's autopoietic organization) multiply instantiatable. The "organization" of the agent is a real entity in its own right. This organizational "closure" definitive of the autonomous agent is a "collective" property not found in any one reaction (*ibid.*: 105). He writes that "The propagating closure that is *an autonomous agent appears to be a new physical concept that we have not known how to see before*" (*ibid.*: 105, emphasis added).

He says, therefore, that "Based on this, I want to say that autonomous agents are parts of the ontological furniture of the universe" (*ibid.*: 128) and that whole organisms are "part of the furniture of the universe". They are not just "atoms in motion in three-dimensional space" (*ibid.*: 129). He resists any attempt to reduce these "emergent" entities to simpler "ontological" elements.

An additional point that Kauffman makes on numerous occasions is that autonomous agents co-evolve. Autonomous agents provide the "environment" for one another. As one agent alters its structure in response to the environment (through mutation and selection, for example), so that structural modulation constitutes a change in environment for some other autonomous agent, requiring a further change, and so on. The term "co-evolution" is, in reality, a way of referring to the fact that the structure of individual species is necessarily determined to a large degree, by even higher-level organization: ecosystems and the biosphere as a whole. The same conclusions of overall unity seem to follow as we have seen emerge in relation to Maturana and Varela's autopoiesis.

Meaning and cognition

Kauffman argues for a force-based account of semantics. He says that from the point of view of a sugar-feeding micro-organism, "the glucose gradient is a sign": "Once there is an autonomous agent, there is a semantics from its privileged point of view" (2000: 111). He writes:

> [C]hemistry allows arbitrary organization of control relations ... It seems legitimate to assign the concepts of sign, signified and significance to the genetic code. It seems legitimate to extend that notion to much of the subtle signalling, chemical and otherwise, within and between autonomous agents. (*Ibid.*: 112)

Here Kauffman's view directly parallels that of Maturana and Varela with respect to their concept of "cognition". Kauffman's semantics and Maturana and Varela's cognition are effectively coextensive with the life process, since they designate the organism's capacity to restructure or modulate in response to the environment, in a manner specified by the organization, such that the organization may be preserved intact. This cognition or semantics is possible because of the self-reproducing character of such entities. The key aspect of this is the determining force of the thing that Kauffman refers to, repeatedly, as the "organization". Here it is the "organization" that determines the "meaning" of aspects of the world with respect to itself *as* an organization. Kauffman asks: what is an act, what is the difference between "actions" and "happenings"? He believes that "the rudiments of semantics, intentionality, value, and ethics arise with autonomous agents". Much like Kant, he argues that "we have the categories of ought and is in the physical universe once we have autonomous agents" (*ibid.*: 118).

Genetic networks

According to Kauffman's view, the molecular sequence of the genome is implicated in a self-reproducing and regulating autocatalytic set. Referring to François Jacob and Jacques Monod's work on the genome, he points out that it constitutes a network of regulatory switching operations. Regulatory genes diffuse chemicals called "trans-acting factors", which, depending on their concentration, regulate the activity of other genes, and, in turn, are themselves regulated by other regulating genes. Each structural gene is, says Kauffman, regulated by up to ten trans-acting factors. So there is a complex web of regulatory connections. This "joint dynamic behaviour" (2000: 161), mediated by trans-acting chemical agents, controls the overall behaviour of the cell, collections of cells and, indeed, processes such as embryonic development. It is through the regulatory network of switches that cells containing the same genome are differentiated into the different cell types of a complex organism. The different cell types are defined by different chemical behaviours that, in turn, are determined by the regulatory network of genes and trans-acting factors. So how can we understand these regulatory networks?

The state of each structural gene can be combined with the states of many other structural genes. So the genome has many possible combinations or "states" available to it, each of which could express a different behaviour of the cell as a whole. Indeed, says Kauffman, there are about 80,000 structural genes in the human genome. Each of these could be "on" or "off" (in fact, each of them can be in any of a far larger number of graded states of activity – but this simplification is sufficient to demonstrate the problem). So, in total, there are $10^{24,000}$ possible state combinations in the human genome. There have only been 10^{17} seconds since the big bang. So, says Kauffman, genomes cannot have explored more than a tiny fraction of the possible states theoretically available to them. The "flow" of a genetic network through its available "state space" from one functional combination of on–off states to another must be "confined" in some way (*ibid.*: 162). If it were not then it would take more time than is available in the total lifespan of the universe to find the functional states on which natural selection might operate. Random mutation and natural selection are not enough. Something more than mere matter and chance must, necessarily, be at work in the guiding of a genetic network through its "state space". What is this?

Boolean networks: attractors and regimes

Such networks can be modelled using Boolean networks by arranging an array of model genes in a two-dimensional array or matrix, connecting them to one another, and then setting up rules according to which each gene state is dependent on the state of the genes connected to it at the previous moment in the "clock time" of the network. So the state of genes at time t determines the state of genes at time $t + 1$. In Boolean network models the model genes generally have simplified on and off states. However, it is possible to produce graded Boolean networks, and the findings that are of interest are not affected by the simplification.

A deterministic Boolean network (unless it is huge and unconstrained) will eventually reach a state that it has encountered before; call it "state x". It will then follow the same series of subsequent states that it followed before, until it again comes back to state x. It will then circulate around this cycle forever, unless there is a perturbation. This is called a "state cycle". It is an "attractor" within the network. A state cycle may be anywhere from one state, to the whole of the state space in length. There may, within the state space, be more than one such state cycle, more than one attractor. Kauffman states that attractors "attract the flow of other states into them" (2000: 163). These are real entities with real determining force. They are clearly allied to the idealist conception of organization that we have already encountered. Indeed it seems that organization can be conceived of as a multiplicity of such attractors:[20] an organized hierarchy of Ideas.

These attractors are then the determinants of the behaviour of the network. Where there are multiple attractors, they define the alternative set of behaviours of the network. This, then, is what the alternative behaviours of organic cell "types" within an organism are determined by: the alternative attractors that inhabit the genomic regulatory network.

However, as we saw earlier, the potential number of states in a genomic network is fantastically large. State cycles that traversed even a relatively small part of the network would take too long to be biologically useful, and there would, potentially, be far more of them than required for the full behavioural repertoire required from organic cells. So how do such networks limit the number and length of state cycles, and the number of attractors? Kauffman says that models of such networks display "three broad regimes of behaviour" (*ibid.*: 165), depending on the "tuning" of three key parameters within the network.

If we take a simplified genetic model, arranged on a two-dimensional lattice, with each "gene" connected to its four neighbours, and we then start it at some random initial state, the overall network will, eventually, display one of three kinds of behaviour. Either (a) there will be a "sea" of "frozen" on or off genes, within which there are small islands of genes that continue to switch on and off in a regular pattern; or (b) there will be a "sea" of genes constantly switching on and off, with islands of "frozen" genes; or (c) there will be large islands of genes switching on and off, just cut off from one another by a "sea" of genes "frozen" in the on or off state. Behaviour (a) has been termed the "ordered" regime, (b) the "chaotic" regime, and (c) the "phase change" regime at the boundary between order and chaos. Kauffman believes that "most complex coordinated behaviour" is in the ordered regime close to the phase transition (*ibid.*: 166). Why is this phase change regime so important? It turns out that in this regime the length of state cycles scales as the "square root" of the number of genes. The human genome has 80,000 genes so, despite the fact that it has a state space of $10^{24,000}$, its attractors will cycle among $\sqrt{80,000}$ states, that is about 270 states, so long as it is held at, or close to, the phase change. This, then, is the domain in which we find what Kauffman calls "order for free". Given the time that it actually takes to turn a real gene on or off, a state cycle of 270 states should take between 4.75 and 48 hours. This is almost exactly what we find in nature since it appears that cell division of human cells takes between 8 and 48 hours. Additionally, in the real genetic network the different state cycles are what determine the different cell types of the organism. Research shows that the number of cell types scales roughly as a square root of the number of genes, as predicted in the phase change regime. This (and other evidence) supports Kauffman's argument that cell behaviours are state cycles, and biologically useful state cycles are produced by holding the genetic network at, or close to, the phase change between order and chaos.

Furthermore, operating in this regime ensures that each state cycle "neighbours" only a few others in the state space. The network requires a perturbation (a chemical signal from outside causing critical state switching) to shift it from one state cycle (attractor) to another. In order, therefore, to move from one state cycle to another that is far away in the state space, it must go through a succession of transitions from state cycle to state cycle. This would imply that we should find cell types located on a series of branching pathways in state space, which, in fact, is the case.

Robust order

Operating in the ordered regime close to the phase change is crucial for the spontaneous emergence of the kind of order found in biological entities then. But it is not just a question of appropriately scaled state cycles. Such constraint also ensures robust resistance to damage. Suppose we flip one gene from on to off at random, thus simulating mutation or damage. Neighbouring genes, too, change their state; the damage spreads in a cascade. If a network is cycling in the ordered regime this cascade of damage is very limited. In the chaotic regime cascades of damage can spread to cover all or most of the network. Such sensitivity to damage (hypersensitivity to initial conditions) is not, says Kauffman, "biologically plausible" (2000: 170).

Another way to think about this is in terms of convergence and divergence along flows in state space. If we take two states that are initially fairly similar to one another and start the clock, will the subsequent states become more alike, less alike or remain with the same "amount" of difference? Will they converge, diverge or neither? In the ordered regime they tend to converge, in the chaotic regime they diverge and in the phase change regime they do neither. Kauffman's argument is that where "flow in state space is mildly convergent" this will "allow the autonomous agents to make the maximum number of reliable discriminations and reliable actions, hence, to play the most sophisticated natural games by which to earn a living" (*ibid.*: 173). This is the answer to Maturana and Varela's difficulty. The autopoietic organism does not need to entirely specify the form of its cognition in order to maintain its own order so long as it lives in the boundary region between order and chaos. Living at the boundary enables the agent to retain organizational integrity while being structurally affected by the environment – such that useful cognition is possible. It is as "sensitive" as it can be without falling apart. At this point the agent is able to make the "maximum number of reliable discriminations without 'trembling hands'" (*ibid.*: 177).

What does this mean for the autonomous agent? It means that multiple perturbations tend to converge into the same structural effect on the agent. In other words, *many similar perturbations are measured as equivalent.* The organism is "buffered against the noise of the environment" (*ibid.*). What this means, then, is that this "convergence" determines that *many (perturbations) are subsumed under the one concept.* The body and the "concept" are simultaneously generated by immanent formative attractors (Ideas). These attractors (Ideas) determine the organization of the autonomous agent within a domain of "convergence". All this can be expressed as a mathematical structuring of the universe because the universe is mathematically structured. The Idea structures nature. It generates both the body and mentality. The Idea is real and the ancient convergence of thought and being is justified in a naturalistic interpretation of Parmenides: "for thinking and being are the same" (Phillips 1955: 553).

Nature's "tuning"

How are such networks held within this crucial domain? Model networks can be "tuned" (as mentioned earlier) via three parameters. The details need not concern us here. The point is that if a network is able to tune these parameters for itself then it can stabilize itself at the crucial phase change boundary. It turns out that organic cells do precisely this. Nature tunes, in particular, the parameter called "canalysation" in order to ensure that autonomous agents remain within the ordered regime.

These findings are extendable to asynchronous networks, and to networks with graded levels of activity rather than just on–off states (Kauffman 2000: 175). To reiterate the point, this is how the genetic network is constrained within a sufficiently small part of its state space, and with state cycles of a sufficiently small size, for it to be biologically practicable. Also, of course, while Kauffman discusses his Boolean networks as models of genetic networks in particular, the point is that this is a general system theory that is applicable to any autonomous agent at any scale. As he puts it, "the ordered and chaotic regimes and the phase transition between them are deeply characteristic of some enormous class of parallel processing nonlinear dynamical systems" (*ibid.*: 177).

Propagating organization

Kauffman writes that "we have established a 'circle of concepts' here – work, constraint, construction, propagating work, measurements, couplings, energy, records, matter, processes, events, information, and organization". But he says that we lack a satisfactory concept of "organization … its emergence, and self-constructing propagation and self-elaboration" to connect these concepts (2000: 104).

Can emergent levels of organization always be reduced to lower levels – more simple statements about sense data? he asks. Is temperature completely reducible to the kinetic energy of atoms? If so, how far can we reduce the "ontological furniture of the universe"? As we saw in the case of the organization of autonomous agents, Kauffman is deeply suspicious of such reductionist impulses. In particular – if the top level of organization can conceivably be multiply instantiated, then it is not reducible. For example, "DNA and RNA and proteins, is an instantiation, a sufficient condition for Darwinian evolution" (*ibid.*: 127), but it is, arguably, not a necessary condition. There may be many other ways of instantiating evolution. Here, again, he is pointing to the "reality" of universal organizational forms and their multiple instantiations. It is the same as the distinction made by Maturana and Varela between "organization" and "structure". The irreducible organizational forms in question are real Ideas.

If we go back to the earlier theme of work cycles in autonomous agents we might ask: what, exactly, is work? Physicists may say that it is just force acting through a distance, but Kauffman argues that it is more than this. "In any specific case of work, the specific process is organised". Work is always "organized". This requires a series of constraints. But, he says, "work is the constrained release of energy, but it often takes work to construct the constraints" (*ibid.*: 83). Kauffman writes that in physics:

> [The] problem of the organization of the process in any specific case of work is hidden from view in the initial and boundary conditions of the usual statement of the physical problem ... But an evolving biosphere is all about the coming into existence in the universe of the complex, diversifying ever-changing initial and boundary conditions that constitute coevolving autonomous agents.
> (*Ibid.*: 96–7)

We cannot, he claims, state the initial and boundary conditions of a biosphere. We have to "grapple with the emergence and propagation of organization itself". There is, he reiterates, something "amiss with the way Newton taught us to do science" (*ibid.*: 97). What Kauffman is voicing concern about here is precisely the problem of grasping the whole within which to understand the workings of the parts that motivated Hegel's logic.

"The heart of the mystery", says Kauffman:

> concerns a proper understanding of "organization" and "*propagating, diversifying organization*". Most profoundly, the mystery concerns the historical appearance since the big bang of connected structures of matter, energy, and processes by which an increasing diversity of kinds of matter, sources of energy, and types of processes come into existence in a biosphere, or in the universe itself.
> (*Ibid.*: 83)

The universe is far from equilibrium, but early on was relatively featureless. Why and how has this transition from an "absence of specific structures and processes" to the situation we find now occurred? How did the "nonequilibrium universe couple that enormous energy to the specific generation of anything at all" (*ibid.*: 84)?

Kauffman proposes a possible fourth law of thermodynamics according to which:

> As an average trend, biospheres and the universe create novelty and diversity as fast as they can manage to do so without destroying the accumulated propagating organization that is the basis and nexus from which further novelty is discovered and incorporated into the propagating organization. (*Ibid.*: 85)

The parallels with Whitehead with respect to centrality of novelty and the propagation of organization are clear. The result of this propagation is constantly increasing numbers of entities in what Kauffman refers to as the "adjacent possible" (*ibid.*).

Adjacent possible

Consider a large set of organic molecules as a substrate that will react to produce a large number of chemical species not found in the founder substrate. Kauffman asks us to "consider the founder set [of molecular species] as the 'actual'. Now consider the molecular species that are one reaction step away from the actual, but do not yet exist. Call this new set the chemically 'adjacent possible'" (2000: 47). Then he asks us to expand this view:

> Four billion years ago, the chemical diversity of the biosphere was presumably very limited, with a few hundred organic molecular species. Today the biosphere swirls with trillions of organic molecular species. Thus, in fact, the sunlight shining on our globe, plus some fussing around by lots of critters, has persistently exploded the molecular diversity of the biosphere into its chemically adjacent possible ... The species diversity of the biosphere has increased as well as the molecular diversity. The diversity of goods and services in our economy is huge compared to the diversity of goods achievable by Paleolithic humans 200,000 years ago ... Indeed, I will be so bold ... as to suggest that this nonequilibrium flow into a persistent adjacent possible may be the proper arrow of time, rather than the more familiar appeal to the second law of thermodynamics in closed thermodynamic systems.
> (*Ibid.*: 47–8)

The adjacent possible is "all those molecular species that are not members of the actual, but are *one reaction step away from the actual*" (*ibid.*: 142); "the biosphere has been expanding ... into the adjacent possible for 4.8 billion years" (*ibid.*: 143). What kind of a thing is this "adjacent possible"? It certainly is no palpable material entity. It certainly is no direct object of experience. And its determining power is no kind of efficient causation. Indeed, if anything, it appears to act *backwards* in time, from the realm of "possible futures" on the realm of actualities. The adjacent possible acts only where there is disequilibrium, so that a system can be "pulled" into an adjacent possible state. In other words, as Deleuze would argue (see ch. 15), it acts through the constant cancellation of difference or disequilibrium that, in turn, is constantly recreated anew.

There has been, Kauffman argues, an expansion of organic molecular species from a few hundred or thousands to hundreds of trillions. Unfortunately, however, we have "no particular theory for this expansion" of diversity (*ibid.*). Finally, Kauffman expresses the purposiveness of the motor of cosmic novelty quite explicitly:

> It follows that every such reaction couple [between actual and adjacent possible species] is displaced from its equilibrium in the direction of an excess of substrates compared to its products. This displacement constitutes a chemical potential driving the reaction toward equilibrium. The simple conclusion is that there is a real chemical potential from the actual to the adjacent possible. Other things being equal, *the total system "wants" to flow into the adjacent possible.* (*Ibid.*, emphasis added)

He intends us to think of this "want" in relation to "the actual molecular diversity of the entire universe" (*ibid.*). He points out that there are in the order of 10^{28} possible reactions between the 100 trillion organic chemical species in the actual. This is an astronomical number. Since a significant number of these "flow from the actual to the adjacent possible ... [t]he total chemical potential from the actual to the adjacent possible is hard to estimate, but it is certainly not small" (*ibid.*: 144). This is the force that drives the arrow of time.[21]

Non-ergodicity

We saw earlier that genetic networks have so many potential states in their state space that if they randomly wandered around that space without constraint, the time it would take to explore that state space would be longer than the time available in the lifetime of the universe. This is a peculiar characteristic of networks of this kind that Kauffman refers to as "non-ergodicity". The capacity of a system to explore all of its state space appears to be closely related to its capacity for entropic decay of information. Non-ergodicity, in contrast, appears to imply resistance to entropy. Indeed increasing non-ergodicity seems, in Kauffman's analysis, to imply generalized negentropy.

Kauffman points out that computer-generated environments for organizational evolution based on algorithmic modelling reach only limited levels of organizational complexity. The continued propagation of complexity characteristic of the biosphere is absent. This, he argues, must be because the biosphere is not properly algorithmic. But how can this be? He argues that it is because it is not possible to state, or define, input data and a program for the biosphere.

> The configuration space of a biosphere cannot be finitely pre-stated ... persistent novelty occurs in the biosphere and universe as a whole ... something is odd with how we have been taught to do our science for in Newtonian physics, Einstein's physics, and Bohr's physics, one can finitely pre-state the configuration space in question. (2000: 123)

To illustrate what he means by this he discusses the theme of "exaptation" as developed by Stephen Jay Gould and Elizabeth Vrba (Gould & Vrba 1982). The idea here is that features of the organism that have evolved performing one particular function (or no particular function) may have an almost infinite possible number of causal consequences in variable environments, and suddenly begin to be selected for the performance of a quite different function. Consequently he argues that there is "no finite description of a simple physical object in its context" (*ibid.*: 133). So, we cannot have an algorithmic description of an organism that includes all possible exaptations of all its features. It is not possible to finitely pre-state all possible exaptations of all organisms in a biosphere. There is, in other words, no finitely pre-statable set of all the possible biological functions. "We cannot say ahead of time all the possible constellations of matter, energy, process, and organization that is a kind of 'basis set' for a biosphere in the sense that the atomic chart of the elements is a finite basis set for all of chemistry" (*ibid.*: 131). We do not even know what the basic building blocks of a biosphere (its "primitives") are. They seem to keep changing over time, he argues (*ibid.*: 136). Similarly, it is not possible, either, to pre-state all the causal consequences of human artefacts that might end up being useful. We, accidentally, *find* new uses for things all of the time. He says that because they are not pre-statable, all these things are "genuine novelties in the universe".

What we are touching on here is the massive connectivity of the physical universe as a whole. Because of the organizational propagation into the adjacent possible "the transformation rules of the biosphere enlarge and change in ways that cannot be pre-specified". A biosphere may have "algorithmic freedom" – while conventional science is algorithmic – which is why there are no higher-order organizational levels in algorithmic models (*ibid.*: 125).

But it is not just the biosphere that has the quality of being resistant to pre-statement of conditions, relations and possibility. The universe itself is "vastly nonergodic" (*ibid.*: 144). Kauffman says that "there is no way in the lifetime of the universe for any knower within the universe to enumerate, let alone work with, all the possible properties or categories and their causal consequences" (*ibid.*: 137). The necessary computations are "transfinite – not infinite, but so vastly large that they cannot be carried out by any computational system in the universe". There are "combinatorial problems" that are greater in scale than "all the events that have happened within any causally connected light cone (since the beginning of the universe) that might … carry out computation" (*ibid.*: 138). He thinks that the inability to pre-state the configuration space of the biosphere is related to this "incapacity to enumerate and predict all the possible detailed dynamics of coupled molecular systems by any computational system in the universe" (*ibid.*: 139). As long as so many species remain in the unexplored adjacent possible towards which the universe is drawn, towards which it "wants" to flow, Kauffman claims, the universe cannot come to equilibrium. Since the ever increasing diversity of the actual implies increasing diversity of the adjacent possible, Kauffman seems to be moving towards a denial of entropy in general. He remains cautious on this point, however.

He concludes:

> The universe is vastly nonequilibrium, vastly nonergodic at the level of complex organic molecules. A fortiori, the universe is vastly nonergodic at the level of species, languages, legal systems, and Chevrolet trucks … the universe is kinetically trapped. It has gotten from wherever it started, by whatever process of flow into a persistently expanding adjacent possible, but cannot have gotten everywhere. (*Ibid.*: 145)

In fact the universe inhabits an increasingly small part of the "possible that it might have reached" (*ibid.*). What does this mean with respect to entropy? he asks.

Can this expansion into the adjacent possible go on for vastly longer than the lifetime of our universe, moving it into a smaller and smaller proportion of the total possibilities that it could have occupied, becoming "ever more kinetically trapped", and ever more "refinely differentiated"? The increasing organizational hierarchy is, he says, a "sink" into which the ever burgeoning complexity of the universe is "dumped".

We can give perfectly good causal accounts of "what happened" after the fact, even though it is impossible to predict ahead of time what features might become functional, or in what way, ahead of time. We can always retrospectively characterize events at the level of trajectories of fundamental particles. But this is after the event has resolved, or actualized, itself at the macroscopic level. The particular level is, perhaps, the last level of resolution or actualization; that is, it is the effect not the cause of things. This seems to be the case if we cannot pre-state possible worlds as we cannot at the atomic level, nor, as Kauffman points out, at the level of organic chemicals, autonomous agents or higher levels of organization. Again, Whitehead argues similarly that this is an inevitable characteristic of a totality that produces conditions of possibility for more than one future, only one of which is actualized. Once the present moment is actualized it appears as though it was inevitable, since the past does, indeed, provide its conditions. At the same time Kauffman is, somehow, convinced that this non-ergodicity is somehow determinant of the real purposefulness of things. He says that because we cannot pre-state the configuration space, we cannot deduce, from initial conditions, what will occur in the biosphere. So we are compelled to tell stories in terms of purposes and choices. By virtue of non-ergodicity efficient causation is not enough; organization and purpose in nature are real.

There is something profoundly reminiscent of both Hegel and Whitehead in the overall picture, in which Kauffman begins to suggest the ontological reality of purpose and direction in the universe, and, also to question classical mechanical determinism quite profoundly. He also explores a number of quantum theoretical arguments for questioning classical determinism (*ibid.*: 147–8). Towards the end of the book he discusses his work with the physicist Lee Smolin, in which they suggest that "if we cannot prestate the configuration space of a universe then 'time' is real and necessary, and ... the way a universe constructs itself may have analogies to the way a biosphere constructs itself" (*ibid.*: 123).

Smolin is another good example of a contemporary scientist influenced by idealist philosophy; however, Smolin is a physicist rather than a biologist. He opens his *The Life of the Cosmos* (1999) with a quote from Leibniz's *Monadology*, which states that the universe tries to obtain "as much variety as possible, but with the greatest order possible, that is ... the way of obtaining as much perfection as possible" ($56–8). Smolin, then, explicitly incorporates a Leibnizian idealist final causality into his theory of the laws of nature. The laws of nature "evolve" according to the "Idea" of the best (maximum). Fellow physicist Julian Barbour also argues that if the Leibnizian theory of maximal variety is correct then physics becomes rather like biology: the universe is an "ecological balance between competing individuals. Each is trying to be as individualistic as possible… to exist is to become differentiated and hence to emerge from the mist of nothingness" (2003: 54). Kauffman's own argument has itself clearly been influenced by Smolin's Leibnizian conclusions. He argues that the decoherence account of the collapse of the wave function in quantum mechanics implies a built-in ontological preference for the complex over the simple; the universe at a macro level is compelled to complexify its adjacent possible in an apparently dialectical movement of self-organization immanent to the whole universe. Neither Smolin nor Barbour makes any attempt to hide the great influence Leibniz has had on his thought and Smolin even argues that Leibniz should be the model for the relationship between the scientist and philosopher. "In the past, philosophers like Leibniz did not hesitate to tell physicists when they were speaking nonsense. Why now, when at least as much is at stake, are the philosophers so polite?" (Smolin 1999: 244).

15. CONTEMPORARY PHILOSOPHICAL IDEALISM

INTRODUCTION

Our discussion of idealism thus far has terminated in a survey of biology, which is only one of the sciences of nature we might have examined. The purpose of this focus on the natural sciences was twofold. First, we wanted to counter the more commonly accepted accounts of idealism – those we find in our standard reference works on philosophy – which present it as having little or nothing to say with regard to the natural sciences in particular or to problems in the philosophy of nature in general. Second, of the two themes emerging from the idealism that dominates in contemporary philosophy, the issue of naturalism has become a focus of activity since McDowell's influential *Mind and World* (1996) and the subsequent school of "Pittsburgh neo-Hegelianism" McDowell shares with Robert Brandom. It is a central theme of Brandom's *Making it Explicit* (1994) that "reason" is not subject to the naturalization agenda favoured by empiricists precisely because it consists in an inherently normative set of practices (interrelated makings-explicit). A second of these emergent themes concerns the normative account of idealism, which motivates the Pittsburgh school's critical concern with nature.

The limits of naturalism also motivate the work of Rescher, Sprigge and Leslie. For nor is experience separable from the experienced, so that what appears as an "antecendent nature" (Brandom 2009: 112) is rather consequent on the conceptual activity that produced it. Naturalism thus mistakes the part (the product) for the whole (the universe that includes the experiencing and conceiving of it) before shaving the latter from the former. While Rescher seeks to reverse this without making nature mind-dependent, since mind, too, is only a small part of what is, Sprigge makes mindedness as such into the condition of existence, proposing a panpsychism of finite centres of experience. Although Leslie shares both Rescher's normative metaphysics and Sprigge's panpsychism, he proposes that nature, just as it is, is the product of a "creatively effective ... ethical requiredness" (Leslie 2007: 2) that something exist. The consequences of all these positions set philosophical naturalism against a normative idealism.

One of the refreshing aspects of idealism's renewed good fortunes has been the emergence of a shared philosophical agenda among contemporary philosophers from both the "analytic" and "continental" traditions. Indeed, the view that the history of philosophy is the *lingua franca* that enables philosophers to speak to one another across traditions was asserted by Wilfrid Sellars (1968: 1), whose avowed Kantianism partly motivated McDowell's and Brandom's reinvestigations of Hegel. This same concern has resulted in a recent resurgence of scholarly interest in the period in which British idealism came under eventually fatal critical pressure from Russell and Moore (see Hylton 1990; Candlish 2007). Meanwhile, the renewed concern among postanalytic philosophers with the critical and idealist legacy of Kant and Hegel (see Redding 2007) shares its generally moral-practical orientation with many European philosophers' engagements with idealism as a development of the sceptical tradition in philosophy. Scepticism is not, as Burnyeat made clear, reducibly an *epistemological* response to problems concerning the existence of the external world, as Descartes presented it; its "prime concern" is ethical, so that "scepticism is a solution to uncertainty about how to act in the world" (Burnyeat 1982: 30). We find the same concern echoed in Paul Franks' (2005) and Markus Gabriel's (2009) studies of the relation between scepticism and idealism in modern and ancient philosophy, respectively. Yet the same problem is being played out again in contemporary philosophy. As we shall see, having rediscovered Fichte's importance, Žižek's declared "moralist idealism" (Gabriel & Žižek 2009: 158) leads him to forge an overtly political metaphysics of "wordlessness" (Žižek 2006: 318) as the sceptical basis for making his "French Hegelian" legacy contemporarily important.

While these philosophers agree with Brandom that the concept "concept" is normative (Brandom 2009: 114), not all contemporary idealisms are of the moral variety. Deleuze is perhaps an unlikely candidate for inclusion in such discussions, but this appearance is, as we shall see, superficial. Notwithstanding his many protests against "platonism", his metaphysics is an elaborate account of the nature of the "problem-idea" he describes as "a natural or spiritual power" (1994: 23), and draws equally on Platonic and Neoplatonic sources. Implicitly criticizing a "moralist idealism" as one-sided, Deleuze insists that philosophy must "embrace all the concepts of nature and freedom" (*ibid.*: 19), and thus reintroduces the philosophy of nature into an idealist philosophical framework. The roots of Deleuze's idealism are therefore shared with the Platonic philosophical cosmology proposed by Leslie, who argues that it is the *need for existence* that "wields creative power" (2007: 18). Although Leslie would dispute Deleuze's account of power, both share the problem of the relation between nature and idea, however differently articulated.

The basic axis of argument across which contemporary idealism ranges therefore extends from nature to freedom. Having taken a broadly naturalistic route towards this discussion, we are able to adopt a critical perspective towards both sets of arguments. Following McDowell, the "nature" at issue is contested with respect to: (a) what it is assumed to comprise according to contemporary naturalisms; and (b) whether a concept of nature so composed is well founded. McDowell shares with Hegel, according, for example, to Pippin (2002: 60), a movement "away from nature and towards spirit". The "moral idealism" at issue, meanwhile, is not reducible to "the pursuit of happiness" by which Burnyeat characterizes the position of the ancient sceptics, but rather confronts an insuperable moment of decision: "at some point or other", writes Gabriel, "we encounter a brute decision – the decision constitutive of rationality – which is neither rational nor reasonable" (in Gabriel & Žižek, 2009: 44). Exactly as for Fichte, the acknowledgment of a groundless decision as the starting point of philosophy entails that our knowing consists of free acts. For Žižek and Gabriel, as for Fichte, therefore, ethics becomes first philosophy.

We may note that these neo-Hegelian and neo-Fichtean repetitions of classical German idealism in contemporary philosophy are not extended to Schelling, although Deleuze repeatedly cites him (see esp. Deleuze 1994: 190–91, 229–31) and Žižek has written extensively on him (Žižek 1996, 1997). This is because Schelling's naturalism is not one, like Hegel's or McDowell's, preparatory to its supersession by "spirit". Our excursion into contemporary biological theory (chs 14–15) self-consciously echoes one of the more fertile fields for Schelling's philosophy of nature at the turn of the nineteenth century.[1] It therefore asks the Hegelian–Fichtean orthodoxy prevailing in contemporary idealism whether nature must be "left behind".

Nature, Freedom, Reason and Idea, then, constitute the constellation of problems whose solutions differentiate contemporary idealist philosophies, just as they did their ancient precursors (ch. 1). This chapter will therefore both summarize the concerns dealt with throughout this book and function as a map for locating the central concepts and problems of idealism where these occur in contemporary philosophy. By noting the chapters dealing with the sources of these concepts, we aim to reconnect them with their histories. While we do not claim that all philosophy is idealism, we are nevertheless suggesting that the histories of these concepts and problems have a continuing role to play in forming contributions to contemporary philosophical discussions, even those where the influence of idealism remains inexplicit.

ANALYTIC HEGELIANISM: JOHN MCDOWELL AND ROBERT BRANDOM

Concept and experience

McDowell's *Mind and World* revives two classic dilemmas of idealist philosophy. The first is how to assert the insuperability of our experience of reality without making reality experience-dependent in turn. The second is how to criticize scientistic naturalism without lapsing into straightforward anti-naturalism.

McDowell addresses the first problem by considering the nature of concepts. Endorsing Davidson's (1984) critique of the "dualism of scheme and content", or of concept and experience, McDowell argues that concepts are formed from our experience, and our experience is shaped by the world. This does not mean that worldly trees, for instance, *cause* the concept "tree", but rather that the concepts we rational animals form have as their content "the layout of the world". There is, as he puts it, simply "no ontological gap" between the sort of thing one can think and the sort of thing that is. Thought and reality, concept and experience, therefore maintain an "equipoise" in the concept, and it is central to McDowell's attempt to resolve the naturalism problem that "we should not look for a priority in either direction" (1996: 28). While scientistic naturalism invites us to hold a view of the world as it is without our thoughts interfering in it, so too a full-blown idealism of the sort McDowell wishes to avoid asserts the absolute mind-dependence of the world.

Kant's solution to this problem was to propose the thing-in-itself as mind-independent. Yet this mind-independent reality must remain inaccessible to experience, separating knowing and acting from what is. Rejecting the ontological cost of this solution, McDowell argues instead for the "unboundedness of the conceptual" (1996: 28ff.). The concept is unbounded in the sense that it has no outward limit that separates it from the world, so that "concepts are things grasped in thoughts" (Hegel 1991: 56). No reality is inconceivable in principle, as fundamental reality is for Kant. What thinking conceives is not something "alien and external to" the world, but rather the conceptual content *of* the world. This objective or "Absolute idealism", McDowell claims (1996: 44), is the Hegelian moment in his metaphysics.

Yet doesn't this, McDowell imagines a critic objecting, risk abandoning the independence of reality from thought, amounting to the most egregious of idealisms that renounces all hope of an independent reality as self-contradictory?

Hegel writes, "It is one of the profoundest and truest insights to be found in the *Critique of Pure Reason* that the *unity* which constitutes the nature of the *Concept* [*Begriff*] is recognized as the ... unity of the *I think*, or of self-consciousness" (1969: 584, trans. mod.). It is McDowell's project to demonstrate that this unity is not that of the thinking subject, but of thinking and being, or mind and world. To avoid a "merely subjective idealism", he follows Hegel's critique of Kant. Hegel argues that Kant's concept of knowing, which hinges on the unity of the subject, cannot be a knowing because it is contradictory: it is not a knowing of what is (reality), but a knowing of what cannot be known (the thing-in-itself). For Kant, the unity of the thinking subject can guarantee that my knowing is "mine" only because we know in advance that such knowing cannot be of the thing-in-itself. Therefore Kant's knowing asserts, writes Hegel: "a duality of opposed factors, the *unity of apperception* and equally a *Thing*; whether the Thing is called an extraneous impulse, or an empirical and sensuous entity, or the Thing-in-itself, it still remains in principle the same, i.e., extraneous to that unity" (Hegel 1977b: 144). Such knowing is "mine" only to the extent therefore that it is "abstracted" or withdrawn from what is. The project of Hegel's *Phenomenology* is to present the experiences in which knowing finds itself, experiences that broaden from sense-certainty to the sociohistorical contexts in which such knowings take place, to the "absolute" thinking that, Hegel says, is the "last shape of Spirit" (*ibid.*: 485). As the *last* shape, "spirit knowing itself as spirit" is the *goal* of experience, and it is in this last shape that this goal or "object" becomes explicit: "For experience is just this, that the content – which is Spirit – is *in itself* substance, and therefore an *object* of *consciousness*" (1977b: 487).

Hegel's claim is that fully elaborated consciousness explicates Spirit as its content, since it is Spirit that, as its substance, underlies experience as experience. McDowell, however, takes a more objective line, emphasizing the world's role in experience: "Experience enables the layout of reality itself to exert a rational influence on what a subject thinks" (1996: 26). The "objectivity" at issue does not, therefore, have, for Hegel, the sense it has for McDowell, since for the latter this is the objectivity of the world's "rational influence", whereas for the former, it is the objectivity of consciousness, or the self-directed *purposive* objectivity of Spirit. The objectivity at issue, therefore, can belong neither to nature nor to consciousness, but is encapsulated in the idea that reality exerts a *rational* influence.

Two questions, therefore, arise regarding the character of McDowell's neo-Hegelianism. First, what is the role of nature in (a) providing experience with traction on reality, and (b) McDowell's idealism? Second, if idealism is to retain traction on reality, and if nature does not in the end provide this, how does McDowell develop the character of objectivity?

The naturalism of second nature

One of McDowell's motivations is to reject the naturalistic realism, which, he holds, has held philosophy in its spell for much, at least, of the twentieth century. If naturalism is to be abandoned, the problem of what the world is must be revisited to avoid asserting naturalistic realism as the *only* possible explanation of the nature of the world without falling into reflex anti-naturalism. McDowell begins by resituating Kant's division of the domains of freedom and nature, such that "the crucial contrast … is between the internal organization of the space of reasons and the internal organization of nature, on a conception that modern natural science invites us to hold" (1996: 71n.). In brief, McDowell's position is that naturalism undermines "the space of reasons" within nature. Reason is, therefore, compromised by the falsely deflationary concept of nature on which naturalistic realism draws. Interestingly, rather than criticize modern philosophical naturalism directly, McDowell castigates it as "rampant Platonism", since it maintains that the objective view of things arises only once it has been abstracted from our experience of it. Naturalism is Platonic to the extent that it withdraws the reality of thought and experience from the domain of nature. McDowell's solution is to assert that the contrast between reason and nature can be maintained on the idealist grounds that "the world is made up of the sort of thing one can think", without in turn reducing that "sort of thing" to "mental stuff" (*ibid.*: 27–8).

It attests to the revisionary nature of McDowell's project that the philosophical contest for the world is between Platonic and Hegelian *idealisms*: only idealism provides a viable address to the problem. If Platonic naturalistic *idealism*, therefore, seeks the world as it is rather than its accidents and becomings, Hegelian idealism considers the world *inclusively*, so that thought about it and actions within it constitute elements of that thinkable, actionable world. To supplant naturalism, therefore, idealism must demonstrate that it is concerned not to abandon nature "in itself", that is, abstracted from that inclusive world, but rather to integrate it into a "naturalism of second nature" (1996: 86), that is, to consider the concept "nature" satisfied *only* once the world is developed in thought, experience and the concept.

In effect, McDowell resituates "nature" as consequent on rather than prior to experience. The concept being "unbounded" and therefore having no outside, the concept of nature is the only nature remaining. The question therefore arises whether this is a concept of nature at all, rather than perhaps a demonstration that the problem of nature *itself* is a pseudo-problem. Once we understand that nothing that takes place does so outside nature, it becomes so non-exclusive as to be contentless. Nature may, then, as McDowell concedes, "drop out of my picture" (2002: 277), just as it does for Hegel. However, that McDowell seeks his Hegel in the *Phenomenology* rather than the *Philosophy of Nature* suggests that it is less nature than experience that is his concern. His rejection of anti-naturalism notwithstanding, McDowell's "second nature" tends in an anti-naturalistic direction, revealing a kinship with contemporary, Bradley-inspired, "pan-experientialist" idealisms for which "there is no conceivable sort of concrete actuality but sentience" (Sprigge 1983: 110).

Second nature as ethical life

It is now clear that, for McDowell, the "unboundedness of the conceptual" means that the world to which thought is answerable is not the bare world of nature as revealed by the natural sciences, but rather already a world encompassed by reason and ethical life. It is here that the sources of both McDowell's idealism and the species of "naturalism" he is concerned to promote become clearer still.

McDowell's critique of scientistic naturalism is that it provides an abstract or "sideways-on investigation of how ethical life and thought are related to the natural context in which they take place" (1996: 83). The "naturalism of second nature" he is concerned to promote is based, by contrast, on placing ethical life or "culture" centre-stage to correct for this philosophical distortion. Yet as he puts it, "second nature is nature too" (2009: 186): nature is experience before being abstracted from it by naturalism's Platonizing objectives. As revealed in experience, nature is not bald but hirsute, because experience *is* nature for communitarian rational animals intimately physiologically, conceptually and practically involved in the world. It is this Aristotelian naturalism concerning cultured or rational experience that McDowell makes "transcendentally prior" for any conceivings of the world:

> If the space of reasons is alien to the space of nature, the idea that conceptual capacities could inform sensibility seems incoherent. ... My reminder about second nature ... was only meant to liberate my conception of experience from that seeming incoherence. What does the transcendental work is the conception of experience, not the appeal to nature. (*Ibid.*: 185–6)

This conception is, moreover, ethically motivated:

> The point of expanding the scope of intellectual freedom is to achieve a genuine balance between subjective and objective, in which neither is prior to the other. Achieving a genuine balance would allow subjectivity to be conceived as engaging with what is

> genuinely objective [and] is exactly not to abandon the independently real in favour of projections from subjectivity.
>
> (*Ibid.*: 152–3)

If conceptual and practical experience are of and by nature – of and by rational animals, that is – then clearly this does not abandon the world as such; yet a question may still be raised concerning the fate of the "independently real" on such a model. If, like Kant, we take the independently real to occupy a domain inaccessible to experience, we are left, argues McDowell, with as much of a "sideways-on view" of what lies outside the "outer boundary" of the space of concepts (1996: 41–2), as we find in scientific naturalism. At the same time as it revokes access to the independently real, such an account demotes the domain of experience to a merely subjective product in contrast to the radical independence of the real itself. Accordingly, Kant's transcendental account becomes precisely that sort of idealism for which reality is lost to experience and reason. To avoid this subjectivist trap, McDowell recommends that species of "absolute idealism" he finds in Hegel: "The way to correct what is unsatisfactory in Kant's thinking about the supersensible is ... to embrace the Hegelian image in which the conceptual is unbounded on the outside" (*ibid.*: 83). McDowell does not, therefore, abandon Kant, but takes the archaeology of experience from Hegel's *Phenomenology* at once to short-circuit the idea of some independently real lying outside any boundary of experience, and therefore as a medium into which to insert the Kantian demand that we recognize our own *responsibility* for our conceivings and judgings as well as for our doings. As Brandom puts the point, it is Kant's "fundamental insight ... that judgments and actions are to be understood to begin with in terms of the special way in which we are *responsible* for them" (1994: 8), so that our conceivings as well as our doings share a "normative" character. To conceive of "Hegel's idealism as a radicalisation of Kant" (McDowell 2009: 69–89), as McDowell and Pippin (1989) do, is then to grasp the transcendental priority of the normative over the division between subjectivity and objectivity in order to serve the aim, itself normative in turn, of "expanding the scope of intellectual freedom". This means, however, that nature itself, or "the independently real", must become a subset of second nature in so far as it is subject to conceivings. In other words, transcendentally speaking, no "independently real" is possible unless it is conceived of as such by experiencers and cognizers, which is to say that no "real" independent of experience is conceivable at all. This is why both McDowell and Brandom remake Hegel on a normatively Kantian blueprint, albeit one not beset, they propose, with the dualisms in that latter scheme that post-Kantian idealism sought to surpass.

Brandom's Hegelianism

Brandom is the more obvious inheritor of late-twentieth-century interpretations of Hegel than McDowell. His Hegel is informed and illuminated by Hartmann's "non-metaphysical view" which takes the "reconstruction" of "experienced fact" into "thought in terms of thought" (Hartmann 1976: 103) for what is living in Hegel. Crucially, Brandom also follows Charles Taylor's influential account, which agrees with Hartmann that "Hegel's logo-ontology" should be "set aside" (Taylor 1975: 569), but differs from him in emphasizing Hegel as a philosopher of "linguistic consciousness". In particular, Taylor makes the Enlightenment account of "expressivism" in Herder and Rousseau crucial to Hegel's model of "linguistic consciousness", all of which Brandom draws on to provide an alternative to the referential model informing the philosophy of language since Frege. Echoing Hartmann's rejection of the "informal and non-formalizable" Hegel resulting from J. N. Findlay's (1958) "re-examination", Brandom offers full-blooded support for Hegel's "rationalism", that is, his commitment to "making explicit" or putting into logical form, and thus conceptually mastering, what is merely implicit in unanalysed awareness. Brandom can thus be seen to be responding to a challenge from the conclusion of Taylor's *Hegel*: "Those who are trying to relate linguistic consciousness to its matrix in unreflective life – once Hegel's logo-ontology is set aside – must necessarily see explicit thought as rooted in an implicit sense of the situation which can never be fully explored" (Taylor 1975: 569). It is just as progressively making fully explicit what is implicit that Brandom takes Hegel to be labouring towards. Brandom nevertheless agrees that we are led "back to Hegel" in what Taylor identified as "the contemporary attempt ... to situate subjectivity by relating it to our life as embodied and social beings, without reducing it to a function of objectified nature" (*ibid.*: 570).

It is as a contribution to this attempt that the Brandom–McDowell revival of Hegelianism in contemporary philosophy is best understood. Brandom, in particular, is explicit about his "reconstruction" of Hegel's concept of Spirit or *Geist* as "normativity aware of itself as such", creating what Pinkard describes as a "self-instituted liberation from nature" (2005: 30). In this respect Brandom, with contemporary Hegel scholars such as Pinkard and Pippin (1989), considers Hegel to have extended or furthered Kant's critique of traditional metaphysics for his own and for the present age, outstripping both the pre-Kantian dogmas Brandom finds in Frege and the post-Kantian critiques of empiricism found in Quine, Davidson and Sellars. Moreover, if Descartes, Spinoza and Leibniz are read "only as their deepest lessons came to be understood within the German Idealist tradition", they, together with that reconstructed contemporary philosophical context, form a continuous legacy that Brandom refers to as "philosophical rationalism" (2009: 1).

History and system in Brandom's philosophy

The historical scope of Brandom's philosophy is not only unusually large, but also an important element of that philosophy. The activity of "recollecting" the history of philosophy is a part of what philosophy does, making explicit what is merely implicit in it while reconstructing it in new contexts. The other lesson Brandom draws from Hegel concerns the "systematic" side of philosophy, which it is the purpose of his celebrated *Making it Explicit* (1994) to deliver. Yet neither side is separable from the other. As he puts it, "the history of systematic philosophy … is itself animated by a systematic philosophical aspiration" (2002: 1). This properly Hegelian understanding of the scope and aspirations of philosophy, at odds with the (historical) self-understanding of the analytic philosophical context in which he is writing, marks out Brandom's project as an important shift in that self-understanding, a shift Rorty has described as Brandom's "attempt to usher analytic philosophy from its Kantian to its Hegelian stage" (in Sellars 1997: 8–9). This Hegelian stage is characterized by Brandom as that of "*objective* idealism", which he presents – somewhat paradoxically – as the thesis that "the structure and unity of the *concept* is the same as the structure and unity of the *self*" (2002: 210). This is at least paradoxical, since if the core of this idealism is said to consist in the identity of subject and concept, rather than, for instance, in that of thinking and being, then such an idealism would seem more subjectivist than objective.[2] To assess the "objectivity" or "subjectivity" of Brandom's idealism, we shall first examine the systematic dimension of his project before taking account of his Hegel.

The core thesis of Brandom's *Making it Explicit* follows from its critique of the semantic bias of the philosophy of logic and language, a "critique", he says "of the logical given". Semantics provides a theory of meaning, and assumes that such meanings may be stabilized and established independently of their application, a strategy Brandom calls "the Frege–Russell–Carnap–Tarski platonistic model-theoretic approach to meaning" (2000: 7). Like McDowell, Brandom contests this "platonistic" idealism by rejecting the idea that there is anything thinkable that is not already conceptually structured. Contrasting the "platonistic" with the Hegelian view, then, Brandom notes that:

> Frege thinks of the senses we grasp in thought and their referents in reality as two different *kinds* of things … It is a central part of Hegel's idealist strategy to take them to be things of the *same* generic kind … [such that] thought and the world thought about can both be seen to be *conceptually* structured.   (2009: 97–8)

According to the view Brandom recommends, Platonists simply do not realize facts of the matter concerning concepts. First, there are no concepts

265

that are not articulated in language. Second, concepts are exclusive occurrences within the domain Brandom comfortably calls "Spirit", or "the peculiar constellation of conceptually articulated comportments that Hegel called '*Geist*'" (2000: 33). Third, therefore, the world in so far as it is thought about is already a world-thought-about, and inseparable *in fact* and *in principle* from that thinking. Finally, not only *is* the world inseparable from thought about it at the ontological level, but nor, "deontologically", *ought* it to be (cf. Brandom 2002: 212).

Brandom's proposal concerning the philosophy of language draws on one of Kant's "great insights[:] that judgments and actions are to be distinguished from the responses of merely natural creatures by their distinctive *normative* status, as things we are in a distinctive sense *responsible for*" (2000: 33). According to this model, *pragmatics*, or "things we do" with language, is prior to semantics, because *claiming* and *knowing* are *actings*, products of that "spontaneity" that, like McDowell, Brandom assimilates to the normative "space of reasons". Rather than being constrained by things, this pragmatics is normatively constrained by reasonings, and the inferential patterns by which our "entitlements and commitments" are made explicit. Thought is not exhausted in accurately tying our meanings to worldly referents, but rather consists in a holistic and systematic working out of the claims we make, the claims and actions these commit and entitle us to, which two sets of practices Brandom categorizes, with Hegel, as being the work of the *understanding* and of *reason*, respectively.

No sooner does Kant resolve the problem of meaning by making it into a doing, than he recreates the dualism of ontology and deontology at another level, a dualism resolved by Hegel:

> Kant ... punted many hard questions about the nature and origins of normativity, of the bindingness of concepts, out of the familiar phenomenal realm of experience into the noumenal realm. Hegel brought these issues back to earth by understanding *normative* statuses as *social* statuses – by developing a view according to which ... *all transcendental constitution is social institution.* The background against which the conceptual activity of making things explicit is intelligible is taken to be implicitly normative essentially *social* practice. (Brandom 2000: 33–4)

Hegel improves on Kant's account of our responsibility for cognitive activity by replacing the noumenal limitations of that responsibility with the social practices in which such responsibilities are assumed, explicated, disputed and acted on. In other words, rather than making ontology and deontology the source of a new dualism, Brandom's Hegel makes normativity into the social source of all claims about the world. Thus, claimants or reasoners are responsible *for* their claims, but also responsible *to* the world about which they are made.

This emphasis on the social sources of cognition achieves two things. First, it disabuses philosophy of its atomism regarding *individual* thought–thing or sense–reference pairs in favour of a holism as regards concepts. "One cannot have just one concept", as Brandom says (1994: 89). Such a holism means that it is only in the context of *expression* and articulation that particular concepts become determined, as opposed to the model-theoretic account of the "logical given" in which conceptual determinacy is a fact of the matter concerning principles and laws. Brandom takes Hegel's account of "mediation" and "determinate negation" to satisfy the account of conceptual explication. He reconstructs mediation as the means by which one concept "serves both as the conclusion of one inference and the premise of another", while determinate negation, or "material incompatibility" becomes "the way the applicability of one concept normatively precludes the applicability of another" (2002: 223). While negation selects among incompatible inferences, mediation articulates inter-conceptual connections. These are not, however, logical givens, but rather *processes*: "moments" in the determination of the concept. Moreover, they are moments by which concepts are differentiated from and connected with one another. It is for this reason that Brandom favourably cites Hegel's claim to *the* Concept (e.g. 2009: 93) as the target and result of all fully explicated rational claims. This is also why concepts are *essentially* rather than merely *accidentally* both historical and social: dynamic processes rather than static entities.[3]

The second such achievement is to make negotiation of conceptual content itself a social practice. Since there is no thought of anything that is not already conceptual, what occurs in the social context is the progressive elaboration or making explicit of that implicit conceptual content. To make something explicit, therefore, is to articulate the conceptual structure of the world. Although this occurs one conceptual determination at a time, such determinations are normatively constrained by the rules of inference, or by *reasonings* by which the world is *finally* articulated whole in its concepts. It is within the normative domain of making these articulations, and in negotiating the commitments and entitlements inferable from them, that subjects appear as selves. Just as the logical atomist presumes conceptually determinate givens, so the social atomist presumes pre-socially determinate selves. The idealist response is to invert, after the "heroic functionalist inversion" undertaken by the pragmatists (2009: 9), the relation between agent and action such that the *doing* precedes the *being*. Neither reasons nor personality are primitive, but rather consequent on social negotiations. A self becomes a self only once it is recognized by other selves as a self, which in turn recognizes those others as selves. It is, as Brandom says, a "social achievement" that:

> merely *biological* beings, subjects and objects of desires, become *spiritual* beings, undertakers and attributors of commitments, by being at once the subjects and the objects of recognitive attitudes. At the same time and by the same means that *selves*, in this normative sense, are synthesized, so are *communities* .... Both selves and communities are normative structures instituted by social recognition. (2002: 217)

It is "only when this 'movement'", this to and fro of recognition and recognized,[4] is completed that "a self is constituted" (*ibid.*). This is Brandom's demonstration of the idealist thesis that "the structure and unity of the *concept* is the same as the structure and unity of the *self*" (*ibid.*: 210). One further Hegelian step remains: the passage from becoming a self to the emergence of self-consciousness.

Since the social constitution of concepts and selves is understood as arising through processes of negotiation – the explication of concepts and of experience – the emergence of self-consciousness must itself involve a synthesis. Whereas in Kant's transcendental unity of apperception the "I think" is transcendentally deduced as necessary if I am to have experience at all, for Hegel, self-consciousness arises through grasping the movements of reason in experience. On the back of the normative social pragmatics whereby conceptual content is explicated and determinacy negotiated, therefore, it is in the making explicit of the reason implicit in these doings that self-consciousness arises. Simple awareness necessarily accompanies the explicit making of claims, such as "Leo is a lion"; but self-consciousness arises when we make explicit our reflections on our making of such claims, or, in Brandom's words, when "we begin to *say* what we are *doing* in *saying* that Leo is a lion" (2000: 20). Self-consciousness, that is, is the expression of the doings involved in our sayings as a second-level saying something about these doings and sayings. In this way, the historical and social dimensions of his philosophizing are *recovered* in its systematic dimension, while both are articulated and expressed as such *self-consciously* only when all the movements of concepts and selves, of pragmatics and inferential semantics, have been run through and *made explicit*. "Making it explicit" therefore consists in taking responsibility for the cognitive and practical doings and sayings in being responsible to the situations in which these doings and sayings arise and the "objects" concerning which these doings and sayings are undertaken. To be self-conscious, then, is to articulate the *consequences* of this reasoning: "The *true being* of man is rather his deed; in this the individual is *actual* ...

[W]hat the deed *is* can be *said* of it. It *is* this, and its being is not merely a sign, but the fact itself. It *is* this, and the individual human being *is* what the deed *is*" (Hegel 1977b: 193–4).

Yet the domain of Spirit is spelt out against the background of the "merely biological". His complex reconstruction of "objective idealism" may therefore satisfactorily reconstruct the *Phenomenology*, but at the cost of nature, on the one hand, or of a nature unconstructed in language, that is a nature not "made explicit" in the space of reasons. Although it is part and parcel of Brandom's idealism to argue that such a move is simply to recast an already conceptual contradiction as an ontological dualism, in so far as the conceptual structure implicit in any entrant into, or emergent in, the domain of Spirit rules out the appearance of what cannot appear, the normative foundations of pragmatically grounded semantics rule out any possible preconceptual domain.

Like Brandom's Hegel, Wolfram Hogrebe's (1989) reconstruction of Schelling is motivated by a critique of a semantics. Hogrebe's complaint is that a complete semantics entails a closed or "discrete" ontology, from which all genesis, all nature, is expelled. Rather than seeking to accommodate this omission, Hogrebe (1992: 123) argues that an "indiscrete ontology" is required, one in which "meaning" is conceived as a product of a "meaningless", chaotic domain that precedes it. As Schelling (1972: 222) put it, "The entire world is as it were caught in reason, but the question is: How did it come to be in this net?" (cited in Hogrebe 1989: 39). If there is simply no outside of conceptual objectivity, then the map produced in, and by, fully explicated self-consciousness must exceed the territory it explicates. While this satisfies a demand for novelty in rational articulation, guaranteeing the progressive nature of Spirit's histories, it does so at the cost of reducing nature to a region of Spirit. That this is not what Brandom wants from his Hegel is clear from the following response to a hypothetical critic of his advocacy of idealism:

> The thought that the world is always already there anyway, regardless of the activities, if any, of knowing and acting subjects, has always stood as the most fundamental objection to any sort of idealism. It is a true and important thought: but it is not an objection to Hegel's objective idealism, as here construed. (2002: 208)

If the objectivity of this idealism is secured on the basis of the double structure of responsibility *for* (one's claims about) and *to* (the world), then it is not owing to the object-nature of the world, so to speak, but rather to *rational objectivity*, that is, the social rather than individual nature of the *conceiving* of it. It is the final consequence, then, of the priority of pragmatics over semantics that doings are not only *deontologically* prior to beings, but that deontology simply *replaces* ontology altogether, so that doings exhaust being. This Fichtean bias is confirmed by Brandom's account of Heidegger's "fundamental ontology" as "the study of the nature of social being – social practices and practitioners" (2002: 322). Such an ontology commits its proponent to "a sort of linguistic assertional practice" that is ultimately a "normative pragmatism" (*ibid.*: 324) by virtue of the "interfusion of being and action" (Hegel 1977b: 240). While the grounds of this sociality are acknowledged to be Hegelian (see Brandom 1994: 67; 2002: 310), Brandom's idealism is importantly Fichtean in that it combines Kant's responsibility thesis regarding action with Fichte's regarding cognition.

In addition to the "sociality of reason" (Pinkard 1994), Hegel maintained nature as the exteriority of the Idea. The question therefore remains whether Brandom's progressive synthesis is sustainable without the nature it disavows in the constitution of Spirit. In so far as his is a more systematic philosophy than McDowell's, Brandom's focus on the domain of Spirit remains an attempt to resolve this problem non-metaphysically, as Hartmann recommended. Yet if we interpret Brandom adequately, his denaturation of nature *ought*, therefore, to recommend a Fichtean rather than an Hegelian solution.

SPRIGGE, LESLIE AND RESCHER: AXIOLOGY, PANPSYCHISM AND NATURE

The idealism championed by the Pittsburgh neo-Hegelians shares with much post-Taylor Hegel scholarship an antipathy towards metaphysics, nature and ontology. It focuses instead on the normative dimensions of Hegel's thought as an alternative to the naturalism that, since Quine, has been dominant in analytic philosophy. Yet Hegel scholarship supplies many alternatives to this post-metaphysical, anti-naturalistic reading (see ch. 8). Nor, as we shall see, does normativity eclipse the metaphysical, ontological and naturalistic dimensions of contemporary idealist philosophy more generally.

It is the shared concern of Sprigge, Leslie and Rescher to provide a systematic idealist philosophy comprising metaphysics, nature and mindedness. This concern sets these philosophers against the intellectual orthodoxies of their age, not least of which is that idealism was successfully eclipsed exactly when Russell successfully "defeated" Bradley at the dawn of analytic philosophy.[5] Yet the issue exemplified between the neo-Hegelians and the overtly metaphysical or even "absolute" idealists is not a trivial one, since it concerns a problem fundamental to the practice and complexion of contemporary philosophy in general. That problem takes many forms, but at its core lies the *possibility* of systematic metaphysics after Kant, on the one hand, and the subsequent success of philosophical naturalism on the other. As we shall see, none of these philosophers hinges their metaphysics on "leaving nature behind", although their philosophies of nature vary considerably.[6] In common with Brandom, they reject the notion that metaphysics is no longer possible after Kant or Quine, thus disputing the claim that Kant exposed fatal errors in his forebears' conception of metaphysics. Thus Rescher (2005) confesses Leibniz to be his philosophical hero; Leslie (2007) pursues a Platonic solution to a Leibnizian problem; while Sprigge (1983, 2006) pursues a Spinozan solution to a Bradleyan problem.

In what follows, we shall approach these philosophers through the issues that unite and divide them in order to provide an outline of problems in contemporary idealist philosophy. We do this in order first to accommodate the enormous bodies of work credited to these philosophers within a brief compass; and second because it is their solutions to these problems that will, in Rescher's words (2005: 1–15), demonstrate the "viability" of their idealisms.

Axiology: existence, value and explanation

We shall begin with the issue of "axiology", the theory of value, which is the topic that most closely allies these idealists with the neo-Hegelians. While the latter understand normativity as premised on a "denial of nature in order to make room for ethics", or, less unkindly, as an alternative conception of sociocultural, logical or experiential phenomena to that based on nature, the normativist is left – as is the physicalist, correlatively, Sprigge notes – with a kind of Kantian dualism between the phenomenal and the noumenal. Sprigge's point can be explicated by noting the parallel McDowell draws between naturalism and the Kantian noumenon, both being fundamental and inaccessible. Either, for physicalists, experience is explained by taking the noumenal to be simply nature, or, for normativists, nature is explained in terms of an experiential domain that already normatively underwrites our conceptions of nature, leaving "nature in itself" inaccessible in turn.

Axiology, by contrast, is not premised on the rejection of naturalistic explanatory models, nor on nature itself, but rather on accounting for the emergence of such models (Rescher), or the emergence of the universe itself (Leslie). In other words, rather than a norm-laden alternative to naturalism, axiology envelops the metaphysics of nature.

Despite considerable *prima facie* similarity, Rescher thinks his own position is divided from Leslie's by precisely the issue of axiology (although Leslie disagrees). The core of the problem concerns the ontological status of value. If values exist to the extent that they are only possibly held by persons or agents, they are not ontologically basic, but dependent on "the evolutionary emergence of agents" (Rescher 2000: 179). Such values, claims Rescher, are ethical rather than strictly axiological. If, on the other hand, values are ontologically primitive, as Bosanquet and Whitehead maintained (see chs 11 and 13, respectively), then either existence itself is "axiogenetic" (Rescher) or values are ontogenetic (Leslie).

In the naturalistic idiom Rescher favours, existence is axiogenetic in so far as "the universe ... gives rise only late in the game" to actual evalutions (2000: 178–9), but prepares the basis for them in its actual selections. An evaluation-enabling nature is accordingly, in so far as it exists, self-evidently one of the values nature prepares. When, therefore, Rescher argues that "value is not *productive* at all, but merely *eliminative*" (2005: 83), he is sending out two signals. The first concerns the roles he allots to *nature* and our conceptions of it; the second expressly rejects an "ontogenetic" or constitutive idealism in the interests of an explanatory one.

Taking these in order, Rescher likes to note that idealism is not "ontophobic" (2000: 118) and to demonstrate this by constant reference to what he takes to be the arbiters of ontology, namely, the natural sciences. For Rescher, nature supplies the ontology our metaphysics strives to explain. As he puts it:

> Traditional ontological idealism of the sort criticized by Russell did indeed center on the idea that thought creates reality [but] the situation is the very reverse: the fact of biological evolution means that natural reality creates thought. It seems best to take the line that thought has gained its key foothold on the world stage not so much by creating it as by virtue of the emergent saliency of its role in nature. (Rescher 2005: 2)

Disregarding the contestable accuracy of the Russell–Moore critique of idealism as the theory that reality is mind-dependent, the position so described is a constitutive idealism because its proponents held it to be metaphysics' task to supply ontology. Rescher contests this by allocating to nature the ontogenetic role such idealists sought to ascribe to mind. The role now to be adopted by what he calls "conceptual idealism"[7] is, in consequence, *explanatory* rather than ontological.

That nature supplies a context in which thought enjoys emergent saliency introduces a twist in Rescher's tale, suggesting that the retrospective purchase thought has on nature is prepared for by nature itself. The kinds of explanations nature itself warrants are in turn explanations not of nature itself but of the *concept* of nature that we in fact successfully deploy, paradigmatically in the natural sciences. The central thesis of conceptual idealism holds that the ascription of properties to physical things is always *relational*, "with some facet of ... minds in general serving as one term of this relation" (2005: 4). In other words, nature is not *ontologically* mind-dependent but only *explanatorily* so. We neither can nor should infer from the fact that we cannot avoid concepts in explaining it that nature is in reality *no more than* such concepts; we especially should not conclude that nature *owes its existence* to them.

Hence the role played by the ontological priority of nature as regards axiology consists expressly in withdrawing the office of *causality* from metaphysics and allotting it exclusively to ontology. Nature produces while minds explain, from a niche within it, the concept of nature that best explains what produces a mind that so explains. So all axiological explanation of an axiogenetic nature is, in Rescher's terms, a species of "retrojustification" (2010: 112–17). Yet a problem arises here. Granted that explanations are retrojustified – evidence selecting, practice and technology endorsing, and so forth – if this applies at all, it must apply to all explanation, in natural science just as much as in philosophy. Doesn't Rescher's ontological–epistemological division of conceptual labour therefore render the ontologies putatively supplied by natural science *further* instances of retrojustificatory explanation? In other words, doesn't this model eliminate the possibility of ontology in the interests of a metaphysics of explanation? And doesn't this metaphysics render nature simply a conceptual artefact? Ultimately, Rescher's responses to such criticisms are of a pragmatic order; what works does so for a reason, which reason is supplied by the evident success of the nature–concept collaboration. There is, however, an additional, "noumenal", dimension of nature to which we shall return below.

For the present, however, we have noted that the division of scientific and philosophical labour between science and philosophy is won at the cost of severing any question of causation from metaphysics. It is from this perspective that Rescher's criticism of Leslie's axiological or "ethical" philosophical cosmology begins. Namely, Leslie grants too much to ethical requirements when he describes them as "creatively powerful" (Rescher 2000: 177, citing Leslie 1970: 286). Before discussing this criticism, we shall quickly sketch Leslie's "Platonic–Spinozistic" philosophical cosmology.

Leslie, who first outlined his thesis that "the world exists because it should" in 1970, starts from the Leibnizian question "Why is there anything rather than nothing?", and has consistently advocated a Platonic solution to it. The solution draws on Plato's theory of the Good, which "is itself not existence, but far beyond existence in *dignity and power*" (*Resp.* 509b). For Plato, the axiological concern with "dignity" immediately entails the ontogenetic concern with "power". Here Leslie draws on the tradition of Plato as a philosopher of "Immanent Law",[8] or *power*: power is immanent law simply because it is in the nature of power to act, other things being equal, as it does, and therefore relies on no exogenous doctrine to institute natural law. Indeed, it is this immanence, the simple endogeneity of Plato's explanation of existence as a function of power, that draws Leslie to recommend it; as he puts it, the world's "ethical requiredness ... *is itself creatively effective*" (2007: 2). Of course, that it is required does not of itself mean that its requiredness is satisfied; but we need not resolve this issue to note that the causation Rescher excises from his metaphysics is central to Leslie's.

What kind of existence is it, however, that Plato's ascription of creative power to the Good produces? From the perspective of naturalistic explanation, it would create what Leslie calls "a blank ..., a situation including no actual existents" (*ibid.*). This is because the Good is, apart from being creatively powerful, an eternal and necessary fact, the being of which does not rely on being thought or instantiated. In order to create more than a "blank", Plato's immanent axiology must be supplemented by an additional thesis, which Leslie takes from Spinoza. Spinoza's claim that "there is a divine mind ... whose reality is due to the eternal ethical need for it" (Leslie 2007: 3) adds to the Platonic thesis a pantheistic unity of God and nature. The Platonic thesis therefore generates more than a blank only when it is coupled with the Spinozistic claim that, in a divine mind, "*thinking* and *being a mind* would be rolled into one" (*ibid.*: 6). The first criterion of the divine mind contemplating the Good is that it be a whole, not simply discrete thises and thats.

Leslie is aware of the awe-inspiringly counter-intuitive nature of his advocacy of a Platonic pantheism. To offset this, he asks us to consider what eidetic memory is like. A slide rule serves its user as a calculating aid; a slide rule pictured by an eidetic memory is one that such a memory's possessor could imagine so vividly that she can use it *as* a calculating aid. From this, Leslie draws the lesson that it is the complexity of the thinking that constitutes the existence of the thought: "When some pattern of great intricacy is pictured in full detail, then a pattern with that kind of intricacy must genuinely exist in the mind that does the picturing, whether or not anything of the sort exists elsewhere as well" (*ibid.*: 37).

Where such a mind is "divine" in the Spinozistic sense, a thinking sufficiently complex is a universe, just as a universe sufficiently complex amounts to a divine mind. What Platonism adds to Spinozism is the doctrine of immanent law; what Spinozism grants Platonism is a nature rather than a "blank". As to the nature of such a universe, Leslie argues that it is simply the one we are and have: a universe worth contemplating owing to its holism and complexity, and one "obedient to physical laws" (*ibid.*: 12). A universe governed by immanent law pantheism simply is the universe we inhabit. Moreover, it is a universe whose ethical requiredness entails that it is not unique, since if it were, there would be only one species of Good, which would be less good than an infinite number. It is not what this Good is good *for* (for intelligent life, arsenic-breathers, diamonds or clouds) that makes it good, but simply that, like our universe, it is sufficiently complex or "fine-tuned" that it would be better that it existed than not. Leslie therefore achieves a multiple-universe account of nature on Platonic grounds, one that tallies significantly with key quantum-theoretical commitments as regards the number of universes.[9]

Ultimately, Leslie's Platonic creation story stipulates only that "an ethical ground for the existence of some possible world would itself lead to that world's actual existence, or it would not" (*ibid.*: 36). The key point here is whether the satisfaction of the principle of sufficient reason – to answer, that is, the question "Why is there anything rather than nothing at all?" – is sufficient in turn to justify or ground a metaphysics. Following Kant's critique of attempts to deduce existence from reason alone, many philosophers think not, with some arguing even that this fact renders metaphysics non-viable. Yet it is important to be clear about what exactly Leslie is arguing. Nothing, he insists, "makes necessary" the fulfilment of the "ethical requirement that there be a cosmos which ... was creatively sufficient *by itself*"; yet neither is there anything that would "make" it "*unable to bring about its own fulfilment*" (*ibid.*: 33–4). Having proved such a cosmos *possible*, Leslie argues that if it exists, the reason for it would simply *be* its creative sufficiency. From its existence it would follow that its nature would involve the unity of thinking and being realized most effectively by a Platonic axiology in Spinoza's pantheistic cosmos, comprising not one but an infinite number of minds, since fewer would be less good.

When, therefore, Rescher says of Leslie's cosmology that it "is predicated on a recourse to specifically ethical considerations" of what is good (2000: 177), he is arguing that such considerations arise only late in the game, and so cannot be ontogenic in the sense Leslie intends. Yet in what sense is Leslie's a theory of the genesis of being? He would dispute that the "ethics" Rescher ascribes to him – the ethics owned or obstructing a rational agent – accurately captures the Platonic understanding of the Good, which would not depend on the "prior existence of any person or object". This is because, if it were real at all, "it would be real *necessarily and eternally*" (Leslie 2007: 34, emphasis added). It is only such a cosmos whose "immanent law" (Whitehead 1933: 154) would turn its "ethically required existence" into something "creatively sufficient by itself instead of being important only thanks to complex processes which proceeded successfully" (*ibid.*: 33). It is clear that the complex processes Leslie intends are the evolutionary ones Rescher cites to argue that ethics is a late acquisition, so that they could not be "creatively powerful" (Rescher 2000: 177). Yet if the Good is eternal and the reason for the universe's existence, Rescher's argument against its creative power would be redundant for two reasons. First, evolutionary evidence presupposes an irreversible arrow of time, while eternity denies genesis: not only would a divine mind "not need to generate its thoughts" (Leslie 2007: 6), but it could not. Second, therefore, Leslie's account is based not on efficient but on final causality.

Whether or not we buy Leslie's solution to the problem of why anything exists at all, we must ask what sort of a nature it is that consists of the eternal thoughts of a divine mind, and in which there is no becoming or change. Meanwhile, the thought that existence is the problem to which nature is a solution will recur in our discussion of the idealist dimensions of Deleuze's philosophy.

Panpsychism: the metaphysical insides of things

Sprigge begins with the question: what is reality? This is a specifically Bradleyan question because the reality intended by the latter necessarily transcends any particular grasp of it in thought or experience. Such aspects of reality that are so grasped are reality's "appearances" or phenomena, and become distorting when considered as isolated entities or parts of a whole, rather than as aspects of reality as such.[10] Sprigge agrees with Bradley that reality itself is the Absolute in which experience inheres. Accordingly, Sprigge contests any response to the question "What is reality?" that asserts it to be reducibly physical on the grounds that such physicalisms are invariably phenomenalistic. This is because physicalism addresses only *part* of reality, not that reality as a whole that *necessarily includes* the psychical. Like Rescher, Sprigge argues that thinking about reality necessarily possesses a conceptual or "psychical" element because thinking about reality is the starting point of all such physicalisms. This is not to say that "reality" is nothing more than a thought – Sprigge contests as "cosmic impiety" any theory that so belittles the "non-human immensities" of the universe (1983: xiii) – but that it *necessarily includes* the thinking. The fallacy of the thesis that reality is mind-dependent, with which Moore charged the idealists, is that it "confuses what one is thinking about with the activity of thinking about it" (Sprigge 1985: 63). Yet physicalism disavows this, making it a separably "noumenal" element, not integral to the reality in question. Sprigge counters this tendency by pointing out that "whatever has a physical, and therefore phenomenal character, also has a noumenal character". Unlike Rescher, Sprigge draws not only epistemological, but also ontological, conclusions from this, arguing that this "noumenal backing … can be known to be somehow psychical", so that "reality in its true nature is psychical through and through" (1983: 39). Sprigge's is thus a *panpsychist* idealism.[11]

Panpsychists ask: where does mindedness come from? If it is not primitively there, then it must arise from unminded elements. While evolutionary biology has little problem explaining this in terms of how developed intelligence enhances survival, while the neurosciences tell us about the neurophysiological constituents by means of which brains work, how does it happen that parts unminded achieve mindedness by assembly? Panpsychists answer these problems by (a) denying that it makes sense to say mindedness is emergent – whether from evolutionary processes or neurophysiological composition – without begging the question; and (b) concluding that mindedness is a primitive constituent of things.

Some panpsychists, such as Strawson (2008), insist that mindedness must be physically primitive, so that there is no part of the physical universe that is not minded, albeit in differing degree. For Sprigge, this is already a psychicalist view, but one that does not draw the ontological consequences it should concerning a properly psychical understanding of reality. We might ask why a good Spinozist such as Sprigge takes such a one-sided view of the problem, however, since Spinoza's point is surely that the physical and the psychical are inalienably identical. How, in other words, can Sprigge agree with Spinoza's claim that there is no physical being where there is no mindedness, and yet disagree that there is no mindedness where there is no physical being? Why, finally, is the physicalist understanding of panpsychism, as offered most recently by Strawson (2008), insufficient?

One answer[12] is that Sprigge is intent not merely on the Spinozist claim as to the *substantial* identity of thought and nature, but on exploring what Findlay (1967: 139ff.) called "the noetic cosmos". While this seems merely to reciprocate physicalism's disavowal of the noumenal with a psychicalist disavowal of the physical, Sprigge denies this, arguing that he treats "the nature of perception and the nature of physical reality ... as a single problem, because perception is ... the primordial basis of our knowledge and conception of the physical" (1983: 42). The perception of an apple, that is, is most richly "intuitively fulfilled" not by its representation in thought, but by biting into it, reminding us of what Brandom calls Hegel's "erotic" theory of how animals classify things, taking foodstuffs as food only when they "fall to without ceremony and eat them up".[13] Despite his talk of "perception" and "conception", Sprigge's concerns are less epistemological – as are Rescher's similar-sounding claims – than ontological; he is concerned to demonstrate that perception forms the "primordial basis" that does not preclude, but rather includes, physical things.

Nevertheless, Sprigge's concerns clearly lie with the noetic rather than the physical cosmos. This is due in part to the character of his panpsychist solution to the "true nature of reality". Mindful of the "cosmic impiety" of reducing things to thoughts about them, Sprigge argues conversely that "all things think",[14] but not all things think all things. That is, reality is composed not of *one* all-suffusing mental *substance*, since the "ultimate constituents of the universe" (1985: 67) are the *activities* of "innumerable momentary centres of experience" (1983: 250). This distinction between substance and activity[15] is key for understanding the respect in which Sprigge argues that reality as a whole is "not physically specifiable" (*ibid.*: 67). Physical things are defined less by material constitution, or by the particulars that make them up, than by the extent to which they exist as "continuants", or by the universal of which they are concrete continuations.

Yet physical things are also what he calls the objective component of experience, or the "not-self aspect of a centre of experience" (*ibid.*: 68). That is, they stand in real relation to the conceiving or perceiving of them. Here again, Sprigge's claims risk falling foul of the mind-dependence accusation: surely if things are real to the extent that they stand in relation to their conception or perception, then in the absence of such relations there can be no reality? Yet Sprigge ascribes reality not to things, but to relations:[16] real relations obtain just when they belong in the same universe. It is equally true, he writes, "that things which are in no relation whatever to each other, things out of all relation to ourselves, are not in anything we can properly call 'the universe'" (*ibid.*: 250). Where no relation obtains, therefore, things belong to different universes. Things do not lose reality by being unrelated; rather, as for Leslie,[17] other universes gain it to the extent that their continuants are bereft of real relation with ours. Crucially, then, actual relations may be distant, but related they must be, simply by belonging to the universe. In so far as the universe is so conceived *as* an interrelated "concrete whole" or Spinozist "one" (*ibid.*: 252), it is conceived *by* a concrete centre of experience necessarily related to that whole. For such a centre of experience, this conception is more or less richly "intuitively fulfilled", that is, the finite character of the perceptual world that does such fulfilling of conceptions is insuperable for any and all such experiential centres.

This, then, is how Sprigge can argue that his absolute idealism does not fall foul of the fallacy of mind-dependence: consisting of innumerable centres of experience, reality is an active thinking that does not reduce the being of physical things to representations within that thinking. Rather, concrete universals (physical things in so far as they are continuants) are transcendent of the finite centres of experience that are the ultimate constituents of the universe. Similarly, they form the not-self aspects of perceptual experience "towards which the self-aspect ... directs itself" (*ibid.*: 68). Moreover, things are not irreducibly concrete universals towards which the self-aspect in perceptual experience directs itself; as Sprigge puts it, things have their "metaphysical insides" too (*ibid.*: 80). And these metaphysical insides consist in their being centres of experience, however inaccessible – that is, however lacking conceptions of such centres happen to be in intuitive fulfilment for the conceiver – such experiences may be to other such centres. Together they form, as Sprigge evocatively puts it, an "ocean of interacting low-level centres of experience, pulsing with dim emotion" (1985: 65).

Sprigge's panpsychism consists not in a single all-pervasive mind in which others participate, or of which apparently physical things are artefacts; but rather a mindedness that is the essential, noumenal component of all things, each constrained in their conceivings and perceivings according to degree, while none is capable, since finite, of intuitively fulfilling the experience of the Absolute to which they belong. For all centres capable of continuant conception, "we can only mean, when we talk of the universe, or of that whole of things …, that system of things to every part of which we stand in some sort of relation, more or less direct" (*ibid.*: 67). Such a view follows from the idea that things are inseparable from, or really related to, their "noumenal backing" or "insides" when it is conjoined with the stipulation of relatedness for all continuants in a single universe. Deriving from the "holistic nature of all real relationship" (1983: 252), Sprigge's "holism constraint" – that conceiving of anything whatsoever places the conceived in a real and inseparable relation to the conceiving – holds at every scale or level at which conception takes place, from the "ultimate constituents" to the universe as a whole. At no level of reality, then, are the unminded particulars by which physicalism seeks to conceive nature, conceivable without either conceding the point to the absolute or panpsychist idealist that mindedness is basic and ineliminable, or leaving that part of reality arbitrarily out of consideration.

Yet the question remains: *why* does the psychical explain the physical, but not the other way round, if the two are ineliminably related at every level of reality? Formally and historically, in terms both of Sprigge's account and its Spinozist inheritance, surely the inseparability thesis regarding thinking and being would entail reversibility in their relatedness? Sprigge's idealism could consistently explain this reversibility in terms of the relations between the noumenal contained in the physical, as its "metaphysical inside", and the physical contained in the noumenal, as the objective component of perception, forming a dynamic interrelatedness of mind and nature. His insistence that physicalist panpsychism is psychicalism unaware of itself does not therefore have a theoretical, but rather, as for Rescher and Leslie, a normative, basis. The question of nature, therefore, while core to the theories offered by all three of our idealists, remains unresolved.

Nature, ontogenesis and transcendence

Each of these philosophers offers a theory of nature. For Rescher, nature supplies the basis of ontology, at least as this is fashioned by the best available natural science. For Leslie, nature is generated by the "creative efficacy" of the Good in any pantheistic universe, but remains nature precisely as it is. Despite the panpsychist basis of his absolute idealism, Sprigge maintains a transcendence of what, while it cannot simply be equated with nature, nonetheless supplies a framework of "non-human immensities" by which experience is inalienably surrounded.

In their concern with nature, their idealisms differ markedly from the alternatives to philosophical naturalism offered by McDowell and Brandom examined earlier in this chapter. It is not philosophical naturalism that concerns them, but the ontological role of nature itself in idealism. Yet Rescher, Leslie and Sprigge share a commitment with the neo-Hegelians to the metaphysics of normativity. Two questions will therefore animate this section. The first concerns the position of nature within each of their metaphysics; the second is whether the normative grounds they share with the neo-Hegelians can facilitate an adequate address to the philosophy of nature that supplies an important component, as we have seen, of ancient, early modern and Kantian and post-Kantian idealisms.

As we have seen, Rescher cedes the role of ontology to the natural sciences, reserving that of explanation to metaphysics. Yet metaphysical explanations "retrojustify" the ontology supplied by natural scientific investigation and explanation. The question arises, then, as to whether nature itself has a place within Rescher's account. If it does not, then retrojustification in effect removes the ontology–epistemology dichotomy from which Rescher starts. Rescher's scientific realism "ultimately rests on a pragmatic basis" (2010: 119), demonstrated not theoretically but by the fact that scientific understanding is successful. Since scientific knowledge is in principle systematic rather than piecemeal, its success allows us to infer that nature is more "rulish" than unruly: "our situation in nature must be such that our local environment is sufficiently systematic (orderly, regular) to permit the orderly conduct of rational inquiry" (2000: 18).

Ontological conclusions concerning what nature *must be* thus follow from the success of the natural sciences. While maintaining a strict division between epistemology and ontology, Rescher simultaneously explains the fact of explanation-capable beings in evolutionary terms: values, explanations and concepts, unlike Platonic Ideas, are late acquisitions selected for by an intelligence-tolerant nature. Epistemologically, there is the question of the warrant for such explanations, which is here supplied both by the findings of evolutionary biology and by the fact that there is intelligence at all. Ontologically, it amounts to the claim that nature generates those values, facts and concepts — that it contains "observation-engendering causes", or "causes of experience" (2005: 42) — subsequently deployed in its explanation.

The critical point is not the circularity, which, Rescher elegantly demonstrates (see esp. Rescher 2010: 93–125), is anything but vicious. It is, rather, the thesis that nature maintains a manifest productive priority over its explanability, a fact explained in turn from the order of being: "ontological systematicity is in fact a sufficient condition for cognitive *systematizability*" (2000: 20). This entails that if nature is explicable in terms of systems, it is because the mental operations used in explaining it "must be inserted into the world as a smoothly functioning integral part thereof" (*ibid*.: 21). This can be explained in two ways. First, we may argue that nature is "unavoidably enmeshed with the operations of mind" (*ibid*.: 6), such that the "doings of minds" are inseparably responsible for "how we standardly conceive of nature". Alternatively, we may argue that nature is transcendent of the minds natively constituent of it. Although Rescher argues consistently for the first – "reality as we conceive it … is unavoidably enmeshed with the operations of mind" (2005: 6) – he does not conclude that *therefore* nature is reducible to "the doings of minds", but rather that thinking is "our only possible access to how things *are*" (*ibid*.: 9).

In arguing for the second, Rescher supplies the rudiments of a philosophy of nature. While thinking irremediably mediates the nature we (scientists, philosophers, poets) conceive, nevertheless, "natural reality creates thought" (*ibid*.: 2). How it does so is not to be decided on the basis of the "causal goings-on" in the world, however, but rather the sort of "extended causality" by which Bernard d'Espagnat (2006: 236–7) considers a "veiled reality" to exert "influences on phenomena".[18] Rescher's version of this extension, while he would reject the ascription of "causality" of any kind to it, is premised on the fit between systematic thought (science) and nature. If science works, then the systematicity of thought cannot be alien to that of nature. The next step is to assert that precisely because thinking is a minor constituent of it, it must be the case that "nature is vastly more complex than the human brain" (2000: 22): hence his thesis concerning "cognitive depth" in nature, or the "cognitive inexhaustibility of things" (2010: 50–51). Since systematic thinking teaches us that "real existence is always involved in an unending elaborateness of detail" (2000: 23), and since non-linearity or unending detail is resistant to simplification, it follows that "nature is non-linear to an extent greater than we like to think", confronting us with a "law of natural complexity" (*ibid*.: 24–6). Rescher's model of the "infinite descriptive depth" of nature makes epistemology "local" to a specific domain of detail (e.g. studies of the house fly), and leaves no science universal. If there remains any trace of the Absolute whose "concise history" Rescher provides (2005: 109–31), it lies in the absolute transcendence of nature as a domain of infinite detail against which all cognition becomes local, contingent. The lesson is that nature's "self-potentiating complexity" (2000: 25) makes it unrecoverably transcendent of the thinking that is part of it, thus insulating his conceptual idealism from Russellian charges of mind-dependency: man is not the measure of what is.

Rescher remarks repeatedly that systematization thus provides a "methodological" or "regulative ideal" and resists granting it ontological purchase in order to lay greater claim to the axiological or regulative *understandings* of mind, world and nature. This axiological understanding is regulative of the *kind of theory* permissible under the constraints he notes: natural complexity, the fact of nature and its invoking of the conceiving involved in the acknowledgement of these facts.

Although sharing this axiological understanding of the philosophy of nature with Leslie, Rescher criticizes the latter's position as "predicated on a recourse to specifically *ethical* considerations so that for him 'the world's existence and make-up' are products of 'a directly active causal necessity' with the result that 'ethical requirements are creatively powerful'" (Rescher 2000: 177, citing Leslie 1970: 286). We have already noted that Rescher's complaint concerns the causality Leslie ascribes to ethical requiredness rather than his ethicism. While it is by withdrawing "creative power" from it that Rescher conceives of what nature is, productive agency is core to Leslie's account of nature as ontogenesis. Yet we have seen that Leslie insists that what nature there is must necessarily be internal to a divine mind, from and to which productive agency flows. On Leslie's model, nature acquires productive power once the good has drawn it into existence, and this is its efficacy. Leslie refuses, in other words, to separate efficient from final causality, so that all production is for the sake of the good, which is existence. Whether this is a philosophy of nature deprived of productivity, or a philosophical "cosmodicy", or justification of the world's existence, Leslie's take on Platonic ontogenesis – the becoming of being – is not the only one possible. The young Schelling (1994c), for example, argued that it is precisely as a theory of the becoming of being that Plato's philosophy of nature must be understood, while Whitehead further develops the Platonic theory of power as nature's "immanent law" (1933: 154).

If it appears that Leslie's nature seems to live on borrowed causes, this is conditioned by the withdrawal of time from it, as Leslie reads the Einsteinian lesson. Relativity physics, Einstein writes, "makes it natural to think of physical reality as a four-dimensional existence instead of, as hitherto, the evolution of three-dimensional existence" (quoted in Leslie 2007: 58). In other words, all that exists, exists eternally and unchangingly. Similarly, although a divine mind is necessary to bring nature into existence, "such a mind would not need to generate its thoughts" since "it would be those thoughts joined together in an unchanging whole" (*ibid.*: 6). Where, for Rescher, a causally impotent nature remains axiologically and ontologically transcendent of its conceivings (in both senses of "its conceiving"), for Leslie, a divine mind is required to impute causal efficacy to a nature that would not exist but for it, and which, even given its actual existence, remains transcended by mind. What, then, is Rescher complaining about when he sees a productive agency in Leslie's cosmodicy? Just as Rescher withdraws causality from his concept of nature in order to increase his conceptual idealism's axiological purchase, so too does Leslie. What remains, however, is a conception of being as a problem never finally resolved by actually existing nature.

Coming finally to Sprigge, we noted in our foregoing discussion of his absolute idealism that, although he is a Spinozist panpsychist, he nevertheless rejects the view of an ontological equivalence or epistemological reversibility between the physical and the psychical. While this might seem to commit Sprigge's absolute idealism to a theory of nature as reducibly mind-dependent, we have also seen the steps Sprigge takes to avoid this. In place, however, of the *physical*, the office of transcendence is offered to "non-human immensities" whose denial amounts to "cosmic impiety".

In many ways, Sprigge is not criticizing concepts of nature so much as the materialist base on which these tend to rely. As he writes, the "attraction of materialism for many lies, I think, in the surely false belief that it is the only properly naturalistic philosophy" (1985: 47). In other words, it is because nature *need not* be conceived on "physicalist" grounds that Sprigge resists the epistemological reversibility between the psychical and the physical registers. The non-human immensities irrevocably transcendent of concrete centres of experience, tied to a "locus of the real" – in particular, "objective components of experience" or "not-self aspects of perception" – constitute nature for Sprigge. And this is a nature that, finally, is active, at least in the sense of being opposed to any substantialist account of what reality ultimately is. Thinking thinks not-self aspects or "physical things" whose physicality forms around their "metaphysical insides". It is not, therefore, physical things that are transcendent of mind, but rather the metaphysical insides, the "noumenal backing" against which phenomenal nature appears, that are transcendent of material being.

As for Leslie's and Rescher's, so too "the metaphysical positions" advocated by Sprigge "belong to a normative rather than a revisionary metaphysics" (Sprigge 1983: xiii). For all three, the axiological component of their idealisms forces them to wrestle nature into new conceptual forms. For Rescher and Sprigge, if not for Leslie, nature remains transcendent of all its conceivings, even if for the former this is a nature without becoming or production; the latter, although he replaces these elements, as swiftly withdraws from it its predominantly physical being. Our examination of these contemporary idealists seems to establish both that all theories of physical nature are importantly incomplete, and that the incoherence introduced by the intrusion of nature into idealist metaphysics is at least as troubling as Sprigge diagnoses it is for all physicalist theories of existence. All three waver between axiology and nature, just as was the case following Fichte's completion of Kant's transcendental idealism. Even if none of the thinkers addressed in this chapter manage to provide a complete idealist naturalism, it is clear that the problematic or antinomic relation of value to nature drives the thinkers we have been examining, and so continues to animate idealist philosophy.

GILLES DELEUZE: THE PROBLEM-IDEA

Gilles Deleuze's work covers a great deal of ground and we are not concerned, here, with that work in its entirety. We wish only to highlight the central role of the Idea. Deleuze has often been interpreted as some kind of materialist. Perhaps the "machinic" language of his first work with Félix Guattari, *Anti-Oedipus* (1984), initially gave rise to this perception. The "geological" language, "assemblages" and "war machines" of *A Thousand Plateaus* (1988) only reinforced this, mistaken, impression. Deleuze is, no doubt, concerned with bodies and the world of things that they connect with. But if the label "materialist" is taken to imply a metaphysics that makes the physical substance of actual things primary and irreducible, then it simply does not fit his purpose. Moreover, if we take that same label to imply some fundamental opposition to the metaphysical primacy of the Idea then it would imply the opposite of Deleuze's intention. As we shall see, in *Difference and Repetition* (1994), Deleuze is quite explicit and overt in his development of a philosophy of the Idea (esp. *ibid.*: ch. 4 and "Conclusion"). There he offers an account in which the Idea is ontologically primary, and actual physical substance a very late abstraction from a world of actualities generated by the Idea. It is our contention that Deleuze is, in fact, a philosophical idealist. We are aware, of course, that there are many complicating issues here, not least the question of Deleuze's relationship to Kant. Among other things, we shall show, however, that Deleuze goes much further than Kant in developing the ontological primacy of the Idea.[19]

Morphogenesis: virtual and actual

Deleuze is a monist, repeatedly asserting that "there has only ever been one ontological proposition: Being is univocal" (1994: 35–42, 66, 303–4). As with other monists, then, Deleuze faces the problem of accounting for the multiplicity of actual manifestations of a unified being. How can a multiplicity of forms arise in the world? He does not take the existence of these particular things as given, but asks how they are generated. It is this that is, perhaps, Deleuze's basic question, informing his entire philosophy.

Perhaps the key move in his approach is the division of being into two aspects. Using a vocabulary derived and modified from the work of Henri

Bergson, Deleuze refers to these two aspects as the "virtual" and "actual" aspects of real existence (1990b; 1994: 191, 201, 207–14, 246, 249, 279). We must not understand these two aspects as two separate substances or irreducible domains;[20] rather, we must understand them in genetic terms. The virtual aspect generates the actual aspect, and is always immanent to it, so that the actual particular things that appear in the world are generated by some underlying virtual activity. To reiterate the point made above, material substance, in all its particular manifestations, is reducible to something more ontologically primitive than itself: something "virtual". Consequently, whatever Deleuze is, he cannot be a materialist in any commonly understood sense.

Morphogenesis without resemblance: the relationship to Plato

So something "virtual" has the power of morphogenesis. What is this something? Deleuze argues that it is the Idea that generates form. His theory of the Idea is that it plays the role of an omnipresent, inexhaustible and eternal potential for the genesis of actual forms. However, Deleuze is emphatic in his distancing of himself from a "crude Platonist" solution to morphogenesis (as he sees it; Deleuze 1994: 66–9, 279). The Idea cannot be a model that actual things, in some way, resemble. The relation of Idea to actuality is not one of original and copy (*ibid.*: 66–9). Deleuze will not allow a domain of forms in this sense.

The distance between Deleuze and Plato should not be overemphasized, however. Deleuze himself distinguishes between good and bad Platonism. He says, for example:

> The task of modern philosophy has been defined: to overturn Platonism. That this overturning should conserve many Platonic characteristics is not only inevitable but desirable .... With Plato [himself] the issue is still in doubt ...: the Idea is not yet the concept of an object which submits the world to the requirements of representation, but rather a bright presence which can be invoked in the world only in function of that which is not "representable" in things. (*Ibid.*: 59)

Hence, "was it not inevitable that Plato should be the first to overturn Platonism?" (*ibid.*: 68).[21]

The point, for Deleuze, in the "overturning of Plato" is not the denial of the theory of Forms – not the denial of the Idea – but simply the denial of resemblance between the Idea and the actuality. In developing a philosophy of the Idea without "resemblance" he is able, of course, to sidestep all of the conventional Aristotelian criticisms of the theory of Forms. Deleuze is not embarking on an attack on idealism, but on a defence of the genetic core of Platonic idealism. In considering the Idea, however, he says "the absolute condition of non-resemblance must be emphasized" (1994: 279). But how could Ideas generate the forms of particular actual things without employing resemblance? What kind of thing could this "non-resembling" Idea be?

Problems and the Ideas of reason

One way that we can conceive of the Idea is in terms of "problems" (Deleuze 1994: ch. 4 and "Conclusion"). In our own lives we are constantly guided by attempts to solve problems: how to be a good parent; how to be excellent in our work; how to grow the perfect rose; how to cook the most delicious food; how to perform the perfect musical recital. What all these problems share is a fundamental irresolvability. Each actual attempt to solve them simply leads to a new arrangement of things that requires a new attempt at the problem. The problems are irresolvable, yet constantly generate new actual forms in the world.[22]

As Deleuze points out, there is a close kinship between this problem-idea and Kant's Ideas of reason (Deleuze 1994: 168–71). As we have seen, the Ideas of reason are regulative guides to our thought and behaviour, but ultimately not determinable. We cannot determine what the whole of the "world" is, but we must retain such a final determination as an ambition in order to guide all our more modest activities of discovery and knowledge creation.[23] So the Kantian Idea of reason is, Deleuze believes, multiply morphogenetic in that it drives all processes of knowledge-building actualization. The Kantian Ideas are then, in Deleuze's words, "undetermined", but they are "determinable" in the objects of experience, and they carry "the ideal of an infinite determination with regard to the concepts of experience" (*ibid*.: 196).

But Deleuze does not think that Kant goes nearly far enough with this. For Kant only the Ideas of reason are indeterminable, but, as we have seen, the forms of intuition and the categories of the understanding are clear and well determined in advance of their application. For Deleuze, however, time, space and concepts are all caught up in the indeterminability of the problem-idea. Moreover, it is not just finite rational beings in their mental activities that encounter the problem-idea. The growing plant has to solve the problem of its own life as it negotiates the conflicting pressures of its soil, seasons, weather and ecosystem. Each of its attempted solutions, each reaching out of a stem, each growth of a bud or opening of a flower, alters all the reciprocal relationships of the many variables that makes up the problem, thus requiring a new attempt at solving the same problem: how to live the life of such a plant. Thus the Idea is not a cognitive mechanism of finite rational beings, but the genetic principle of *all* being. The infinite determinability of the Idea is not with respect just to the "concepts of experience" but to every actual thing that exists. Hence Deleuze's monistic claim that being is *univocal*. Whether that being can be said, with Parmenides, to be fully rational is another matter, as we shall see.

Intensive difference and the genesis of quantity and extension

The problem-idea is not simply a problem in the sense of a conceptual problem, then (although that might be one of its manifestations); rather, Deleuze describes its general nature as consisting in an unresolved, and unresolvable, tension between forces, powers and "intensities". These are forces whose identity cannot be absolutely determined, since there is nothing absolute for them to be determined in relation to.[24] The identity of such forces can only arise in relations of "reciprocal determination". Intensities are such only by virtue of being differentiated one from another by degree.[25] It is, therefore, in the nature of intensities to be (a) plural and (b) differentiating. Ideas can be conceived of, then, as mobile arrangements of such reciprocally determined intensities. These intensive differentia are constantly attempting to resolve themselves (water flows downhill, electrons flow from negative to positive, photons flow from the Sun to the Earth, fires burn up their fuel, organisms metabolize their food, clocks run down, neurons fire action potentials and so on). All of these flows, constituted by intensive difference, are constantly moving from intensive disequilibrium towards a point of equilibrium, although, as we shall see, the latter is a point never to be reached.

Deleuze says two things about this intensive flow. First, it is what gives rise to actual qualities. That is to say, genesis is differentiation. This, then, is the answer to Deleuze's core question regarding the problem of the genesis of particular, actual things. Actual qualitative particular things are the outward manifestation of immanent intensive flows arising from these intensive differentia (Deleuze 1983: 40–41). This is what he means when he says that quality arises from quantity, or from quantitative difference of intensity. He says that "qualities are nothing but the corresponding difference in quantity between two forces whose relationship is presupposed" (*ibid.*: 40). This explains how the problem-idea, as an immanently differentiating intensive series, generates beings that do not resemble it, resolving the relation of Deleuze's Idea to its Platonic precursor.[26] It also explains how Being can be univocal yet have both virtual and actual aspects, because virtual intensive flows are not different from their actual manifestation, the actuality is simply the outward expression of the inner virtual intensity. Virtual intensities are genetically pre-individual, pre-objective, but ontologically rather than temporally. The virtual is always immanent to the actual; it is the latter's immanent genetic element.

The eternal return of difference

Deleuze additionally insists that these intensive differences are ultimately irresolvable, which is why the Idea always presents a problem that particular beings are attempted resolutions of. The universe is in a permanent state of intensive disequilibrium. As fast as intensive differentia resolve themselves (a battery goes flat, a flower shrivels, a thought fades, a love dies, a star dims and collapses), somewhere at the heart of being the engine of difference regenerates disequilibrium. This is his interpretation of Nietzsche's "eternal return". For Deleuze, nothing returns or repeats but intensive difference itself. And since it is generative of qualitative things it must return for as long as there is something rather than nothing: for as long as there is being. Being is the eternal return of pure difference (Deleuze 1983: 43–5) or its repetition (1994: esp. ch. 1 and "Conclusion").

Why are we not consciously aware of the immanent intensive genesis of all the things we experience? Because consciousness itself and all its mental contents are themselves products of the same "cancellation" of difference that gives rise to all actual things. Thought is, literally, "forced" into existence (*ibid.*: 136). But mental actualities are blind to the intensive differences or forces that give rise to them. Intensive difference always remains unconscious. It is this blindness to the underlying intensive genesis of things that leads us into the illusions of "representation", in which we conceive of mental contents as representations of given particular things in the world. As a consequence, says Deleuze, philosophy has constantly subordinated difference to the "identical": difference as the difference *between* already established actualities (*ibid.*: esp. "Introduction" and ch. 1). Even science, says Deleuze, is obsessed with equilibrium. Its materialism turns our view of reality upside down, and makes the final product of the intensive flow, the particular material body, into the fundamental principle (1983: 41–2). But difference must not be subordinated to the identical. It is evident, then, that Deleuze's problem-idealism makes disequilibrium primary.[27]

Intensive multiplicity and singularities: the domain of complexity

What, exactly, does "intensity" mean? Intensity refers to those things to which we can attribute quantity, while they are not extensive. We have various names for these quantities including temperature, density, pressure, electrical potential, gravitational potential and so on. We are able to attribute differing quantitative measures to these properties at different points in time and space, but they do not designate temporal or spatial properties themselves. Rather, it is the eternal cancellation of intensive differences, and establishment of new intensive differences, that gives rise to things, and therefore to the spatial and temporal extensions that things constitute.[28] Deleuze writes: "Every relationship of forces constitutes a body – whether it is chemical, biological, social, or political. Any two forces being unequal, constitute a body as soon as they enter into a relationship" (1983: 37).[29] He is describing his interpretation of Nietzsche's metaphysics but, as elsewhere, this is Deleuze's own appropriation of Nietzsche, for his own purposes. What Deleuze is describing here is his own emerging metaphysical outlook, as is confirmed in *Difference and Repetition*. What he is saying here is that it is these "forces" or intensive differences that are ontologically primary. Whenever we seem to see a constant, substantial thing or body, with qualities and extension – there is really a complex network, or field, of intensive differences immanent to that thing, giving rise to its extensive and qualitative existence.[30] Moreover, those intensive differences must reproduce, and sustain, that thing continuously if it is to have any apparently consistent identity over time.

What we see, then, is, effectively, an extension of the iterative becoming that we have seen in accounts of autopoiesis, dissipative structures and self-organization extended to all things.[31] This also, clearly, shares a great deal with Whitehead's account of apparently material things being, in effect, "societies" of actual occasions (see ch. 13).

Deleuze often refers to these networks, or fields, of intensive difference as "multiplicities" (1994: esp. chs 4 and 5). When he does so, it is important to differentiate intensive multiplicity from extensive plurality. Extensive pluralities of actual things come at the end of a process of individuation that has its genetic origin in the virtual realm. As such they are pluralities of separate and countable things. Intensive differences, on the other hand, cannot be separate and countable things since they are what give rise to separate and countable things. They are pre-individual and pre-objective. Therefore the multiplicity of intensive difference is one of continuous variation or "variety" (*ibid.*: 187). Again, borrowing terms from Bergson, these intensive differences are "continuous" multiplicities, in contrast to discrete multiplicities or pluralities.

The whole virtual domain is a network, or field, of intensive differences structured as continuous multiplicities. This structuring takes place by means of what Deleuze calls "singularities" (*ibid.*). These are "significant" points that give rise to bifurcations, phase changes or transformations at the level of actual things. They are, arguably, functionally identical to the "attractors" that we encountered in earlier chapters.[32]

While constant cancellation of intensive differences gives rise to extended and qualified actual things, that cancellation is never final. A final cancellation would amount to the heat death of the universe, or the complete cancellation of qualitative and quantitative differences.[33] Instead there is a constant regeneration of difference: an eternal return or repetition of difference. This reliance of form on constant generation of intensive difference or disequilibrium, together with the singularities or attractors that organize the intensive spatium, can be linked directly back to our earlier discussions of complex dissipative systems, autopoietic entities and autonomous agents. We earlier maintained that when complex systems thinkers refer to the constitutive role of real, yet immaterial, "attractors" they are, in fact, developing a variety of idealism. Arguably, Deleuze's contribution to idealist philosophy is to have made this link explicit through the theory of the problem-idea. That this link draws not on the practical idealism associated with much contemporary "neo-Hegelian" philosophy, but rather on the philosophy of nature (see e.g. Deleuze 1994: 256), makes this an uncommon approach, but in no way detracts from its idealist character.

Chaos and the unground

As already stated, Deleuze does not think that Kant goes far enough in his account of the indeterminability of the Ideas of reason. For Kant the Ideas of reason are constant guides for the reasoning activities of finite rational beings. As we saw, Deleuze extends the problem-idea well beyond the boundaries of the finite rational mentation. The problem-idea is the morphogenetic element immanent to the whole of nature. This has a further and profound implication, however. Since the problem-idea is indeterminable, the whole of nature is indeterminable. Nature is not a unified rational structure, as we find it in Hegel's account, and in that of many of the British idealists. For Deleuze, the world itself must remain eternally incomplete, leaving an "irreducible remainder", as for Schelling (see ch. 7).

The intensive spatium gives rise to order and structure at the level of actualities, that is, of nature in general. Yet because it is itself pre-objective, it does not resemble this domain of actuality or nature in any way, as the crude Platonist would understand the relation between the Idea and its copy. Rather, it throws off a little actual order here and there by "chance" (Deleuze 1994: 115–16, 126, 198–200, 202, 282–4, 312). Furthermore, there is no inevitability, no mechanical determinacy, about the way in which the intensive resources of the virtual give rise to the actual world. It is not just in the domain of human freedom that indeterminacy reigns, as dualistically inclined philosophers have long argued. Instead there is indeterminacy right the way down through nature. The virtual is "chaos" (*ibid.*: 68, 213–14, 280–81, 299; Deleuze & Guattari 1994: "Conclusion"). There is no rational ground for things; rather, there is a chaotic "unground" – the generative principle out of which emerge small and ephemeral islands of order (Deleuze 1994: 275–7). The "thingness" of actuality stands out in a kind of relief against this background of unthingness or chaos. There is no total system, no absolute Idea.[34] Rather, there is a chaotic intensive maelstrom, out of which emerges something concrete, for a short time, before disappearing again into the whirlwind of intensities.[35] And it is the problem-idea that enables this emergence and perishing of actual order from the chaotic unground of intensity.

Transcendental empiricism

In *Difference and Repetition* Deleuze states:

> Empiricism becomes truly transcendental, and aesthetics an apodictic discipline, only when we apprehend directly in the sensible that which can only be sensed, the very being of the sensible: difference, potential difference and difference in intensity as the reason behind qualitative diversity … The intense world of differences, in which we find the reason behind qualities and the being of the sensible, is precisely the object of a superior empiricism.
> (1994: 56–7)

Why does Deleuze call his philosophy "transcendental"? It is transcendental because it is concerned with the deduction of *a priori* conditions. However, it cannot be a transcendental idealism (like Kant's), since it is not concerned merely with the *a priori* conditions for the thought of a finite rational being. Rather, as we have seen, it is concerned with the conditions for the generation of all things in the world. So it is a transcendental philosophy, but Deleuze has to distinguish it from Kantian transcendental idealism.

On the other hand, it is an empiricism because, methodologically, it relies directly on our senses. It is in our sense-perception that qualities are directly produced through the cancellation of intensive differences. All the qualities of things rely on sensations. These sensations are not things, but energetic processes. Sensations are not mental processes – but the means by which intensive quantities generate all actual qualities. Qualities are always sensations. But rather than taking this to mean that all of reality is inside mind (as we have seen with Berkeley, for example) Deleuze argues that sensation is everywhere in the world. The particular things that exist in the world must be generated via universal sensation. We, and everything else, are composed of the results of sensation. Everything senses everything else constantly as intensive difference is reciprocally determined and the things in the world are thereby iteratively reproduced from moment to moment.[36]

Consequently, the problem that guides Deleuze's transcendental enquiry is how we can know intensive difference if it is cancelled in its "explication". How can we encounter the being of the sensible? The method that Deleuze employs must rely on sensation in order to deliver to the philosopher the truth of the genesis of things. However, we can see that sensation is not concerned merely with the perception of things once they have been constituted (an "inferior" empiricism?), but is a part of the intensive processes that underlie them: the transcendental "conditions" of the sensible. Since, as we have seen, these processes are the realm of the problem-idea, this is an *empiricism of the Idea*. Empiricism becomes transcendental when it engages with the Idea.

Deleuze develops this view of the importance of our "encounter" with intensity in, among other things, his accounts of learning and of modern art. Consider the example of learning to swim (Deleuze 1994: 192). It is not gained through the observation and representation of particular things, but through feeling the intensive forces giving rise to me in the world from moment to moment. This is, in fact, common to all learning, since it must originate in intensive forces that have the capacity to change us. Similarly, he also claims that modern art is concerned with the intensive genesis of things. He claims that "the work of art leaves the domain of representation in order to become 'experience', transcendental empiricism or science of the sensible" (*ibid*.: 56).

Deleuze's idealism

This returns us to the nature of the idealism to which Deleuze may be considered a contributor. We have already noted that this takes the contemporarily unusual route to the Idea through the philosophy of nature. In the foregoing discussion, however, we broached the problem of "freedom", which, we concluded, is a condition affecting not simply some particular parts of nature, but rather nature as such considered from the perspective of production. Does this amount to a reduction of the problem of freedom to naturalistic indeterminacy, or does the concept of freedom supply a reason for the metaphysics of forces, powers and intensities? While the foregoing may sound like a naturalistic reduction, we have already noted Deleuze's rejection of materialism, making such a strategy unlikely at best. Nor does Deleuze advocate an ethics-based metaphysics inspired by the "good beyond being" that Plato's *Republic* (509b) hypothesized. On the contrary, drawing Spinozist lessons, Deleuze notes that since all things are generated by and composed of intensities or powers, an understanding of their behaviours and nature already constitutes an "ethical vision of the world" (Deleuze 1990b: 257). As opposed, therefore, to those contemporary idealisms that oppose normativity to nature that we examined above, Deleuze's metaphysics satisfies the ampliative or inclusivist stakes idealist philosophy set itself since Plato, rearticulating rather than eliminating ethics in accordance with nature, but both in accordance with the problem-idea.

SLAVOJ ŽIŽEK AND FRENCH HEGELIANISM

Mainland European philosophical discussion of idealism centres overwhelmingly on scholarship around German idealism. In Germany in particular, an enormous amount of scholarly attention is lavished on the works of Kant, Fichte, Schelling and Hegel. When Hegel entered French intellectual life, on the other hand, in the early to mid-twentieth century, it was less for reasons of scholarship than politics: as Marx's crucial forerunner, the analysis of Hegel was, therefore, a matter of neither the past nor the conceptual, but of the analysis of and action in the present. Since this legacy was crucial in the development of twentieth-century French philosophy in general, what follows will show Žižek as its pre-eminent inheritor before briefly looking for contemporary developments in philosophical idealism.

Two philosophers introduced and defined French Hegel studies during the Second World War: Alexandre Kojève and Jean Hyppolite. Both rejected the Hegel of the Absolute defended by Jean Wahl, and the overtly religious Hegel represented by Gabriel Marcel. The vivid Hegel that emerged instead was riven between materialism and the philosophy of consciousness, between Marxism and phenomenology. A polarization emerged around Kojève's influential Sorbonne lectures on the *Phenomenology*,[37] and Hyppolite's translation of and commentary on it.[38] The former presented an anthropological reading of Hegel's work that supplanted the Absolute with "man" and made desire the motor of history. The latter, by contrast, foregrounded the *Phenomenology*'s contradiction by the *Logic*, rejecting Kojève's attempt to conjoin philosophy and anthropology. While Jean-Paul Sartre, Merleau-Ponty, Georges Bataille, Emmanuel Levinas and Jacques Lacan were all attendees at Kojève's lectures, Jacques Derrida, Michel Foucault, Deleuze and Badiou were all, at various times, students of Hyppolite's.[39] We may thus speak of these poles as an erotic Hegel and a rationalist Hegel: while Kojève participated in and was fêted by Bataille and the members of the College of Sociology,[40] Hyppolite debates Platonism, negation and the philosophy of nature with Lacan.[41]

Not only this polarity, but also the near-universal anti-Hegelianism on the part of precisely that generation to have been introduced to Hegel by Kojève and Hyppolite, dominated French philosophical life until the century's end,[42] formulating, in Foucault's words, "the most fundamental problems of our age" (1972: 237). These are problems, Foucault stated in his inaugural lecture for the Collège de France, ultimately determined by Hegel, that may remain insoluble, so that, even as anti-Hegelians, philosophers remain indebted to Hyppolite for having "tirelessly explored ... the path along which we may escape from Hegel". In the end, however, "we shall find ourselves brought back to him" (*ibid.*: 235).[43] As if in confirmation, Badiou's formula "The dialectic is exhausted. We must rise up against the negative" (2008: 121) indicates the extent to which Hegel remains "unsurpassable" in the new century. While not all agree – Catherine Malabou's *The Future of Hegel* (2005) is a case in point – the problem of what is to replace this long, negative, Hegelian dominion over post-war French philosophy remains.

In this invention of the philosophy of the future, Badiou and Deleuze take the "path of an ontology" (Deleuze in Hyppolite 1997: 194) opened by Hyppolite. Thus, in a review of Hyppolite's *Logic and Existence*, Deleuze reaffirms Hyppolite's equation of philosophy with ontology while disputing the equation of ontology with logic, as understood in Hegelian terms (Deleuze in Hyppolite 1997: 191–5): there is more to being than what can be recovered in the logical overcoming of contradictions. Hence Deleuze's reassertion of the philosophical rights of difference over contradiction as its phenomenal or "anthropological" form (*ibid.*: 195) is precisely an attempt to surpass (Hyppolite's) Hegel, leading, as we have seen, towards broadly Platonic problematics. Yet Deleuze would also return, in his celebrated intellectual partnership with Félix Guattari, to the philosophy of desire that would be their Kojèvian inheritance, in *Anti-Oedipus*. As Deleuze would later report, however, their ongoing project had been to produce a philosophy of nature that, although there are scattered contributions to it, would never be completed.

Similarly, Badiou's ontological investigations have eschewed the equation of logic with the "sense" or "meaning" that Hyppolite advanced as the medium of the Absolute,[44] since "meaning" introduces finitude into ontology (meaning for what or whom?). In consequence, Badiou takes the Platonic line that mathematics gets us closer to being than does sense, precisely because it opposes the real infinities with which the former works (logic) to the finitude of experience (phenomenology). Badiou's *Logics of Worlds* (2009), however, finds him returning to the logic of appearances, by way of Hegel. He calls the logic developed in that work the "'greater logic'", after Hegel, although he wishes to wrest it from "the constraint of language" (*ibid.*: 93), which Hyppolite (1997) had considered the medium of the Absolute's self-articulation, in the direction of a "transcendental logic". Badiou's, in other words, is a recovery of Hegel from Hyppolite's path, in the interests of a materialism that has as its starting point the postulate "every atom of appearing is real" (Badiou 2009: 94). That the "logic of appearing" is the logic of the real suggests an unexpected Kojèvian turn in the history and development of French Hegelianism, one premised on the *political* problematic that, Badiou overtly acknowledges, animates his ontology. In this we see what Žižek (2006: 325) calls Badiou's "Fichteanism" come to light. Fichte, too, had his transcendental logic, but, more importantly, advocated the primacy of activity over being, which is only the "exhausted residuum" of the former.

It is this thesis, taken as a political imperative, and echoed in what Badiou calls "an essential national tendency" to make knowledge "subordinate to ethics" (2008: 121), that ultimately lies behind Kojève's Hegel. We find it in its most undiluted contemporary form in Žižek's long-term investment in idealist philosophy, which began with his doctoral thesis on Hegel, completed in France, and published as *Most Sublime of Hysterics* (1988). Žižek shares Badiou's formulation of materialism against the reductive materialisms evident, for example, in neuroscientific philosophies of mind, maintaining that a radical materialism "is by definition nonreductionist" (Žižek 2006: 168): if materialism holds that "nothing is not-matter", then either everything that exists and appears must be material, or the materialism is of what Marxists used to call the "vulgar" variety, limited to the abstractions of the so-called "natural" sciences. These are abstractions or merely formal understandings because they set up an object standing over and against a subject, whose interventions are held to alter nothing of the truth of the object in itself. As Kojève makes the case in his Hegel lectures, a materialist account of natural phenomena must acknowledge that "science is born from the desire to transform the World in relation to Man". Accordingly:

> [S]cientific knowledge is never absolutely passive, nor purely contemplative and descriptive. Scientific experiment disturbs the Object because of the active intervention of the Subject .... What it reveals, therefore, is neither the Object taken independently of the Subject, nor the Subject taken independently of the Object, but only the result of the *interaction* of the two or, if you prefer, that interaction itself.   (Kojève 1969: 176–7)

As a result, "science never attains the autonomously real, the 'thing in itself' of Kant and Newton" (*ibid.*). The reason for this constructivist–instrumentalist account of experiment is to insert the subject – consciousness – into the production of natural phenomena. As Žižek puts it, what he still calls the "materialist" moment consists in how it happens that "I myself am included in the picture *constituted by me*" (2006: 17, emphasis added). What is striking about this account is the final phrase concerning the constitutive authority of the subject over the picture in which I am included. This is a genuinely Fichtean assertion of what Brandom would call the *responsibility* of the subject for its objects, for which reason scholars have noted that much of what Brandom appreciates in Hegel "is in fact Fichtean" (Franks 2007: 63). Just as the starting point of Fichte's *Science of Knowledge* is the claim that facts are first "acts" (*Tathandlungen*) (see ch. 6), so "responsibility", with its normative-political entailments, does not claim *authorship* of the object, but only that the subject is actively and insuperably involved in its articulation, its conception and its applications. Yet Žižek goes further than this, simultaneously eliminating the possibility of any "autonomous real" and therefore of any ontological role played by "nature", even to the point of "wordlessness" (2006: 318). Lately, therefore, Žižek has enthusiastically endorsed "Fichte's position with regard to the *status* of nature".[45] The activity of the conscious subject prevents not only *access to* a thing-in-itself, but withdraws from it any ontological "status" in the interests of a practical one. According to Žižek's Fichte, then, it is only when:

> reality is primordially *experienced* as the obstacle to the I's practical activity ... that nature (the inertia of material objects) exists only as the stuff of our moral activity, that its justification can only be practical-teleological. This is why Fichte rejects all attempts at a speculative philosophy of nature.
> (Gabriel & Žižek 2009: 160, emphasis added)

Thus nature becomes nothing more than "the subject's prehistory" (Žižek 1992: 49), which the subject experiences as drives. When, therefore, Žižek addresses Schelling, the role of nature in the latter's philosophy is supplanted by that of the drives, which are not nature, but rather a "proto-ontological domain", a "not yet fully constituted reality" (2004: 32). It is clear, then, that Žižek's materialism derives from his engagement with Hegel's reception in France, especially in its Kojèveian form, which presents Hegel as the philosopher of desire. It is through this practical category that his materialism is articulated: a materialism of the drives in his psychoanalytical account of Schelling; a materialism of decision in his political account of Fichte; and a materialism of consciousness in his account of Hegel. Yet the subordination of ontology to ethics draws a direct line from Žižek through Kojève to Fichte, from whence this idealism originates. It is Fichte's *science of knowledge* as deriving fundamentally from the acts of a subject – whether this is understood as individual, collective, state or species – for which objects present obstacles to activity.[46]

The fundamental form, therefore, of French idealism, contemporarily typified by Žižek, was impressed upon it by Kojève. Even Malabou's *The Future of Hegel* repeatedly cites Kojève but makes no mention of Hyppolite.[47] Contemporary French philosophy in general – to which we may, given his themes, background and allegiances, assimilate Žižek – is being played out between Hyppolitean ontology and the Kojèvean elimination of the "autonomous real", between science and desire, knowing and willing; and both poles derive in turn from Hegel. One of the elements Kojève brought with him to Paris was his familiarity with Heidegger's work, from which we may derive a fitting formula for the Hegelian movement he inaugurated: "the natural is not the real and the real not natural" (Heidegger 2002: 110). By contrast, as we have seen, the Hyppolitean trajectory on which Deleuze set out carried him in the Schellingian direction – equally idealist, just not Fichtean – of a philosophy of the Idea and of nature. The struggle for the future of French philosophy is therefore a struggle over the legacy of idealism.

It is perhaps a fitting irony of history that we might conclude this chapter with a consideration of the contemporary situation in philosophy. Introducing a volume of their studies of the idealist tradition, Žižek and Gabriel note:

> [T]here is a group of philosophers who deem the Post-Kantian speculative-historical approach to philosophical thought the highest achievement of philosophy which we have not yet even fully understood. They believe that many of the central insights of German Idealism still wait to be translated into contemporary philosophy. (Gabriel & Žižek 2009: 4)

It is striking that the same sentiments exactly are expressed by Brandom. How surprising it is, therefore, that Hegel, the very philosophical presence around which the analytic tradition took its distance from philosophy in general at the beginning of the twentieth century should, at the beginning of the next, be the cause of their reunion.

NOTES

INTRODUCTION

1. In particular, we regret the omission of medieval and Renaissance philosophy, the Cambridge Platonists, and the phenomenological tradition's idealist inheritance.
2. Quotations from the *Critique of Judgement* are from the Pluhar translation (Kant 1987), unless otherwise noted.
3. We must be wary of attributing to Hegel any theory regarding natural selection, since this is not what he could be denying in the early nineteenth century.
4. The following abbreviations are used for Plato's dialogues: *Prm.* = *Parmenides*; *Phd.* = *Phaedo*; *Phlb.* = *Philebus*; *Resp.* = *Republic*; *Soph.* = *Sophist*; *Ti.* = *Timaeus*.

1. PARMENIDES AND THE BIRTH OF ANCIENT IDEALISM

1. In dictionaries and encyclopaedias of philosophy, this remains so even when the entries are authored by self-confessed idealists such as T. L. S. Sprigge in the *Routledge Encyclopaedia of Philosophy* (Craig 1998: 662–3) and Nicholas Rescher in the *Cambridge Dictionary of Philosophy* (Audi 1999: 412). The entries in the *Oxford Dictionary of Philosophy* (Blackburn 1994) and the *Oxford Companion to Philosophy* (Honderich 2005) repeat the claim that idealism is "Any doctrine holding that reality is fundamentally mental in nature" (Blackburn 1994: 177).
2. Fragments are numbered according to Diels and Kranz (1960) and cited in Cornford's (1939) translation.
3. Burnyeat continues: "Just as materialism is the monism which asserts that ultimately nothing exists or is real but matter and material things, so idealism is the monism which claims that ultimately all there is is mind and the contents of mind" (1982: 8).
4. "What I have ascribed to antiquity is an unquestioned, unquestioning assumption of realism: something importantly different from an explicit philosophical thesis" (*ibid*.: 33).
5. Eliminative materialists in the philosophy of mind argue that precisely this distinction is critical and that, as neuroscience progresses, our ontology will be revised. This yields the odd conclusion, however, that some existents are merely mental constructions that have no material reality, so the eliminative materialist either produces or presupposes a dualistic ontology of material and exclusively mental phenomena.

NOTES

6. The model in question is most overtly provided by H. B. Action in his entry on idealism in Edwards (1967: 110).
7. Scholars estimate that we possess 90 per cent of the first part, and 10 per cent of the second. Burnet (1930: 171 n.3) cites Hermann Diels to this effect.
8. Since Cornford does not quote the second sentence from the above passage, the appended line comes from Waterfield (2000: 57).
9. For panpsychism, see Skrbina (2005). Sprigge gives a partial defence of panpsychist idealism (1983: 153–61; 2006: 478–86), but remains "inclined to think that ... brain process breaks the normal laws of nature" (2006: 486).
10. Hegel explicates the indeterminacy of pure Being as the starting point for thinking: "When thinking is to begin, we have nothing but thought in its pure lack of determination, for determination requires both one and another; but at the beginning we have as yet no other. ... This starting point is to be found in ... Parmenides" (1991: 137–8).
11. In another version of these lectures, Fichte argues that this identity means "that the I itself arises only through the unification of being and thinking" (1992: 381).
12. Since Cornford's phrasing of fragment B2 is archaic, the above translation is Waterfield's (2000: 58).

2. PLATO AND NEOPLATONISM

1. Plato's *eidos* is rendered by the capitalized "Idea" throughout, rather than by "Form".
2. Aristotle repeats Plato's argument against its author at *Metaphysics* 990a35–91b8; 1038b1–39a23; *Sophistical Refutations* 178b37–9a5, and in "On Ideas" (in Fine 1993: 18–19).
3. Lloyd Gerson has recently argued that "It is ... misleading to characterize Platonism in terms of dualism(s) such as mind (soul)/body or even intelligible/sensible. The hierarchical explanatory framework of top-downism is conceptually prior to these dualisms" (2005: 35).
4. References to Plotinus are to the *Enneads*, compiled and arranged after their author's death by his pupil Porphyry into six books, divided into chapter and section numbers.
5. Gerson (2005) discusses these issues in his provocatively titled *Aristotle and Other Platonists*.
6. Dodds presents Proclus' *Elements of Theology* in his introduction as "the one genuine systematic exposition of Neoplatonic metaphysic that has come down to us" (Proclus 1963: ix).
7. A. H. Armstrong, responding to Burnyeat's (1982: 16) dismissal of Plotinus as an idealist, disputes that mind-dependency makes Plotinus' philosophy into a subjective idealism: "Plotinus' *logoi* ... are living thoughts. This is no subjective idealism. The minds which the universal thoughts constitute are themselves both universal and individual or substantial .... If we want to suppose a kind of 'Consciousness *überhaupt*' we need not be too afraid of anachronism" (Armstrong 1990: 134).
8. Dominic J. O'Meara (1996: 70–71) emphasizes the ontological dimension of the Platonic theory of value as stemming from this passage.

3. PHENOMENALISM AND IDEALISM I: DESCARTES AND MALEBRANCHE

1. In fact, we have endeavoured to show that even the D1 definition is too restrictive.
2. Hibbs's evidence of pre-Cartesian idealism refers to Plotinus and Richard Sorabji's

work on the Christian Neoplatonist Gregory of Nyssa. He also directs the reader to Dermot Moran's work on the medieval idealist Eriugena.
3. Margaret Wilson (1978) associates this view with G. E. Moore, Norman Malcolm and Henri Frankfurt.
4. This view is associated with W. H. Walsh.
5. See Berkeley, *Principles* §18, for his own version of the DA3 argument and thus its importance for his idealism.
6. By "mind", Descartes means a "one and the same 'I'", which is a "thinking thing" that "doubt, understands, affirms, denies, is willing, is unwilling, and also imagines and has sensory perceptions" (AT VII.28; CSM II.19), that is, perceives ideas.
7. We have used blocks in order to make the diagram as simple as possible; however, it must be remembered that this is an abstraction used to aid the discussion. Descartes distinguishes three types of matter: the first type is "subtle" and has no determinate shape; the second can be conceived of as very minute spherical particles; and the third is much bulkier. "The sun and fixed stars are composed of the first element, the heavens from the second, and the earth with the planets and comets from the third" (AT VIIIA.105; CSM I.258).
8. Descartes does recognize that this is conceptually difficult and in a letter to Princess Elizabeth writes: "It does not seem to me that the human mind is capable of forming a very distinct conception of both the distinction between the soul and the body and their union; for to do this it is necessary to conceive them as a single thing and at the same time to conceive them as two things; and this is absurd" (AT III.693; CSM III.227).
9. See Scott (2000). The fine details of this account of causation are the subject of much debate. Some particularly good discussions include Nadler (1994), Rozemond (1999) and Wilson (1999b).
10. While Descartes, in the *Meditations*, makes a distinction between three types of ideas – adventitious, fabricated and innate – there is a sense in which all ideas are innate. Jolley points out that Descartes implies a distinction between "weak" and "strong" innate ideas. While all ideas are innate for Descartes, those abstract truths such as mathematical truths and the idea of God are innate in the strong sense. Adventitious and fabricated ideas are still innate, but only in the weak sense.
11. Jolley (1990) claims that Malebranche goes some way towards tidying up the mess that Descartes left behind.
12. For example, Augustine reports that the "original form resides" in God, as "the source of all creation" (*City of God* VIII.8; 2003: 308).

4. PHENOMENALISM AND IDEALISM II: LEIBNIZ AND BERKELEY

1. In a letter to Magnus Wedderkopf, written in 1671, Leibniz writes: "For essences of things are just like numbers, and they contain the very possibility of entities, which God does not bring about, as he does existence, since these very possibilities – or ideas of things – coincide rather with God himself" (A II.i.117; CP 3).
2. For a concise and well-argued defence of this position see Rutherford (1995a).
3. It is also arguable that Berkeley's "abstract universals" may not be precisely the same as the universals employed by Hegel and Whitehead.
4. For Berkeley, "no idea or archetype of an idea can exist otherwise than in a mind" (GBW II.213), and Leibniz writes: "considering the matter carefully, it may be said that there is nothing in things but simple substances, and in them, perception and appetite" (G II.270; AG 181).

NOTES

5. IMMANUEL KANT: COGNITION, FREEDOM AND TELEOLOGY

1. See Chapter 14 for a discussion of "attractors" in late-twentieth-century sciences.
2. See Chapter 15 for a discussion of Deleuze's "problem-idea".
3. Although, as we have seen in Chapter 4, Berkeley explicitly denies that he is a sceptic of this kind.
4. This, of course, is the core of Jürgen Habermas's (1984) neo-Kantian account of "communicative rationality".
5. An excellent paper by Linda Palmer (2008) argues that there is neuroscientific evidence to support Kant's suggestion that there is an "inner sense" of pleasure associated with judgement. In particular, parts of the amygdala may be functional in generating this pleasurable "feeling" of cognition. It is this that drives unsupervised exploration and learning, without any external reward. This is why we are curious creatures in the first place.

6. FICHTE AND THE SYSTEM OF FREEDOM

1. "The First System-Programme of German Idealism" was first published in 1917. Schelling, Hegel or Hölderlin may be its author.
2. "[M]y system", wrote Fichte, "is the first system of freedom" (1988a: 385).
3. On this, see Rockmore (1980) and Ameriks (2000b).
4. It is important that the reader know the German term, since important Fichte translators such as Breazeale (Fichte 1988a,b, 1992) preserve the German "*Wissenschaftslehre*", translated as "science of knowledge" in Fichte (1982), but as "science of knowing" in Fichte (2005b).
5. Heidegger's criticism masks his own transformation, in "On the Essence of Ground" (1998), written contemporaneously with his Fichte lectures, of nature from the ground to the consequence of freedom. Fichte was constantly defending himself against Schelling's criticism that nature "neither *is* nor *exists*" (SW VII.10) in the *Wissenschaftslehre*.
6. Although Spinoza does not use the term "principle of sufficient reason", he provides one in *Ethics* I, P11, Second proof: "For every thing a *cause or reason* must be assigned either for its existence or non-existence" (1992: 37).
7. Fichte was an enthusiastic proponent of the French Revolution, writing a *Correction of the Public Judgment of the French Revolution* in 1793 (W VI.37–287).
8. It is interesting in this regard to note Kant's criticism of Fichte's *Wissenschaftslehre* as a "vain effort … to cull a real object out of logic" (Ak. XII.370–71).
9. David Woodruff Smith reports that Husserl read Fichte "during the years leading up to *Ideas* I" (2007: 96).
10. Phenomenology's debt to Fichte has been widely acknowledged since the 1950s. See Hyppolite (1959), Franks (1999) and Rosen (1999).
11. Husserl defines intentionality thus: "Universally it belongs to the essence of every actional *cogito* to be conscious of something" (1989: §36).
12. Heidegger's *Collected Works* contain two books each on Kant (vols 3, 41), Schelling (42, 49) and Hegel (32, 68), with one on Fichte (28).
13. Heidegger's extensive 1929 lectures on Fichte are published under the title *German Idealism* as volume 28 of the *Gesamtausgabe*. Despite the three names, the bulk of the material is devoted to Fichte. For the concept of "projection", see Heidegger (1998: 126–9).

7. IDEALIST PHILOSOPHY OF NATURE: F. W. J. SCHELLING

1. This is a constant of Schelling's account of Kant, his last work presenting Kant's as a "critique of natural cognition" (SW XI.526).
2. Ultimately, as Schelling notes, Kant "accords the ideas no reality except insofar as they are moral by nature" (1994a: 174), which is also a criticism of Fichte.
3. Schelling's theories of self-construction, irreversibility and forces have brought several recent commentators, none of whose work is available in English, to examine the extent to which Schelling's philosophy of nature should be regarded as the philosophical precursor of the sciences of complexity. See Chapter 15, below, for our discussion of these sciences and their relation to Schelling's idealism.
4. See Snow (1996: ch. 5) for an excellent discussion of this point.
5. Schelling's *Introduction to the Philosophy of Mythology* (SW XI.371) tells us that he used this phrase only once, referring his reader to the *Presentation of My System of Philosophy* (cf. 2001: 348).
6. See, for example, Habermas (2004) and Žižek (1996). They see Schelling as a precursor of Marx's historical materialism.

8. HEGEL AND HEGELIANISM: MIND, NATURE AND LOGIC

1. See Beiser (1987: chs 2–5) for an excellent account of Jacobi's influential work, and the conflicts that grew around it.
2. Sprigge (2006) provides a sympathetic examination of this thesis, not only in Spinoza and Hegel, but throughout the British idealist movement and on to his own philosophical position.
3. Major figures of German Romanticism were Friedrich Hölderlin, Friedrich Daniel Ernst Schleiermacher, August Wilhelm and Friedrich Schlegel, and Novalis (Georg Philipp Friedrich Freiherr von Hardenberg). Associated with this movement and substantially overlapping it was the philosophical movement later known as German idealism (see Beiser 2006).
4. The idealists may, as we have seen, be divided into an earlier phase of "transcendental" idealism, mostly associated with Kant and Fichte, and a later phase of "absolute" or "speculative" idealism, mostly associated with Hegel and Schelling.
5. The concept of "negation" plays a purely systemic role. It indicates that the indentity of any part of the totality is only what it is by virtue of not being everything that it is not. Each thing "negates" its other in order to be itself. Thus identity and negation collapse into one another dialectically. This can only be so, of course, in a system in which every identity is derived relationally from its place in the whole. The movement from unity, through multiplicity, to unity in multiplicity can, therefore, be thought of as the movement from identity, through the negation of identity, to the location of the identical and non-identical in the relations within the whole.

9. BRITISH ABSOLUTE IDEALISM: FROM GREEN TO BRADLEY

1. It did not completely die down. Both J. N. Findlay and Charles Taylor produced major works on Hegel in 1958 and 1975, respectively, while Alistair MacIntyre's collection of essays in 1972 continued English-language Hegel scholarship. More recently, there has been a neo-Hegelianism in the work of John McDowell, Robert Brandom, Robert Pippin, Terry Pinkard and Frederick Beiser.

NOTES

2. See Bradley (1930: ch. 21) for Bradley's full critique of solipsism. "If solipsism is to be proved it must transcend direct experience. Let us then ask, (*a*) first, if transcendence of this kind is possible, and, (*b*) next, if it is able to give assistance to Solipsism. The conclusion, which we shall reach, may be stated at once. It is both possible and necessary to transcend what is given. But the same transcendence at once carries us into the universe at large. Our private self is not a resting-place which logic can justify" (*ibid.*: 221).

10. PERSONAL IDEALISM: FROM WARD TO MCTAGGART

1. Andrew Seth Pringle-Pattison was known as just "Andrew Seth" until 1898, when he took on an additional surname to fulfil the terms of a bequest of a distant relative's widow, in which he was given a country estate (The Haining, Selkirkshire) together with 7000 acres.
2. This has recently become a favoured argument by the Pittsburgh neo-Hegelians. See Chapter 15.
3. Like Pringle-Pattison, John McTaggart Ellis McTaggart's extraordinary double surname was the condition of a bequest. See Geach (1979: 9).
4. Unlike Bradley, McTaggart refutes the premise that there can be degrees of reality. Either an existent is real or it is not an existent at all, although it is often argued that possibility is real without being actual. McTaggart is opposed to this claim; all possibility is, he argues, a limitation of our knowledge. We may say "It is possible that it may rain tomorrow" but what we really mean is "I don't know whether or not it will rain tomorrow"; it does not mean that before the event there are a number of possible worlds and in one of them it rains and in another it does not. Only the actual is real.
5. P. T. Geach argues that "between" is still a confusing and unnecessary term. McTaggart, he claims, would have been better off regarding relations as functions: "use of the 'between' jargon blurs one of the most important traits of relations, lack of symmetry. If C is R to B, B need not be R to C; this is not clarified but obscured by saying, 'R may hold between C and B but not between B and C'" (1979: 48–50).
6. McTaggart uses the term "characteristics" to refer to both qualities and relations at the same time.
7. See Geach (1979: ch. 3), for an interesting defence of this principle against Broad's critique: "McTaggart, like Wittgenstein in the *Tractatus*, is committed to the view that the Universe could be *completely* described in completely general terms, with no irreducible use of a 'non-connotative' proper name; and I think this view ought to be accepted" (*ibid.*: 54).
8. "[I]f any substance, A, other than the universe, has a quality X, the universe has the quality of containing a part with the nature of A, which has the quality X. We may call this quality of the universe X'. It is clear that the possession of X by A, and the possession of X' by the universe, intrinsically determine one another … it would be unjustifiable to assert that, if A had not the quality X, any of the qualities of the universe would remain the same. For if A had not the quality X, the universe could not have the quality X', and X'' extrinsically determines all the other qualities of the universe.

In the same way, it would be unjustifiable to assert that, if any of the qualities of the universe were not the same, A would still possess X. For it could not possess X unless the universe possessed X', and X' is in reciprocal extrinsic determination with all the other qualities of the universe" (McTaggart 1921: 150).
9. "Determining Correspondence may be defined as follows: A relation between a sub-

stance C and the part of a substance B is a relation of determining correspondence if a certain sufficient description of C, which includes the fact that it is in that relation to *some* part of B, (1) intrinsically determines a sufficient description of the part of B in question, B!C, [! Is McTaggart's notation for "determines"] and (2) intrinsically determines sufficient descriptions of each member of a set of parts of each of such members and so on to infinity" (*ibid*.: 214).

10. Much later in *The Nature of Existence*, McTaggart introduces another, arguably better, argument for the dependence of the B-series on the A-series. The direction of the B-series depends on the A-series because the B-series moves from earlier to later, and its dependence on change means that time must move from future to present to the past, and until these terms are introduced conceptions of earlier and later make no sense: "until the terms are taken as passing from future to present, and from present to past, they cannot be taken as in time, or as earlier or later; and not only the concept of presentness, but those of pastness and futurity, must be reached before the conceptions of earlier and later, and not *vice versa*". (1927: 271 n.1). The very meaning of earlier and later cannot be established until the distinctions of the A-series are introduced. Therefore, there can be no doubt that the B-series *must* depend on the A-series.

11. This is, of course, a highly speculative claim. McTaggart agrees that he knows of no valid reports of anyone actually perceiving others' perceptions but this does not mean that it is an impossibility.

11. NATURALIST IDEALISM: BERNARD BOSANQUET

1. See, for example, Sweet (1996), which provides an informative account of the main trends in the critical literature surrounding Bosanquet.
2. "There is more analogy between the work of thought and solid and complete reality, than Mr. Bradley, treating thought as solely discursive, seems to allow" (Bosanquet 1911: vol. 2, 288 n.).
3. Bosanquet references Spinoza and Hegel in support of this claim: "Hegel's 'actual soul' is the perfection of a living body highly trained and definitely habituated. We do not know, Spinoza warns us in a wonderful passage, how much the body may be capable of doing" (1912: 178).
4. Other than Alexander, these philosophers are: C. Lloyd Morgan, C. D. Broad and G. H. Lewes. G. Dawes Hicks (1938) provides a later, excellent survey of this material.
5. Alexander (1920) is considered the foundational work for early-twentieth-century "emergentism".
6. Bosanquet writes: "Plato's law of Contradiction – what does or suffers 'opposites' … in the same relation must in itself be two and not one" (1912: 224). Socrates gives an overt account of contradiction: "Clearly one and the same thing cannot act or be affected in opposite ways at the same time in the same part of it and in relation to the same object; so if we find these contradictions, we shall know we are dealing with more than one faculty" (*Resp.* 436b–c).
7. Discussing the context in which Bosanquet began his logical investigations, J. H. Muirhead writes: "It is hard for the present generation to realise the chaos that prevailed in this department in the [18]70s" (1923: 400). It is in this context that Hermann Lotze's and Hegel's logical works were received (the former in Bosanquet's translation), and the invention Bosanquet and Bradley brought to philosophical logic made them antipsychologistic allies in philosophical logic with the likes of Russell, Frege and Husserl.
8. McTaggart was moved by this analysis to assert that "Almost every word that Dr

NOTES

Bosanquet has written about the relations of Mind and Matter might have been written by a complete Materialist" (1912: 422).
9. For further discussion, see "Hegel, British Idealism, and the Curious Case of the Concrete Universal" (Stern 2009: ch. 5); Sprigge's (1983: 11–13) discussion is incisive and economical. For Hegel's distinction between the concrete and abstract universals, see Hegel (1991: 239–42).
10. "Teleology, Professor Burnet points out, has not really to do with *telos* as an external end, but with *teleion*, 'complete'" (Bosanquet 1917b: 270).

12. CRITICISMS AND PERSISTENT MISCONCEPTIONS OF IDEALISM

1. Moore gives his realist credentials away in separating "awareness" from the necessary components of real objects: "awareness is and must be in all cases of such a nature that its object, when we are aware of it, is precisely what it would be, if we were not aware" (Moore 1903: 453).
2. Russell's attempted refutation of Bergson is premised on a similar argument. In his response to Wildon Carr he argues that "I did not attempt to prove that 'Bergson's philosophy is not true'" (1914: 33); rather, he wanted to prove that the arguments it is based on are fallacious, and without stable arguments it remains merely an imaginative possibility of a cosmic poet.
3. The contemporary metaphysicians advancing a "powers-ontology" claim to inherit the notion of power from Locke (see Shoemaker 1980) but an epistemological argument for a powers-ontology – that nature must be powerful in order to create sensation – is at heart more Leibnizian than Lockean, even if the solution differs.
4. The speculative philosopher, writes Bosanquet, "considers the outer world, the world of nature, as it does every factor of experience, at its fullest …. It is altogether free from the assumption … that to advance toward the real you must look to what persists under the minimum of conditions" (1917a: 9).
5. See, for example, Bosanquet's claim, in *A Companion to Plato's Republic*, that Plato is a causal realist (1925: 241).
6. It is important to emphasize that not all idealists are organicists, although most subscribe to the priority of an organization or a system of nature.
7. See Monod (1970) for a manifesto for informational microbiology or, as Monod calls it, "molecular cybernetics", and Jacob (1989) for its critique.
8. This connection is not continued by all idealists. McTaggart notes, in his review of Bosanquet's *The Principle of Individuality and Value*, that "organic unity is an inadequate category – a view for which I can at any rate plead the authority of Hegel, however unpopular it may be among the Hegelians" (1912: 419n.).

13. ACTUAL OCCASIONS AND ETERNAL OBJECTS: THE PROCESS METAPHYSICS OF ALFRED NORTH WHITEHEAD

1. See Beiser (2002) for a full account of the anti-subjectivist character of German speculative idealism.
2. These are questions that we shall see, in Chapter 14, are raised again, urgently, by contemporary idealist biologists such as Stuart Kauffman.
3. Whitehead did not, however, agree with Einstein's theory in its entirety and dedicates his *The Principle of Relativity* (1922) to his own version of the theory.
4. For a convincing account of Russell's influence on Whitehead's metaphysics see

Pierfrancesco Basile's *Leibniz, Whitehead and the Metaphysics of Causation* (2009), in which he shows the importance for the development of Whitehead's philosophy of Russell's critique of substance and subject–predicate logic in *A Critical Exposition of Leibniz's Philosophy* (1967b).
5. This attempt was also made by Lord Haldane in *Reign of Relativity* (1922) and H. Wildon-Carr in *Theory of Monads* (1922).
6. By this means, Whitehead's account of time avoids Zeno's paradox (1929: 158).
7. This is a thought that we shall see developed in the context of theories of cognition within contemporary biology (see ch. 14).
8. Whitehead distinguishes "simple" and "complex" eternal objects. Simple eternal objects have the "grade of zero complexity" and cannot be further analysed: "such as a definite shade of green"; a definite set of such simple eternal objects is itself a "complex" eternal object (1926: 207).
9. It seems likely that there are interesting comparisons to be made here between the transition from indistinct potentia to actualities in Whitehead, with the relation between the "virtual" and the "actual" in both Bergson and Deleuze (see Chapter 15).
10. This is a question that is mirrored in Kauffman's biological semantics (see Chapter 14).

14. SELF-ORGANIZATION: THE IDEA IN LATE-TWENTIETH-CENTURY SCIENCE

1. We have already seen the Idea articulated as the concept of "organization" in Schelling and Bosanquet, in particular, of course.
2. See our brief comments on the work of Lee Smolin and Julian Barbour, for example, at the end of the chapter.
3. It is possible to understand Maturana and Varela's denial of "purpose", perhaps, because the perceived existence of "parts" might be understood to be a feature only of the domain of description. In reality, autopoietic unities, one might argue, do not have discrete parts but smooth continuous processes of autoproduction. My immune system can be separated from the rest of my body only by a process of analytical cognition, observation and description. If autopoietic entities do not have parts, then we cannot attribute "purposes" to parts. There are two problems with this interpretation. First, Maturana and Varela never state it in anything like these terms, and second, even without the "purposes" of parts within the whole, we still have the overall "purpose" of identity maintenance.
4. This is a fact that would also become central to the idealist metaphysics of Gilles Deleuze (see ch. 15).
5. Or autopoietic systems must feed on "pure difference", as Deleuze would put it (see ch. 15).
6. The extent of explicit idealist influence is suggested by the fact that Isabelle Stengers (Prigogine's close collaborator and co-author) has published an entire book on Whitehead's metaphysics (2002). Prigogine himself often refers to Whitehead approvingly.
7. A simple example of such homeostatic feedback is a thermostatic control operating as part of a central heating system. By means of feedback the temperature is regulated "autonomously".
8. Such a move is common in this kind of scientific idealism, as we shall see with Kauffman's work.
9. Varela, Thompson and Rosch insist that there is no information *in* the "genetic code". The gene can only do what it does when embedded within a metabolic network. The

organization determines what the genetic sequences can do. Only as part of a unity does the sequence become active as part of the "emergent regularities" of the cellular network (1993: 101). Only under these circumstances does it gain a "purpose" and "meaning", one might say.
10. See, for example, their constructionist account of scientific reasoning (1998: 28).
11. Indeed, Whitehead's "prehension" and Maturana and Varela's "cognition" are virtually identical concepts.
12. The title is a deliberate allusion to Ludwig Wittgenstein's "break with logical atomism" (Kauffman 2000: ix).
13. This is evidently a development of the cybernetic feedback theories alluded to earlier in the chapter.
14. While each reaction in the network consists of new chemical particles, the network itself is sustained. The network is a mechanism composed of what Deleuze would call the "repetition of difference". This is true of all dynamic self-reproducing systems. Human networks, similarly, are sustained networks composed of non-repeating interactions. It has occurred to us, therefore, that the autocatalytic set can be conceived as a perfect example of what Deleuze calls a "problem-idea". The organism emerges as matter flows through the network in a never-ending quest to "cancel" or "solve" the difference or disequilibrium that gives rise to it (see Chapter 15; Deleuze 1994: 168–221).
15. Again, compare this to Deleuze's account of the importance of disequilibrium in the genesis of life (1983: 42).
16. A steam engine, for example, may potentially occupy states in which its fire is out, or where its boiler has melted. These states, while part of its potential state space, clearly cannot be part of its work cycle. Consequently, we can see that only a constrained part of the steam engine's state space can be included in its work cycle.
17. Again, we shall see that Deleuze describes precisely the same arrangement in terms of "pure difference" (see ch. 15).
18. Of course, we would suggest that he must look towards the resources of idealist metaphysics to find the "proper concept of organization" for which he is searching.
19. This is reminiscent of Leibniz's own employment of calculus and, as we shall see, that of Deleuze (ch. 15).
20. Again, the same conception is to be found in Deleuze's theory of the problem-idea (see ch. 15).
21. It also occurs to us that this is the true character of what Deleuze, following Nietzsche, would call the "will-to-power", and the "eternal return of difference". This is precisely the quantitative difference of force that Deleuze's Nietzsche refers to: the one that can only ever express itself in the qualitative differentiation of the universe as it is driven from the actual to the adjacent possible (Deleuze 1983; ch. 15).

15. CONTEMPORARY PHILOSOPHICAL IDEALISM

1. For an account of recent German-language scholarship on Schelling's philosophy of nature, see Richards (2002) and Grant (2008).
2. This worry is echoed in Paul Franks's comment that although Brandom "typically appeals to Hegel rather than to Fichte, much of what he appreciates in Hegel is in fact Fichtean" (2007: 63).
3. Hegel "proposes to replace this static way of thinking about the determinateness of the *relations* that articulate conceptual contents with a dynamic account of the *process* of determin*ing* those contents" (Brandom 2009: 89).

4. This to and fro of recognition and recognized is documented by Hegel (1977b) in the famous dialectic of "lordship and bondage".
5. On Russell's "victory" over Bradley, and its importance for both the complexion of subsequent philosophical developments in the English-speaking context and for the problems that philosophy considers core, see Candlish (2007). See also our discussion of Moore's "refutation" in Chapter 12.
6. Hinging metaphysics on "leaving nature behind" is what Pippin (2002) advises modern idealists to do.
7. This is how Rescher (1973) characterizes his position.
8. This is Whitehead's (1933: 154) term.
9. Leslie (1996) explores this in detail, wheras he skims its compatibility with Einsteinian relativity and Bohmian quantum physics (2007: 45–51).
10. See Chapter 9 on Bradley. Sprigge (1993) discusses Bradley at length (see also Sprigge 1985: ch. 3; 2006: ch. 6), but Bradley's metaphysics saturate Sprigge's work: "my own idealism is a form of absolute idealism, very close to that of F. H. Bradley" (2006: 473).
11. For the history of panpsychism, see Skrbina (2005). For contemporary panpsychisms including Strawson's, see Skrbina (2009).
12. Another answer would take as its starting point the *phenomenological* inheritance in Sprigge's work. Although he does not discuss this in detail, he clearly shares with Husserl certain convictions regarding the methodological importance of starting with the presentations of consciousness. As he puts it while discussing Heidegger, "phenomenology tends to lead on to some kind of idealism, since its method suggests that what things truly are is no more and no less than what they are for our consciousness. This was an implication that Husserl himself, after some early doubts, embraced" (1985: 117; see also 1983: 77).
13. Brandom (1994: 87) cites this passage from Hegel's discussion (1977b: 65) of "the being of sensuous things". Of the apple, Sprigge writes: "It is … an essential element of the core conception that that constituent in the not-self aspect of its centre of experience to which the self-aspect directs itself in perceptual experience is not a representation of the thing perceived, the apple say which arouses my appetite, but that thing, that apple, itself" (1983: 68).
14. "All things think" is how Plato's *Parmenides* (132c) characterizes the young Socrates' theory of ideas.
15. The distinction between substance and activity echoes Fichte (ch. 6) and Whitehead (ch. 13).
16. As Sprigge makes the point in discussing Bradley, 'The idea is not necessarily that physical things … are themselves experiences or mental activities, but that they are elements in these which cannot be thought of as existing in separation from them" (1985: 62).
17. David Lewis's theory of possible worlds bears marked similarities to Sprigge's, as he acknowledges (Sprigge 1983: xii). For Lewis (1986), where things enjoy spatiotemporal relations with one another, they belong to the same world; but this is true for all possible worlds, as is the consequence that unrelateds belong to different worlds.
18. Bernard d'Espagnat (2006) praises Kant and the idealists for asserting the non-equivalence of reality and a "pure x".
19. There is the issue, for example, of his triumphing of "transcendental empiricism", and his transcendentalism in general, a point we shall deal with further below. At one level, this could be resolved by asking whether "transcendental empiricism" is a starting point or a consequence of the philosophy of the idea; that is, should the idea be treated as one among many objects of a transcendental empiricism, or does the latter result from the subjection of all things to the problem-idea? At another level,

that Deleuze offers a contribution to the philosophy of the idea derived, in the main, from idealist sources (Plato, the Neoplatonists, Leibniz, Maimon and, latterly, Hegel and Schelling in *What is Philosophy?*) raises the issue of the relation between transcendental philosophy and idealism at a general level, while immersing both, more particularly, in the context of the idealist philosophical heritage. This has been partly explored by Catherine Malabou (2005) and, very recently, by Elena Ficara (2009).

20. Some commentators and critics have questioned the basis on which a unitary and univocal being can be said to have both virtual and actual aspects even if they are not distinct substances. In particular, see Badiou (2000).
21. See also Deleuze's critique of an Aristotelianized Plato (1994: 59–60).
22. James Williams gives the excellent example of the idea of the perfect surgical intervention. It has many parameters ("How many stitches? What convalescence? What should the survival rate be?"), some of which conflict with one another ("There's always going to be some degree of cellular damage, and yet cellular damage is undesirable"), and so is not finally determinable. It is not an object that can be actually experienced, but a problem that is only expressable by "an unstable set of contradictory questions and answers" (Williams 2003: 141).
23. Kant calls this the "transcendental substrate" or "whole of reality (*omnitudo realitatis*)" (CPR A575/B603), while maintaining that "reason demands the unconditioned", that is the *Absolute* (A565/B593).
24. Deleuze's theory is, in the language of the contemporary physical sciences, "background independent". That is, space, time, geometry and matter emerge from the theory of forces rather than forming a background to those forces.
25. Deleuze uses the term "perplication" to signify the coexistence of Ideas and the way that each Idea enters into each other Idea in relations of reciprocal determination. Deleuze uses the example of the Idea of colour, which he argues is "like white light which perplicates in itself the genetic elements and relations of all the colours, but is actualised in the diverse colours with their respective spaces" (1994: 206). The Idea of sound too is the perplication of white noise.
26. Deleuze's Platonism is therefore of that "one-world" variety we encounter in Proclus, Bosanquet and Whitehead and, of course, in Plato's own works. See Chapters 2, 11 and 13, above. It crucially informs the theory Deleuze (1990b) ascribes to the "intelligent dynamist".
27. It is also clear that Deleuze takes the classically idealist theme of appearance versus reality and transforms it into one of the genesis of forms.
28. The intensive generation of spatial extension appears throughout Deleuze's work. He provides a detailed account of the intensive genesis of time in Chapter 2 of *Difference and Repetition* (1994). Importantly, of course, this account of space and time as part of the intensive fabric of Being further sets him apart from Kant, for whom, as we have seen, time and space figure merely in the faculties of the finite rational mind.
29. Arguably, Deleuze's derivation of bodies (matter) from difference of force (energy) in a "background independent" context is closely allied to field theory in general, and relativistic field theory in particular (Einstein 1954).
30. This virtual network or field of intensive differences goes under various names. In *Anti-Oedipus* (Deleuze & Guattari 1984), for example, it is called the "body without organs" (because, of course, it is the intensive body that generates the actual body *with* organs), and the intensive processes (as difference cancels itself to produce actualities) are called "desiring production". In *A Thousand Plateaus* (1988) it is also called the "plane of consistency".
31. Deleuze refers to this iterative character of actuality as "systems of simulacra" (1994: 66–9, 277).

32. Manuel DeLanda (2002) provides an excellent account of the clear relationship between Deleuzian metaphysics and complex systems science. Oddly, however, considering his focus on the Deleuze of *Difference and Repetition*, he avoids explicit engagement with Deleuze's idealism.
33. It seems that Deleuze, with Nietzsche, identifies this urge to find equilibrium with nihilism, life denial and reactivity (Deleuze 1983: 42). Similarly, as Michel Foucault has observed, he identifies the urge to find a final solution or determination, to indeterminable problem-ideas, with all fascistic impulses (Deleuze & Guattari 1984: xi–xiv).
34. This is why Deleuze is opposed to Hegel. See, for example, Deleuze (1994: 42–5, 49–50, 263–4).
35. In one of their most thought-provoking passages of joint writing, Deleuze and Guattari describe the "thought-brain" as the site at which philosophy, art and science confront this "chaosmos" (Deleuze & Guattari 1994: Conclusion).
36. Again we can see similarities to Whitehead's claim that the actual things in the world are composed of actual occasions, which reproduce themselves through "experience". Indeed, it would be quite appropriate to call Whitehead a transcendental empiricist too. Or, perhaps, both Whitehead and Deleuze should, more accurately, be called transcendental empirical idealists.
37. Kojève gave these lectures between 1933 and 1939. Raymond Queneau, always in attendance, had a complete set of Kojève's lecture notes, which he edited and published in 1947, an abridged translation of which was published (Kojève 1969).
38. Hyppolite's French translation of Hegel's *Phenomenology* appeared at the onset of the Second World War (1939–41), with his two-volume commentary (1946–7), published in English as *Genesis and Structure of Hegel's Phenomenology of Spirit* (1974), following after its cessation.
39. For details of these influences and struggles, see Leonard Lawlor's brief but excellent introduction to Hyppolite (in Hyppolite 1997). See also John Heckman's introduction to Hyppolite (in Hyppolite 1974). See Badiou (2008: "Jean Hyppolite") for his recollections of attending Hyppolite's lectures on Fichte at the École Normale Supérieure in 1957.
40. See Denis Hollier's (1988: 85–7) comments on Kojève's involvement in and influence on what was known as the College of Sociology, and Bataille's almost Kierkegaardian response (*ibid.*: 89–93).
41. See Hyppolite's interventions and ongoing debates with Lacan in Lacan (1988a).
42. See Baugh (2003) for an account of Hegelianism in France.
43. The point is echoed by Derrida in his "Introduction" to Malabou (2005); he notes (albeit in a different context) that "we always finish by finding Hegel at the very origin of all these thematized or schematized *ends*" (*ibid.*: xviii), that is, the ends of "history", of "man" and so forth.
44. As Deleuze notes: "Following Hyppolite, we recognize that philosophy, if it has meaning, can only be an ontology and an ontology of sense" (in Hyppolite 1997: 194).
45. Žižek had previously disputed Fichte's position. See Žižek's (2007) response, "With Friends Like These …", to I. H. Grant's (2007) essay on his Schellingianism.
46. This theme has been expressly developed by, among others, Franck Fischbach (2002).
47. Derrida notes this in his introduction to that work (Malabou 2005: xxv).

BIBLIOGRAPHY

Adamson, R. 1881. *Fichte*. Edinburgh: Blackwood.
Alexander, S. 1920. *Space, Time and Deity*, 2 vols. London: Macmillan.
Allison, H. E. 2004. *Kant's Transcendental Idealism: An Interpretation and Defense*. New Haven, CT: Yale University Press.
Ameriks, K. (ed.) 2000a. *The Cambridge Companion to German Idealism*. Cambridge: Cambridge University Press.
Ameriks, K. 2000b. "The Legacy of Idealism in the Philosophy of Feuerbach, Marx and Kierkegaard". In Ameriks (2000a), 258–81.
Ameriks, K. 2006. *Kant and the Historical Turn: Philosophy as Critical Interpretation*. Oxford: Oxford University Press.
Aquinas [1255] 2007. *De Principiis Naturae*. In *Medieval Philosophy: Essential Readings with Commentary*, G. Klima, F. Alhoff & A. J. Vaidya (eds), 156–67. Oxford: Blackwell.
Aristotle 1984. *The Complete Works of Aristotle*, 2 vols, J. Barnes (ed.). Princeton, NJ: Princeton University Press.
Aristotle 1989. *On Sophistical Refutations, On Coming to Be or Passing Away, On the Cosmos*, E. S. Forster & D. J. Furley (trans.). Cambridge, MA: Harvard University Press.
Armstrong, A. H. 1990. *The Anatomy of Neoplatonism*. Oxford: Oxford University Press.
Audi, R. 1999. *Cambridge Dictionary of Philosophy*, 2nd edn. Cambridge: Cambridge University Press.
Augustine 2003. *City of God*, H. Bettenson (trans.). London: Penguin.
Ayer, A. J. [1936] 1983. *Language, Truth and Logic*. Harmondsworth: Penguin.
Ayer, A. J. [1973] 1984. *The Central Questions of Philosophy*. Harmondsworth: Penguin.
Badiou, A. 2000. *Deleuze: The Clamor of Being*, L. Burchill (trans.). Minneapolis, MN: University of Minnesota Press.
Badiou, A. 2008. *Pocket Pantheon*, D. Macey (trans.). London: Verso.
Badiou, A. 2009. *Logics of Worlds*, A. Toscano (trans.). London: Continuum.
Barbour, J. 2003. "The Deep and Suggestive Principles of Leibnizian Philosophy". *Harvard Review of Philosophy* **11**: 45–58.
Barnes, J. 1982. *The Presocratic Philosophers*. London: Routledge.
Barrett, C. 1933. "Is Idealism Realism? A Reply in Terms of Objective Idealism". *Journal of Philosophy* **30**(16): 421–9.
Basile, P. 2009. *Leibniz, Whitehead and the Metaphysics of Causation*. Basingstoke: Palgrave.
Baugh, B. 2003. *French Hegel: From Surrealism to Postmodernism*. London: Routledge.
Beach, E. A. 1994. *The Potencies of God(s)*. Albany, NY: SUNY Press.
Beierwaltes, W. 1972. *Platonismus und Idealismus*. Frankfurt: Klostermann.

Beierwaltes, W. 2000. *Platonisme et idéalisme*, M.-C. Challiol-Gillet, J.-F. Courtine & P. David (trans.). Paris: Vrin.
Beierwaltes, W. 2007. *Procliana: Spätantikes Denken und seine Spuren*. Frankfurt: Klostermann.
Beiser, F. C. 1987. *The Fate of Reason: German Philosophy from Kant to Fichte*. Cambridge, MA: Harvard University Press.
Beiser, F. C. 2002. *German Idealism: The Struggle Against Subjectivity*. Cambridge, MA: Harvard University Press.
Beiser, F. C. 2005. *Hegel*. London: Routledge.
Beiser, F. C. 2006. *The Romantic Imperative: The Concept of Early German Romanticism*. Cambridge, MA: Harvard University Press.
Beiser, F. C. (ed.) 2008. *The Cambridge Companion to Hegel and Nineteenth-Century Philosophy*. Cambridge: Cambridge University Press.
Berkeley, G. 1948–57. *The Works of George Berkeley Bishop of Cloyne*, 9 vols, A. A. Luce & T. E. Jessop (eds). London: Nelson.
Blackburn, S. 1994. *Oxford Dictionary of Philosophy*. Oxford: Oxford University Press.
Böhme, G. 2000. *Platons theoretische Philosophie*. Stuttgart: Metzler.
Bolzano, B. 1972. *Theory of Science: Attempt at a Detailed and in the Main Novel Exposition of Logic*, R. George (ed. & trans.). Berkeley, CA: University of California Press.
Bosanquet, B. 1883. "Logic as the Science of Knowledge". In *Essays in Philosophical Criticism*, A. Seth & R. B. Haldane (eds), 67–101. London: Longmans, Green.
Bosanquet, B. 1911. *Logic, or The Morphology of Knowledge*, 2 vols, 2nd edn. Oxford: Oxford University Press.
Bosanquet, B. 1912. *The Principle of Individuality and Value: The Gifford Lectures for 1911*. London: Macmillan.
Bosanquet, B. 1913. *The Distinction between Mind and its Objects*. Manchester: Manchester University Press.
Bosanquet, B. 1917a. "Realism and Metaphysic". *Philosophical Review* **26**(1): 4–15.
Bosanquet, B. 1917b. "The Relation of Coherence to Immediacy and Specific Purpose". *Philosophical Review* **26**(3): 259–73.
Bosanquet, B. 1920. *Implication and Linear Inference*. London: Macmillan.
Bosanquet, B. 1921. *The Meeting of Extremes in Contemporary Philosophy*. London: Macmillan.
Bosanquet, B. 1923a. *The Value and Destiny of the Individual: The Gifford Lectures for 1912*, 2nd edn. London: Macmillan.
Bosanquet, B. 1923b. *The Philosophical Theory of the State*, 4th edn. London: Macmillan.
Bosanquet, B. 1924. "Life and Philosophy". In *Contemporary British Philosophy*, J. H. Muirhead (ed.), 49–100. London: George Allen & Unwin.
Bosanquet, B. 1925. *A Companion to Plato's Republic for English Readers: Being a Commentary adapted to Davies and Vaughan's Translation*, 2nd edn. London: Rivington's.
Bosanquet, B. 1927. *Science and Philosophy and Other Essays*. London: George Allen & Unwin.
Boucher, D. & A. Vincent 2000. *British Idealism and Political Theory*. Edinburgh: Edinburgh University Press.
Boucher, D. & A. Vincent, forthcoming. *British Idealism: A Guide for the Perplexed*. London: Continuum.
Bowie, A. 1996. "John McDowell's *Mind and World*, and Early Romantic Epistemology". *Revue Internationale de Philosophie* **197**: 515–54.
Bradley, F. H. 1909. "On Our Knowledge of Immediate Experience". *Mind* **18**(69) (January): 40–64.
Bradley, F. H. 1914. *Essays on Truth and Reality*. Oxford: Oxford University Press.

Bradley, F. H. 1922. *The Principles of Logic*, 2nd edn, revised with commentary and terminal essays. Oxford: Oxford University Press.
Bradley, F. H. 1927. *Ethical Studies*, 2nd edn. Oxford: Oxford University Press.
Bradley, F. H. 1930. *Appearance and Reality: A Metaphysical Essay*, 2nd edn. Oxford: Oxford University Press.
Brandom, R. B. 1994. *Making it Explicit: Reasoning, Representing and Discursive Commitment*. Cambridge, MA: Harvard University Press.
Brandom, R. B. 2000. *Articulating Reasons: An Introduction to Inferentialism*. Cambridge, MA: Harvard University Press.
Brandom, R. B. 2002. *Tales of the Mighty Dead: Historical Essays in the Metaphysics of Intentionality*. Cambridge, MA: Harvard University Press.
Brandom, R. B. 2009. *Reason in Philosophy: Animating Ideas*. Cambridge, MA: Harvard University Press.
Breazeale, D. & T. Rockmore (eds) 1994. *Fichte: Historical Contexts/Contemporary Perspectives*. Atlantic Highlands, NJ: Humanities Press.
Breazeale, D. & T. Rockmore (eds) 2002. *New Essays on Fichte's Later Jena Wissenschaftslehre*. Evanston, IL: Northwestern University Press.
Breazeale, D. & T. Rockmore (eds) 2008. *After Jena: New Essays on Fichte's Later Philosophy*. Evanston, IL: Northwestern University Press.
Burnet, J. 1930. *Early Greek Philosophy*, 4th edn. London: Adam & Charles Black.
Burnyeat, M. F. 1982. "Idealism and Greek Philosophy: What Descartes Saw and Berkeley Missed". *Philosophical Review* **91**(1) (January): 3–40.
Caird, E. 1883. *Hegel*. Edinburgh: Blackwood.
Candlish, S. 2007. *The Russell/Bradley Dispute and its Significance for Twentieth-Century Philosophy*. Basingstoke: Palgrave Macmillan.
Capra, F. 1996. *The Web of Life: A New Synthesis of Mind and Matter*. London: HarperCollins.
Carlson, D. G. 2007. *A Commentary to Hegel's Science of Logic*. Basingstoke: Palgrave Macmillan.
Cassirer, E. 1981. *Kant's Life and Thought*, J. Haden (trans.). New Haven, CT: Yale University Press.
Clarke, A. 2001. *Being There: Putting Brain, Body and World Together Again*. Cambridge, MA: MIT Press.
Cornford, F. M. 1932. *Before and After Socrates*. Cambridge: Cambridge University Press.
Cornford, F. M. 1935. *Plato's Theory of Knowledge*. London: Routledge & Kegan Paul.
Cornford, F. M. 1939. *Plato and Parmenides*. London: Routledge & Kegan Paul.
Cottingham, J. (ed.) 1992. *The Cambridge Companion to Descartes*. Cambridge: Cambridge University Press.
Courtine, J.-F. 2003. *Les Catégories de l'être: Études de philosophie ancienne et médiévale*. Paris: Presses Universitaires de France.
Craig, E. (ed.) 1998. *Routledge Encyclopaedia of Philosophy*, 10 vols. London: Routledge.
Cunningham, G. 1933. *The Idealistic Argument in Recent British and American Philosophy*. New York: Books for Libraries Press.
Damascius 2010. *Problems and Solutions regarding First Principles*, S. Ahbel-Rappe (trans.). New York: Oxford University Press.
Davidson, D. 1984. "On the Very Idea of a Conceptual Scheme". In *Inquiries into Truth and Interpretation*, 183–98. Oxford: Oxford University Press.
DeLanda, M. 2002. *Intensive Science and Virtual Philosophy*. London: Continuum.
Deleuze, G. 1983. *Nietzsche and Philosophy*, H. Tomlinson (trans.). London: Athlone.
Deleuze, G. 1990a. *Bergsonism*, H. Tomlinson & B. Habberjam (trans.). New York: Zone.
Deleuze, G. 1990b. *Spinoza: Expressionism in Philosophy*, M. Joughin (trans.). New York: Zone.

BIBLIOGRAPHY

Deleuze G. 1994. *Difference and Repetition*, P. Patton (trans.). London: Continuum.
Deleuze, G. 2006. *Nietzsche and Philosophy*. London: Continuum.
Deleuze, G. & F. Guattari 1984. *Anti-Oedipus: Capitalism and Schizophrenia*, R. Hurley, M. Seem & H. R. Lane (trans.). London: Continuum.
Deleuze, G. & F. Guattari 1988. *A Thousand Plateaus: Capitalism and Schizophrenia*, B. Massumi (trans.). London: Athlone.
Deleuze, G. & F. Guattari 1994. *What is Philosophy?*, H. Tomlinson & L. Burchill (trans.). London: Verso.
Descartes, R. 1974–89. *Oeuvres de Descartes*, 12 vols, C. Adam & P. Tannery (eds). Paris: Vrin.
Descartes, R. 1984–91. *The Philosophical Writings of Descartes*, 3 vols, J. Cottingham, D. Stoothoff & D. Murdoch (eds). Cambridge: Cambridge University Press.
Descartes, R. 1998. *The World and Other Writings*, S. Gaukroger (ed. & trans.). Cambridge: Cambridge University Press.
Diels, H. & W. Kranz 1960. *Die Fragmente der Vorsokratiker*, 3 vols, 10th edn. Berlin: Wiedmann.
Dudley, W. 2007. *Understanding German Idealism*. Stocksfield: Acumen.
Edwards, P. (ed.) 1967. *Encyclopedia of Philosophy*, 8 vols. New York: Macmillan.
Einstein, A. 1954. *Relativity: The Special and General Theory*. London: Methuen.
Epperson, M. 2004. *Quantum Mechanics and the Philosophy of Alfred North Whitehead*. New York: Fordham University Press.
Eriugena, J. S. 1976. *Periphyseon: On the Division of Nature*, M. Uhlfelder & J. Potter (trans.). Indianapolis, IN: Bobbs-Merrill.
d'Espagnat, B. 2006. *On Physics and Philosophy*. Princeton, NJ: Princeton University Press.
Ferrier, J. F. 1854. *Institutes of Metaphysics*. London: William Blackwood.
Ficara, E. 2009. "Hegel's Dialectic in Twentieth-Century Continental Philosophy: Benedetto Croce and Gilles Deleuze". *Idealistic Studies* **39**(1–3): 87–98.
Fichte, J. G. 1964. *J. G. Fichte: Gesamtausgabe der Bayerischen Akademie der Wissenschaften*, R. Lauth, H. Jacob & H. Gliwitsky (eds). Stuttgart: Frommann-Holzboog.
Fichte, J. G. 1971. *Fichtes Werke herausgegeben von Immanuel Hermann Fichte*, 11 vols, I. H. Fichte (ed.). Berlin: Walter de Gruyter.
Fichte, J. G. 1976. "The Science of Knowledge in General Outline", W. E. Wright (trans.). *Idealistic Studies* **6**: 106–17.
Fichte, J. G. 1976– . *Gesamtausgabe der Bayerischen Akademie der Wissenschaften*, R. Lauth, H. Jacobs & H. Gliwitzky (eds). Stuttgart-Bad Canstatt: Frommann Holzboog.
Fichte, J. G. 1978. *Attempt at a Critique of All Revelation*, G. Green (trans.). Cambridge: Cambridge University Press.
Fichte, J. G. 1982. *The Science of Knowledge*, P. Heath & J. Lachs (trans.). Cambridge: Cambridge University Press.
Fichte, J. G. 1984. "On the Spirit and the Letter in Philosophy", D. Breazeale (trans.). In *Fichte: Early Philosophical Writings*, 185–215. Ithaca, NY: Cornell University Press.
Fichte, J. G. 1987a. *The Vocation of Man*, Peter Preuss (trans.). Indianapolis, IN: Hackett.
Fichte, J. G. 1987b. *A Crystal Clear Report to the General Public Concerning the Actual Essence of the Newest Philosophy: An Attempt to Force the Reader to Understand*, J. Botterman & W. Rasch (trans.). In *Fichte, Jacobi and Schelling: Philosophy of German Idealism*, E. Behler (ed.), 39–115. New York: Continuum.
Fichte, J. G. 1988a. *Concerning the Concept of the Wissenschaftslehre*. In *Fichte: Early Philosophical Writings*, D. Breazeale (ed. & trans.), 94–135. Ithaca, NY: Cornell University Press.
Fichte, J. G. 1988b. "On the Spirit and the Letter in Philosophy". In *Fichte: Early Philosophical Writings*, D. Breazeale (ed. & trans.), 185–215. Ithaca, NY: Cornell University Press.

Fichte, J. G. 1992. *Foundations of Transcendental Philosophy (Wissenschaftslehre nova methodo 1795–99)*, D. Breazeale (ed. & trans.). Ithaca, NY: Cornell University Press.
Fichte, J. G. 1994. *Attempt at a New Presentation of the Wissenschaftslehre*, D. Breazeale (trans.). In *Introductions to the Wissenschaftslehre and Other Writings*, 1–118. Indianapolis, IN: Hackett.
Fichte, J. G. 1996. *Reclamation of the Freedom of Thought from the Princes of Europe, Who Have Oppressed It Until Now*, T. E. Wartenberg (trans.). In *What is Enlightenment? Eighteenth-Century Answers and Twentieth-Century Questions*, J. Schmidt (ed.), 119–41. Berkeley, CA: University of California Press.
Fichte, J. G. 1997. *Darstellung der Wissenschaftslehre*, R. Lauth & P. K. Schneider (eds). Hamburg: Meiner.
Fichte, J. G. 2000a. "Review of Aenesidemus". In *Between Kant and Hegel: Texts in the Development of Post-Kantian Idealism*, 2nd edn, G. di Giovanni & H. R. Harris (eds), 136–57. Indianapolis, IN: Hackett.
Fichte, J. G. 2000b. *Foundations of Natural Right According to the Principles of the Wissenschaftslehre*, F. Neuhouser (ed.), M. Baur (trans.). Cambridge: Cambridge University Press.
Fichte, J. G. 2005a. *The System of Ethics According to the Principles of the Wissenschaftslehre*, D. Breazeale & G. Zöller (eds & trans.). Cambridge: Cambridge University Press.
Fichte, J. G. 2005b. *The Science of Knowing*, W. E. Wright (trans.). Albany, NY: SUNY Press.
Findlay, J. N. 1958. *Hegel: A Reexamination*. London: Allen & Unwin.
Findlay, J. N. 1967. *The Transcendence of the Cave*. London: George Allen & Unwin.
Fine, G. 1993. *On Ideas: Aristotle's Criticism of Plato's Theory of Forms*. Oxford: Oxford University Press.
Fischbach, F. 2002. *L'Être et l'acte: Enquête sur les fondements de l'ontologie moderne de l'agir*. Paris: Vrin.
Foucault, M. 1972. "The Discourse on Language". In *The Archaeology of Knowledge*, 215–37. New York: Pantheon.
Franks, P. 1999. "Transcendental Arguments, Reason, and Scepticisim: Contemporary Debates and the Origins of Post-Kantianism". See Stern (1999), 111–45.
Franks, P. 2005. *All or Nothing: Systematicity, Transcendental Arguments and Skepticism in German Idealism*. Cambridge, MA: Harvard University Press.
Franks, P. 2007. "From Quine to Hegel: Naturalism, Anti-Realism, and Maimon's Question Quid Facti". In *German Idealism: Contemporary Perspectives*, E. Hammer (ed.), 50–69. London: Routledge.
Frege, G. 2000a. *The Frege Reader*, M. Beaney (ed.). Oxford: Blackwell.
Frege, G. [1892] 2000b. "On Sense and Reference". See Frege (2000a), 151–71.
Frege, G. [1892] 2000c. "Comments on Sense and Reference". See Frege (2000a), 172–80.
Frege, G. [1918] 2000d. "Thought". See Frege (2000a), 325–45.
Fritz, A. D. 1954. "Berkeley's Self: Its Origin in Malebranche". *Journal of the History of Ideas* **15**(4) (October): 554–72.
Gabriel, M. 2009. *Skeptizismus und Idealismus in der Antike*. Frankfurt: Suhrkamp.
Gabriel, M. & S. Žižek 2009. *Mythology, Madness and Laughter: Subjectivity in German Idealism*. London: Continuum.
Garber, D. 1985. "Leibniz and the Foundations of Physics: The Middle Years". In *The Natural Philosophy of Leibniz*, K. Okruhlik & J. Brown (eds), 27–130. Dordrecht: Reidel.
Garber, D. 1995. "Leibniz: Physics and Philosophy". In *The Cambridge Companion to Leibniz*, N. Jolley (ed.), 270–352. Cambridge: Cambridge University Press.
Garber, D. 2009. *Leibniz: Body, Force, Monad*. Oxford: Oxford University Press.
Gatti, M. L. 1996. "Plotinus: The Platonic Tradition and the Foundation of Neoplatonism". In *The Cambridge Companion to Plotinus*, L. P. Gerson (ed.), 10–37. Cambridge: Cambridge University Press.

Geach, P. T. 1979. *Truth, Love and Immortality: An Introduction to McTaggart's Philosophy.* Berkeley, CA: University of California Press
Gerson, L. P. (ed.) 1996. *The Cambridge Companion to Plotinus.* Cambridge: Cambridge University Press.
Gerson, L. P. 2005. *Aristotle and Other Platonists.* Ithaca, NY: Cornell University Press.
Goudeli, K. 2002. *Challenges to German Idealism: Schelling, Fichte and Kant.* Basingstoke: Palgrave Macmillan.
Gould, S. J. & E. S. Vrba 1982. "Exaptation: A Missing Term in the Science of Form". *Paleobiology* **8**(1): 4–15.
Grant, I. H. 2007. "The Insufficiency of Ground: on Žižek's Schellingianism". In *The Truth of Žižek*, P. Bowman & R. Stamp (eds), 82–98. London: Continuum.
Grant, I. H. 2008. *Philosophies of Nature after Schelling.* London: Continuum.
Green, T. H. 2003. *Prolegomena to Ethics*, D. O. Brink (ed.). Oxford: Oxford University Press.
Habermas, J. 1984. *Theory of Communicative Action, Volume One: Reason and the Rationalisation of Society*, T. McCarthy (trans.). London: Heinemann.
Habermas, J. 2004. "Dialectical Idealism in Transition to Materialism: Schelling's Idea of a Contraction of God and its Consequences for the Philosophy of History". In *The New Schelling*, J. Norman & A. Welchman (eds), 43–89. London: Continuum.
Haldane, V. R. B. 1922. *The Reign of Relativity.* New Haven, CT: Yale University Press.
Hammer, E. (ed.) 2007. *German Idealism: Contemporary Perspectives.* London: Routledge.
Harris, H. S. 1972. *Hegel's Development: Towards the Sunlight, 1770–1801.* Oxford: Oxford University Press.
Harris, H. S. 1983. *Hegel's Development: Night Thoughts (Jena 1801–1806).* Oxford: Oxford University Press.
Harris, H. S. 2000. *Between Kant and Hegel: Texts in the Development of German Idealism*, 2nd edn. Indianapolis, IN: Hackett.
Harris, R. B. (ed.) 2002. *Neoplatonism and Contemporary Thought*, 2 vols. Albany, NY: SUNY Press.
Hartmann, K. 1976. "Hegel: A Non-metaphysical View". In *Hegel: A Collection of Critical Essays*, A. MacIntyre (ed.), 101–24. Notre Dame, IN: University of Notre Dame Press.
Hartmann, N. 1923–29. *Die Philosophie des Deutschen Idealismus.* Berlin: de Gruyter.
Hartz, G. 2006. *Leibniz's Final System.* London: Routledge.
Hatfield, G. 1979. "Force (God) in Descartes' Physics". *Studies in the History and Philosophy of Science* **10**: 113–40.
Hatfield, G. 1992. "Descartes' Physiology and its Relation to Psychology". In *The Cambridge Companion to Descartes*, J. Cottingham (ed.), 335–70. Cambridge: Cambridge University Press.
Hegel, G. W. F. 1939–41. *La Phénoménologie de l'esprit*, 2 vols, J. Hyppolite (trans.). Paris: Aubier.
Hegel, G. W. F. 1967. *Philosophy of Right*, T. M. Knox (trans.). Oxford: Oxford University Press.
Hegel, G. W. F. 1969. *Science of Logic*, 2 vols, A. V. Miller (trans.). London: George Allen & Unwin.
Hegel, G. W. F. 1970a. *Werke in zwanzig Bänden. Werkausgabe*, 20 vols, E. Moldenhauer & K. Michel (eds). Frankfurt: Suhrkamp.
Hegel, G. W. F. 1970b. *Philosophy of Nature: Part Two of the Encyclopaedia of the Philosophical Sciences*, A. V. Miller (trans.). Oxford: Oxford University Press.
Hegel, G. W. F. 1971. *Philosophy of Mind: Part Three of the Encyclopaedia of the Philosophical Sciences*, W. Wallace (trans.). Oxford: Oxford University Press.
Hegel, G. W. F. 1977a. *The Difference Between Fichte's and Schelling's System of Philosophy*, W. Cerf & H. S. Harris (trans.). Albany, NY: SUNY Press.
Hegel, G. W. F. 1977b. *Phenomenology of Spirit*, A. V. Miller (trans.). Oxford: Oxford University Press.

Hegel, G. W. F. 1991. *The Encyclopaedia Logic: Part One of the Encyclopaedia of the Philosophical Sciences*, T. F. Geraets, W. A. Suchting & H. S. Harris (trans.). Indianapolis, IN: Hackett.
Heidegger, M. 1985. *Schelling's Treatise on the Essence of Human Freedom*, J. Stambaugh (trans.). Athens, OH: Ohio University Press.
Heidegger, M. 1988a. *Pathmarks*, W. McNeill (trans.). Cambridge: Cambridge University Press.
Heidegger, M. 1988b. "On the Essence of Ground". In *Pathmarks*, W. McNeill (trans.), 97–135. Cambridge: Cambridge University Press.
Heidegger, M. 1997. *Der deutsche Idealismus (Fichte, Schelling, Hegel) und die philosophische Problemlage der Gegenwart. Gesamtausgabe* vol. 28. Frankfurt: Klostermann.
Heidegger, M. 2000. *Introduction to Metaphysics*, G. Fried & R. Polt (trans.). New Haven, CT: Yale University Press.
Heidegger, M. 2002. *Off the Beaten Track*, J. Young & K. Haynes (trans.). Cambridge: Cambridge University Press.
Henrich, D. 2003. *Between Kant and Hegel: Lectures on German Idealism*. Cambridge, MA: Harvard University Press.
Hibbs, D. 2009. "On the Possibility of Pre-Cartesian Idealism". *Dialogue* **48**: 643–53.
Hicks, G. D. 1938. *Critical Realism: Studies in the Philosophy of Mind and Nature*. London: Macmillan.
Hogrebe, W. 1989. *Prädikation und Genesis*. Frankfurt: Suhrkamp.
Hogrebe, W. 1992. *Metaphysik und Mantik*. Frankfurt: Suhrkamp.
Hollier, D. (ed.) 1988. *The College of Sociology*. Minneapolis, MN: University of Minnesota Press.
Honderich, T. (ed.) 2005. *The Oxford Companion to Philosophy*, 2nd edn. Oxford: Oxford University Press.
Houlgate, S. (ed.) 1998. *Hegel and the Philosophy of Nature*. Albany, NY: SUNY Press.
Husserl, E. 1989. *Ideas Pertaining to a Pure Phenomenology I*, F. Kersten (trans.). *Collected Works of Edmund Husserl*, vol. 2. Dordrecht: Kluwer.
Husserl, E. 1995. "Fichte's Ideal of Humanity. Three Lectures", James G. Hart (trans.). *Husserl Studies* **12**: 111–33.
Hutchison, K. 1983. "Supernaturalism and the Mechanical Philosophy". *History of Science* **21**: 297–333.
Hylton, P. 1990. *Russell, Idealism and the Emergence of Analytic Philosophy*. Oxford: Oxford University Press.
Hyppolite, J. 1946–7. *Genèse et structure de la Phénoménologie de l'esprit de Hegel*. Paris: Aubier.
Hyppolite, J. 1959. "L'idée fichtéene de la doctrine de la science et le projet husserlien". In *Husserl und das Denken der Neuzeit*, H. L. van Brenda & J. Taminaux (eds), 173–82. The Hague: Nijhoff.
Hyppolite, J. 1974. *Genesis and Structure of Hegel's* Phenomenology of Spirit, S. Cherniak & J. Heckmann (trans.). Evanston, IL: Northwestern University Press.
Hyppolite, J. 1997. *Logic and Existence*, L. Lawlor & A. Sen (trans.). Albany, NY: SUNY Press.
Inge, W. R. 1923. *The Philosophy of Plotinus*, 2 vols, 2nd edn. London: Longmans, Green.
Jacob, F. 1989. *The Logic of Life: A History of Heredity and the Possible and the Actual*, B. E. Spillmann (trans.). Harmondsworth: Penguin.
Jameson, F. 2010. *The Hegel Variations*. London: Verso.
Jaspers, K. 1955. *Schelling: Grösse und Verhängniss*. Munich: Piper.
Jolley, N. 1990. *The Light of the Soul: Theories of Ideas in Leibniz, Malebranche and Descartes*. Oxford: Oxford University Press.
Jolley, N. (ed.) 1995. *The Cambridge Companion to Leibniz*. Cambridge: Cambridge University Press.

Jowett, B. 1902. *Select Passages from the Introductions to Plato*, L. Campbell (ed.). London: John Murray.
Kahn, C. H. 2009. *Essays on Being*. Oxford: Oxford University Press.
Kant, I. 1889. *Kant's Critique of Practical Reason and Other Works on the Theory of Ethics*, 4th rev. edn, T. Kingsmill Abbott (trans.). London: Kongmans, Green.
Kant, I. 1902. *Kants gesammelte Schriften*, 29 vols, Königlich Preussische Akademie der Wissenschaften (ed.). Berlin: Walter de Gruyter.
Kant, I. 1909. *Kant's Critique of Practical Reason and Other Works on the Theory of Ethics*, T. Kingsmill Abbott (trans.). London: Longman.
Kant, I. 1929. *Critique of Pure Reason*, N. Kemp Smith (trans.). London: Macmillan.
Kant, I. 1987. *Critique of Judgment*, W. S. Pluhar (trans.). Indianapolis, IN: Hackett.
Kant, I. [1928] 1991. *Critique of Judgement*, J. Creed Meredith (trans.). Oxford: Oxford University Press.
Kant, I. 1993. *Opus Postumum*, E. Förster (ed. & trans.). Cambridge: Cambridge University Press.
Kant, I. 1997. *Critique of Practical Reason*, M. Gregor (trans.). Cambridge: Cambridge University Press.
Kant, I. 1998. *Groundwork of the Metaphysics of Morals*, M. Gregor (trans.). Cambridge: Cambridge University Press.
Kant, I. 2007. *Critique of the Power of Judgment*, P. Guyer & E. Matthews (trans.). Cambridge: Cambridge University Press.
Kauffman, S. 1993. *The Origins of Order: Self-Organization and Selection in Evolution*. New York: Oxford University Press.
Kauffman, S. 1995. *At Home in the Universe: The Search for Laws of Complexity*. New York: Oxford University Press.
Kauffman, S. 2000. *Investigations*. New York: Oxford University Press.
Kojève, A. 1969. *Introduction to the Reading of Hegel*, A. Bloom (ed.), J. H. Nichols (trans.). New York: Basic Books.
Kroner, R. 1921–24. *Von Kant bis Hegel*, 2 vols. Tübingen: Mohr.
La Vopa, A. J. 2001. *Fichte: The Self and the Calling of Philosophy*. Cambridge: Cambridge University Press.
Lacan, J. 1988a. *The Seminar of Jacques Lacan, Book I: Freud's Papers on Psychoanalysis 1953–1954*. Cambridge: Cambridge University Press.
Lacan, J. 1988b. *The Seminar of Jacques Lacan, Book II: The Ego in Freud's Theory and in the Technique of Psychoanalysis, 1954–1955*. Cambridge: Cambridge University Press.
Leibniz, G. W. 1839–40. *Opera Philosophicae quae exstant Latina, Gallica, Germanica omnia*, J. E. Erdman (ed.). Berlin: Eichler.
Leibniz, G. W. 1848–63. *Mathematische Schriften*, 7 vols. Berlin: Asher/Halle.
Leibniz, G. W. 1875–90. *Die Philosophischen Schriften*, 7 vols, C. I Gerhardt (ed.). Berlin: Wiedmann.
Leibniz, G. W. 1923– . *Sämtliche Schriften und Briefe*. Berlin: Akademie-Verlag.
Leibniz, G. W. 1967. *The Leibniz–Arnauld Correspondence*, H. T. Mason (ed. & trans.). Manchester: Manchester University Press.
Leibniz, G. W. 1985. *The Theodicy*, E. M. Huggard (trans.). Chicago, IL: Open Court.
Leibniz, G. W. 1989a. *Philosophical Essays*, R. Ariew & D. Garber (eds). Indianapolis, IN: Hackett.
Leibniz, G. W. 1989b. *Gottfried Wilhelm Leibniz: Philosophical Papers and Letters*, L. Loemker (ed.). London: Kluwer.
Leibniz, G. W. 1992a. *New Essays on Human Understanding*, P. Remnant & J. Bennett (eds & trans.). Cambridge: Cambridge University Press.

Leibniz, G. W. 1992b. *De Summa Rerum: Metaphysical Papers, 1675–1676*, G. H. R. Parkinson (ed. & trans.). New Haven, CT: Yale University Press.
Leibniz, G. W. 2005. *Confessio Philosophi: Papers Concerning the Problem of Evil, 1671–1678*, R. C. Sleigh, Jr (ed. & trans.). New Haven, CT: Yale University Press.
Leibniz, G. W. 2007. *The Leibniz–Des Bosses Correspondence*, B. Look & D. Rutherford (eds). New Haven, CT: Yale University Press.
Lennox, J. G. 2001. *Aristotle's Philosophy of Biology*. Cambridge: Cambridge University Press.
Leslie, J. 1970. "The Theory that the World Exists Because it Should". *American Philosophical Quarterly* 7: 286–98.
Leslie, J. 1979. *Value and Existence*. Oxford: Blackwell.
Leslie, J. 1996. *Universes*. London: Routledge.
Leslie, J. 2001. *Infinite Minds*. Oxford: Oxford University Press.
Leslie, J. 2007. *Immortality Defended*. Oxford: Blackwell.
Levinas, E. 1989. "Ethics as First Philosophy". In *The Levinas Reader*, S. Hand (ed.), 75–87. Oxford: Blackwell.
Lewis, D. 1986. *On the Plurality of Worlds*. Oxford: Blackwell.
Lindgaard, J. 2008. *John McDowell: Experience, Norm and Nature*. Oxford: Blackwell.
Malabou, C. 2005. *The Future of Hegel: Plasticity, Temporality and Dialectic*. London: Routledge.
Malebranche, N. 1958–67. *Oeuvres completes de Malebranche*, 20 vols, A. Robinet (ed.). Paris: Vrin.
Malebranche, N. 1992. *Treatise on Nature and Grace*, P. Riley (trans.). Oxford: Oxford University Press.
Malebranche, N. 1997a. *The Search After Truth*, T. M. Lennon & P. J. Olscamp (trans.). Cambridge: Cambridge University Press.
Malebranche, N. 1997b. *Dialogues on Metaphysics and on Religion*, N. Jolley (ed.), D. Scott (trans.). Cambridge: Cambridge University Press.
Martin, W. R. 1998. *Idealism and Objectivity: Understanding Fichte's Jena Project*. Stanford, CA: Stanford University Press.
Mates, B. 1986. *The Philosophy of Leibniz: Metaphysics and Language*. Oxford: Oxford University Press.
Maturana, H. & B. Poerksen 2004. *From Being to Doing: The Origins of the Biology of Cognition*. Heidelberg: Carl-Auer Verlag.
Maturana, H. & F. Varela 1980a. *Autopoiesis and Cognition: The Realization of the Living*. Dordrecht: Reidel.
Maturana, H. & F. Varela [1972] 1980b. "Autopoiesis: The Organization of the Living". In *Autopoiesis and Cognition: The Realization of the Living*, 73–87. Dordrecht: Reidel.
Maturana, H. & F. Varela 1998. *The Tree of Knowledge*. London: Shambhala.
McDowell, J. 1996. *Mind and World*, 2nd edn. Cambridge, MA: Harvard University Press.
McDowell, J. 1998. *Mind, Value & Reality*. Cambridge, MA: Harvard University Press.
McDowell, J. 2002. "Responses". In *Reading McDowell on Mind and World*, N. H. Smith (ed.), 269–305. London: Routledge.
McDowell, J. 2009. *Having the World in View: Essays on Kant, Hegel and Sellars*. Cambridge, MA: Harvard University Press.
McRae, R. 1976. *Perception, Apperception & Thought*. Toronto: University of Toronto Press.
McTaggart, J. M. E. 1896. *Studies in the Hegelian Dialectic*. Cambridge: Cambridge University Press.
McTaggart, J. M. E. 1901. *Studies in Hegelian Cosmology*. Cambridge: Cambridge University Press.
McTaggart, J. M. E. 1908. "The Unreality of Time". *Mind* **17**: 456–73.

McTaggart, J. M. E. 1912. Review of *Principle of Individuality and Value*. *Mind* **21**(83): 416–27.
McTaggart, J. M. E. 1921. *The Nature of Existence*, vol. 1. Cambridge: Cambridge University Press.
McTaggart, J. M. E. 1923. "*The Idea of Immortality*, by A. Seth Pringle-Pattison". *Mind*, New Series, **32**(126) (April): 220–24.
McTaggart, J. M. E. 1927. *The Nature of Existence*, vol. 2. Cambridge: Cambridge University Press.
Merleau-Ponty, M. 2003. *Nature*, R. Vallier (trans.). Evanston, IL: Northwestern University Press.
Metz, R. 1938. *A Hundred Years of British Philosophy*, J. H. Muirhead (ed.), J. W. Harvey, T. E. Jessop & H. C. Sturt (trans.). London: George Allen & Unwin.
Monod, J. 1970. *Chance and Necessity*, A. Wainhouse (trans.). London: Fontana.
Moore, G. E. 1903. "Refutation of Idealism". *Mind* **12**(48): 433–53.
Moran, D. 1989. *The Philosophy of John Scottus Eriugena: A Study of Idealism in the Middle Ages*. Cambridge: Cambridge University Press.
Muehlmann, R. G. 1992. *Berkeley's Ontology*. Indianapolis, IN: Hackett.
Muirhead, J. H. 1923. "Bernard Bosanquet". *Mind* NS **32**(128): 393–407.
Muirhead, J. H. 1927. "How Hegel Came to England". *Mind* **36**(144): 423–47.
Muirhead, J. H. 1931. *The Platonic Tradition in Anglo-Saxon Philosophy: Studies in the History of Idealism in England and America*. London: George Allen & Unwin.
Murray, A. H. 1937. *The Philosophy of James Ward*. Cambridge: Cambridge University Press.
Nadler, S. 1992. *Malebranche and Ideas*. Oxford: Oxford University Press.
Nadler, S. 1994. "Descartes and Occasional Causation". *British Journal for the History of Philosophy* **2**: 35–54.
Nadler, S. (ed.) 2002. *A Companion to Early Modern Philosophy*. Oxford: Blackwell.
Neuhouser, F. 1990. *Fichte's Theory of Subjectivity*. Cambridge: Cambridge University Press.
Newton, I. 2004. *Philosophical Writings*, A. Janiak (ed.). Cambridge: Cambridge University Press.
Nicholson, P. 2006. "Green's 'Eternal Consciousness'". In *T. H. Green: Ethics, Metaphysics, and Political Philosophy*, M. Dimova-Cookson & W. J. Mander (eds), 139–59. Oxford: Oxford University Press.
Nietzsche, F. [1887] 1998. *On the Genealogy of Morality*, M. Clark & A. Swenson (trans.). Indianapolis, IN: Hackett.
Novalis 2003. *Fichte Studies*, J. Kneller (ed.). Cambridge: Cambridge University Press.
O'Meara, D. J. 1996. "The Hierarchical Ordering of Reality in Plotinus". In *The Cambridge Companion to Plotinus*, L. P. Gerson (ed.), 66–81. Cambridge: Cambridge University Press.
Omnès, R. 1999. *Quantum Philosophy*. Princeton, NJ: Princeton University Press.
Owen, G. E. L. 1986. *Logic, Science and Dialectic: Collected Papers in Greek Philosophy*. London: Duckworth.
Palmer, L. 2008. "Kant and the Brain: A New Empirical Hypothesis" www.hss.cmu.edu/philosophy/palmer/KantBrainExt.pdf (accessed November 2010).
Phemister, P. 2005. *Leibniz and the Natural World*. Dordrecht: Springer.
Phillips, E. D. 1955. "Parmenides on Thought and Being". *Philosophical Review* **64**(4): 546–60.
Pinkard, T. 1994. *Hegel's Phenomenology: The Sociality of Reason*. Cambridge: Cambridge University Press.
Pinkard, T. 2000. *Hegel: A Biography*. Cambridge: Cambridge University Press.
Pinkard, T. 2005. "Speculative *Naturphilosophie* and the Development of the Empirical Sciences: Hegel's Perspective". In *Continental Philosophy of Science*, G. Gutting (ed.), 19–34. Oxford: Blackwell.

Pippin, R. 1989. *Hegel's Idealism: The Satisfactions of Self-Consciousness*. Cambridge: Cambridge University Press.
Pippin, R. 2002. "Leaving Nature Behind: Or Two Cheers for 'Subjectivism'". In *Reading McDowell on Mind and World*, N. H. Smith (ed.), 58–75. London: Routledge.
Plato 1914. *Euthyphro, Apology, Crito, Phaedo, Phaedrus*, H. N. Fowler (trans.). Cambridge, MA: Harvard University Press.
Plato 1925a. *Lysis, Symposium, Gorgias*, W. R. M. Lamb (trans.). Cambridge, MA: Harvard University Press.
Plato 1925b. *Statesman, Philebus, Ion*, H. N. Fowler & W. R. M. Lamb (trans.). Cambridge, MA: Harvard University Press.
Plato 1926. *Cratylus, Parmenides, Greater Hippias, Lesser Hippias*, H. N. Fowler (trans.). Cambridge, MA: Harvard University Press.
Plato 1928. *Theaetetus Sophist*, H. N. Fowler (trans.). Cambridge, MA: Harvard University Press.
Plato 1929. *Timaeus, Critias, Menexenus, Epistles*, R. G. Bury (trans.). Cambridge, MA: Harvard University Press.
Plato 1935. *Republic*, 2 vols, P. Shorey (trans.). Cambridge, MA: Harvard University Press.
Plotinus 1966. *Enneads*, 7 vols, A. H. Armstrong (trans.). Cambridge, MA: Harvard University Press.
Prigogine, I. 1997. *The End of Certainty: Time, Chaos, and the New Laws of Nature*. Glencoe, IL: Free Press.
Prigogine, I. & I. Stengers 1984. *Order out of Chaos: Man's New Dialogue with Nature*. London: Flamingo.
Pringle-Pattison, A. S. 1922. *The Idea of Immortality*. Oxford: Oxford University Press.
Proclus 1963. *The Elements of Theology*, E. R. Dodds (trans., intro., comm.). Oxford: Oxford University Press.
Proclus 1987. *Commentary on Plato's Parmenides*, G. R. Morrow & J. M. Dillon (trans.). Princeton, NJ: Princeton University Press.
Proclus 2001. *On the Eternity of the World*, H. S. Lang & A. D. Macro (intro., trans., comm.). Berkeley, CA: University of California Press.
Pyle, A. 2003. *Malebranche*. London: Routledge.
Radner, D. 1985. "Is There a Problem of Cartesian Interaction?" *Journal of the History of Philosophy* **23**: 35–49.
Redding, P. 2007. *Analytic Philosophy and the Return of Hegelian Thought*. Cambridge: Cambridge University Press.
Remes, P. 2008. *Neoplatonism*. Stocksfield: Acumen.
Rescher, N. 1973. *Conceptual Idealism*. Oxford: Blackwell.
Rescher, N. 1992. *G. W. Leibniz's Monadology*. Pittsburgh, PA: University of Pittsburgh Press.
Rescher, N. 2000. *Nature and Understanding: The Metaphysics and Method of Science*. Oxford: Oxford University Press.
Rescher, N. 2005. *Studies in Idealism: Collected Papers vol. III*. Frankfurt: Ontos.
Rescher, N. 2010. *Reality and its Appearance*. London: Continuum.
Richards, R. J. 2002. *The Romantic Conception of Life: Science and Philosophy in the Age of Goethe*. Chicago, IL: University of Chicago Press.
Rockmore, T. 1980. *Fichte, Marx and the German Philosophical Tradition*. Carbondale, IL: Southern Illinois University Press.
Rockmore, T. 2003. *Before and After Hegel: An Historical Introduction to Hegel's Thought*. Indianapolis, IN: Hackett.
Rorty, R. 1997. "Introduction". In W. Sellars, *Empiricism and the Philosophy of Mind*, 1–12. Cambridge, MA: Harvard University Press.
Rosen, M. 1999. "From Kant to Fichte: A Reply to Franks". See Stern (1999), 147–53.

Royce, J. 1892. *The Spirit of Modern Philosophy*. Boston, MA: Houghton, Mifflin.
Rozemond, M. 1999. "Descartes on Mind–Body Interaction: What's the Problem?" *Journal of the History of Philosophy* **37**(3): 436–67.
Russell, B. 1914. *The Philosophy of Bergson: With a Reply by Mr H. Wildon Carr and a Rejoinder by Mr Bertrand Russell*. London: Macmillan.
Russell, B. 1962. *An Inquiry into Meaning and Truth*. Harmondsworth: Penguin.
Russell, B. [1946] 1967a. *History of Western Philosophy*. London: Allen & Unwin.
Russell, B. 1967b. *A Critical Exposition of the Philosophy of Leibniz*. London: George Allen & Unwin.
Rutherford, D. 1995a. "Metaphysics: The Late Period". In *The Cambridge Companion to Leibniz*, N. Jolley (ed.), 124–75. Cambridge: Cambridge University Press.
Rutherford, D. 1995b. *Leibniz and the Rational Order of Nature*. Cambridge: Cambridge University Press.
Sandkühler, H. J. (ed.) 1984a. *Natur und geschichtlicher Prozess: Studien zur Naturphilosophie Schellings*. Frankfurt: Suhrkamp.
Sandkühler, H. J. 1984b. "Natur und geschichtlicher Prozeß: Von Schellings Philosophie der Natur und der Zweiten Natur zur Wissenschschaft der Geschichte". In *Natur und geschichtlicher Prozess: Studien zur Naturphilosophie Schellings*, H. J. Sandkühler (ed.), 13–80. Frankfurt: Suhrkamp.
Schelling, F. W. J. 1856–61. *Schellings Werke*, 14 vols, K. F. A. Schelling (ed.). Stuttgart: Cotta.
Schelling, F. W. J. 1946. *Die Weltalter: Fragmente. In den Urfassungen von 1811 und 1813*, M. Schröter (ed.). Munich: Beck.
Schelling, F. W. J. 1972. *Grundlegung der positiven Philosophie: Münchener Vorlesung WS 1832/33 und SS 1833*, H. Fuhrmanns (ed.). Turin: Bottego del Erasmo.
Schelling, F. W. J. 1975. "On the Possibility of a Form for all Philosophy", F. Marti (trans.). *Metaphilosophy* **6**(1): 1–24.
Schelling, F. W. J. 1978. *System of Transcendental Idealism*, P. Heath (trans.). Charlottesville, VA: University Press of Virginia.
Schelling, F. W. J. 1980. *The Unconditional in Human Knowledge: Four Early Essays (1794–1796)*, F. Marti (ed. & trans.). Lewisburg, PA: Bucknell University Press.
Schelling, F. W. J. 1988. *Ideas for a Philosophy of Nature*, E. E. Harris & P. Heath (trans.). Cambridge: Cambridge University Press.
Schelling, F. W. J. 1994a. *Idealism and the Endgame of Theory: Three Essays by F. W. J. Schelling*, T. Pfau (ed. and trans.). Albany, NY: SUNY Press.
Schelling, F. W. J. 1994b. *History of Modern Philosophy*, A. Bowie (trans.). Cambridge: Cambridge University Press.
Schelling, F. W. J. 1994c. *Timaeus (1794)*, Horst Buchner (ed.). Stuttgart: Frommann-Holzboog.
Schelling, F. W. J. 1997. "On the Nature of Philosophy as Science", M. Weigelt (trans.). In *German Idealist Philosophy*, R. Bubner (ed.), 210–43. Harmondsworth: Penguin.
Schelling, F. W. J. [1815] 2000. *Ages of the World*, J. M. Wirth (trans.). Albany, NY: SUNY Press.
Schelling, F. W. J. 2001. *Presentation of My System of Philosophy*, M. Vater (trans.). *Philosophical Forum* **32**(4): 339–71.
Schelling. F. W. J. 2003. *First Outline of a System of the Philosophy of Nature*, K. R. Peterson (trans.). Albany, NY: SUNY Press.
Schelling, F. W. J. 2006. *Philosophical Investigations into the Essence of Human Freedom*, J. Love & J. Schmidt (trans.). Albany, NY: SUNY Press.
Schelling, F. W. J. 2007. *The Grounding of Positive Philosophy*, B. Matthews (trans.). Albany, NY: SUNY Press.
Schelling. F. W. J. 2010. *On the World Soul*, I. H. Grant (part trans.). *Collapse* **6**: 88–117.
Schmaltz, T. M. 2002. "Nicola Malebranche". In *A Companion to Early Modern Philosophy*, S. Nadler (ed.), 152–66. Oxford: Blackwell.

Schmidt, J. (ed.) 1996. *What is Enlightenment? Eighteenth-Century Answers and Twentieth-Century Questions.* Berkeley, CA: University of California Press.

Schrödinger, E. 1954. *Nature and the Greeks.* Cambridge: Cambridge University Press.

Scott, D. 2000. "Occasionalism and Occasional Causation in Descartes' Philosophy". *Journal of the History of Philosophy* **38**(4): 503–28.

Scruton, R. 2001. *Kant: A Very Short Introduction.* Oxford: Oxford University Press.

Seidel, G. J. 1993. *Fichte's Wissenschaftslehre of 1794: A Commentary on Part 1.* West Lafayette, IN: Purdue University Press.

Sellars, W. 1968. *Science and Metaphysics: Variations on Kantian Themes.* London: Routledge.

Sellars, W. 1997. *Empiricism and the Philosophy of Mind.* Cambridge, MA: Harvard University Press.

Seth, A. 1887. *Hegelianism and Personality.* London: William Blackwood.

Seth, A. & R. Haldane (eds) 1883. *Essays in Philosophical Criticism.* New York: Burt Franklin.

Shoemaker, S. 1980. "Causality and Properties". In *Time and Cause: Essays Presented to Richard Taylor*, P. van Inwagen (ed.), 91–104. Dordrecht: Reidel.

Sinnerbrink, R. 2007. *Understanding Hegelianism.* Stocksfield: Acumen.

Siorvanes, L. 1996. *Proclus: Neo-Platonic Philosophy and Science.* New Haven, CT: Yale University Press.

Skrbina, D. 2005. *Panpsychism in the West.* Cambridge, MA: MIT Press.

Skrbina, D. (ed.) 2009. *Mind that Abides: Panpsychism in the New Millenium.* Amsterdam: John Benjamins.

Sloman, H. & J. Wallon 1855 (eds & trans.). *The Subjective Logic of Hegel.* London: John Chapman.

Smith, D. W. 2007. *Husserl.* London: Routledge.

Smith, N. H. (ed.) 2002. *Reading McDowell on Mind and World.* London: Routledge.

Smolin, L. 1999. *The Life of the Cosmos.* Oxford: Oxford University Press.

Snow, D. E. 1996. *Schelling and the End of Idealism.* Albany, NY: SUNY Press.

Solomon, R. C. & K. M. Higgins (eds) 1993. *The Age of German Idealism.* London: Routledge.

Sorabji, R. 1983. *Time, Creation and the Continuum.* London: Duckworth.

Spinoza, B. 1992. *Ethics, Treatise on the Emendation of the Intellect and Selected Letters*, S. Feldman (ed.), S. Shirley (trans.). Indianapolis, IN: Hackett.

Spinoza, B. 2002. *Complete Works*, M. L. Morgan (ed.), S. Shirley (trans.). Indianapolis, IN: Hackett.

Sprigge, T. L. S. 1983. *A Vindication of Absolute Idealism.* Edinburgh: Edinburgh University Press.

Sprigge, T. L. S. 1985. *Theories of Existence.* Harmondsworth: Penguin.

Sprigge, T. L. S. 1993. *James and Bradley: British Reality and American Truth.* Chicago, IL: Open Court.

Sprigge, T. L. S. 1994. "Idealism *contra* Idealism". *Philosophy and Phenomenological Research* **54**(2): 409–14.

Sprigge, T. L. S. 2006. *The God of Metaphysics.* Oxford: Oxford University Press.

Stengers, I. 2002. *Penser avec Whitehead: Une libre et sauvage création de concepts.* Paris: Seuil.

Stern, R. (ed.) 1999. *Transcendental Arguments: Problems and Projections.* Oxford: Oxford University Press.

Stern, R. 2009. *Hegelian Metaphysics.* Oxford: Oxford University Press.

Stewart, J. (ed.) 2002. *Miscellaneous Writings of G. W. F. Hegel.* Evanston, IL: Northwestern University Press.

Stirling, J. H. 1865. *The Secret of Hegel: Being the Hegelian System in Origin, Principle, Form and Matter.* Edinburgh: Oliver & Boyd.

Strawson, G. 2008. *Real Materialism and Other Essays.* Oxford: Oxford University Press.

Strawson, P. F. 2006. *The Bounds of Sense: An Essay on Kant's Critique of Pure Reason*. London: Routledge.
Sweet, W. 1996. "Bradley and Bosanquet". In *Philosophy After F. H. Bradley*, J. Bradley (ed.), 31–56. Bristol: Thoemmes.
Taylor, A. E. 1925. "F. H. Bradley". *Mind* NS **34**(133) (January): 1–12.
Taylor, C. 1975. *Hegel*. Cambridge: Cambridge University Press.
Tilliette, X. 1992. *Schelling: Une philosophie en devenir* 2e, 2 vols. Vol. I: *Le Système vivant*. Vol. II: *La Dernière philosophie*. Paris: Vrin.
Tilliette, X. 2007. *Une Introduction à Schelling*. Paris: Honoré Champion.
Varela, F., E. Thompson & E. Rosch 1993. *The Embodied Mind: Cognitive Science and Human Experience*. Cambridge, MA: MIT.
von Uexküll, J. 1957. "A Stroll Through the World of Animals and Men". In *Instinctive Behaviour*, C. H. Schiller (ed. & trans.), 5–80. New York: International Universities Press.
Ward, J. 1911. *The Realm of Ends: Pluralism and Theism*. Cambridge: Cambridge University Press.
Ward, J. [1899] 1915. *Naturalism and Agnosticism*, 4th edn. London: A. & C. Black.
Ward, J. 1927. *Essays in Philosophy*. Cambridge: Cambridge University Press.
Waterfield, R. 2000. *The First Philosophers: The Presocratics and the Sophists*. Oxford: Oxford University Press.
Whitehead, A. N. 1920. *Concept of Nature*. Cambridge: Cambridge University Press.
Whitehead, A. N. 1922. *The Principle of Relativity*. Cambridge: Cambridge University Press.
Whitehead, A. N. 1926. *Science and the Modern World*. Cambridge: Cambridge University Press.
Whitehead, A. N. 1929. *Process and Reality*. London: Macmillan.
Whitehead, A. N. 1933. *Adventures of Ideas*. Cambridge: Cambridge University Press.
Whitehead, A. N. 1934. *Nature and Life*. Cambridge: Cambridge University Press.
Whitehead, A. N. 1938. *Modes of Thought*. Cambridge: Cambridge University Press.
Whitehead, A. N. & B. Russell 1910, 1912, 1913. *Principia Mathematica*, 3 vols. Cambridge: Cambridge University Press.
Wiener, P. P. (ed. & trans.) 1951. *Leibniz Selections*. New York: Charles Scribner's Sons.
Wildon-Carr, H. 1922. *A Theory of Monads*. London: Macmillan.
Williams, B. 2008. "The Legacy of Greek Philosophy". In his *The Sense of the Past: Essays in the History of Philosophy*, M. Burnyeat (ed.), 3–48. Princeton, NJ: Princeton University Press.
Williams, J. 2003. *Gilles Deleuze's Difference and Repetition*. Edinburgh: Edinburgh University Press.
Williams, R. R. 1992. *Recognition: Fichte and Hegel*. Albany, NY: SUNY Press.
Wilson, M. 1978. *Descartes*. London: Routledge.
Wilson, M. D. 1999a. *Ideas and Mechanism: Essays on Early Modern Philosophy*. Princeton, NJ: Princeton University Press.
Wilson, M. D. 1999b. "Descartes on the Origin of Sensation". See Wilson (1999a), 41–68.
Wilson, M. D. 1999c. "Berkeley and the Mind-Dependence of Colours". See Wilson (1999a), 229–42.
Wilson, M. D. 1999d. "The Phenomenalisms of Leibniz and Berkeley". See Wilson (1999a), 306–21.
Woolhouse, R. & R. Francks 1997. *Leibniz's "New System" and Associated Contemporary Texts*. Oxford: Oxford University Press.
Woolhouse, R. & R. Francks 1998. *Philosophical Texts by Gottfried Wilhelm Leibniz*. Oxford: Oxford University Press.
Žižek, S. 1988. *Le Plus sublime des hystériques: Hegel passe*. Paris: Point Hors Ligne.
Žižek, S. 1992. *Enjoy Your Symptom!* London: Verso.

Žižek, S. 1996. *The Irreducible Remainder: An Essay on Schelling and Related Matters*. London: Verso.
Žižek, S. 1997. "The Abyss of Freedom". In *The Abyss of Freedom/Ages of the World*, S. Žižek & F. W. J. Schelling, J. Norman (trans.), 1–112. Ann Arbor, MI: Michigan University Press.
Žižek, S. 2004. "Everything you Ever Wanted to Know about Schelling (But were Afraid to Ask Hitchcock)". In *The New Schelling*, J. Norman & A. Welchman (eds), 30–42. London: Continuum.
Žižek, S. 2006. *The Parallax View*. Cambridge, MA: MIT Press.
Žižek, S. 2007. "With Friends Like These …". In *The Truth of Žižek*, P. Bowman & R. Stamp (eds), 197–254. London: Continuum.
Zöller, G. 1998. *Fichte's Transcendental Philosophy: The Original Duplicity of Intelligence and Will*. Cambridge: Cambridge University Press.

INDEX

Absolute, the 5–7, 97, 119, 124, 137–8, 143, 146–7, 160, 164, 168, 170–73, 175, 177, 180–82, 187–8, 276, 293–4, 310n23
   and Idea 150, 152, 154
   and sentient experience (Bradley) 170
accident 25, 94, 169–70, 211–13, 225, 232, 261, 267
actual occasion 210–11, 213–19, 220–21, 230, 237–8, 242, 289, 311n36
aesthetics 109, 111, 291
aggregates 61–2, 65, 68, 70–72, 75–6, 79, 81, 178
Alexander, S. 6, 175–6, 192, 305n3
algorithm, algorithmic 252–3
anti-realism, idealism's putative 4–5, 11
appearance 64, 74, 91–2, 96–7, 132, 134, 159, 168–73, 177, 184, 187–8, 190–92, 201, 249, 276, 294, 310n27
a priori 82, 86, 90–95, 99–102, 104, 106–7, 114, 149, 168, 182, 259, 269, 291
Aristotle 24, 27–9, 34, 55, 93, 95, 127–8, 150, 166, 193, 211, 224, 300n2
   and Green 166
   and Leibniz 55
Armstrong, A. H. 300n7
atom 40, 62, 69, 195, 198–9, 208, 214, 219–20
atomism 5, 8, 165, 176, 210, 213ff., 243, 248, 254, 267, 308n12
attractor 97, 240, 245–7, 289–90
Augustine 7, 46, 301n12
autonomy 102, 225, 230–31, 235, 238
autopoiesis 224, 227, 230–31, 233, 235–7, 241, 243, 289

autonomous agent 241–4, 247–9, 254, 290
autocatalysis 240–41
axiology 270–71, 274–5, 283

Badiou, A. 174, 293–5, 310n20, 311n39
Barbour, J. 3, 254–5, 307n2
Basile, P. 306–7n4
Bataille, G. 293, 311n40
beauty 4, 21, 23, 55–6, 107, 110–11, 149
being/Being 20–23, 27–33, 51, 63, 76, 117, 119, 123, 128, 130, 137–8, 140, 157, 191, 270, 275, 287–8, 280, 282–4, 292, 294, 300n10, 309n13
   as activity, as substance 122, 124–5, 132, 225, 267, 295
   affect of 126
   and not-being 19–20
   and thinking, identity of 11, 13–18, 25–6, 30–33, 131, 142, 205, 223, 247, 265, 274, 279, 300n11
   univocity of 284, 310n20, 310n28
   and will 139
Beiser, F. C. 145, 149, 152–3, 157, 303n1, 306n1
Bergson, H. 194, 199, 285, 289, 306n2, 307n9
body, bodies 33, 36–45, 47–53, 55–8, 61, 69–72, 76–81, 83, 85–6, 98, 113, 125, 134–5, 148, 157, 161–2, 167, 171–3, 179, 181, 191–2, 211–12, 216, 220–21, 223, 247, 284, 288–9, 395n1, 300n3, 301n8, 307n3, 310n29, 310n30
Bolzano, B. 126
Brentano, F. 126

327

INDEX

Broad, C. D. 6, 304n7, 305n3
Burnyeat, M. 10–13, 15, 25, 33–7, 201, 205–9, 257–8, 299n3, 300n7
by itself 21–4, 275

Caird, E. 205
Candlish, S. 257, 309n5
Cassirer, E. 149
categories 30, 82, 92–6, 103–4, 107, 110, 130, 168, 208, 244, 253, 286
causation 2, 4, 8, 11, 22–3, 27–30, 32–3, 37–8, 40, 42–5, 53, 55–7, 64, 74–7, 81–3, 86, 94, 96–7, 101, 113–15, 125, 137, 146, 148–50, 152, 154, 161–3, 167, 173, 195, 220, 223, 230, 237, 241, 253–4, 273, 276, 280–82, 302n6
categorical imperative 99–104, 110, 124, 243
chaos 138, 140, 142–3, 165, 246–7, 290–91, 305n6
cognition 13, 92, 98, 100, 103–4, 109, 131, 137, 169, 195, 221, 223, 227, 234–8, 247, 302n5, 303n1, 307n7, 308n11
cognitive depth (Rescher) 281
complexity 8, 252, 274, 281–2, 288ff., 303n3, 307n8
concrescence 214–19
concrete notion (Stirling) 160
concrete particulars 218
concrete universal 7–8, 145–6, 198, 278, 306n3
concept 7–8, 27, 45–6, 65, 111, 144–5, 147, 151, 198, 257–9, 265–8, 273, 286–7, 308n3
  as powers 135, 137
  space of 263
  unboundedness of 259, 261–2
continuants (Sprigge) 278–9
contradiction 17, 146–7, 155, 172, 186, 192–4, 294, 305n5
Cornford, F. M. 14, 18, 23, 299n2, 300n8, 300n12
cosmology 2–3, 23, 40, 138, 141–2, 177, 180–81, 224, 257, 273, 275
Cousin, V. 159
creativity, creative advance 108–9, 178, 180, 210, 213–15, 221, 275

Darwin, C. 3, 6, 195, 197, 209, 248
Davidson, D. 259, 264

Dawes-Hicks, G. 305n3
De Landa, M. 311n32
Deleuze, G. 284–93
Derrida, J. 293, 311n43, 311n47
description
  domain of 223, 225–9, 307n3
  exclusive and sufficient (McTaggart) 185–7, 305n9
desire 26, 69, 99–102, 104, 268, 293–7
decision 69, 99–101, 103, 210, 215, 217, 219–221, 238, 258, 296
d'Espagnat, B. 3, 281, 309n18
dialectic 154–6, 234, 303n5
  generative 143
  Hegelian 18, 31, 144–7, 151, 155, 157
  Kant and 89
  Platonic 19, 31–2
dichotomy 120, 126, 135, 146
difference 28, 61, 193, 288, 294
  as disequilibrium 251
  of force 137, 223, 310n28
  intensive 187, 287–92
  repetition of 308n14, 308n20
dissipative structures 232, 239, 289
disequilibrium 231–2, 241, 251, 287–8, 308n14, 308n15
Dodds, E. R. 300n6
dreams, argument from (Descartes) 36–7, 46, 83–4
duty 5, 99ff., 101–3
  moral, to be "non-moral" 174

Einstein, A. 6, 212, 216, 239, 252, 282, 306n3, 309n9, 310n29
empiricism 57, 161, 205, 264
  transcendental 291–2, 309n19
epigenesis 178–9
Eriugena, John Scottus 12–13, 33, 300–301n2
essence 21, 47, 61, 66–7, 72, 87, 116, 137, 139, 145, 173, 191, 225, 232, 301n1, 302n11
eternal consciousness (Green) 161, 163–4, 166–7, 171
eternal objects 218–19
ethical life 262
  requiredness of existence 257, 271–5, 282
  vision of the world 293
ethics, the ethical 2, 116, 128, 139, 161, 167, 173–4, 190, 244, 275, 293

as first philosophy 116, 128, 139, 258, 292, 296
evil 66, 139, 158, 174, 184, 192
evil demon (Descartes) 37–8
experience 44, 73, 82, 95, 111, 114, 173, 221, 262
  centres of 16, 156, 169, 177, 256, 277–8, 283, 309n13
  immediate 80, 168, 172–3
extension 35, 39, 43, 46, 52, 55, 61, 75, 77–80, 87, 91, 168, 210, 213, 281, 287, 289, 310n28
  Leibniz's rejection of the Cartesian theory of 58–62
  infinite (Malebranche) 47, 54, 57, 72
externality 91, 97, 145, 151, 158, 191–2, 195–6, 204

faculty 44, 47, 109, 120, 171, 238
  of desire 99–101
  of imagination 80
  of intuition 91, 93
  of judgement 106, 108, 110–111, 114, 149
  of principles 119
  of understanding 96, 103, 107, 148, 153–5
Fallacy of Misplaced Concreteness (Whitehead) 213
far from equilibrium 223, 231–2, 239–42, 249
feeling 15, 38, 107–12, 126, 161, 163, 170, 172–3, 218–19, 221, 292, 302n5
Ferrier, J. 160–61
Ficara, E. 310n19
final cause, finality 3, 23, 27, 29, 106, 113, 141, 146, 149–50, 152, 154, 178, 210, 220, 223, 229–30, 237, 241, 254, 276, 282, 290, 311n33
force/forces 42, 47, 59–65, 67, 69–71, 112, 120, 132–5, 140, 143, 157, 208, 217, 226, 243, 245, 249, 251, 287–9, 292, 303n3, 308n20, 310n24, 310n29
form 7–8, 25, 45, 59, 62–3, 66, 71, 73, 80, 86–92, 94–6, 100, 103–4, 110–11, 113, 141, 156, 164, 166, 195, 197, 211–12, 214, 216–19, 238, 247–9, 284–6, 300n1, 310n27, 301n12
Foucault, M. 293–4, 311n33
Frank, M. 129
Frankfurt, H. 391n3

Franks, P. 257, 296, 302n10, 308n2
freedom 95, 99, 101–7, 112, 114–17, 120–21, 123, 125–9, 138–9, 140–41, 161–2, 207, 210, 220–21, 253, 257–8, 261–3, 290, 292, 302n2, 302n5
Frege, G. 195, 205–7, 264–5, 305n6
Freud, S. 139, 156
function 108, 114, 146–56, 167–8, 178–9, 192–4, 197, 215, 218, 221–3, 228, 235, 242–4, 252–5, 264, 267, 281, 285, 289, 302n5, 304n5

Gabriel, M. 257–8, 296–7
Gatti, M. 25–6
Geach, P. T. 183, 304n3, 304n5, 304n7
gene, genetic 85, 120, 143, 178, 223, 236, 243–6, 248, 251, 287–9, 307–8n9, 310n25
Gerson, L. 300n3
God 37–8, 40, 42, 45–7, 49–50, 52–60, 63–7, 73, 79, 81–7, 96, 152, 173, 175, 178, 180, 221, 238, 274, 301n10, 301n13, 301n1 (ch. 4)
  vision in (Leibniz) 72ff.
  vision in (Malebranche) 48–51
Good, (Idea of) 21, 23, 26–31, 128, 174, 178, 180, 273–5, 279, 282, 285, 292
Grant, I. H. 308n1, 311n45
Gregory of Nyssa 12–13, 32–3, 300–301n2
ground 33, 59, 65, 118–19, 139–43, 170, 174, 180
  of existence/reality 30, 88, 127, 137–8, 139, 161, 172
  ethical/normative 101, 161, 275, 280, 302n5
  and unground 140–41, 290–91
  grounding principles 120–21, 123–4, 132
Guattari, F. 284, 291, 294, 310n30, 311nn34–5

Habermas, J. 105, 129, 302n4 (ch. 5), 303n6
Hartmann, K. 144, 264, 270
Hartmann, N. 129
Heidegger, M. 15, 119, 127–9, 138, 143, 270, 297, 302n5, 302nn12–13, 309n12
Hibbs, D. 34–5, 300n2
Hogrebe, W. 269
holism 159, 240, 267, 274, 279

INDEX

Husserl, E.   126–8, 205, 302n9, 302n11, 305n6, 309n12
Hylton, P.   165, 257
Hyppolite, J.   293–5, 297, 302n10, 311nn38–9, 311n41, 311n44

idealism
  absolute   150, 153, 155, 161, 175, 177, 259, 263, 270, 278–9, 283, 303n4, 309n10
  conceptual   272, 281, 283
  naturalistic   2–3, 18, 26, 132, 138, 143, 262, 270, 283
  objective   11, 15–16, 26, 31, 144–5, 148, 208, 259, 262, 265, 269
  phenomenalist   35–6, 46, 59, 64, 69
  real-   30, 131
  subjective   12, 15–16, 25–6, 30–31, 170, 196, 260, 300n7
idea/Idea
  absolute (Green)   164
  in Berkeley   73, 75, 78–80, 82–4, 86–8, 301n4
  in Bradley   8, 173
  complete system of   110, 116–17; see also idea, as organization; science, philosophy as
  in Deleuze   285, 288, 310n19, 310n25
  in Descartes   35–6, 38, 44–5, 47–8, 61, 301n6, 301n10
  in Hegel   144–52, 154–8, 270
  in Kant   89, 90, 96–7, 99, 104–6, 148, 303n2
  in Leibniz   59, 61, 66–7, 72, 81, 254, 3021n1
  in Malebranche   46, 48–57, 59, 72
  in McTaggart   181
  in Neoplatonism   27, 30–33
  as organization   8, 106–7, 109, 223–5, 229, 232, 245, 247, 249
  in Plato   4, 7–8, 19–24, 26–8, 47, 85, 131, 153, 178, 210, 17, 223, 300n1 (ch. 2), 300n2 (ch. 2)
  realism about the   6, 26, 45, 131
  of reason   90, 112, 124, 290
  problem-   257, 284–7, 290–93, 308nn14, 308n19, 311n33
  in Schelling   137–8, 143, 307n1
  in Sprigge   309n16
  in Whitehead   210, 212, 217–18, 225
  in Williams   310n22

identity   17, 176, 211, 225, 232, 237, 277; see also being and thinking, identity of
  absolute   128, 137–8, 140, 147
  and dissimilarity of the diverse (McTaggart)
  of identity and non-identity   136, 146
  of indiscernibles   182
  and negation   303n5
  and organization   223, 232
  over time   211, 232, 237–8, 289, 307n3
  personal   169
  principle of ("like is known by like")   139
  system of   129, 131, 135–7
  of the transcendental and the dynamic (Schelling)   132–3
imagination   48, 53, 79, 80, 82, 84, 88, 107–8, 109, 111–12, 115
immaterialism   13, 73, 84
indeterminacy/indeterminate   14–15, 20, 103, 210, 217, 300n10
indeterminability   286, 290
inference   80, 194, 267
ingression   216–18, 220
in-itself, thing   7, 77, 78, 93, 97, 104, 110, 116, 118, 122–3, 127, 130–31, 133, 136–7, 140, 143, 157, 165, 167, 195, 232–3, 238, 259–61, 271, 295–6, 305n5; see also "by itself"
innate ideas   35, 44, 46–9, 50, 86, 301n10
intellect, intellection   14, 25, 28–30, 33, 48, 79–80, 84, 94, 121–2, 153–4, 172, 231
intensity   187–8, 287–8, 291–2; see also force
intensive differences   287–92, 310n28, 310n30
intentionality   127, 152, 244, 302n11
intrinsic determination   184, 304n8
intuition   89–97, 107, 109, 114, 122, 149, 154, 158, 286

Jacobi, F. H.   152, 303n1
Jaspers, K.   129, 134, 142

Kahn, C   13, 16–17
Kauffman, S.   238–55
Kojève, A.   293–7, 311n37

Lacan, J.   293, 311n41
Laplace, P.-S.   215

330

law 52–3, 56, 64, 66, 121, 143, 148, 231, 239, 267
  immanent 6, 138, 196, 273–5, 282
  moral 101–6
  of motion 40, 57, 83
  of natural complexity (Rescher) 281
  of nature 57–8, 60, 65, 84, 95, 165, 178–9, 195, 249–50, 254, 273–4, 300n9
  of non-contradiction 17, 146, 192–4, 305n5
  of mind 132
Lewes, G. H. 305n3
Lewis, D. 309n17
Levinas, E. 128, 293
life 5, 35, 106, 113–15, 188–9, 195, 202, 224–5, 227–8, 233–5, 239–40, 243, 262, 264, 286
Lloyd-Morgan, C. 6, 175, 305n3
Locke, J. 1, 87–8, 165, 203, 225, 306n3
logic 3, 6, 17, 26, 31–3, 53, 66, 117, 144–7, 151, 154–5, 181, 192–5, 197, 206, 211–12, 234, 264–5, 267, 294–5, 302n8, 305n6, 306–7n4, 308n12
Lotze, H. 305n6
love 20, 50–51, 55, 181ff., 188–9

Malabou, C. 294, 297, 310n19, 311n43, 311n47
Malcolm, N. 301n3
Marcel, G. 293
Marx, K. 105, 126, 293, 295, 303n6
materialism 11–13, 74, 117, 126, 168, 171, 181, 209, 212, 283, 288, 292–3, 295–6, 299n3, 303n6
  eliminative 299n5
  mechanical 5–6, 58, 113, 165, 197, 202, 229
matter 3, 6–7, 12, 25, 29, 33, 35, 39–43, 46–7, 52, 58–9, 61–5, 69–71, 73, 75, 77, 79, 81, 83–4, 93, 98, 124, 134, 156, 160–64, 166, 170–72, 188, 191, 194, 197, 202–4, 208, 211–14, 239–41, 244, 248–9, 252, 299n3, 301n7, 301n4 (ch. 4), 305–6n7, 308n14, 310n24, 310n29
  unreality of (McTaggart) 185, 187
  self-construction of (Schelling) 133
  as the phenomenon of force 133–4
Maturana, H. 224–38
mechanism 57–8, 90, 92, 97, 149, 176–9, 191, 195–7, 204, 215, 224, 226, 232, 240

mind 3–6, 11–13, 15–16, 25, 33–4, 39, 44–57, 67, 72–80, 82–7, 96, 100, 132, 135, 137, 155–6, 158, 176, 179, 196–200, 204, 206–8, 211–13, 251, 256, 260, 270, 272–5, 278–9, 281–3, 299n3, 299n5, 300n7, 301n6, 301n8, 301n4, 305–6n7
  bodily basis of 18, 190–93
  mind–body dualism 43, 300n3
monadology 177–8, 180, 299n3
monism 11–13, 16, 21, 23, 118ff., 155ff., 159, 206, 211–12
  spiritual (Ward) 177
Monod, J. 244, 206n7
Moore, G. E. 1, 3, 10–11, 201–9, 257, 272, 276, 301n3, 306n1, 309n5
Moran, D. 12, 33, 300–301n2
morphogenesis 284–6, 290
morphology 3, 195, 209
motion 21, 23, 29, 40–42, 44–5, 47, 54–5, 57–8, 60–61, 77–80, 83, 86, 134, 161–2, 176, 188, 204, 208, 238, 243, 278
Muirhead, J. H. 160, 305n6
multiplicity 134, 154–5, 157, 181, 184, 214, 245, 284, 288–9, 303n5

nature 5–6, 23, 25–6, 30–33, 55, 58, 83, 110, 12, 115–17, 122, 125, 149, 154–5, 157–8, 161–2, 165–7, 171, 190–92, 195–6, 198–9, 209–10, 224, 256, 269, 270–73, 279–83, 290, 292
  idealism's engagement with 2–3, 8, 207, 224, 257
  philosophy of 31, 129, 131–41, 143–6, 148, 150–51, 296–7, 303n3
  second 261–4
natural attitude, the (Husserl) 126
naturalism 1, 3, 58, 127, 138, 144, 155, 176, 190, 208, 256–9, 261–2, 270–71, 280, 283
negation 17–18, 20, 23, 74, 94, 123, 134, 147, 155, 164, 206, 293, 303n5
  determinate and indeterminate 22, 267
Newton, I. 2, 5, 58, 113, 210, 212, 214–15, 221, 239, 249, 252, 295
Nietzsche, F. 7, 139, 288–9, 308n20, 311n33
nominalism 66, 84–5, 99, 104, 211
non-ergodicity 251–4

331

INDEX

normativity 1–3, 105, 127, 144, 256–7, 263–4, 266–8, 269–71, 279–80, 283, 293, 296
noumenon 3, 93, 101, 157, 271
nature, laws of see law of nature
novelty 178, 250, 252, 269

objective immortality 215, 225
occasionalism 54–6
 and Leibniz 55
 and Malebranche 54
O'Meara, D. J. 300n8
order for free 246
organization 2, 8, 71, 96, 114, 117, 138–41, 149–53, 155, 191–2, 194, 198, 208–9, 216, 223–33, 235–43, 245, 247–55, 261, 289, 192, 306n6, 307n1, 307–8n9, 308n17
organic 71–2, 85, 148–9, 151–2, 154–5, 157, 167, 188, 197, 199, 208–9, 218, 220–21, 224, 226, 232–5, 237, 241, 245, 248, 250–51, 253–4, 306n8
organicism 306n6
organism 5, 8

panpsychism 14, 256, 270, 276–7, 279, 300n9, 309n11
pantheism 274
perception and expression 65–6, 72, 111
phenomenalism 34ff., 59ff., 67, 201
 perceptions and 64ff.
phenomenon 12, 70, 81, 101, 133–4, 157, 200, 226
phenomenology, phenomenological 78, 85ff., 126–8, 146, 176, 225–7, 236, 293–4, 302n10
physicalism 276–7, 279
Pinkard, T. 144, 264, 270, 303n1
Pippin, R. 144, 258, 263–4, 303n1, 309n6
Platonism 3, 6–8, 19–20, 22–4, 26, 46, 57, 67, 86–7, 180, 205–6, 257, 261, 274, 285, 293, 310n26
 overturning of 285
 and two-worlds metaphysics, error of 6–7, 24, 120–21, 164, 300n3
positing, and counterpositing 117, 121–5, 127, 130, 157
potentia/potential/potentiality 109, 178, 226, 242, 245, 251, 285, 287, 289, 291, 308n16

in Aristotle 28, 62, 226
in Schelling 135
in Whitehead 214–21, 307n9
powers 7, 32–3, 39, 44–5, 57, 60, 62, 72, 83, 86–7, 109–10, 112–13, 115, 119, 121, 157, 166, 202, 211, 223, 238, 251, 257, 308n20
 and forces 42, 47, 63, 208, 287, 292–3
 inert 120
 natural (Malebranche) 50, 55, 58
 ontology of 23, 27–31, 132–3, 135, 137–8, 140, 143, 231, 274–5, 282, 285, 306n3
 passive (Leibniz) 59, 64–5
practical, the, primacy of 117, 177
 in Fichte 124, 126, 295
 in Kant 119
prehension/prehend 137, 210, 215–16, 218–19, 221, 237–8, 308n11
Prigogine, I. 215, 231–2, 307n6
primary matter 59, 61–3
primitive force 59, 60–61, 63–5, 69
process 6, 27, 47, 114, 134–5, 145, 156, 164, 167, 179, 191, 194, 196–7, 210, 214, 216–20, 224, 226–7, 229, 231, 237, 240–41, 243–4, 249, 252–3, 267, 275, 277, 289, 291–2, 300n9, 307n3, 310n30
problem-idea see idea, problem-
purpose 89, 106–10, 114–15, 145–6, 149–50, 152–3, 195–6, 198, 219ff., 224, 226–30, 232–3, 239, 241–2, 254, 307n3, 307–8n9

qualities 19, 23, 45, 48, 62–6, 76, 94, 161, 164, 172, 182–3, 185–7, 202, 212, 225, 287, 289, 291, 304n6, 304n8
 primary and secondary, distinction between 39, 41, 53, 75, 77–9, 85, 168, 204
quantity 33, 40, 62, 94, 123–4, 207
 and difference 137, 287–8, 290, 308n20
quanta of being and activity 123
Quine, W. V. 264, 270–71

rationality 104, 112, 121, 153, 180, 258
rationalism 224
 philosophical (Brandom) 264
realism
 about ideas, idealism as 6, 80, 218, 229; see also ideas, realism about

332

contrasted with idealism 4–5, 11, 13, 145, 151, 190, 192, 199–200, 203, 205–8, 261
and phenomenalism 201
reality 82, 84, 92, 192, 195, 200
  absolute 170, 172, 188
  as appearance 36, 168–71, 191, 207, 305n1
  of the effect 43
  and experience 75, 93–7, 106, 113–14, 260–61
  and externality 138, 234
  and freedom 99, 105
  ground of 137
  and mind-dependency 3–4, 12, 77, 83, 202, 208, 259, 272–9, 299n1 (ch. 1), 299n5
  physical character of 21, 46, 73, 120, 203, 278
  quanta of (Fichte) 123–4
  and subjectivity 154
  thought-creating 288
reason
  ideas of 89ff., 96, 90, 105, 286, 290
  practical 99, 100–102, 104, 106, 114, 119, 124
  principle of sufficient 119, 140, 275, 302n6
  principle of unreason 140
  pure 96, 100, 105–6, 110, 113–14
reasons, space of (McDowell) 261–2, 266, 269
recognition 141, 156, 268, 309n4
refutations of idealism 3, 97–8, 159, 201, 203, 206, 309n5
relations 55, 92, 159, 171, 177, 193, 227, 253, 304n5, 308n3, 309n17
  accidental 232
  in Bosanquet 196
  in Bradley 168–9, 172–3
  causal 29, 63, 191
  in Green 161–2, 164–7
  holistic nature of all real 197, 278
  in Kauffman 243
  in Maturana and Varela 226, 229
  in McTaggart 181–6, 189, 304n6
  monadological 62, 179
  in Whitehead 214, 216
res cogitans, res extensa 35, 42–3, 46
Romanticism 5, 148, 150, 152–4, 156, 210, 303n3

Russell, B. 1, 6, 75, 205–6, 212, 257, 265, 270, 272, 281, 305n6, 306–7n4, 309n5
Sartre, J.-P. 127, 293
Schopenhauer, A. 139
science (*Wissenschaft*)
  idealism and 2–3, 5–6, 118, 143, 152, 180, 194, 233, 237, 240, 256, 261–2, 272, 279–280, 303n3
  philosophy as 32, 117, 126, 130, 142, 144, 154, 273, 295
self, the 156, 169–70, 172, 175, 181, 187, 189–90, 211, 259–60, 265
self-organization 106ff., 113–14, 149, 165, 167, 223–4, 232, 235, 237, 255, 289
Sellars, W. 257, 264–5
sensation 37–8, 43–6, 50, 53–4, 65, 72, 76–82, 110, 162, 166–7, 177, 203–6, 291–2, 306n3
sensible 15, 21, 68, 71, 74–6, 80–86, 94, 112, 193, 202, 205, 212, 291–2, 300n3
  and supersensible 114, 120, 263
Seth, A. Pringle-Pattison 175, 304n1
Shoemaker, S. 396n3
Smith, D. W. 302n9
Smolin, L. 254–5, 307n2
Snow, D. 202, 303n4
space and time 90–98, 107, 113, 148, 150, 152, 165, 168, 173, 212, 245, 254, 286, 289, 310n24, 310n28
speculative philosophy 3, 105, 118, 146, 180, 190, 192–3, 195, 199–200, 204, 206–7, 210–11, 225, 296–7, 303n4, 306n4
spirit 11, 33, 44, 75, 83–4, 86, 135–6, 144–6, 148, 151–2, 154, 157–8, 166, 177, 179–80, 185, 187–8, 203–4, 258, 260, 264, 266, 269–70
Spinoza, B. 13, 20, 31, 37, 118–19, 152, 156, 207, 264, 271, 274–5, 277, 302n6, 303n2, 305n2
spontaneity 121, 178, 246, 266
Stengers, I. 231–2, 307n6
Stern, R. 306n8
Stirling, J. H. 160–61
Strawson, G. 12, 277, 309n11
structure 17, 26, 29, 61, 117, 199, 208, 243, 265, 268
  a priori 92, 99
  dissipative 232, 239, 289

333

and organization 225–6, 236–8, 249, 290
  plasticity of 235
sublime 111–12, 295
subjectivism 12, 73, 92, 198
subject–predicate logic 75, 170, 193, 306–7n4
substance 30, 33–5, 40, 42–3, 46–7, 50, 59–60, 62–7, 69–72, 74–7, 79, 84, 87, 94, 118–19, 122, 156, 161, 177, 182–5, 187–8, 202, 204, 211–14, 225, 260, 277, 285, 304n8, 304–5n9, 306–7n4, 309n15, 310n20
  simple 59, 64–5, 87, 184, 301n4, 307n8
Sweet, W. 305n12
system 8, 24–6, 31, 33, 40, 116–20, 136–42, 146–57, 163, 193–4, 196–7, 210, 215, 223, 225–8, 231, 233, 241–2, 251–3, 265, 270, 281, 291, 303n1, 306n6, 308n14
  and asystasy 143
  autopoietic 167, 224, 232, 290, 307n5, 307n7

tanquam sensations 38, 46
Taylor, C. 144, 173, 264, 270, 303n1
teleology 23, 29, 89ff., 106–7, 113–15, 126–7, 149, 152, 180, 195–9, 223, 227–30, 238, 296, 306n9
theism 180, 182
time, unreality of (McTaggart) 186, 192
totality 94, 96–7, 106–7, 110, 112, 142, 148–9, 151–5, 157, 180, 192–3, 303n5
transcendental, the 93, 96, 98, 101, 116, 122, 125–7, 133, 135–6, 149, 171, 262–3, 266, 291–2, 295–6, 310n23

identity of the dynamic and (Schelling) 132

unconditioned 89–90, 96–7, 101–2, 121, 124, 130–31, 154–5, 310n23
understanding, the 8, 47–8, 53, 66–7, 87–8, 92–6, 101, 103, 105–6, 108–11, 126, 146–8, 153–5, 161–4, 227, 236, 266, 286, 293
unground 140–41, 290–91
universal
  abstract 7–8, 73, 78–80, 85, 87, 91, 145–7, 301n3, 306n8
  concrete 7–8, 87, 144–6, 149, 160, 198, 218, 278, 306n8
  Platonic 7, 85, 95, 149, 157, 237
  realism concerning 79, 218
universality, test of 193–4

Varela, F. 224–38
virtual 284–5, 287–90, 291, 307n9, 308n11, 310n20

Wallace, W. 205
Walsh, W. H. 301n4
Wildon-Carr, H. 307n5
Williams, B. 10–11, 15
Williams, J. 310n22
Wilson, M. 36–7, 45, 70, 201, 301n3 (ch. 3), 301n9
work cycle 241–2, 245–9, 308n16

Zeno 161, 213, 307n6
Žižek, S. 129, 139, 257–8, 293, 295–7, 303n6, 311n45

334